THE
PASTORAL
COMPANION

THE PASTORAL COMPANION

A Handbook of Canon Law

by

MARCIAN J. MATHIS, O.F.M., J.C.D.

and

NICHOLAS W. MEYER, O.F.M., S.T.D.

Professors of Canon Law at St. Joseph

Seminary, Teutopolis, Illinois

Twelfth Edition

1961

FRANCISCAN HERALD PRESS

Publishers of Franciscan Literature

Chicago 9, Illinois

Imprimi Potest

> Dominicus Limacher O.F.M.
> *Minister Provincialis*
> Sancti Ludovici, Mo. die 25 jan., 1961

Nihil Obstat

> Amos E. Giusti, J.C.D.
> *Censor Librorum*
> Campifonte in Illinois, die 23 febr., 1961

Imprimatur

> †Gulielmus A. O'Connor, D.D.
> *Episcopus Campifontis in Illinois*
> Campifonte in Illinois, die 23 febr., 1961

Twelfth Edition, 1961

THE PASTORAL COMPANION, Library of Congress Catalog Card Number: 61-11199, copyright 1961 by Franciscan Herald Press, 1434 West 51st Street, Chicago 9, Illinois. Produced by Publication Associates. Made in the United States of America.

FOREWORD

The purpose of *The Pastoral Companion* is not to present an exhaustive exposé of all the Canons of the Code of Canon Law, but to treat in a concise way those subjects of Canon Law that easily escape memory and cause doubts and perplexities in the sacred ministry. This practical purpose has been the guide in the selection and limitation of the material presented in this book. Theological and canonical discussion are beyond the scope of this work, for *The Pastoral Companion* is meant to be the busy priest's practical handbook of Canon Law. The priest engaged in the care of souls will find in this book those canons of the Code and decisions of the Holy See which pertain to the daily work of his sacred ministry.

The authors acknowledge a debt of gratitude to their provincial and local superiors for granting them leave of absence from other duties during the time this new edition was in preparation; to Frater Cary Fox, O.F.M., for his work in preparing the manuscript for the printer; and to all others who have helped to bring this work to a successful conclusion.

JAN 1 6 1984

TABLE OF CONTENTS

THE
PASTORAL
COMPANION

PART I
GENERAL PRINCIPLES

CHAPTER I
Jurisdiction — Dispensations — Rescripts

I. JURISDICTION

A. *Division*

1. Jurisdiction of the *external forum* concerns primarily the common and public good, regulates the social action of the faithful, is exercised publicly, and has public juridical effects.

> The powers to make laws, exercise judgment in court, establish censures, give parishes, etc., are powers of the external forum.

Jurisdiction of the *internal forum* or the forum of conscience, concerns primarily the private actions of the faithful, regulates the moral relations of the faithful to God, is exercised privately, often secretly, and has no juridical effects unless these are expressly granted by law or by a competent superior.

> Jurisdiction of the internal forum is *sacramental* when it must be exercised only in the sacrament of penance or in connection with it (v.g. the power to absolve from sins); it is *extra-sacramental* when not subject to this restriction (v.g. the power to dispense from fasting when exercised outside the occasion of sacramental confession but yet in a private manner).

2. *Ordinary* jurisdiction is that which is attached to an office by law; all other jurisdiction is *delegated*. (Cf. Can. 197.)

Two essential conditions are required for jurisdiction to be classified as ordinary, namely: 1) the office to which the jurisdiction is attached must be an office *in the strict sense* (v.g. office of local Ordinary, pastor, superior in an exempt clerical religious institute), and 2) the jurisdiction must be attached to that office by law, either by the common law or particular law or by legal custom (v.g. jurisdiction given to pastors by Canon 1245 to dispense from feasts and fasts).

Delegated jurisdiction, therefore, lacks one or both of the essential qualities mentioned in the preceding paragraph. Thus the power given by law to confessors to absolve from censures in an urgent case is delegated power because the confessor holds an office only in the broad sense, not in the strict sense; the Bishops' quinquennial faculties are delegated power because they are given not by law but by special concession; the simple confessor's faculties to absolve from sins is delegated power both because it is given not by law but by special concession of the Ordinary and because the confessor does not hold an office in the strict sense.

3. *Judicial* jurisdiction is that which is exercised with the formalities described in the fourth book of the Code (court proceedings), *and also the power to absolve from sins.*

Voluntary jurisdiction includes all jurisdiction that is non-judicial, hence, the power to make laws, grant favors and dispensations, grant permissions for alienation of property, etc.

B. *Delegation*

1. One who has *ordinary* power of jurisdiction can delegate it in whole or in part to another, unless the law expressly provides otherwise. (Can. 199 § 1.)

Although pastors have ordinary jurisdiction for confessions, they, as well as priests who have universal delegated jurisdiction, cannot delegate or subdelegate this power to others. (PCI, 16 Oct., 1919.)

2. Jurisdiction *delegated by the Holy See* can be subdelegated, either for one act, or even habitually, unless the person delegated was chosen for his personal qualification, or subdelegation was forbidden. (Can. 199 § 2.)

Habitually — i.e., for a certain number of cases (v.g. ten times) or for a certain time (v.g. during lent).

For one act — only for one case.

3. Jurisdiction *delegated ad universitatem negotiorum* by one who has ordinary power but beneath the Roman Pontiff can be subdelegated in single cases. (Can. 199 § 3.)

Ad universitatem negotiorum — i.e., comprehending all cases or all cases of a certain kind (v.g. all matrimonial impediments).

In single cases — not only for one case, but also for several cases provided they are specifically determined (v.g. power to dispense John Jones and Joe Smith from fasting).

4. In other cases *delegated power* can be subdelegated only in case the faculty to subdelegate has been expressly granted. (Can. 199 § 4.)

For example, the pastor delegates you to assist at a marriage and states that you may subdelegate this power to some other priest.

5. No *subdelegated power* can be again subdelegated unless the power to do so has been expressly granted (Can. 199 § 5) by the person who first delegated by ordinary power.

C. *Use*

1. The power of jurisdiction can be exercised directly only upon one's subjects. (Can. 201 § 1.)

Laws and indults granting faculties to dispense usually also explicitly include the power to dispense *peregrini*. If such a clause is not contained in the grant of faculties, it seems that the one having jurisdiction may nevertheless use his power (whether ordinary or delegated) in favor of all those actually in the territory whether they are his subjects or not. (Cf. Beste, p. 218; S.R.R., case, coram Mannucci, 25 May, 1925.)

2. *Judicial power,* whether ordinary or delegated, cannot be exercised for one's own benefit, nor outside the territory, except as provided in Canons 401 § 1, 881 § 2, and 1637. (Can. 201 § 2.)

Ordinary power to absolve from sins and censures can be exercised on one's own subjects anywhere on earth. (Canons 401 § 1, 881 § 2.)

3. *Voluntary power* can be exercised for one's own benefit, or while one is outside one's own territory, or upon a subject who is outside the territory, unless the contrary is evident from the nature of the case or from law. (Can. 201 § 3.)

Thus, for example, an assistant pastor who has obtained delegated power to dispense from fasting can dispense himself, unless the power has been restricted to the sacramental forum.

4. An act of jurisdiction, whether ordinary or delegated, conferred for the *external forum,* is valid also for the internal forum; but the converse is not true. Power conferred for the *internal forum* can be exercised also in the internal extra-sacramental forum, unless the sacramental forum is demanded. If the forum for which the power was granted was *not specified,* the power is understood as granted for both fora, unless the contrary is evident from the nature of the case. (Can. 202 §§ 1-3.)

D. *Cessation*

1. *Delegated power* expires: a) when the business is finished; b) when the time has expired or the number of cases is exhausted; c) when the motive cause of the delegation has ceased; d) when it is revoked by the one who delegated, upon direct notice thereof to the delegate; e) when it is renounced by the delegate, upon direct notice to and acceptance thereof by the one who delegated. Delegated power *does not expire* with the expiration of the authority of the person who delegated, except in the two cases mentioned in Canon 61, namely, a) when the delegation was thus limited by clauses attached to it (v.g. "according to our good pleasure") and b) where one was delegated to grant a favor to specified persons, and the business is still to be begun. (Can. 207 § 1.)

Note well: when power was granted for the *internal forum,* an act of the power placed through inadvertence after the lapse of time or the expiration of the number of cases is valid. (Can. 207 § 2.)

2. *Ordinary power* expires only with the loss of the office to which it is attached. (Cf. Can. 208.)

E. *Supplied Jurisdiction*

1. *In case of inadvertence.* In the case of jurisdiction granted for the *internal* forum, an act is valid if through *inadvertence* it has been placed after the time for the faculties has expired or the number of cases for which one had the faculties has been exhausted. (Can. 207.)

2. *In common error.* In common error the Church supplies jurisdiction for both the internal and external forum. (Can. 209.) The error concerns the possession of jurisdiction. The error is common if it affects some sort of community, v.g., a diocese, parish, monastery. The error is common factually if in a place it is generally believed that a priest has jurisdiction when as a fact he has not. The error is common legally if there exists a public circumstance or set of circumstances from which the majority of reasonable persons, without any error of law, would naturally conclude that jurisdiction exists, whereas in fact it does not exist, and even though no one actually forms any judgment concerning the case. In other words, the error itself need not be common or public, but it suffices that the foundation of the error be public and common. For instance, a pastor announces from the pulpit that a religious priest will be present to help with confessions at Easter. The pastor forgets to obtain faculties for this priest. Common error exists, and the Church supplies jurisdiction by Canon 209, if in these circumstances, the religious priest hears confessions.

Note that common error is based on an actual consideration, a reasonable conclusion, and *not* on a mere assumption, on mere ignorance. General erroneous beliefs are insufficient foundation for common error.

For the *licit* use of jurisdiction supplied in common error the authors require a grave cause. Since, however, the Code itself says nothing about such a cause, we may hold that a priest may licitly act in cases of common error if on days of precept or some other such occasion the faithful wish to confess, and no other priest is present or cannot be had without difficulty, or if a great number of penitents is at hand so that the service of all available confessors is required. In the last analysis, we believe that a reasonable petition on the part of the faithful, i.e., a reasonable cause, suffices for the licit use of jurisdiction supplied in common error. (Cf. Cappello, *De Sacr.*, I, n. 31.) This presupposes that common error exists. If there is question of placing the cause or foundation for common error, a truly *grave* cause is absolutely required.

3. *In positive and probable doubt of law or of fact,* the Church supplies jurisdiction for both the internal and the external forum. (Can. 209.) A doubt is positive and probable when there is a serious or good reason to believe that one has jurisdiction, although there is also reason for the opposite belief. A doubt of law regards the existence, the extent or the meaning of the law; v.g., I doubt whether or not a marriage before a Justice of the Peace is a reserved sin in this diocese. A doubt of fact regards the existence of some circumstances which the law certainly requires that an act fall under its ambit; v.g., I doubt whether or not a person is really in danger of death, whether or not this case has all the requisites necessary to be a reserved case, etc. Note that in the last analysis, the doubt always comes back to this: do I have jurisdiction in this case? To have jurisdiction supplied by Canon 209 it is necessary that there be good reason to say that one has jurisdiction, even though perhaps there is also good reason to say that one has not.

For the *licit* use of jurisdiction supplied in positive and probable doubt, no special reasons are required.

Appendix: the power of orders entrusted to a person or attached to an office by the competent ecclesiastical superior cannot be transferred to another unless its transfer is expressly permitted by law or indult. (Can. 210.)

> Thus the faculty of pastors to administer the sacrament of confirmation to those in danger of death cannot be transferred or delegated to others. (S.C.Sacr., 14 Sept., 1946.)

II. DISPENSATIONS

A. *Power to Dispense*

1. *Ordinaries*

a. Laws, even invalidating and incapacitating laws, do not bind in case of a positive doubt of law; in a case of positive doubt of fact Ordinaries may dispense, provided the law is one from which the Holy See usually dispenses. (Can. 15.)

b. Ordinaries subordinate to the Roman Pontiff may dispense in particular cases from general laws of the Church, but only in cases in which recourse to the Holy See is difficult and there is danger of grave harm in delay, and provided that the dispensation is one which the Holy See is wont to grant. (Can. 81.)

> The ordinary means of communication is by mail. Communication with the Holy See is considered morally impossible if the danger of grave harm cannot be avoided except by the use of extraordinary means of communication. In law, extraordinary means are telephone, telegraph, or the sending of a courier by train, motor car, plane, ship, or other vehicle. (Cf. PCI, 12 Nov., 1922; Abbo-Hannan, I, n. 81.)

> The clause "recourse to the Holy See is difficult" is not verified when the Ordinary can easily have recourse to the Legate of the Roman Pontiff in the country, who is in communication with the Holy See. (PCI, 26 June, 1947.)

> The dispensing power granted in Canon 81 does not extend to reserved vows or to the obligation of clerical celibacy binding deacons and subdeacons. (PCI, 26 Jan., 1949.)

c. The Code gives Ordinaries power to dispense from many of the more common obligations and impediments of ecclesiastical law; further powers are enjoyed by local Ordinaries in virtue of the quinquennial faculties and by religious Ordinaries in virtue of privileges. These various powers are mentioned in *The Pastoral Companion* under the specific obligations and impediments in question.

d. Bishops and other local Ordinaries can dispense from diocesan laws and, in particular cases only, from laws of a provincial or plenary council, not however from laws which the Roman Pontiff has specially enacted for that particular territory, except according to the norm of Canon 81. (Canons 82, 291 § 2.)

2. *Pastors and Confessors*

The Code grants pastors and confessors faculties to dispense from many of the more common obligations, and in urgent cases from more important obligations. Further faculties are enjoyed by delegation from the local Ordinary and by privilege. These various faculties are mentioned in *The Pastoral Companion* under the specific obligation in question.

B. *Just Cause for Dispensation*

A dispensation from ecclesiastical law is not to be granted without a just and reasonable cause, taking into consideration the gravity of the law from which the dispensation is given; otherwise the dispensation, if given by one inferior [to the legislator] is both illicit and invalid. In doubt as to the sufficiency of the reason, the dispensation is lawfully petitioned and licitly and validly granted. (Can. 84.)

C. *Use of a Dispensation*

1. A dispensation which is personal can be used anywhere, v.g., an individual dispensed from fasting need not fast even when he is outside his own diocese.

2. A dispensation which is local is restricted to a determined place, v.g., a diocese, city, parish. It can be used

by all who are in that place, but by no one outside that place.

3. A dispensation which is mixed, i.e., both personal and local, may be used by anyone in the territory and by the residents or subjects of the territory even when they are outside the territory.

Dispensations given for a whole diocese or city by general indult are presumed to be local or territorial and not personal unless the contrary is evident from the wording of the dispensation.

D. *Cessation of Dispensation*

1. A dispensation which is called *unica* or *simplex,* v.g., from today's fast, from the impediment of consanguinity, etc., once it is granted, does not cease when its motive cause ceases. However, as long as the dispensation has not been used, it can be recalled by the legislator.

If one is dispensed from a matrimonial impediment for the reason of legitimating a child, and the child dies before the marriage is celebrated, the dispensation is still valid.

2. A dispensation which has *recurring application,* v.g., from fasting during lent, *expires:*

a. by revocation, provided the dispensed person is notified of this;

b. by renunciation, provided the renunciation is accepted by the dispensing superior;

c. by lapse of the time for which the dispensation was given; also by lapse of the number of times for which the dispensation was given;

d. by the certain and complete cessation of the motive cause for the dispensation. (Cf. Canons 86, 60 § 1, 71, 72, 77.)

Note that the cessation of non-motive causes (*causae impulsivae*) do not affect the dispensation. Likewise, for the dispensation to cease it is required that all (not only some) motive causes cease certainly (not only probably) and completely (not only partially).

3. A dispensation which has *recurring application* does *not* expire:

a. on the expiration of the authority of the person who gave the dispensation, unless he gave it *ad beneplacitum* (v.g., at my good pleasure, as long as I am Bishop etc.);

b. by death of the person dispensed if the dispensation was given to the office he held rather than to the person holding the office;

c. by non-use or by contrary use provided that the dispensation is not burdensome to others (v.g., a dispensation from fasting), but if the dispensation places a burden on others, it ceases if legitimate prescription or tacit renunciation takes place. (Cf. Canons 81, 73, 74, 75, 76.)

III. RESCRIPTS

Since matrimonial dispensations from the Holy See and from the local Ordinary are granted by rescripts, the following canons will help the pastor judge the validity of matrimonial (as well as other) dispensations.

1. *Truth of the causae.* In all rescripts this condition is presupposed even if it is not expressly stated, namely, *if the request be founded on truth.* (Can. 40.)

> Hence, if the reasons for which the dispensation was granted are false, the dispensation is invalid. However, the rule of Canon 40 is further specified by other canons.

a. According to Canon 42 this is the essential truth that must be contained in one's petition in order to obtain a valid rescript, namely: 1) the concealment of the truth (*subreptio*) in one's petition does not prevent a rescript from being valid and effective, as long as one mentioned all those things which the *stylus curiae* demands for validity. (Can. 42 § 1.)

> What is demanded, of course, can be learned only by experience since the various tribunals and congregations as well as the various chanceries demand different information.

2) the allegation of falsehood (*obreptio*) does not invalidate a rescript provided that the single cause given be true, or if several causes are given that at least one motive cause be true. (Can. 42 § 2.)

b. An exception to paragraph 1 of Canon 42 is made in Canon 45. Rescripts granted with the clause *motu proprio* are valid even though certain matters which should have been mentioned in the petition are suppressed; not, however, if the single motive cause alleged is false. (Can. 45.)

> Hence, when the superior grants a favor *motu proprio* he affirms that he does so out of his generosity just as if he had not been asked for it. He limits this generosity to a case of subreption or the hiding of the truth and does not extend it to the case where not even one motive cause given is true.

c. An exception to paragraphs 1 and 2 of Canon 42 is made in Canon 1054. A dispensation granted from a matrimonial impediment of minor degree is not invalidated by any defect, whether of obreption or of subreption, even if the only motive cause stated in the petition is false. (Can. 1054.)

> Hence no omission and no falsehood will invalidate a dispensation from a matrimonial impediment of minor degree. Note however that the dispensation is valid only for the impediment that was mentioned in the petition. As is evident a dispensation granted from the impediment of consanguinity is not valid if the impediment actually existing is that of crime.

d. Time when the petition must be truthful: in rescripts in which no executor is required (i.e., rescripts *in forma gratiosa*) the petition must be founded on truth at the time when the rescript is issued; in all others (i.e., rescripts *in forma commissoria*) at the time of execution. (Can. 41.)

> This rule is a practical application of Canon 38 which states that rescripts by which a favor is granted without the ministry of an executor take effect from the moment at which the rescript is issued; all others from the time of execution. Note that

rescripts from the Holy See are usually *in forma commissoria;* from the local Ordinary, ordinarily *in forma gratiosa.*

2. *Mistakes in the rescript.* Rescripts are not invalidated by an error in the name of the person to whom or by whom they are granted, or by a mistake in the place where the person dwells, or by an error concerning the favor itself, provided that, in the judgment of the Ordinary, there is no doubt as to the identity of the person or as to the matter in question. (Can. 47.)

For the validity of the rescript it is required that there be no doubt as to the person or matter meant; the Ordinary's judgment affects only the licit use of the rescript.

3. *The execution of rescripts*

a. The executor of a rescript performs that function invalidly before he has received the rescript and has satisfied himself of its authenticity and integrity, unless advance notice of the rescript has been sent him on the authority of the granter. (Can. 53.)

As is evident, this canon deals with rescripts *in forma commissoria;* the one to whom some faculty has been granted by the rescript cannot validly use that faculty until he receives the rescript and examines it to find if it is authentic. He may use the faculty granted before he actually receives the rescript only if the one granting the faculty, or some qualified official acting on this person's behalf, informs him in advance of the faculty granted. If, however, one acts invalidly because the prescription of this canon has not been observed, he does not lose that faculty granted by the rescript and hence can use the faculty once the rescript arrives. (Cf. Can. 59 § 1.)

b. The executor of a rescript must use his faculty according to the norm of his mandate, and the execution is invalid unless he fulfills the essential conditions expressed in the rescript and follows the substantial form of procedure required. (Can. 55.)

If a person fails against the prescription of this canon, he does not lose his faculty, but can execute the rescript anew. (Cf. Can. 59 § 1.)

4. *Conditions appended to rescripts.* Conditions appended to rescripts are essential to their validity only when they are expressed by the particles, *si, dummodo,* or others of the same meaning (Can. 39), v.g. *nisi, non aliter, tantum.*

> In regard to conditions expressed in the ablative absolute, the general rule is that they are not for the validity of a rescript unless the nature of the case or the *stylus curiae* evidently demand their fulfillment for the validity of the favor, faculty, etc. granted. (V.C., II, n. 322.) Thus the following are looked upon as essential conditions: *audita prius eius confessione; in actu sacramentalis confessionis tantum; remoto fidei periculo.* Certainly affecting the licitness only are: *imposita gravi poenitentia, remoto scandalo, de consensu Ordinarii, praemissis proclamationibus, etc.*

5. *Cessation of rescripts*

a. A rescript which has been revoked by a special act of the superior remains in effect until the revocation has been made known to the person who obtained the rescript. (Can. 60 § 1.)

b. Rescripts are never revoked by a contrary law unless the law itself so provides, or unless the law is made by the superior of the granter of the rescript. (Can. 60 § 2.)

c. A rescript of the Holy See or of an Ordinary is not invalidated by the vacancy of the Holy See or of the diocesan see, unless it should appear otherwise from the appended clauses, or unless the rescript confers on some person the power of granting a favor to particular persons named in it and the execution has not yet reached even its initial stage (*res adhuc integra sit*). (Can. 61.)

> The clauses *ad beneplacitum nostrum* and *donec voluero* would invalidate the rescript on a vacancy of the see; not, however, the clauses *ad beneplacitum Sedis* or *donec revocavero*. Note that the second exception refers to a rescript which grants to some person a special faculty to grant a favor to some other persons who are mentioned in the rescript and nothing

has yet been done about the granting of this favor, i.e., not even a preparatory act for the execution of the rescript has been placed.

CHAPTER II

Subjects of the Law — Domicile

I. Subjects of Ecclesiastical Law

Bound to the observance of merely ecclesiastical laws are the baptized who have attained the use of reason and have completed their seventh year of age, unless the contrary is expressly provided for in the law. (Cf. Can. 12.)

The completion of the seventh year of age is computed according to the norm of Canon 34 § 3, 3°. The seventh year is completed at the midnight which falls between one's seventh birthday and the following day.

Children who have sufficient use of reason are bound to the paschal precept even though they are not yet seven years of age. (Cf. Canons 859 § 1 and 906.)

Baptized Protestants are expressly exempted from the form of marriage and from the impediment of disparity of cult. (Canons 1099 and 1070.) In general, validly baptized Protestants are objectively bound by ecclesiastical law except in those cases where they are expressly exempted. Ignorance excuses them from the observance of many laws (v.g., fast and abstinence), not however from invalidating laws. (Cf. Can. 16.)

II. Subjects of Particular Law

1. Bound by the laws made for a particular territory are the persons for whom they are made, who have a domicile or quasi-domicile there and at the same time are actually staying there, the prescriptions of Canon 14 remaining intact. (Can. 13 § 2.)

Hence, that one be bound by the particular ecclesiastical laws of some diocese, province, or nation it is required that he be both *de territorio* in as far as he has a domicile or quasi-domicile there, and *in territorio* in as far as he is actually in the diocese, province, nation and is not travelling elsewhere. Exceptions to this principle are given in Canon 14.

2. a. *Peregrini* are not bound by the particular laws of their territory while they are absent from it, unless the transgression of the laws would bring harm to the territory, or unless the laws are personal. (Can. 14 § 1, 1°.)

b. *Peregrini* are not bound to the particular laws of the territory in which they are staying, with the exception of those laws which look to the tuition of the public order or which determine the formalities of legal acts. (Can. 14 § 1, 2°.)

> *Peregrini* are bound to the general laws of the Church only in as far as these laws are binding in the territory in which they are staying; *peregrini* are not bound to general laws of the Church which are not binding in the territory in which they are staying. (Cf. Can. 14 § 1, 3°.)
>
> *Vagi* (persons who have no domicile or quasi-domicile anywhere) are obliged to both the general and the particular laws which are binding in the place where they are staying. (Can. 14 § 2.)

III. DOMICILE

1. *Acquisition of Voluntary Domicile*

a. Domicile is acquired either by living in a parish, diocese, etc., with the intention of remaining permanently unless called away, or by actually living in this place for ten years. (Can. 92 § 1.)

b. Quasi-domicile is acquired either by living in a parish, diocese, etc., with the intention of staying there at least for the greater part of the year unless called away, or by actually living in this place for the greater part of the year. (Can. 92 § 2.)

> When domicile or quasi-domicile are acquired by actual residence for a period of 10 years or of over 6 months, the time need not be absolutely continuous; moral continuity suffices; hence brief absences do not break the continuity of the period of time.
>
> Domicile (or quasi-domicile) acquired in a parish is called parochial; acquired in a diocese but not in a parish, is called diocesan. (Can. 92 § 3.)

2. *Acquisition of Legal (Necessary) Domicile*

a. A wife not legally separated from her husband necessarily retains the domicile of her husband; an insane person, the domicile of his guardian; a minor, the domicile of his parents or legal guardians. (Can. 93 § 1.)

These domiciles are assigned by law irrespective of the actual place of residence of a wife or minor and irrespective of any personal intention to live there, or even to not live there. Once the status of subjection to the authority of a husband or parents ceases, the legal domicile is lost, and voluntary domicile is acquired if the conditions specified in Canon 92 are fulfilled.

A minor who has completed his seventh year can acquire a quasi-domicile of his own; a wife, not legally separated from her husband, can acquire a quasi-domicile of her own; a wife legally separated from her husband can acquire a domicile of her own. (Can. 93 § 2.)

b. By analogy of law we assign a legal domicile to religious. Religious have a domicile at the house to which they are permanently assigned by their superiors. Religious have a quasi-domicile in a place, outside their own house, where they are commanded to reside for a greater part of the year, or where under obedience, they actually do reside for the greater part of the year. — This is a simple solution to the problem of a religious' domicile and quasi-domicile, supplying the silence of the Code, according to the norm of Canon 20. (Cf. V.C., I, n. 217; Coronata, I, n. 128.)

3. *Effect of Domicile*

By both domicile and quasi-domicile a person obtains his proper pastor and Ordinary. The proper pastor and Ordinary of a *vagus* is the pastor and local Ordinary of the place where the *vagus* is actually staying. Those, also, who have only a diocesan domicile or quasi-domicile obtain as their proper pastor the pastor of the place in which they are actually staying. (Can. 94.)

It frequently occurs that a person has several proper Ordinaries and pastors by reason of domicile in one place and quasi-domicile in another. Which proper Ordinary or pastor is to be preferred in various cases (as for baptism, marriage, burial) is often determined either by law or by legal custom; in other cases one has the liberty to choose whichever proper Ordinary or pastor one prefers.

4. *Loss of Domicile*

Domicile and quasi-domicile are lost by departure from the place with the intention not to return, the prescription of Canon 93 remaining intact. (Can. 95.)

Hence mere absence, even for a number of years does not cause loss of domicile or quasi-domicile as long as the intention to return exists.

Legal (necessary) domicile is not lost by departure even with the intention never to return) it is lost only when subjection to authority of a husband, parents, or guardian ceases. (Cf. Can. 93.)

CHAPTER III

The Computation of Time

In computing the hours of the day the common usage of the place is to be followed; however in the private celebration of Mass, in the private recitation of the canonical hours, in the reception of Holy Communion, and in the observance of the law of fast or abstinence, although the computation of time in local usage is different, one can follow either the local true or mean sun time, or the legal time, whether regional or extraordinary. (Can. 33 § 1.)

The private celebration of Mass is a celebration that is not public in the juridical sense, hence any Mass which is not a capitular or conventual Mass or the parish Mass; *the reception of Holy Communion,* i.e., in computing the hour when Holy Communion may be distributed; *fast or abstinence,* i.e., in determining the moment when the obligation begins or ends.

Local time is either true or mean. True sun time is determined by the position of the sun; it is true noon for any place when the sun reaches its highest position. But days measured from noon to noon according to the passage of the sun across the meridian are not of equal length; such days vary in length according to the seasons of the year. To avoid the inconvenience of these daily variations a mean solar time has been devised, to obtain days of equal duration. According to mean sun time, therefore, the time from noon to noon is twenty-four hours or the average length of the solar day.

Legal time is either regional (standard) or extraordinary (daylight saving, war time). Standard time is the time computed from a standard meridian. In the United States the following meridians are used as standards, designated from Greenwich (Observatory of London): For Colonial time, the 60th degree of longitude; Eastern time, the 75th degree; Central time, the 90th degree; Mountain time, the 105th degree; Pacific time, the 120th degree. Daylight saving time (summer time, as used in some cities) is an hour ahead of standard time.

The difference between the mean and the standard time may be ascertained in a simple manner by looking up in a geographical map the nearest standard meridian, and finding out how many degrees (east or west) your locality is from said meridian. Multiply the difference of degrees by 4 to get the difference in time (1 degree equals 4 minutes; a quarter degree is equal to 1 time minute). For instance, Minneapolis is 3 and ¼ degrees west of the 90th degree of longitude. Hence, multiply 3¼ by 4. Thus Minneapolis will be found to be 13 minutes west of the standard meridian. Observe the general rule: If your locality is east of the standard meridian, your local (mean) noon or midnight is ahead of the noon or midnight of your clock; if it is west of the standard meridian, your local (mean) noon or midnight is later than the noon or midnight of your clock.

After one manner of computing time has been chosen for one type of action, a person may in virtue of Canon 33 choose another manner of computing time for another action that is formally different. (PCI, reply, 29 May, 1947.) Hence, one may choose different kinds of time for fulfilling different obligations in which an option is given.

Thus, one may choose standard time to end one obligation and at the same time use mean sun time to begin another obligation. For example, on Thursday night in Omaha, if I have not yet finished my breviary when the clock strikes midnight according to standard time, I may excuse myself from whatever part of that day's office I have not had a chance to say; at the same time by using mean time I may take a meat sandwich until 23 minutes after 12 on the clock, since according to mean time the Friday abstinence has not yet begun. Though such action is not encouraged, it is lawful.

CHAPTER IV
Oriental Law

I. CATHOLICS OF THE ORIENTAL RITE

1. The original Oriental rites are the Byzantine, the Alexandrian, the Antiochene, the Chaldean, and the Armenian.

The district, autonomous Oriental rites now in existence are:
a. Coptic, Ethiopic (Alexandrian)
b. Malankar, Maronite, Syrian (Antiochene)
c. Bulgarian, Georgian, Greek, Melkite, Italo-Albanian, Rumenian, Russian, Serbian, Ruthenian (Byzantine)
d. Chaldean, Malabar (Chaldean)
e. Armenian (Armenian).

2. Baptism determines the rite, Latin or Oriental (and the Oriental rite in particular) to which a person belongs. Amongst the various Catholic rites, a person belongs to the rite in whose ceremonies he was baptized, unless perhaps baptism was conferred by a minister of a rite different from that of the parents either through fraud, or in case of grave necessity when a priest of the proper rite could not be at hand, or finally by apostolic or episcopal dispensation, when permission has been given for someone to be baptized in a certain rite without thereby being ascribed to this rite. In these three cases the person belongs to the rite in whose ceremonies he should have been baptized. (Cf. Can. 98 § 1; *Cleri Sanctitati*, Can. 6; PCI, 16 Oct., 1919.)

A child is to be baptized in the rite of the parents. If one parent belongs to the Latin rite, the other to the Oriental, the child is to be baptized in the rite of the father unless a contrary ruling is prescribed by particular law. If only one of the parents is Catholic, the child must be baptized in the rite of this parent. (Can. 756 §§ 1-3.)

A woman can transfer to the rite of her husband, either at the time of entering marriage or any time during the marriage;

when the marriage is dissolved, she is free to return to her former rite. (Can. 98 § 4; *Cleri Sanctitati,* Can. 9.)

II. LAW TO WHICH ORIENTALS ARE SUBJECT

1. The codification of the law of the Oriental Church was begun in 1929. To date four sections of Oriental law are promulgated and in force, namely:

Mp, *Crebrae allatae,* 22 Feb., 1949 — marriage legislation;

Mp, *Sollicitudinem nostram,* 6 Jan., 1950 — law for judicial procedure;

Mp, *Postquam Apostolicis,* 9 Feb., 1952 — law on religious, ecclesiastical goods, and the signification of legal terms.

Mp, *Cleri Sanctitati,* 2 June, 1957 — the law of persons, with introductory canons on the Oriental rites.

Dissident Orientals are considered bound to these laws, unless they are expressly exempted in particular matters by the law itself. (Cf. Coussa, I, n. 15.)

Orientals (Catholic and dissident) are bound to the laws of the Latin Code only when a canon of this Code expressly mentions Orientals, or when the Code treats of matters which by their very nature affect also Orientals.

2. Orientals are also bound to the particular laws of their own individual rite; however by reason of domicile outside their own patriarchal territory they are not bound to the disciplinary laws of the local Oriental synods since they are not subject to the jurisdiction governing the places for which these synodal laws are constituted. On the other hand, Orientals subject to Latin Ordinaries are subject to the disciplinary laws emanating from the jurisdiction of the local hierarchy where they have their domicile, as long as these laws are not detrimental to their respective rites. (Cf. Ap. Lett., *Orientalium dignitas,* 30 Nov., 1894, n. 9.)

III. JURISDICTION OVER ORIENTALS

A. *Proper Ordinary and Proper Pastor*

1. Ruthenians in the United States are subject to their own Ordinaries of the Byzantine rite.

The Byzantine Rite Eparchies of Philadelphia and Stamford have jurisdiction over Ruthenians who come from (roughly) the Austrian half of the former Austro-Hungarian Monarchy; also over the descendants of such persons and women married to these persons if they comply with Canon 98 § 4; etc. The jurisdiction of the Eparchy of Philadelphia extends territorially to all the lands under the sovereignty of the United States excepting the territory of the Eparchy of Stamford which comprises the New England States and the State of New York. The people of these Eparchies call themselves Ukranians.

The Byzantine Rite Apostolic Exarchy of Pittsburg has jurisdiction over Ruthenians coming from (roughly) the Hungarian half of the former Austro-Hungarian Monarchy; also over the descendants of these people, etc. — as mentioned above. The jurisdiction of the Exarchy extends territorially to all lands under the sovereignty of the United States. These people refer to themselves as Orientals of the Byzantine Slavonic Rite.

2. All non-Ruthenian Orientals in the United States (Syrians, Maronites, Melkites, etc.) are subject to the jurisdiction of the Latin hierarchy according to the norms of the Apostolic letter *Orientalium dignitas,* 30 Nov., 1894, and of Canon 22 § 3 of the Mp, *Cleri Sanctitati,* 2 June, 1957.

3. Ruthenian Orientals in the United States ordinarily have pastors of their own rite and diocese and are subject to the jurisdiction of these pastors. If there is no pastor of their own diocese in the place, they then become subject to the pastor of another diocese of their Byzantine rite.

If there is no Ruthenian parish at all, then their Hierarch (Ordinary) is to appoint a priest of another rite (Latin or Oriental) to be their pastor. (*Cleri Sanctitati,* Can. 22 § 2.) If this is not done, then these people are to be considered subject to the Latin rite pastor of their domicile or quasi-domicile.

4. Non-Ruthenian Orientals in the United States re-

ceive their pastors from the Latin Ordinaries to whom they are subject. This pastor may be one of their own rite or one of a different Oriental rite or finally one of the Latin rite. (Cf. *Cleri Sanctitati,* Can. 22 §§ 2-3.)

> If no such appointment is made for places where these Orientals have no parish of their own rite, they automatically become subject to the Latin pastor of their domocile or quasi-domicile.

B. *Use of Faculties in Favor of Orientals*

1. Ordinaries of the Latin rite do not have jurisdiction over the faithful of the Ruthenian rite in the United States. (Cf. Coussa, I, n. 305.)

2. Ordinaries of the Latin rite may use their ordinary power as well as power delegated to them by their quinquennial faculties in favor of non-Ruthenian Orientals in the United States who are their subjects. (Cf. S.C.E.O., 24 July, 1948; Diederichs, CUA, n. 229, p. 49.)

> Note: Concerning confessional jurisdiction see below, p. 23.

IV. SACRAMENTS — FEASTS — BURIAL

1. *Sacraments:* The priest of the Latin rite may administer the sacraments of penance, Eucharist, and, in case of necessity, extreme unction to the faithful of the Oriental rite whether Ruthenian or non-Ruthenian; under certain conditions he may also administer baptism and assist at marriage. The priest always follows the rubrics and ceremonies of his own rite in the administration of the sacraments. (Cf. Canons 881 § 1; 866 §§ 1-2; 938 § 2.)

> Orientals follow the same prescriptions for the Eucharistic fast as do Latins.

2. *Feasts and Fasts:* All Orientals in the United States may follow either the prescriptions of their own rite concerning Holydays, fasts and abstinence, or those of the Latin rite, if the former are inconvenient for them. This

privilege is granted to individuals and families, not to communities as such. (Cf. S.C.E.O., decr., 1 March, 1929; reply, 19 Dec., 1928.) The Paschal precept exists also in the Oriental rites. (Fonti, Serie II, Fasc. XVII, 58.)

> Orientals may satisfy their obligation of attending Mass through attendance at Mass in the Latin rite. (Cf. S.C.E.O., decl., 11 June, 1930.)

> Latin rite pastors and Ordinaries may dispense their Oriental rite subjects from the law of feasts and fasts. (Cf. Pospishil, p. 61.)

3. *Burial:* The Latin priest may bury Orientals who were his subjects; the celebration of funerals for families of mixed rite pertains to the pastor of the rite to which the deceased belonged. (Cf. S.C.E.O., decr., 1 March, 1929.)

> The ceremonies for burial will be those of the officiating priest's rite. (Cf. *Cleri Sanctitati,* Can. 2 § 1.)

V. CONFESSIONAL JURISDICTION

A. *Absolution from Sins*

1. The Latin confessor can absolve the faithful of any Oriental rite who come to confession to him. (Can. 881 § 1.)

> However, a priest of the Latin rite cannot validly and licitly hear confessions and give absolution in a church or oratory which is subject to the exclusive jurisdiction of the Ordinary of the Byzantine rite, unless the latter has expressly granted him the faculty to do so. (S.C.P.F., 2 Dec., 1932.)

2. Priests of the Oriental rite, who receive confessional jurisdiction from the Latin Ordinary, may absolve all penitents irrespective of rite who approach their confessionals. (Cf. Canons 881 § 1; 905; Walsh, CUA, n. 320, pp. 36-37, 48; Diederichs, CUA, n. 229, p. 96.)

> If the faculties given to the Oriental priest are not restricted to his particular church but are given for the entire diocese, he can hear confessions, upon invitation of the pastor, in Latin churches, or in churches of Oriental rites different from his own but under the jurisdiction of the Latin Ordinary.

3. Ruthenian priests receive confessional jurisdiction from their own Hierarchs (Ordinaries). This jurisdiction may be used also in favor of penitents of the Latin rite or of other Oriental rites who approach the confessional of the Ruthenian priest. (Cf. Can. 905.)

However, a priest of the Byzantine rite approved by his Ordinary for confessions, cannot validly and licitly absolve in a church or oratory which is subject to the exclusive jurisdiction of the Ordinary of the Latin rite, unless the latter has expressly granted him the faculty to do so. (S.C.E.O., 26 Aug., 1932.)

B. *Absolution from Reservations*

1. *Oriental confessors:* until the complete Oriental Code is promulgated, there seems to be sufficient reason to maintain that confessors of the Oriental rites may make use of the extensions of the material competence of their jurisdiction according to the conditions described in Canons 882 (danger of death), 900 (reserved sins), 990 § 2 (irregularities), 2252 and 2254 (censures), 2290 (vindicative penalties), of the Latin Code.

However, the provision of paragraph 3 of Canon 900 which states that an episcopal reservation ceases if the penitent goes outside the diocese to confess, does not hold if a Latin penitent goes to a Ruthenian church. Just because the Ruthenian church is outside the jurisdiction of the Latin Ordinary, Ruthenian priests cannot absolve the faithful of the Latin rite from censures and reserved sins established by the Latin Ordinaries. (Cf. S.C.E.O., decr., 1 March, 1929, n. 31.)

2. *Latin Confessors* (or Oriental confessors with jurisdiction from the Latin Ordinary): the laws by which more ample faculties are granted in certain circumstances (882, 900, 990 § 2, 2252, 2254, 2290) do not restrict the use of these faculties to the members of one's own rite. Consequently confessors of the Latin rite may make use of their extraordinary material competence in favor of penitents of Oriental rites. (Cf. Walsh, CUA, n. 320, p. 101; see also Diederichs, CUA, n. 229, p. 122.)

However, just because the Latin church is outside the jurisdiction of the Byzantine Ordinary, Latin confessors cannot absolve the Ruthenian faithful from censures and reserved cases established by the Byzantine Ordinaries, without the latter's permission. (Cf. S.C.E.O., decr., 1 March, 1929, n. 31.)

APPENDIX

Use of English in the Administration of the Sacraments

1. The new *Collectio Rituum ad Instar Appendicis Ritualis Romani Pro Dioecesibus Statuum Foederatorum Americae Septentrionalis* was approved by a rescript of the Sacred Congregation of Rites, 3 June, 1954. It contains the rites and ceremonies to be used for the administration of the sacraments of baptism, confirmation (by a priest), Holy Communion (and Viaticum), and extreme unction; also the rite for the celebration of matrimony, the apostolic blessing *in articulo mortis,* the prayers for the dying, the burial service, and finally, twenty-six of the more frequently used blessings. The prayers are given in both Latin and English and the English may, in most instances, be used instead of the Latin. However, *the English may be used only with the permission of the local Ordinary,* who can, if he wishes, approve the use of the vernacular or not, or grant approval with certain restrictions.

2. According to the rescript of the Sacred Congregation, the following must still be said in Latin:

a. In the administration of baptism of infants: the exorcisms, the formulas of the anointings and blessings, the form of baptism itself.

b. In the administration of baptism of adults: besides the above, also the psalms and the other introductory prayers.

c. In the administration of extreme unction: the oration for the imposition of the hands, the words of the anointings and the prayers following the anointing.

d. In the celebration of matrimony: the blessing of the ring and the formula, "Ego coniungo vos."

In the nuptial blessing outside of Mass, given by apostolic indult when Mass is not celebrated, the prayers in the Roman Ritual may be recited in English.

e. In the burial service: the prayers and absolutions (i.e., the "Libera" service after the Mass).

The *Praenotanda* to the *Collectio Rituum* adds this general rule: The sacramental forms, exorcisms, and all anointings are to be read in the Latin language alone. However, the English version, printed at the bottom of the page, may be read before or after the forms, exorcisms or anointings are performed in Latin.

3. *Pro Praxi:*

According to the principle given in the *Praenotanda* we may construct this rule of thumb:

a. If the English version is placed *next to the Latin text,* it suffices to say the prayers in English.

b. If the English version *is not printed alongside the Latin,* it means that the priest must say those prayers in Latin, but before or after the Latin, he may say the prayers also in English, using the English text printed at the bottom of the page.

Note: It is the right of the Ordinary to approve the use of the vernacular as given in the *Collectio Rituum* or not. Hence one must consult the diocesan regulations, for the use of the *Collectio Rituum* may not be approved in one's diocese; or perhaps only certain parts of it are approved for use in one's diocese.

PART II

BAPTISM

CHAPTER I

Subject of Baptism

I. INFANT BAPTISM

1. No one shall be baptized *while enclosed in his mother's womb* as long as there is a probable hope that baptism can be conferred after delivery. A fetus that had been baptized in the womb must be baptized against conditionally after delivery. (Can. 746 §§ 1, 5.)

> If the infant presents its head and danger of death is imminent, the infant shall be baptized on the head; and if later the infant is born alive, it shall not be rebaptized conditionally. If the infant presents some other member, the infant shall be baptized conditionally on that member if danger impends; but in that case if the infant is alive at birth, it shall be baptized again, conditionally. (Can. 746 §§ 2-3.)

2. *If a pregnant mother dies* the fetus is to be extracted by those whose responsibility it is to do so, and if it is certainly alive, it shall be baptized absolutely; if it is doubtful whether it is alive, conditionally. (Can. 746 § 4.)

> The priest has at most the duty to urge the relatives and the surgeon to perform the operation after the mother's death has been ascertained and as soon as the laws of the state permit.

3. Care must be taken that every *aborted fetus,* no matter at what period of gestation it is aborted, shall be baptized absolutely if it is certain that the fetus is alive; if there is doubt that it is alive, it shall be baptized conditionally. (Can. 747.)

4. *Monstrous and unusual forms of fetus* shall always be baptized at least conditionally; in doubt whether the fetus is one or many human beings, one shall be baptized absolutely, the others conditionally. (Can. 748.)

> In instructions to bridal couples, doctors, nurses and midwives, the pastor should remind them of the obligation to secure the baptism of the fetus in the above cases, as well as of any infant that is in danger of death. Manuals of pastoral medicine indicate the manner in which an abortive fetus is to be baptized.

5. *Infants who have been abandoned* shall be baptized conditionally if after careful investigation there is no certainty about their baptism. (Can. 749.)

6. *An infant child of non-Catholic parents* (infidel, heretical, schismatic or apostate), even if its parents are unwilling, is licitly baptized when its life is so threatened that it can prudently be foreseen that it will die before it attains the use of reason. (Canons 750 § 1; 751.)

> An infant of non-Catholic parents may lawfully be baptized even despite the objection of the parents if the danger of death is such that it may be prudently judged that the child will die before it comes to the use of reason.

Outside the danger of death, if there is sufficient guaranty of its Catholic education, the infant may be licitly baptized: a) If its parents or guardians, or at least one of them, assents; b) If its parents, that is, its father, mother, grandfather, grandmother and guardians are deceased or if they have been deprived of their parental right over the infant or have been effectively enjoined from exercising it in any way. (Can. 750 § 2.)

> If one of the parents was a Catholic but is now dead, no further consent is needed, but baptism is not to be conferred until there is sufficient assurance that the child will be reared as a Catholic. Care must be taken not to act contrary to the secular laws, with consequent harm to the faith.

7. Offspring shall be baptized *in the rite of the parents*. If one of the parents belongs to the Latin rite, the other to

the Oriental, offspring shall be baptized in the rite of the father unless a contrary ruling is prescribed by particular law. If only one of the parents is Catholic, offspring must be baptized in the rite of this parent. (Can. 756 §§ 1-3.)

Children who at the request of the parents, contrary to the prescriptions of Canon 756, have been baptized by a minister of a rite not their own, belong to the rite in which they should have been baptized according to Canon 756. (PCI, 16 Oct., 1919.)

II. ADULT BAPTISM

1. An adult shall not be baptized except with his own knowledge and consent and after due instruction; moreover he must be admonished to be sorry for his sins. (Can. 752 § 1.)

The baptism of children who have reached the use of reason is governed by Canon 752, and not by Canons 750 and 751. (Cf. Can. 745 § 2, 2°.) If such children ask for baptism, it may be conferred only if there is reasonable assurance that they will be reared as Catholics. In such cases, care must be taken not to run afoul of secular law. (Abbo-Hannan, I, n. 752.)

2. *In danger of death,* however, if the adult cannot be instructed more thoroughly in the principal mysteries of the faith, it suffices for the conferring of baptism that he should in some way manifest that he assents to these mysteries and sincerely promises that he will observe the precepts of the Christian religion. If he is not even able to ask for baptism, but has either previously or in his present condition given some probable indication of his intention to receive baptism, he should be baptized conditionally; if later he recovers and doubt remains concerning the validity of the baptism conferred, baptism should again be administered conditionally. (Can. 752 §§ 2-3.)

In extreme cases, if the sick person can no longer manifest his intention to receive baptism, a probable opinion allows conditional baptism on the presumption of a probable intention. (Genicot, II, n. 58.) If, therefore, dying adults are found unconscious, he who administers baptism in such cases is not to be censured. (Cf. V.C., II, n. 35.) In perfect agreement with these views is the prescription of the Second Plenary Council of Baltimore: "To be baptized are all (unconscious) dying adults whenever it can be prudently judged that they did not certainly reject the grace of faith." (Balt. II, n. 230.) Hence, in our country every unconscious dying person can be baptized with the condition *"si capax es"* unless one is positive the person refused baptism before becoming unconscious.

If a dying Protestant has some knowledge of the Blessed Trinity, the Incarnation and the Redemption but does not know the difference between the churches, *per se,* he is to be led to make a formal profession of faith in the Catholic Church. If, however, on account of imminent death a short instruction is impossible or would only serve to destroy his good faith, the dying person should be incited to an act of contrition and an intention to do all God wishes him to do. He may then be re-baptized, absolved, and anointed — all conditionally. (Cf. Arregui, n. 589.)

CHAPTER II

Manner of Baptism

I. CEREMONIES

1. Baptism shall be conferred *solemnly,* the prescription of Canon 759 remaining intact. (Can. 755 § 1.)

Baptismal water must be used in solemn baptism. If the blessed water in the baptistry is so diminished in quantity as to be deemed insufficient, water that is not blessed may be added, even more than once, but in quantity less than the blessed water. But if the water is corrupted, or has evaporated, or in any other way has become unavailable, the pastor shall pour fresh water in the font after the latter has been thoroughly cleaned and polished and shall bless it according to the rite as given in the *Rituale Romanum,* Title II, Chapter 8. (Cf. Can. 757.)

For reasons of cleanliness or prevention of contagion, *the touching of nose and ears* with saliva may be omitted. (S.R.C., decr., 14 Jan., 1944.)

Pastors should see to it that *a Christian name* be given the person baptized; but if they are not able to prevail in this matter, they should add to the name chosen by the parents the name of some saint and they shall record both names in the baptismal register. (Can. 761.)

2. It is lawful to confer baptism *privately* in danger of death. (Can. 759 § 1.)

If it is conferred by a minister who is neither priest nor deacon, only that shall be done which is necessary for the validity of the baptism; if by a priest or a deacon, the ceremonies that follow baptism shall also be observed, if time allows. The ceremonies, however, which for any reason were omitted in the conferring of baptism, shall be supplied as soon as possible in church. (Can. 759 §§ 1, 3.)

3. For a grave and reasonable cause the local Ordinary may permit the ceremonies prescribed for the baptism of infants to be used in the baptism of adults. (Can. 755 § 2.)

In many dioceses such permission is given by the diocesan pagella of faculties. In the absence of such a permission all those who have obtained the use of reason are to be baptized with the ceremonies prescribed for the baptism of adults. (Cf. Can. 745.)

4. When baptism is *repeated conditionally,* the ceremonies which were omitted in the previous baptism should be supplied; if they were performed in the previous baptism, they may be repeated or omitted at the second baptism. (Can. 760.)

The local Ordinary may permit *private baptism* in case of adult converts from heresy who are to be baptized conditionally, in which case also the ceremonies need not be supplied. (Cf. Can. 759 §§ 2-3.)

II. Sponsor

1. No one shall be *solemnly baptized* unless, so far as this is possible, he has a sponsor. (Can. 762 § 1.) Only one sponsor, even of different sex than that of the person baptized, or at most two, one man and one woman should be employed. (Can. 764.)

Even *in private baptism* a sponsor should be employed if it is easy to provide one; if a sponsor was not employed, one should be used in the supplying of the ceremonies, but in this case he does not contract any spiritual relationship. (Can. 762 § 2.)

When *baptism is repeated conditionally,* the same sponsor, who acted at the first baptism should, if possible, be employed; otherwise a sponsor is not required in conditional baptism. (Can. 763 § 1.)

2. In order that one may *validly* act as sponsor, it is necessary:

a. That he be baptized, have the use of reason and the intention to act as sponsor;

b. That he belong to no heretical or schismatic sect; be not, by a condemnatory or a declaratory sentence, excommunicated, infamous by infamy of law, or excluded from legitimate acts; be not a deposed or degraded cleric;

c. That he be not the father, mother, or spouse of the person to be baptized;

d. That he be designated by the person to be baptized or the latter's parents or guardians or, in default of these, by the minister;

e. That he himself personally or by proxy physically hold or touch the person being baptized in the very act of baptism or that he immediately lift or receive the person baptized from the sacred font or from the hands of the person baptizing. (Can. 765.)

3. In order that one may *licitly* be admitted as a sponsor, it is necessary:

a. That he shall have reached the fourteenth year of his age, unless for a justifying reason the minister judges otherwise;

One reaches his fourteenth year the day after his 13th birthday. A just cause for admitting a younger sponsor is, v.g., the difficulty of finding another among the relatives. (V.C., II, n. 48.)

b. That he be not, on account of a notorious delict, excommunicated or excluded from legitimate acts or infamous by infamy of law, even though sentence was not pronounced against him; and that he be not under interdict or otherwise publicly marked by crime or factual infamy;

> Catholics publicly living in an invalid civil marriage are excluded from being lawful sponsors, but not excluded are those who have not made their Easter duty.

c.   That he should know the rudiments of faith;

d.   That he be not a novice or a professed member in a religious institute, except in a case of necessity, and then only with the express permission of at least the local superior;

e.   That he be not in sacred orders, unless he has obtained the express permission of his proper Ordinary (Can. 766.)

> In doubt whether one can be admitted to the valid or the lawful exercise of the function of sponsor, the pastor shall, if time allows, consult the Ordinary. (Can. 767.)

4.   *Sponsor by proxy:* if the sponsor cannot be present in person, he may appoint another person to represent him, but the appointment must be made in such wise that there is certainty as to the person who takes the responsibility as sponsor. Ordinarily the appointment of the proxy should be made by the sponsor in writing or before two witnesses, in order that there be certainty as to who is the responsible person. The custom of leaving the appointment of the proxy to the parents of the infant or to the baptizing priest, tends to make sponsorship doubtful, and is to be reprobated. The real sponsor must give a mandate directly or indirectly (through the agency of others but with his consent) to the proxy. In the record of baptism or confirmation the names of both the sponsor and the proxy should be entered. (S.C.Sacr., instr., 25 Nov., 1925.)

Protestants and schismatics may not act as proxy. (Cf. Abbo-Hannan, I, n. 765.)

III. PLACE

1. The proper place for the administration of solemn baptism is the baptistery *in a church or public oratory*. (Can. 773.)

If, owing to distance or other circumstances, the person to be baptized cannot, without serious inconvenience or danger, come or be carried to the parish church or to some other church which enjoys the right to have a font, solemn baptism may and should be conferred by the pastor in the nearest church or public oratory within the parish limits, even though it should not have a baptismal font. (Can. 775.) The inconvenience or danger must be serious, to be judged by the pastor. It should be noted that this canon is speaking of the proper pastor within his parish limits.

2. Solemn baptism is *reserved to one's proper pastor*. If, however, the child cannot be taken to the proper pastor easily and without delay, any pastor may baptize it within the limits of his parish. (Cf. Can. 738.)

Chaplains in hospitals and orphanages are not *per se* allowed to confer solemn baptism. If, however, these places have been withdrawn from the jurisdiction of the pastor by the Ordinary (Can. 464), it would seem that the Ordinary could permit a font to be erected there (Coronata, *De Sacr.*, I, n. 154) and grant the chaplain permission to administer solemn baptism there when special circumstances warrant a departure from the ordinary ruling of the Code that infants are to be baptized in the parish church.

3. Ordinarily solemn baptism may *not* be administered in *private homes* unless the bishop permits it for a just cause in some extraordinary case. (Cf. Can. 776.)

Solemn baptism may never be administered in the homes of non-Catholics, not even in the case of necessity or danger of death. (S.R.C., 17 Jan., 1914.)

IV. RECORD

1. Pastors are obliged to record exactly and without delay in the baptismal register the names of persons bap-

tized, making mention of the minister, the parents, the sponsors, the place and the day on which baptism was conferred. (Can. 777 § 1.)

> In the case, however, of *illegitimate children,* the name of the mother is to be entered, if her motherhood is publicly known with certainty or if she voluntarily requests it in writing or in the presence of two witnesses. The name of the father is to be entered, only if he voluntarily requests this of the pastor either in writing or in the presence of two witnesses or if he is known to be the father from a public authentic document. In other cases, the baptized child shall be recorded as the child of an unknown father or of unknown parents. (Can. 777 § 2.)

2. If the baptism was conferred neither by the proper pastor nor in his presence, the minister shall as soon as possible notify the proper pastor by reason of domicile of the fact of the administration of baptism. (Can. 778.)

> Notification must also be sent in the case of private baptism.
>
> Children baptized in another rite in danger of death, or born and baptized in a place where the father's pastor was not at hand, belong to the rite of the father; and the priest who performed the baptism, must send a record of it to the proper pastor. (Cf. S.C.E.O., 1 March, 1929.)

CHAPTER III

Admitting Converts

Converts should be received with great care, especially if they are strangers to the pastor. The pastor should above all try to ascertain their motives. If material considerations (intended marriage) are impelling motives, he should apprise them that such motives are not sufficient. He should not, however, for that reason refuse to instruct them, since grace often builds up on extrinsic and natural motives.

I. REPORT TO THE BISHOP

If it can be done conveniently, the baptism of adults should be referred to the local Ordinary, so that if he so desires, he himself or a delegate may baptize with greater solemnity. (Can. 744.)

> The bishops of the United States do not insist upon this right.
>
> Conditional baptism is not reserved to the Ordinary by the common law. In some dioceses, however, the petition of the catechumen must be referred to the bishop, who then gives permission for his reception into the Church and, in case the catechumen has been validly baptized in some Protestant sect, grants the faculty to absolve him in the external forum from excommunication incurred because of heresy.

II. RE-BAPTIZING THE CONVERT

Since error and unbelief on the part of the minister do not *per se* affect the validity of baptism, the baptism administered by heretics is without doubt valid if the right matter, form and intention are not wanting. Hence, in each case diligent inquiry shall be made as to the validity or invalidity of the non-Catholic baptism of the prospective convert. If, after the investigation has been made, there still remains a probable doubt concerning the validity of the baptism, then it is to be repeated conditionally.

> In case the investigation cannot be made easily or it is clear from the circumstances that no certainty can be obtained, baptism may, as a rule, be repeated conditionally without any further ado. (Cf. Noldin, III, n. 74.)

III. ACT OF RECEPTION

1. If it is *certain* that the *heretical baptism is invalid,* absolute baptism must be administered with the ceremonies for the baptism of children in case the person to be baptized has not attained the use of reason; otherwise the ceremonies for the baptism of adults must be used, unless the bishop has granted permission to use the rite for the baptism of children. The abjuration of heresy, absolution from censure, and confession are omitted.

2. If the *former baptism is dubiously valid* and the convert is to be re-baptized conditionally, the following are to be observed:

a. Profession of faith and abjuration of heresy;

b. Conditional baptism;

c. Confession with conditional absolution.

3. If the *heretical baptism is valid,* the order of procedure is:

a. Profession of faith and abjuration of heresy;

b. Absolution in the external forum from excommunication;

c. Confession and absolution from sins.

Faculties for the absolution from the excommunication must be obtained from the local Ordinary. Confer your diocesan pagella.

In the case of children not yet fourteen years of age, the absolution from censure is omitted.

4. The Holy Office set down the following conditions regarding *a new short formula for Profession of Faith* for use in the United States:

a. The shorter formula is essentially for those only who have not attained puberty or who are uneducated. Moreover, in the judgment of the Ordinary, all those can be considered uneducated who do not have the religious development to understand the longer formula.

b. However, the longer formula must be used by the better educated adults. (S.O., 13 June, 1956.)

5. *If the convert is married to a Catholic,* the *benedictio sponsae* and the nuptial Mass may take place, as also the other ceremonies; not, however, the renewal of the consent.

6. The Code desires that both the priest who baptizes an adult, and the adult to be baptized, if he is in good health, be fasting. Unless grave and urgent reasons prevent it, the baptized adult should, immediately after baptism, assist at Mass and receive Holy Communion. (Cf. Can. 753.)

IV. ORIENTAL DISSIDENTS

With regard to converts from the Oriental dissident Churches a further problem arises, namely, to which rite will the convert belong upon reception into the Catholic Church?

1. If the convert was *never baptized* (but is of dissident parents), he may, upon embracing the Faith, freely choose the rite he wishes to belong to. (Cf. *Cleri Sanctitati,* Can. 12.)

2. If the convert was *already baptized* in a dissident Church, he may, upon entering the Catholic Church, embrace whichever rite he prefers; it is *desirable,* however, that he retain his own rite. (*Cleri Sanctitati,* Can. 11 § 1.)

> A cleric who in virtue of delegated power [from his local Ordinary] receives a baptized non-Catholic of an Oriental rite into any rite of the Catholic Church different from his own must inform the Hierarch (Ordinary) of the rite adopted. Moreover, it is expedient that, before he receives the person, he should consult the aforesaid Hierarch. (*Cleri Sanctitati,* Can. 11 § 2.)

3. The rules given in nos. 1 and 2 apply to converts who have reached puberty; before puberty, if the child is of unbaptized parents, these may select a rite for the child, but if the child is of baptized non-Catholic parents, the child is to be baptized in the rite of the parents. (Wojnar, *The Jurist,* XIX, pp. 235-237.) If the parents also convert to the Church, their children under the age of puberty become members of the rite which the parents enter upon conversion. (*Cleri Sanctitati,* Can. 10.)

> The doctrine given here differs from that concerning the selection not of rite, but of religion. In this latter case the parents substitute their will for the will of the child only before the child has reached the use of reason. (Cf. Can. 745 § 2.)

APPENDIX

Change of Rite

1. No one can validly transfer to another rite except by permission of the Apostolic See; and after a lawful transfer one cannot revert to his former rite except by permission of the Apostolic See. (Can. 98 § 3; *Cleri Sanctitati,* Can. 8 § 1.)

However a woman may transfer to the rite of her husband either at the time she enters marriage or any time during the marriage; and when the marriage is dissolved she is free to resume her former rite. (Can. 98 § 4; *Cleri Sanctitati*, Can. 9.)

2. If a father, or in a mixed marriage the Catholic mother, lawfully transfers to another rite, the children who have not attained puberty are transferred by the law itself to the same rite. (*Cleri Sanctitati*, Canons 10, 15.)

In this case it seems that adolescent children (boys 14, girls 12 years of age — Can. 88 § 2) may either remain in their own rite or follow the parent into the new rite. (Coussa, I, n. 28.) To make the matter certain, these children should be mentioned in the letter of petition for transfer of rite in case they too wish to embrace the parent's new rite.

3. Unless the rescript of the Apostolic See provides otherwise, the transfer to another rite has its effect from the moment when the declaration is made before the proper Hierarch (Ordinary) or pastor of the new rite, or a priest delegated by either of them and two witnesses, except in the transfer which is made by a woman entering into marriage, but she must declare herself in writing beforehand. (*Cleri Sanctitati*, Canons 13 § 1, 15.)

This declaration must be written into the baptismal register without delay, and notice of it must be sent by the pastor of the new rite to the pastor where the baptism of the one who changed rite was registered according to the norms of law, so that a notation of the change of rite can be made in the baptismal register; and if this is a second transfer notification must be sent also to the pastor of the rite previously adopted. (*Cleri Sanctitati*, Canons 13 § 2, 15.)

PART III

CONFIRMATION

I. SUBJECT

Persons who have not been baptized cannot be validly confirmed. To receive confirmation licitly and with fruit, the recipients must be in the state of grace, and if they have the use of reason, they must be sufficiently instructed. (Can. 786.)

> Though the sacrament of confirmation is not absolutely necessary for salvation, no one may neglect to receive it if he has the opportunity. The pastor should see to it that the faithful receive confirmation at the proper time. (Can. 787.)

II. AGE

Although in the Latin Church confirmation is usually deferred until about the seventh year of age, it may be conferred before this age if an infant is in danger of death, or if the minister for good and weighty reasons thinks it expedient to administer the sacrament earlier. (Can. 788.)

> In countries where it is customary to confirm the children immediately after baptism, this custom may be continued for grave and just reasons. Ordinarily, first Holy Communion should come after confirmation. Nevertheless, children who have reached the years of discretion are not to be prohibited from receiving Holy Communion though they have not yet had a chance to receive confirmation. (S.C.Sacr., reply, 30 June, 1932.)

III. SPONSOR

1. In accordance with a very ancient usage of the Church, a sponsor should, if possible, be procured for confirmation. (Can. 793.) The sponsor should stand for one

40

or two persons only, unless the minister for a just cause allows him to stand for more; and no candidate for confirmation shall have more than one sponsor. (Can. 794.)

> The *practice* of having only a few sponsors for a large number of candidates is not approved of by the Holy See, and violates the rubrics of the Roman Pontifical, which rules that one sponsor should not present more than one or two, unless necessity persuades the bishop to deviate from this rule.

2. In order that a person may be sponsor *validly,* the same conditions are required as for valid sponsorship at baptism; and in addition, the sponsor himself must be confirmed. (Can. 795.)

3. Also in order that a person may be sponsor at confirmation *licitly,* the same conditions are required as for sponsorship at baptism and, in addition, that he be not the same person as was sponsor at baptism, unless for a good reason the minister of confirmation thinks it proper to allow an exception to this rule, or unless confirmation is lawfully conferred immediately after baptism. The sponsor shall be of the same sex as the person confirmed unless in a particular case the contrary shall seem to the minister to be justified for a good reason. (Can. 796.)

IV. RECORD

The pastor must record in the confirmation register the names of the minister, the persons confirmed, the parents, the sponsors, and also the date and place of confirmation. Besides, he must make note of the confirmation in the baptismal register as demanded by Canon 470. (Can. 798.)

> If the confirmed person's own pastor was not present at the confirmation, he must be notified of the confirmation as soon as possible. (Can. 799.)

V. FACULTY OF PASTORS TO CONFIRM

1. By a decree of the S.C. Sacr., 14 Sept., 1946, the

faculty to confer the sacrament of confirmation is given to
the following priests under the conditions and in the cases
mentioned below:

a.   To pastors who have a territory of their own, exclusive therefore, of personal and family pastors unless
these also have their own proper, even though cumulative,
territory. (Pastors of national parishes would, therefore,
have the faculty.)

b.   To Vicars econome (administrators of vacant parishes) and to vicars of moral persons to whom parishes
have been entrusted (religious pastors).

c.   To priests to whom the full care of souls with all
the rights and obligations of pastors has been entrusted in
an exclusive and stable manner with a definite territory
and with a determinate church.

> This faculty to confirm is *not* extended to military chaplains
> (S.C.Sacr., reply, 2 Jan., 1947), nor to chaplains of hospitals
> and other institutions. (S.C.Sacr., reply, 30 Dec., 1946.) How-
> ever, on 25 Oct., 1948, the Congregation of the Sacraments
> granted the faculty to chaplains of maternity homes, hospitals
> for expectant mothers, and orphanages in the United States.
> The faculty was given to the chaplain who is permanently at-
> tached to the institution, and if there are several chaplains, to
> the senior (primus) chaplain only. The faculty was used only
> in cases of danger of death, in favor only of infants (pueruli)
> and only when *no bishop and not even the pastor of the place
> were available.* (Cf. *The Jurist,* IX, pp. 261-262.) The faculty
> was renewed several times, but expired in 1959 and has *not*
> been renewed since.

2.   The aforesaid ministers may confer the sacrament
of confirmation:

a.   Only upon the faithful who are staying in their territory, including persons in places which have been withdrawn from the parochial jurisdiction (v.g., seminaries,
sanitaria, religious houses howsoever exempt).

> Hence, it seems that the faculty may be used in favor of *vagi*
> and *peregrini* also. The faculty may be used also in favor of

the faithful of Oriental rites who are under the spiritual charge of the Latin clergy according to the norms of the Apostolic Constitution *Orientalium Dignitas,* which provided that every Oriental who is staying outside his patriarchal territory shall be under the administration of the Latin clergy. (S.C.E.O., decr., 1 May, 1948.)

b.   They must confer the sacrament personally.

Therefore, they cannot delegate the faculty to others.

c.   Only upon those faithful *who are in danger of death from grave illness.*

Hence, the danger of death must arise from an intrinsic cause, v.g., sickness, infirmity of old age, wounds, *not* from an extrinsic cause (v.g., air-raid, battle, etc.).

d.   The faculty may be used either in the episcopal city itself or outside of it, provided the bishop of the diocese cannot be had or is lawfully impeded from conferring the sacrament in person, and no other bishop is at hand who might take his place without grave inconvenience.

Note: Of the conditions mentioned under a-d, it seems that for the *valid* use of the faculty it is required:

1) That the one to be confirmed be in true danger of death from illness;

2) That the minister use the faculty personally and within the limits of his territory.

For the *lawful* use of the faculty it is also required that there be no bishop in the territory or that he be lawfully impeded.

3.   Annotation: The minister shall make the usual record in the confirmation register and add: confirmation conferred by apostolic indult, the person being in danger of death from grave illness. The usual annotation is also made in the baptismal register, and if the person confirmed belongs to another parish, his proper pastor is notified. The minister must also send to the local Ordinary an authentic notice of the confirmation which he has conferred.

4.   Rubrics: The rubrics and ceremonies to be used by the priest conferring the sacrament of confirmation may be found in the new *Collectio Rituum.*

5. Warning: A priest who dares to administer confirmation without having the faculty to do so, is to be suspended (a *ferendae sententiae* penalty); if the minister has the faculty to confirm but presumes to overstep the limits of the faculty, he is *ipso facto* deprived of the faculty. (Can. 2365.)

Note that since the law uses the terms *"ausus fuerit"* and *"praesumpserit,"* any diminution of imputability excuses from contracting these penalties.

The sacrament is to be conferred without charge on any ground. (S.C.Sacr., decr., 14 Sept., 1946.)

PART IV

HOLY EUCHARIST

CHAPTER I

Holy Mass

I. CONCERNING THE PRIEST WHO OFFERS MASS

A. *State of Grace*

No matter how contrite he may believe himself to be, a priest conscious of mortal sin, shall not dare to celebrate Mass without previous sacramental confession; but if, lacking a confessor to whom he is obliged to confess and being at the same time obliged by necessity to celebrate, he then celebrate Mass after having made an act of perfect contrition, he must go to confession as soon as possible. (Can. 807.)

The necessity to celebrate must be grave, as it is, v.g., when the priest cannot omit Mass (even daily Mass) without grave infamy or scandal arising, or when one must celebrate *ex officio* that the people may hear Mass, etc.

The impossibility to confess may arise from various sources: v.g., there is no confessor at hand at the time one must celebrate and one cannot get to a confessor without grave inconvenience (which is prudently judged from the distance to go, the time one has, one's age and physical condition, etc.); or, v.g., because of extraordinary shame one cannot bring himself to confess to the confessor it is possible to reach, as when an uncle or aged pastor would have to confess a very shameful sin to his nephew or his young assistant respectively; or, v.g., one cannot go to a confessor who is present without danger of infamy as when going to confession immediately before Mass is, according to the circumstances, an admission to others that one has committed a mortal sin. (Cf. Genicot, II, n. 191.)

The confession to be made *as soon as possible* is interpreted as obliging within three days. One is to abstain from further Masses until he gets to confession unless in the meantime it is still necessary to celebrate and it is still impossible to get to confession.

B. *Bination*

1. By the common law, the local Ordinary may grant permission to binate only when on account of scarcity of priests a considerable part of the faithful are otherwise not able to hear Mass on a day of obligation. (Can. 806.) By special indult Ordinaries may receive from the Holy See faculties to grant priests permission to binate on First Fridays and on other special occasions.

If a pastor has received permission to binate, his substitute may also use this privilege, for the authors consider the faculty granted to be local, not personal.

2. Authors generally permit the faculty to binate to be presumed when emergencies arise and the bishop cannot be contacted without inconvenience.

3. The faculty to binate ceases with the necessity. If, for instance, another priest is present who is able and willing to say Mass at an hour convenient for the people, this privilege cannot be used. (V.C., II, n. 78.)

On *Christmas and All Souls' Day* all priests may say three Holy Masses, also those who owing to poor eyesight have the privilege of saying the Votive Mass of the Blessed Virgin every day (S.R.C., instr., 3 Sept., 1942; instr., 15 Dec., 1957.) On Christmas a stipend may be taken for each Mass; on All Souls' Day only for one Mass. Whoever says three Masses on All Souls' Day, must apply one for all the faithful departed and one for the intention of the Holy Father. He who says but two Masses, may take a stipend for the one, but the other he must apply for the souls in general. A remuneration for the second and the third Mass *ex titulo extrinseco* (for instance, on account of distance or late hour) is, however, allowed by Canon 824. But it is not permissible to postpone the two prescribed intentions, in order to apply holy Mass for three stipends on All Souls' Day. (S.C.Conc., 15 Oct., 1915.)

C. *The Celebret*

1. A priest who wishes to celebrate Mass in a church to which he is not attached *is to be permitted* to celebrate Mass, if he presents an authentic and still valid commendatory letter of his Ordinary if he is a secular priest, or of his superior (at least of his local superior) if he is a religious, or of the Sacred Congregation for the Oriental Church if he belongs to an Oriental rite — unless it is evident that in the meantime he has been guilty of some offense which would require that he be debarred from the celebration of Mass. (Can. 804 § 1.)

If the priest has no such "celebret," but it is evident to the rector of the church that he is in good standing, *he may be permitted* to say Mass; if the priest is not known to the rector, he may still be permitted to say Mass once or twice, provided that he is attired in ecclesiastical garb, that he receives no remuneration whatsoever from the church in which he says Mass and that he notes his name, office, and diocese in a book specially kept for this purpose. (Can. 804 § 2.)

2. Special regulations made by the local Ordinary in this matter, *provided they are not contrary to the Code,* must be observed by all, even by exempt religious, unless there is question of giving to religious permission to celebrate Mass in a church of their own institute. (Can. 804 § 3.)

D. *The Server*

1. The priest shall not celebrate Mass without a *server* to wait upon him and answer the prayers. The server shall not be a woman unless no man can be had, and even then the woman must answer the prayers from a distance, and she must in no wise approach the altar. (Can. 813.)

Non-Catholics (even baptized non-Catholic children) are not allowed to serve Mass. (S.O., 20 Nov., 1850, 30 June and 7 July, 1864.)

2. Holy Mass may be said without a server:

a. When Holy Viaticum must be prepared for a sick person and no server is at hand;

b. To celebrate Mass for the people on a day of precept;

c. In time of epidemic when it is difficult to find a server and the priest would otherwise be obliged to abstain from celebrating for a notable time;

d. When the server leaves during the Mass, even though it be before the offertory;

e. When one has an apostolic indult to celebrate without a server, in which case, however, it is necessary that someone of the faithful be in the church during the Mass. (S.C. Sacr., instr., 1 Oct., 1949.)

> Relying on the principle that a proportionately grave cause excuses from the observance of an ecclesiastical law, it seems probable that a priest could occasionally say Mass without a server when it is seriously inconvenient to miss Mass just because no server can be had, v.g., to say Mass for a dying parent, or, v.g., the priest is so devoted to his Mass that to miss saying Mass really is a great hardship for him. (Cf. *Theological Studies,* XI, pp. 577-583.) Indeed, relying on customary interpretation of Canon 813, it seems probable that a priest could occasionally say Mass without a server even though no great inconvenience is experienced if Mass were omitted. (Cf. *Theological Studies,* XXI, pp. 256-270.)

E. *The Calendar*

1. In churches and public oratories, other than his own, a priest celebrates Mass according to the *calendar of the place* and not according to his own calendar. The same rule obtains when a priest celebrates in the principal semi-public oratory of a seminary, college, religious community, hospital, jail, etc. (*Cod. Rubr.,* n. 275.)

> The calendar of the place is ordinarily the calendar of the diocese except in the following cases:
>
> a. The calendar of the religious is used in churches which have been perpetually or indefinitely entrusted to an order or

congregation enjoying its own calendar. (Cf. S.R.C., 15 Dec., 1899; 22 April, 1910; *Cod. Rubr.,* n. 283.)

b. In oratories of nuns and sisters who have their own calendar, Mass is to be celebrated according to this calendar. Brothers and Sisters of the Third Order Regular must use the religious calendar and missal in their oratories. (Cf. S.R.C., 15 April, 1904; 28 Feb., 1914; 15 Dec., 1899; *Cod. Rubr.,* nos. 54, 283.)

2. In semi-public oratories of convents, schools, hospitals, etc., which do not have their own calendar, Mass is to be celebrated according to the calendar of the diocese even by religious priests who have their own calendar and who are perhaps chaplains in such places. In secondary oratories of convents, schools, etc., as well as in private oratories, a priest may use the calendar of the place or his own calendar. (Cf. *Cod. Rubr.,* nos. 276-277.)

3. *The Military Vicar* has authority to produce the directory of the divine office and Mass for the use of military chaplains. This directory may be used by the military chaplains everywhere when they celebrate Mass for the benefit of military personnel, and by priests who celebrate in churches or oratories reserved for the military. (S.C. Consist., instr., 23 April, 1951.)

Religious who are military chaplains may also, according to the prudent judgment of their superiors, follow the directory of the Military Vicar for the recitation of the divine office and celebration of Mass. (S.C.Rel., instr., 2 Feb., 1955.)

F. *Application of the Fruits of the Mass*

1. *Capable* of enjoying fruits of the Mass are sinners, infants, heretics, infidels and in general everyone, both living and dead, *except* the saints in Heaven, the damned in Hell and infants who have died without baptism.

Public application of Mass is forbidden for any living excommunicate, and for any deceased person who was denied ecclesiastical burial. (Canons 2262, 1241.)

Private application (known to one or the other only)

may be made in favor of all capable of receiving some fruits of the Mass, whether faithful or infidel, living or dead; for an excommunicate vitandus, however, only for his conversion. (Canons 809, 2262.)

> Hence, the private application of Mass is allowed for a deceased non-Catholic.

2. The local Ordinary may, for a reasonable cause, permit the pastor to offer the *Missa pro populo* on a day other than that on which he is obliged to offer it (Can. 466); hence, the pastor may, with the Ordinary's permission, celebrate marriage or funeral Masses for the intention of the couple or for the deceased respectively, and defer the application of the *Missa pro populo* to some other day.

3. Religious superiors may command their subjects even in virtue of holy obedience to celebrate Mass according to the intention prescribed by the constitutions or by the superiors themselves, the exceptions, however, allowed by the constitutions or legitimate custom remaining intact. (S.C. Rel., reply, 23 Mar., 1914.)

II. TIME AND PLACE FOR THE CELEBRATION OF MASS

A. *Time of Day*

1. Holy Mass should not be begun earlier than an hour before dawn, nor later than one hour after midday. (Can. 821 § 1.)

> In the private celebration of Mass one may compute the hour according to either true or mean sun time or standard or daylight time. (Cf. Can. 33.)

2. *On Christmas,* at midnight, unless there be a special indult, *only* the parochial or conventual Mass may be said or sung in the churches (Can. 821 § 2), at which Holy Communion may also be distributed.

In the oratories of religious or pious houses (hospitals,

seminaries, etc.) where the Blessed Sacrament is reserved, one and the same priest may say one or the three [also two] Masses at midnight, at which also all the faithful present satisfy their obligation of hearing Mass, and may also receive Holy Communion. (Can. 821 § 3; cf. Coronata, *De Sacr.*, I, n. 235.)

The interpretation of some authors that these Masses may be said only *"januis clausis"* can no longer be sustained. (Cf. PCI, 5 March, 1954 — *Commentarium pro Religiosis et Missionariis*, XXXIII, pp. 329-352.)

By the quinquennial faculties (S.C.Rel., n. 2) the local Ordinary may permit three Masses on Christmas night in churches of religious which are not included in Canon 821 § 3, with permission to those present to receive Holy Communion on condition, however, that the three Masses be said by the same priest. (*Digest*, IV, p. 76.)

3. *Evening Mass.* Local Ordinaries, except Vicars General without a special mandate, can permit the celebration of Mass in the afternoon hours every day, if the spiritual good of a notable part of the faithful requires it. (Mp, *Sacram Communionem*, 19 March, 1957.)

A "notable part" of the faithful may be interpreted as being about 20 persons, more or less, or some community of persons, v.g., a convent, hospital, etc. It was asked: "Can the bishop permit an evening Mass on feast days together with the celebration of a marriage ceremony?" The Sacred Congregation of Rites responded: "He can permit it if the good of a notable part of the faithful demands it, not, however, for the convenience of a single family." (S.R.C., 21 June, 1957.)

If one evening Mass suffices for the spiritual good of the faithful, several Masses cannot be permitted; if several Masses are necessary, then the local Ordinary can permit them even in the same church. (S.R.C., 21 June, 1957; cf. also *Periodica*, XLVI, p. 225.)

Priests cannot say Mass in the morning and evening of the same day unless they have received faculties to binate. (S.O., instr., 6 Jan., 1953.)

Whether or not the Mass may be said anytime in the afternoon or must begin no earlier than four o'clock is disputed by the authors. (Cf. *Clergy Review*, XLII, pp. 325, 593-594, 601.) In a private response, the Sacred Congregation of Rites asserted

that it may not be said before 4 P.M. (S.R.C., 21 June, 1957.)
No one doubts that it can be said in the early evening hours.

B. *Holy Week*

1. *Holy Thursday*. The Mass of the Lord's Supper is
to be celebrated in the evening, not earlier than 4:00 P.M.
and not later than 9:00 P.M. In order that all the faithful
may be present at Holy Mass and receive Holy Communion, the local Ordinary may also permit one or the other
low Mass to be said in churches and public oratories; in
semi-public oratories the Ordinary may permit only one
low Mass; and when the Mass of the Lord's Supper cannot
be celebrated, the local Ordinary, for pastoral considerations, can permit two low Masses to be said in churches
and public oratories, and one low Mass in semi-public
oratories. All these private Masses must likewise be said
not earlier than 4:00 P.M. and not later than 9:00 P.M.
(S.R.C., decr., 16 Nov., 1955; decl., 1 Feb., 1957.)

According to approved custom, once the permission to say a
low Mass in a church or oratory is obtained, it need not be
renewed every year. (Noldin, III, n. 202.)

On Holy Thursday, if in a church pertaining to regulars, the
sacred functions of the *Triduum Sacrum* cannot be carried
out, the Superior may say Mass privately and with the doors
closed in the oratory or church, in order to give Holy Communion to his subjects. (S.R.C., 31 Aug., 1839.)

2. *Good Friday*. On Good Friday the liturgical service
is to be celebrated in the afternoon hours, usually around
3:00 P.M. If, however, pastoral considerations suggest it,
the services may be begun already from 12:00 noon, or
held at a later hour, but not later than 9:00 P.M. (S.R.C.,
decr., 16 Nov., 1955; decl., 1 Feb., 1957.)

3. *Holy Saturday*. The vigil service is to be begun at
an hour which will allow the Mass itself to begin approx-
imately at midnight between Holy Saturday and Easter
Sunday. Because of circumstances of time and place the

local Ordinary may allow the vigil service to be held at an earlier hour; but it may not begin before dusk or certainly not before the setting of the sun. (S.R.C., decr., 16 Nov., 1955; 1 Feb., 1957.)

The priest who has the Mass of the paschal vigil at midnight may also say Mass on Easter Sunday, and if he has the necessary indult, also two or three Masses on Easter Sunday. (S.R.C., instr., 16 Nov., 1955.)

The paschal vigil can be celebrated also in churches or oratories where the functions of Holy Thursday and Good Friday did not take place; and it may likewise be omitted in churches and oratories where those functions were celebrated. (S.R.C., decl., 1 Feb., 1957.)

C. *The Place*

1. The local Ordinary, or in the case of a house of an exempt religion the major superior, can grant permission to celebrate Mass on a consecrated stone *outside of a church or oratory* in a proper place (even out-of-doors), but never in a bedroom, whenever a just and reasonable cause warrants it in some extraordinary and individual case. (Can. 822 § 4.)

The permission may be given, however, for several days, or for as long as the justifying reason and extraordinary case continues, v.g., for the whole period during which a parish church is undergoing repairs.

2. To celebrate *Mass at sea* a *special* papal indult is required over and above the faculty or privilege one may already have of celebrating Mass on a portable altar. (Can. 822 § 3.) Cardinals and bishops are granted this special privilege by law (Canons 239, 349); others may obtain it from the Apostolic Delegate.

According to a probable opinion, if a ship has its own oratory, any priest may use the oratory to say Mass on its altar, without obtaining a special indult for the celebration of Mass at sea. (Cappello, *De Sacr.,* I, n. 712; Coronata, *De Sacr.,* I, n. 257; Welsh, CUA, n. 305, p. 65.)

III. MASS STIPENDS

A. *General Rules*

1. It is the right of the local Ordinary to fix the stipend for Masses in his diocese, and no one may demand a larger one. If no such decree exists, the custom of the diocese determines the amount of the stipend. Even exempt religious are obliged to abide by the decree of the local Ordinary or by the custom of the diocese in this matter. (Can. 831.)

> A priest may accept a larger stipend if it is offered; and unless the local Ordinary has forbidden it, also a smaller one. (Can. 832.)

2. If anyone give a sum of money for the application of Masses without indicating the number, this is to be determined on the basis of the stipend of the place where the donor was staying, unless a contrary intention on his part ought to be lawfully presumed. (Can. 830.)

> Hence, in computing the number of Masses in this case, neither the domicile of the donor, nor the place where the stipend is received, nor the place where the Mass is celebrated, but the place where the donor is staying is considered, i.e., the place where the stipend is offered, or if sent by letter, the place from which it is sent.

3. If a priest celebrates Mass more than once a day and has to apply one Mass by a title of justice (v.g., *Missa pro populo*), he may not receive a stipend for another Mass, except on Christmas; he may, however, receive some compensation, based on a claim extrinsic to the application of the Mass (v.g., late hour, distance, singing). (Can. 824.)

> For Masses said at a privileged altar no larger stipend may be demanded by reason of the privilege. (Can. 918.)
>
> The mere necessity of binating does not constitute an extrinsic claim to a compensation. (S.C.Conc., 13, 17, Nov., 1937.)
>
> The obligation of applying Mass for departed members of Priests' Unions is not *ex iustitia* but only *ex fidelitate et caritate,*

and may, therefore, be satisfied by a bination Mass. (S.C.Conc., 14 Sept., 1878.)

4. It is presumed that the donor wishes only the application of the Mass; if, however, he expressly specifies certain circumstances to be observed in the celebration of Mass (place, time, votive, sung, Gregorian, etc.) the priest who accepts the stipend must carry out his intention. (Can. 833.)

> If these certain circumstances are demanded as substantial conditions, then one does not satisfy his obligation unless the Mass is said according to the manner specified. Often, however, these circumstances are added as non-essential conditions, so that one's obligation is substantially satisfied even if they are not observed, and a reasonable cause would excuse one from their observance altogether. (Genicot, II, n. 130.)

B. *Time for Fulfilling Mass Intentions*

As to the time when Holy Mass is to be applied, the following rules must be observed:

1. If the time was expressly specified by the donor of the stipend, Holy Mass must positively be said at that time. (Can. 834 § 1.)

2. If in case of manual stipends the donor did not expressly specify a time, then Masses ordered for an urgent intention must be said as soon as possible, and within a time proper to obtain the purpose; in all other cases the Masses must be said within a short time, that is, a time that is reasonable according to the larger or smaller number of Masses requested. (Can. 834 § 2.)

> In computing the time allowed, the following equation may be found useful (V.C., II, n. 106): $X = N + \dfrac{N}{2} + 30$. X is the time given to satisfy the obligations. N equals the number of Masses given by one donor. Hence, with 100 Masses given by one donor, $X = 100 + 50 + 30$. Hence, 180 days are granted for the fulfillment of these 100 intentions. If the priest needs more time to satisfy the obligation, he should make this

known to the donor when accepting the stipends. Moreover, the number of days granted is not to be taken so strictly as not to allow a week or two leeway.

3. If the donor expressly leaves the time for saying the Masses to the discretion of the priest, the same may say them as he finds it convenient. (Can. 834 § 3.) However, no one is allowed to accept more Masses to be said by himself than he can say within a year. (Can. 835.)

Masses which have not been said within a year after receiving the stipends, must be sent to one's own Ordinary, unless the donor of the stipends has allowed a longer time for satisfying the obligation. (Cf. Can. 841.)

4. Computation of the required time for the celebration of Masses begins on the day on which the priest who is to celebrate them receives the stipends, unless the contrary is evident from the will of the donor. (Cf. Can. 837.)

Hence, a priest who receives Masses from his Ordinary, if nothing is said concerning the time of the celebration, begins the computation of the *tempus utile* from the day on which he received the stipends from his Ordinary and not from the day on which the stipends were offered by the faithful. (S.C.Conc., 27 Feb., 1905.)

5. In churches where, on account of the special devotion of the faithful, stipends are offered in such numbers that it is impossible to say all the Masses there within the required time, the faithful should be informed by notices placed in conspicuous places that the Masses will be said either there, when it is convenient to do so, or elsewhere. (Can. 836.)

C. *Disposing of Stipends*

1. One who has a number of stipends which he is permitted to transmit to others, may send them to priests of his own choice, provided that he knows them to be of good reputation or to be recommended by their own Ordinary. (Can. 838.)

The Ordinary cannot, except by special indult, forbid his

priests to send *manual* stipends outside the diocese. He may forbid the transference of stipends derived from the income of endowments, i.e., of pious foundations. (S.C.Conc., 19 Feb., 1921.)

Religious may not give extra stipends to others. These stipends become the property of the institute just as any other alms, and hence the religious is not free to distribute them without the permission of his superior according to the constitutions, unless the donor gives stipends to the religious with the express declaration that the religious distribute them to priests of his choice. (Coronata, *De Sacr.*, I, n. 278.)

2. He who transmits to others Masses which he has received from the faithful, or which have in any way been entrusted to him, is held responsible for them until he has been notified of the receipt of the stipends and of the acceptance of the obligation. (Can. 839.)

Though Mass stipends may have been lost without fault of him who has the responsibility to say the Masses, the obligation does not cease. (Can. 829.)

3. He who transmits manual stipends to others, must transfer the entire stipend. He may not retain part of the stipend unless the donor expressly permits it or it is certain that what was offered in excess of the diocesan stipend, was given for the benefit of the immediate recipient. (Can. 840 § 1.)

Benedict XIV called it a detestable abuse for the priest who transmits the stipends to ask the celebrant to let him keep a portion of the stipend. (Ap. Const., *Quanta cura,* 3 June, 1741.) Some authors will, however, permit one to ask that a part of the stipend be kept, provided that the one receiving the smaller stipend is in no wise put under pressure to consent to this arrangement. (Cf., v.g., Cappello, *De Sacr.*, I, n. 667.)

For funeral and nuptial Masses, the celebration of which is reserved to the pastor by law or by custom, a larger stipend is usually given. If the Mass is celebrated by another, the pastor may keep what is in excess of the diocesan stipend for the Mass. (Noldin, III, n. 192.) Let him remember, however, to give the celebrant a stipend for the Mass itself, for the pastor has no right whatsoever to it.

4. With stipends *ad instar manualium,* unless the in-

tention of the founder rules otherwise, it suffices to transmit only the diocesan stipend as determined in the diocese
in which the Mass is to be celebrated, and the remainder
may be retained, if the higher stipend represents in part
the endowment of the benefice or pious cause. (Can. 840
§ 2.)

> Stipends *ad instar manualium* are stipends for *founded
> Masses* when these cannot be applied at the place designated
> or by the persons obligated in the articles of the foundation
> but in accordance with law or indult are sent to other priests
> that the obligations may be satisfied. (Can. 826.)

D.   *Gregorian Masses*

1.   Gregorian Masses are a series of thirty Masses said
on thirty consecutive days. It is required that the Masses
be said for a deceased person and for only one not for
several deceased persons. (S.C.Indulg., 14 Jan., 1889; 24
Aug., 1888.)

> It is not required that all the Masses be said by the same
> priest, but only that they be said each day without interruption,
> whether by the same priest, or by a different priest. It is not
> necessary to take the Requiem Mass on days permitted by the
> rubrics. The last three days of Holy Week do not interrupt the
> Gregorian sequence, and hence the series may be interrupted
> on these days, and begun again on Easter Sunday. (Cf. Noldin,
> III, n. 329.)

2.   *Must the series of Masses be begun anew if once
interrupted?* If the interruption is culpable, the series is
to be begun anew, unless the donor of the stipend permits
the opposite. If, however, the interruption is not culpable,
the priest is probably not bound to begin the series anew,
but it seems to suffice if he simply completes the remaining number of Masses. To begin anew would be an intolerable burden, and it is not at all evident that the soul of
the deceased suffers any great harm from the interruption,
especially if the priest says one or the other of the Masses
at a privileged altar. (Thus, Priimmer, II, n. 269; Cap-

pello, *De Sacr.,* I, n. 722; Coronata, *De Sacr.,* I, n. 273 and others.)

Hence unless the priest when accepting the stipend agrees to begin the series anew in case of an interruption, there is no obligation to repeat in case of a non-culpable interruption.

IV. DIALOGUE MASS (MISSA RECITATA)

1. The dialogue Mass, or a Mass in which the faithful participate by giving the liturgical responses to the celebrant, etc., admits of four degrees of participation:

a. The faithful give the easiest responses: *Amen, Et cum spiritu tuo, Deo gratias, Gloria tibi Domine, Laus tibi Christe, Habemus ad Dominum, Dignum et iustum est, Sed libera nos a malo.*

b. The faithful also give those responses which the server must give according to the rubrics, and if Holy Communion is given during the Mass, also recite the triple *Domine non sum dignus.*

c. The faithful also recite together with the celebrant these parts of the Ordinary of the Mass: the *Gloria in excelsis Deo,* the *Credo,* the *Sanctus-Benedictus,* and the *Agnus Dei.*

d. The faithful also recite together with the celebrant the parts pertaining to the Proper of the Mass: the Introit, Gradual, Offertory verse, and Communion prayer. (S.R. C., instr., 3 Sept., 1958, n. 31.)

2. The entire *Pater noster* may be recited with the celebrant, the *Amen* also being added. (S.R.C., 3 Sept., 1958, n. 32.)

3. In making these responses and in joining in the above mentioned prayers the Latin language must be used. (S.R.C., instr., 3 Sept., 1958, n. 14b.)

V. DEFECTS

1. *Concerning a defect of the wine:* if the priest is aware of this (that wine was not used but water) after consuming the Sacred Host or the water, he takes another host and puts wine and water in the chalice; he then offers, consecrates, and consumes both. *Or if the Mass is celebrated in a public place, where many people are present,* so that scandal might be avoided, the priest may take wine and water, and, having made the oblation as mentioned above, consecrate, and immediately consume the Sacred Species and continue as usual. (*Missale Romanum, de defectibus,* IV, 5.)

2. The place where the *Sacred Host falls,* is to be covered immediately with some clean article and afterwards washed. If it falls on the communion cloth, the place is to be marked and afterwards washed in the same way.

The rubric, according to the common opinion, does not oblige *sub gravi;* however, there is a grave obligation to wash the place where the Sacred Species of wine has fallen.

If the Host falls on the face, beard, or clothing of the communicant, the purification is to be omitted, because it is better to avoid the astonishment and bewilderment, or even perhaps the offense of the people, than to observe a rubric which obliges only lightly. (Ferreres, II, n. 393.)

3. If through negligence some of the *Precious Blood spills* either on the ground or on the altar table, It is to be licked up with the tongue, and the place is to be scraped as much as is necessary, and the scrapings are to be burned; the ashes are to be placed in the sacrarium. If It spills on the altar-stone, the priest is to lick up the drop, the place is to be well washed, and the water with which it was washed is to be poured into the sacrarium. If It falls on the altar linens and goes through to the second cloth, or even to the third: the linens are to be washed three times

where the drop fell, and the water which was used to wash the linens should be poured into the sacrarium. If It falls only on the corporal, or on the priest's vestment, they must be similarly washed, and the water used should be placed in the sacrarium. If It falls on the covering of the floor or the rug, these should be well washed, as indicated above. (*Missale Romanum, de defectibus*, X, 12.)

CHAPTER II

Holy Communion

I. THE EUCHARISTIC FAST

A. *Introduction*

The law of the Code on the eucharistic fast (Canons 808 and 858) was mitigated by the Apostolic Constitution *Christus Dominus* (6 Jan., 1953) and its annexed Instruction of the Holy Office (6 Jan., 1953) and for the most part changed by the *Motu proprio, Sacram Communionem* (19 March, 1957).

B. *The Law*

The law of the eucharistic fast in force today can be stated as follows:

1. The time for the keeping of the eucharistic fast by priests before Mass and by the faithful before Holy Communion, either in the morning hours or in those after noon, is limited to three hours as to solid food and alcoholic drink, and one hour as to non-alcoholic drink; the fast is not broken by drinking water. (*Sacram Communionem,* n. 2.)

2. The eucharistic fast for the time stated above is to be observed also by those who celebrate Mass or receive Holy Communion at midnight or in the first hours of the day. (*Sacram Communionem,* n. 3.)

3.   The sick, even though not confined to bed, can take non-alcoholic drink and true and proper medicines, either liquid or solid, without limitation of time, before celebrating Mass or receiving Holy Communion. (*Sacram Communionem,* n. 4.)

4.   One who has not observed the eucharistic fast as described above, cannot be admitted to Holy Communion, except in case of danger of death or of a need to prevent irreverence toward the Sacrament. (Cf. Can. 858 § 1.)

C.   *Commentary on Certain Points of the Law*

1.   *Solid food* is considered to be whatever men commonly say they eat; *liquids,* whatever people commonly say they drink. Whether or not food is solid food or merely drink depends on the form in which it is put into the mouth. Thus mints, life-savers, etc. are considered solid food even though they are broken down into liquid form before they are actually swallowed.

2.   *Liquid* is whatever is drunk, or at least can be drunk. The drink can be nourishing either naturally (v.g., milk) or by the addition of some substance (v.g., ovaltine). The idea of drink is, in practice, admitted to be something taken *per modum potus,* i.e., liquid food in which is mixed some substance such as bread crumbs and the like, provided the whole mixture continues to have the nature of liquid food. Quite allowable therefore are the following: coffee (with sugar), fruit juices, milk-shake, soup with cracker crumbs, weak cereal, etc. (Cf. Coronata, *Jus Seraphicum,* IV, p. 555.)

3.   *Alcoholic drink* is, v.g., beer, wine, gin, brandy, whiskey, etc., whether taken straight or mixed with non-alcoholic liquid, v.g., a "high-ball." Parvity of matter is not admitted in this connection. The reason for this severity is: the danger of abuse; also the demand of the highest

reverence which we owe to the supreme dignity of the Body and Blood of the Lord.

4. *Water* is whatever men consider to be plain water, even though, as found in its natural state it contain iron, sulphur, calcium, or dust. Chemicals added in city water supplies do not exclude such water from being considered plain water.

5. *Medicine* is whatever is taken by cure, ease, or prevent illness, whether prescribed by a physician or recognized by all as truly a medicine. An inquiry into the nature of the medicine, whether or not is to be alcoholic in a greater or lesser degree is no longer necessary since the law makes no distinction between alcoholic and non-alcoholic medicines; both may be used. Hence it is not necessary to avoid a medicine which contains alcohol as long as it is truly and properly called a medicine.

6. *The infirm* are those who suffer a diminuation or deficiency of health. But not every slight indisposition is judged an infirmity by men of sound judgment. In the present law, infirmity is a wide term which may be broadly interpreted to cover any physical ailment or disorder from severe sickness and senile debility to a bad headache, a cold, a bout of indigestion. Those who suffer from the following may be considered to be infirm: colds, ulcers, diabetes, asthma, ills of pregnancy, insomnia, headache, high or low blood pressure, distressing cough, rheumatism, arthritis, hay fever, the weakness of old age.

> Concerning the sick we should add that *Sacram Communionem* gives no hint as to how sick one must be or how great an inconvenience one must feel before one can take liquid food and/or solid or liquid medicine up until the time of Mass or Communion. Relying on the law of *Christus Dominus* as our norm of interpretation, we hold that to take the liquid food it ought to be a real inconvenience for one to do without it because of his infirmity, but that the medicine can be taken by

reason of its own need as a medicine and not only when the fast would be really difficult without it. Thus a person with a headache, even though it is not severe enough to make fasting difficult, would be permitted an aspirin up to the time of Mass or Communion because he is sick and an aspirin is real medicine.

Note that a person who knows from experience that he will get sick from, v.g., a boat ride, an auto ride, a bination or trination Mass, can take medicine (or liquid food) now when he is feeling well in order to prevent the sickness from occuring.

7. *Three hours . . . one hour* etc. — see our commentary below (E, 3).

D. *Causes Exempting or Excusing from the Law of Eucharistic Fast*

1. According to the *Code* there are two causes *exempting* one from the observance of the eucharistic fast, and both refer to the reception of Holy Communion but not to the celebration of Mass:

a. *Danger of death.* One is not bound to the law of the eucharistic fast if he is in probable danger of death, either from a natural or from an external cause. (Serious operation, difficult childbirth, internal hemorrhages, advanced stage of consumption, — also, soldiers in the front lines, sailors in combat waters, etc.). Many authors require that the one in danger of death from an extrinsic cause observe the fast if he can do so without inconvenience. However, this opinion has little foundation in law, and we may say that such a person is simply exempted from the law of the eucharistic fast and hence may receive without fasting, whether it is convenient to fast or not. (Cf. Anglin, CUA, n. 124, p. 99.)

In doubt as to whether or not the danger of death is present, Holy Communion may be given to one not fasting *per modum Viatici* since the Church does not wish anyone to be exposed to the danger of dying without Viaticum.

Note that as long as one is in danger of death, he is exempted from the law and hence may receive Communion even *daily* without fasting.

b. *Avoidance of irreverence.* Hence, if danger of irreverence is imminent in time of war or persecution, the priest may distribute the hosts to the faithful even though they be not fasting. In the absence of a priest, the faithful may consume the hosts from their own hands.

2. The causes *excusing* one from the observance of the law of eucharistic fast are, according to the unanimous opinion of the authors:

a. *To integrate the sacrifice.* Hence, if the priest already at the altar remembers that he has broken the fast and he is already at the consecration, he may proceed with the Mass. Indeed, because of scandal and infamy, he is practically never obliged to stop the Mass, even though he remember he is not fasting long before the consecration. (Genicot, II, n. 203.)

b. *To avoid the danger of scandal or infamy.* Thus, if on a day of precept, the priest has broken his fast, he may ordinarily say Mass, because if he does not people will be greatly offended; likewise, many may neglect to go elsewhere for Mass even though they could easily do so. (Noldin, III, n. 156; Genicot, II, n. 203 and others.)

> If a young priest before his first solemn Mass, or a child before his first Holy Communion accidentally breaks the fast, they may be allowed to celebrate Mass and receive Holy Communion respectively, as long as scandal be avoided.

c. *To administer Viaticum.* Hence, if no consecrated host is available, a priest who has already broken his fast may say Mass in order to obtain a host for Viaticum.

E. *Breaking the Eucharistic Fast*

1. That the eucharistic fast be broken it is required that:

a. What is taken have the *ratio cibi vel potus,* that is,

that in the common estimation of men it be something that can be digested, or can be drunk.

b. That it be taken *into the mouth and swallowed.* Hence, the fast is not broken by an injection, even a nutritive one, nor by inhaling steam for medical purposes. The fast is not broken by a stomach lotion, even though a small portion of the liquid or some of the lubricating grease from the instrument remains in the stomach.

c. That what is *taken is taken as food and drink* not after the fashion of saliva, breath, or water. Hence, small pieces of tobacco, insects, etc. which get into the mouth and are accidentally swallowed do not break the fast.

> What is taken after the fashion of a drink of water and is accidentally swallowed does not break the fast. Thus the remnants of medicine, food, alcoholic drink, etc. which may adhere to a glass one uses for water do not break the fast provided they are swallowed *praeter intentionem,* i.e., accidentally.

> What is taken together with the Sacred Species does not break the fast. Hence, if a priest who binates swallows something that has fallen into the chalice at the first Mass, he may simply proceed to the celebration of the second Mass.

2. If one doubts whether or not he has broken the eucharistic fast he may approach the Sacred Banquet, for unless it is certain that the fast has been broken, one is not bound to abstain from receiving. (Noldin, III, n. 146.)

3. The law of eucharistic fast obliges *sub gravi,* and it does not admit of parvity of matter in regard to the quantity of food or drink. Most probably (*probabilissime*) the stated times of three hours and one hour of fasting are to be taken exactly and mathematically, not morally.

> Hence a very small piece of candy, a minute portion of alcohol, etc. will break the eucharistic fast; and the fast is broken even though one take these things accidentally except in the case where they are not taken *per modum cibi vel potus* but rather *per modum salivae, respirationis vel aquae* (as explained above).

> The three hour and one hour periods of fasting before Holy

Mass (by the celebrant) or before Holy Communion (by the communicant) are to be computed mathematically. A fast of almost three hours and almost one hour does not fulfill the obligation of the law. However a lack of only a few minutes to complete the prescribed periods of time would not seem to constitute grave matter, so that one could for a very reasonable cause occasionally excuse himself from the lack of a few minutes of fasting in order to be able to communicate. (Cf. *Theological Studies*, XX, pp. 258-260.) We do not propose this opinion for the general consumption of the faithful, but rather for the use of prudent confessors who advise penitents who occasionally find themselves in special circumstances suggesting the use of this opinion.

APPENDIX

The Ablutions at Mass

1. All priests who are going to celebrate Mass twice or three times, *may* in the prior Masses take the two ablutions prescribed by the rubrics of the Missal, but using only water, which according to the new principle does not break the fast. However, a priest who on Christmas or All Souls' Day celebrates three Masses, one immediately after the other, is obliged to observe the rubrics as regards the ablutions. (S.O., instr., 6 Jan., 1953, n. 7.)

One celebrates without intermission, or celebrates one Mass immediately after the other, when he does not leave the altar between consecutive Masses.

2. But if a priest who must celebrate Mass a second or a third time inadvertantly takes wine also in the ablution, he is not prohibited from celebrating the second or third Mass. (S.O., instr., 6 Jan., 1953, n. 8.)

The words "must celebrate" are certainly verified when the priest is obliged to celebrate a second or third time for the good of the people; they are probably verified when the priest desires to celebrate out of devotion only, as on All Souls' Day. (Regatillo-Zalba, III, n. 132; Moriarity, Reed, and others. Cf. *Theological Studies*, XIV, p. 217.)

If a priest inadvertently takes the wine ablution into the chalice at his earlier Mass and notices it before consuming the wine, he is not obliged to dispose of it in some way but can consume it. (Werts, Moriarity, and others. Cf. *The Jurist,* XIV, p. 17.)

A priest who is to celebrate his second Mass not less than three hours after his first Mass, not only may but ought to perform the ablution of the first Mass with water and wine as prescribed by the rubrics. (Cardinal Ottaviani, June, 1957 — cf. *The Digest,* IV, pp. 288-289.)

II. STATE OF GRACE

No one conscious of mortal sin, no matter how contrite he may believe himself to be, shall go to Holy Communion without previous sacramental confession; but if one lacks a confessor to whom he is obliged to confess, and is at the same time obliged by necessity to communicate, he shall first make an act of perfect contrition. (Can. 856.)

The necessity to communicate must be grave, v.g., to avoid infamy or grave scandal which can arise if one does not go to Communion at a wedding Mass, a family Communion, etc.

The impossibility to confess has been explained above, p. 45.

Note: contrary to the opinion of many moralists, it seems to us that the necessity to communicate and the impossibility to confess are, in practice, quite frequently verified in small communities of religious sisters.

III. FIRST COMMUNION OF CHILDREN

1. In danger of death, that Holy Communion may and should be administered to children, it suffices that they know enough to distinguish the Body of the Lord from ordinary food and reverently to adore It. (Can. 854 § 2.)

Hence, when a child five or six years of age is placed in danger of death, the pastor should investigate its capability of receiving the Holy Eucharist, and if he finds the child mentally capable should, after an apt instruction, administer the sacrament.

2. Outside of danger of death a more thorough knowledge of Christian doctrine and a more accurate preparation are properly required, namely, that according to which the child has some knowledge of the mysteries of faith necessary by necessity of means for salvation, and can with fit-

ting devotion approach the Holy Eucharist. (Can. 854 § 3.)

3. The decision regarding the sufficient disposition of a child for its admission to first Communion belongs to the confessor and to the child's parents or guardians. (Can. 854 § 4.)

This canon refers to the child's admission to first Communion as a private individual or in a private way. Admission to first Communion in solemn form is in many places reserved to the pastor either by particular law or by custom.

Moreover, it is the pastor's right and duty to take care that children do not approach the holy sacrament before they attain the use of reason or without sufficient preparation, and at the same time to provide that those who have attained the use of reason and who are sufficiently prepared are refreshed with this divine food as soon as possible. (Cf. Can. 854 § 5.)

IV. TIME AND PLACE

A. *The Time*

1. Holy Communion may be distributed *every day* of the year. (Can. 867 § 1.)

On *Holy Thursday* Holy Communion may be distributed to the faithful only at the principal Mass of the Lord's Supper and at all the other low Masses which the local Ordinary has permitted, or immediately after the Masses. On this day Holy Communion may be brought to the sick in the morning or in the afternoon. (S.R.C., decl., 1 Feb., 1957, nos. 11, 12.)

On *Good Friday* Holy Communion may be distributed only at the solemn afternoon liturgical service, except to persons in danger of death. (S.R.C., decl., 1 Feb., 1957, n. 18.)

On *Holy Saturday* Holy Communion may be distributed only during Mass or immediately after Mass. This restriction does not affect Communion for the sick in danger of death. (S.R.C., instr., 16 Nov., 1955, n. 18.)

Pastoral note: It would seem permissible to distribute Holy Communion on the mornings of Holy Thursday, Good Friday and Holy Saturday for a just and reasonable cause, v.g., if otherwise a person would not be able to communicate on those days. The restrictions placed by the Code on the time of the distribution of Holy Communion on Good Friday and Holy Saturday were looked upon by the authors as probably obliging only *sub levi*; an obligation, therefore, from which a just and reasonable cause excused. (Cf. Cappello, *De Sacr.*, I, nos. 368-369; V.C., II, n. 136; Abbo-Hannan, I, n. 867.) The decrees and instructions of the Sacred Congregation of Rites do not seem to make the obligation any stricter.

2. Holy Communion may be distributed outside of Mass, (cf. Can. 846), but only *at the hours when Mass may be said,* unless there be good reason to distribute it at some other hour. (Can. 867 § 4.)

The late afternoon and early evening are not times when Mass can be said *by law,* hence according to the norm of Canon 867 § 4 Holy Communion may not be distributed apart from Mass at these hours, unless a reasonable cause excuses. (Cf. S.O., 13 April, 1957; S.R.C., 21 June, 1957.) Holy Communion may however be distributed immediately before or immediately after afternoon and evening Masses. (S.O., instr., 6 Jan., 1953, n. 15.) Likewise, when these Masses are not had, the local Ordinary may permit the distribution of Holy Communion in connection with [i.e., before, during, or after] some sacred function or devotion held in the afternoon or evening hours in churches, whether parochial or non-parochial, or in the oratories of hospitals, jails, and schools. The specific kind of sacred function or devotion at which Holy Communion may be distributed is to be determined by the local Ordinary. (S.O., decr., 21 March, 1960.)

The distribution of Holy Communion (*sacris vestibus indutus*) immediately before or after a *Missa solemnis, cantata* or *conventualis* is not permissible. (S.R.C., 19 Jan., 1906.) However, owing to contrary custom, introduced by the frequency of high Mass, this decree is generally not enforced by local Ordinaries.

3. Holy Viaticum may be administered on any day and at any hour of the day or night. (Can. 867 § 5.)

Holy Viaticum is here taken in the broad sense, namely for any Holy Communion received by one in danger of death, and is not restricted to the Viaticum of necessity.

B. *The Place*

1. Holy Communion may be distributed wherever Holy Mass may be said, even in private oratories, unless the bishop of the diocese, for good reasons, forbids it in some particular case. (Can. 869.)

2. The local Ordinary may, in individual cases and by way of act, permit that when Holy Communion is taken to the sick in distant places, it may also be distributed in some decent and suitable place, to others who are not sick, but who cannot go to a church on that day, or to those who are in the same house with the sick person. This is ordinary power and hence may be delegated to pastors and others at the discretion of the local Ordinary. (S.C.Sacr., reply, 5 Jan., 1928.)

> Interpreting this reply, Cappello states that the faithful living in the same house with the sick person may also be given Holy Communion when it is brought to the sick, and the Ordinary's permission is not needed for this case. (Cappello, *De Sacr.,* I, n. 375.)

V. CEREMONIES AND RUBRICS

1. *Rite.* In cases of necessity when a priest of the different rite is not available, it is lawful for a priest of an Oriental rite which uses leavened bread to distribute Holy Communion under the appearance of unleavened bread; likewise it is lawful for a priest of the Latin rite or of an Oriental rite which uses leavened bread to distribute Holy Holy Communion under the appearance of leavened bread; but each must observe the ceremonies of his own rite in the act of ministration. (Can. 851 § 2.)

> A case of necessity is here taken in a broad sense and can be said to be verified as often as the faithful would be impeded in receiving Holy Communion on that day unless the priest made use of the concessions granted by this canon.

2. *Paten.* When Holy Communion is distributed to the faithful a white cloth should be extended in front of the communicants. In addition, the faithful should hold a silver or gold-plated paten without engravings under their chins; the paten may also be held by the server. If, however, a bishop, or a prelate using the pontificals, distributes Communion, or if it is distributed during solemn high

Mass, a priest or a deacon should hold the paten under the chins of the communicants.

> If Communion has been distributed during Mass, the fragments should be very carefully removed from the paten into the chalice with the aid of the fingers; if it has been distributed outside of Mass, the fragments should be put in the ciborium. (S.C.Sacr., instr., 26 March, 1929.)

3. *Vestments.* In case of real necessity it is lawful to distribute Holy Communion without lights or vestment. Outside of the case of necessity, to distribute Communion without any sacred vestment at all is a grave sin. To omit only the stole, or only the surplice, or only the lights or prayers would be a venial sin.

4. *Dividing Hosts.* If necessary, the consecrated host may be divided into two or three parts. It is even permitted to break off a part from the priest's host, if a host is needed for Viaticum or if one or the other communicant cannot wait any longer in order to go to Communion. (Noldin, III, n. 131.)

5. *Communion for the Sick.* When Holy Communion is given to several sick persons who are in the same house or in the same hospital but in different rooms, the priest shall recite only in the first room all the prayers (in the plural) that are to be said before the Communion of the Sick according to the Roman Ritual (Tit. IV, cap. 4). In the other rooms he shall say only the following: *Misereatur tui . . . Indulgentiam . . . Ecce Agnus Dei,* once *Domine non sum dignus . . . Accipe frater (soror) . . .* or *Corpus Domini.* In the last room he shall add *Dominus vobiscum* with the response and the oration *Domine sancte,* and then, if a Sacred Particle is left over, bless the sick with the Sacrament. Finally, in church, he shall say the other prayers as prescribed, in replacing the ciborium in the tabernacle. (S.R.C., instr., 9 Jan., 1929.)

The instruction permits but does not prescribe the above-mentioned rite. Hence, the long established custom of saying the prayers *once in plurali* at one specially prepared table on each floor or corridor may still be retained. (*L'Ami du Clergé*, 1929, p. 164; 1930, p. 392.)

The Roman Ritual (Tit. IV, cap. 4) prescribes that the water used to purify the priest's fingers after giving Holy Communion to the sick be poured into the sacrarium, or if there is no sacrarium, into the fire, or that it be drunk by the communicant.

CHAPTER III

The Reservation and Worship of the Most Holy Eucharist

I. RESERVATION

1. *The Place*

a. The Blessed Sacrament *must* be reserved in cathedral churches, etc., and in all parish churches as well as in all churches attached to houses of exempt religious. With the permission of the local Ordinary, it *may* be reserved in the principal public or semipublic oratory of pious or religious houses and of ecclesiastical colleges conducted by the secular clergy or by religious. (Cf. Can. 1265 § 1.) The Blessed Sacrament may be reserved *habitually* only on one altar of the same church (Can. 1268 § 1), ordinarily, the main altar. (Cf. Can. 1268 §§ 2,3.)

In order that the Blessed Sacrament may be reserved in the above-mentioned churches and oratories, Canon 1265 demands that there be a responsible person to guard it and that, as a rule, Mass be said there at least once a week. However, an occasional omission of the weekly Mass for some good reason is permissible.

Pious houses and ecclesiastical colleges include: retreat houses, hospitals, asylums, orphanages, sanatoria, — if run by the Church; seminaries, scholasticates; schools and colleges operated by religious or clerics.

In churches and oratories having the privilege of perpetual adoration, the Blessed Sacrament must be reserved on two altars; on one for the perpetual adoration, and on the other for the purpose of distributing Holy Communion. (S.R.C., 18 May, 1878; 23 Nov., 1880.)

b. For a good reason the local Ordinary may grant permission to reserve the Blessed Sacrament also in other churches or public oratories but only *per modum actus,* that is to say, for a given occasion and not perpetually. (Can. 1265 § 2.)

The permission may be granted for as long as the justifying reason continues, e.g., for the whole period during which a parish church is undergoing repairs. (Abbo-Hannan, II, n. 1265.)

c. In religious or pious houses, the Blessed Sacrament may be reserved only in the church or principal oratory, and in convents of nuns it may not be reserved within the choir or the precincts of the enclosure; all privileges to the contrary are revoked. (Can. 1267.)

The meaning of Canon 1267 is this: if a religious or pious house is connected with a public church which the members use for their daily spiritual exercises, the Blessed Sacrament may be reserved only in the church; otherwise (i.e., if the daily exercises are carried on in an oratory) it may be reserved in the principal oratory of the respective house (without prejudice to the right of the church, if any), but nowhere else, unless in the same building there exist groups so distinct from one another as to constitute separate houses of religion or piety. (PCI, reply, 3 June, 1918.) For example, the Blessed Sacrament may, with the local Ordinary's permission, be reserved in one oratory for the seminarians, and in another for the sisters who have charge of the culinary department; or in the chapel of that part of the house reserved to the religious, and in the seminary chapel, in the case of a secular seminary operated by religious.

2. *The Tabernacle.* The most holy Eucharist must be kept in an immovable tabernacle placed on the middle of the altar. (Can. 1269 § 1.) The priest in charge of the church or oratory is obliged *sub gravi* to guard the tabernacle key with extreme care. (Can. 1269.)

The priest must see to it that the key is not left in the tabernacle door or on the altar. He must keep the key in personal custody or lock it up in a safe and secret place, the key of which place must remain in his exclusive charge, and in his absence it must be entrusted to another priest or to the sacristan.

In the convents of women religious the key must be kept in the sacristy; but after the sacred functions are finished and especially at night, it is to be kept in a safe place locked with two keys, the one of which must remain in charge of the superioress or her assistant, the other in charge of another nun, ordinarily the sacristan. (S.C.Sacr., instr., 26 May, 1938.)

3. *The Lamp.* Before the tabernacle in which the Blessed Sacrament is reserved at least one lamp, fed either with olive oil or beeswax, shall be kept burning day and night. Where olive oil is not obtainable, the local Ordinary may allow the use of other oils, which should, in as far as possible, be vegetable oils. (Can. 1271.)

The color of the lamp is ordinarily white. However, a green or red lamp is tolerated. (S.R.C., decr., 2 June, 1883.) The two candles used at Mass and the Paschal Candle are to be of beeswax *in maxima parte* (67%); other candles placed on the altar are to be of beeswax *in maiore parte* (51%). (Cf. S.R.C., 14 Dec., 1904.) It is desirable also that the sanctuary candle, which in most places is used instead of the sanctuary lamp, be of beeswax *in maxima parte*. However, it is left to the Bishops' meeting in each country to determine precisely to what percentage the quantity of beeswax, olive oil, or other vegetable oils may be diminished and the candles (Mass candles, Paschal Candle, sanctuary lamp or candle) still be permitted for liturgical use. In places where it is not the practice to have Bishops' meetings, the local Ordinaries are to make the decision. (S.R.C., decr., 13 Dec., 1957.)

Also, in case *beeswax* for the altar candles can be procured only at great inconvenience, at least two beeswax candles must be provided for a private Mass, and four for a chanted Mass or for a solemn high Mass, and for solemn exposition of the Blessed Sacrament, supplying with other lights for any larger number which may be required. (S.R.C., 18 Aug., 1949.)

4. *Renewal of the Sacred Species.* The consecrated hosts, whether reserved for the Communion of the faithful or for the exposition of the Blessed Sacrament, shall be fresh and they shall be renewed frequently, those remaining from a previous consecration being duly consumed, so

that all danger of corruption is avoided. The instructions of the local Ordinaries in these matters are to be sedulously observed. (Can. 1272.)

> Hosts should not be consecrated, as a rule, unless they have been baked within three or at the most within four weeks immediately preceding the consecration. Renewal of the Sacred Species, according to the *Caeremoniale Episcoporum* and the decree of the II Plenary Council of Baltimore (n. 268) should take place every week. Most authors allow that renewal take place every two weeks. (Cf. V.C., II, n. 597.)

II. EXPOSITION

1. *Public exposition*

a. Public exposition of the Blessed Sacrament with the monstrance is allowed on the feast of Corpus Christi and on every day within its octave, at Mass and at Vespers, in all churches and public oratories; at other times, however, public exposition is allowed only for a grave cause, especially a public cause, and with the permission of the local Ordinary even though the church belongs to an exempt religion. (Can. 1274; PCI, reply, 14 July, 1922.)

> The II Plenary Council of Baltimore authorized public exposition on not a few days of the year. However, this decree of the Council is now abrogated by Canon 1274, and, hence, the local Ordinary's permission must be obtained to have public exposition on days over and above those granted by the Code. (Barrett, CUA, n. 83, p. 153.)
>
> It is probable that exempt religious do not need the permission of the local Ordinary when the exposition is for the community and held in the oratory attached to the house, or even in their churches when closed to the public. (*Matters Liturgical*, n. 410, h.)

b. By a special decree of Pope Leo XIII, public exposition of and benediction with the Blessed Sacrament are permitted in connection with the public recitation of the rosary in all parochial churches during the month of October. (S.R.C., decr., 20 Aug., 1885.)

c. In all parish churches and in others in which the

Blessed Sacrament is habitually reserved, the Forty Hour's Devotion shall be observed each year on days determined according to the mind of the local Ordinary; and if, because of special circumstances, this devotion cannot be carried out without grave difficulty and with the reverence due to so great a sacrament, the local Ordinary shall see to it that on certain days the Blessed Sacrament shall be exposed with due solemnity for at least several continuous hours. (Can. 1275.)

> The Mass of exposition and of reposition are celebrated at the altar of exposition at the close of Forty Hour's Devotion. In other cases it is forbidden to celebrate Mass or distribute Communion from the altar of exposition except in case of necessity or some other grave cause, or except if it is allowed by special indult. (S.R.C., 11 May, 1878; 17 April, 1919.)

> Masses during the "octave" of Corpus Christi are not to be celebrated *coram Sanctissimo Exposito*. (S.R.C., 17 April, 1957 — *Acta Minorum,* LXXVI, p. 228.)

d. Public exposition or benediction may be held more than once in the same church on the same day, provided that the permission of the local Ordinary has been obtained if required. (S.R.C., *Decr. Auth.,* n. 3438.)

2. *Private exposition,* that is with the ciborium, may be held for any good reason, and without the permission of the Ordinary, in churches and oratories authorized to reserve the Blessed Sacrament. (Can. 1274.)

> For private exposition the door of the tabernacle is opened and the covered pyx or ciborium remains in the open tabernacle, placed near the opening, (so the worshipers can see it) but not outside the tabernacle. The Blessed Sacrament may be incensed, and after the *Tantum Ergo* which has been sung or recited, the blessing may be given with the ciborium, over which the priest drapes the ends of the humeral veil. Exposition of the ciborium *in throno* is contrary to the Roman rite and therefore forbidden. (S.R.C., decr., 16 March, 1876.)

> *Private exposition* of the Blessed Sacrament is forbidden during Mass. (S.R.C., decr., 27 July, 1927.)

3. *Commemoration.* The commemoration of the Bless-

ed Sacrament must be made in the Mass celebrated at the altar where the Blessed Sacrament is exposed, or at the altar where immediately after the Mass the Blessed Sacrament is to be exposed for some time and for a public cause; the commemoration is never made in Masses celebrated at other altars during the time of exposition. (S.R.C., 2 June, 1955, n. 9; 11 Jan., 1928.)

The words, "for some time," are understood as an exposition and adoration of the Blessed Sacrament which last for at least a half-hour. Hence, the oration need not be said if there is question merely of exposition, a brief devotion and benediction. "For a public cause," means, v.g., for the greater solemnization of a feast day; on the occasion of a mission; to promote the devotion of the faithful on days of precept, or during a novena in preparation for a great feast.

This commemoration is to be omitted if the Mass or a commemoration occurring in the Mass are of a feast of Our Lord or a Sunday. (*Cod. Rubr.*, n. 355.)

4. *Relics.* When the Blessed Sacrament is exposed, it is permitted to expose relics on *other* altars; but kissing the relic and blessing the people with it shall be omitted as long as the Blessed Sacrament remains exposed. (S.R.C., 17 June, 1900.)

PART V
PENANCE

CHAPTER I
Jurisdiction

I. ORDINARY JURISDICTION

The following have ordinary jurisdiction to hear confessions:

1. The *local Ordinary* in his own territory. (Can. 873 § 1.) The term "local Ordinary" includes also the vicar general, and during a vacancy of the diocese, the diocesan administrator. (Can. 198.)

2. *Pastors* and those who have a status equivalent to pastors, in their own territories (parishes). (Can. 873 § 1.)

> Therefore, in addition to the pastors the following have ordinary jurisdiction to hear confessions: *quasi-pastors* in vicariates and prefectures apostolic (cf. Canons 216 and 451); the *vicar of a moral person,* when a parish is completely united to a moral person (v.g., to a religious house); the *vicar econome* (administrator), who after appointment by the bishop, rules the parish during a vacancy; the *vicar substitute,* who, with the permission of the Ordinary, rules the parish when the pastor is away for more than a week's time; the *vicar adjutor* who is appointed by the Ordinary to take care of the affairs of the parish because of the old age, mental infirmity, blindness, or other permanent affliction of the pastor, but only if he is given complete parochial authority (cf. Canons 471-475); *not,* however, the vicars cooperator (assistant pastors).

> Those with ordinary power to absolve may use this power in favor of *their own subjects* everywhere (Can. 881 § 2), i.e., they may hear the confession of their own subject, even though

both pastor and parishioner be outside the parish and/or diocese.

3. *Superiors* in exempt religious institutes according to
the norm of their constitutions. (Can. 873 § 2.) *Per se*
this includes local superiors also, unless the constitutions
restrict the power to the major superiors.

For details on who the subjects of the religious superior are
in matters of confessional jurisdiction, see below, II, 1, b.

II. DELEGATED JURISDICTION

1. Those empowered to delegate jurisdiction for the
sacrament of penance are the following:

a. *The local Ordinary* of the place in which the confessions are to be heard grants delegated jurisdiction for
the confessions of all persons, whether lay or religious, to
priests both secular and religious, even exempt; religious
priests should, however, not use this jurisdiction without
at least the presumed permission of their own superior.
(Can. 874 § 1.) To hear confessions validly, one needs
jurisdiction *expressly* granted either orally or in writing.
(Can. 879 § 1.)

Hence, tacit and presumptive concessions of jurisdiction are
excluded. However, implicit concession may be admitted, v.g.,
if the local Ordinary should send a priest to be an assistant
without explicitly granting him delegation for the hearing of
confessions. (Abbo-Hannan, II, n. 879.)

Pastors, parochial vicars, or priests invested with universal
delegated powers, *cannot* delegate to priests, either secular or
religious, jurisdiction to hear confessions; to grant faculties
they need special power from the local Ordinary to delegate.
(PCI, reply, 16 Oct., 1919.)

b. *The religious superior.* In exempt clerical institutes,
delegated jurisdiction is also granted by the proper superior according to the constitutions, for the confessions of
the professed, the novices, and others who live day and
night in the religious house by reason of services to be
rendered, education, hospitality, or health; the same su-

perior may grant these faculties also to priests of the secular clergy and to those belonging to another religious institute. (Can. 875 § 1.)

Hence, confessional jurisdiction over exempt religious and their *familiares* may be received from either the local Ordinary or from the religious superior. The religious superior of Canon 875 is also the local superior, *unless* the constitutions of his institute say otherwise. The constitutions may very well, as is the case with the Friars Minor, reserve this power to the major superiors.

2. Concerning *the use of delegated jurisdiction,* note the following:

a. Since the religious superior in a clerical exempt institute has jurisdiction which is not territorial but personal, one delegated by him can hear the confessions of the superior's subjects in every place, i.e., *ubique terrarum.* (Coronata, *De Sacr.,* I, nos. 349 and 358.)

b. All priests, secular and religious, who are approved in a given place for the hearing of confessions, whether their jurisdiction be ordinary or delegated, can also validly and licitly absolve *vagi* and *peregrini* who come to them from another diocese or parish, as well as Catholics of any Oriental rite. (Can. 881 § 1.)

A Catholic has the right to confess his sins to the confessor of his choice, even though the confessor belong to another rite, provided that he is lawfully approved. (Can. 905.) However, a priest of the Latin rite cannot validly or licitly hear confessions and give absolution (even to faithful of the Latin rite) *in a church or oratory which is subject to the exclusive jurisdiction of the Ordinary of an Oriental rite,* unless the latter has expressly granted him the faculty to do so. (Cf. S.C.P.F., 2 Dec., 1932.) Likewise, a priest of an Oriental rite cannot validly absolve (even faithful of his own rite) in a church or oratory which is subject to the exclusive jurisdiction of an Ordinary of the Latin rite, unless the latter has expressly granted him faculties. (Cf. S.C.E.O., 26 Aug., 1932.)

Priests of the Latin rite cannot absolve faithful of the Greek-Ruthenian rite from censures and sins reserved by the Greek-Ruthenian Ordinary without his permission. In turn, the same is to be said of Greek-Ruthenian priests relative to censures and reservations established by an Ordinary of the Latin rite. (S.C. E.O., decr., *Cum data fuerit,* 1 March, 1929.)

3. *Cessation of delegated jurisdiction.* The ordinary ways in which delegated jurisdiction comes to an end are: by the lapse of time or the exhausting of the number of cases for which the jurisdiction has been granted by the revocation of faculties, which revocation must be directly communicated to the one delegated; on the contrary, one's faculties *do not cease to exist* with the loss of office on the part of the delegating superior, except when the faculties were granted by the superior *"ad beneplacitum nostrum,"* or in the case where one received a special faculty to grant some favor to a particular penitent, and in both cases, the case has not yet been begun (*res adhuc integra*). (Can. 207.)

In case a confession has been begun but not yet finished and either the time for which one's faculties were granted elapses or the superior who granted the faculties *ad beneplacitum* dies or loses his office, one's faculties last until the case is finished. (Arregui, n. 600; Abbo-Hannan, I, n. 207.)

Since Ordinaries very seldom grant faculties *ad beneplacitum,* one's faculties usually do not cease when the Ordinary dies or loses his office.

By leaving the diocese before the term of delegated jurisdiction has expired, the faculties are not lost unless the Ordinary in granting them has specified otherwise. Thus, if a religious obtains the faculties of the diocese for as long as he is attached to a certain house or position, he retains such faculties until he is definitely transferred elsewhere. If one receives faculties for the time during which he will be helping Father X, the faculties continue even though the delegated priest goes into another diocese on a visit during the time he is helping Father X.

III. JURISDICTION DELEGATED IN EXTRAORDINARY CIRCUMSTANCES

1. *In Danger of Death.* In danger of death, whether it be from some internal (sickness) or external cause (dangerous voyage, difficult childbirth, dangerous operation),

any priest, though not approved for confessions, and though censured, irregular, apostate, schismatic, heretical or degraded, and even though an approved confessor be present, can validly and licitly absolve any penitent from all sins and censures, no matter in what manner reserved or notorious. (Cf. Can. 882.)

> However, the absolution of one's accomplice in a sin of impurity, though valid in danger of death, is licit only in case of necessity. (Can. 882 and 884.)

> The obligation of having recourse, should the penitent recover, is binding only in case of absolution from censures *ab homine* or *specialissimo modo* reserved to the Holy See, and in the case of absolving a priest who has attempted marriage and for very grave reasons must continue to live under the same roof with the woman. (S.P., 18 April, 1936.)

2. *At Sea and in the Air*

a. All priests who are on a *sea voyage,* provided they have duly obtained the faculty of hearing confessions from their own Ordinary or from the Ordinary of the port of embarkation or from the Ordinary of any intervening port at which they will call during the voyage, can, throughout the entire voyage, hear aboard ship the confessions of all the faithful who are making the voyage with them, even though the ship should, in the course of the journey, pass through or even call at various places subject to the jurisdiction of several Ordinaries. (Can. 883 § 1.)

b. The provisions of Canon 883 regarding the faculty of hearing confessions on the part of priests taking an ocean journey, shall apply and be extended, with the appropriate adjustment of the clauses to fit the case, to priests who make a *voyage by air.* (Pius XII, *motu proprio,* 16 Dec., 1947.)

> For a religious, the proper Ordinary of this canon is not his own major superior (PCI, 30 July, 1934), but the local Ordinary of the place where the religious house to which he is attached is located.

> In case a religious is transferred from a house in one diocese

to a house in another diocese, and is making the journey by air or sea: usually he loses the faculties of the diocese upon his definitive departure from the territory; however, for obtaining the faculties of Canon 883 for the duration of the voyage, it suffices that the faculties of the diocese from which the ship or plane departs be in existence, and that they have not been revoked by some positive act, up to the time at which the traveler boards the ship or plane. (Cf. Jorio, III, n. 431.)

Sea voyage: authors understand this as a true voyage (not merely a brief sight-seeing trip), but do not demand that the voyage be made on, or over, an ocean. A voyage on the Great Lakes or the Mississippi River would be comprehended by Canon 883. (Cf. Coronata, *De Sacr.,* I, n. 360; Jorio, III, n. 431.) The voyage by plane need not be over water. A trip from Chicago to Detroit would fall under Canon 883. (Cf. Danagher, *Homiletic and Pastoral Review,* LV, pp. 650-655, 740-749.) Neither Canon 883 nor the *motu proprio* require any determinate time or distance for the use of the faculties. Hence, when one can say that he is actually *making a voyage,* the faculties are in effect.

c. As often as the ship, in the course of the voyage, puts in at a port, these priests can hear the confessions, both of the faithful who for any reason board the ship, and also of those who wish to confess to them when they incidentally go ashore, and they can validly and licitly absolve the faithful even from cases reserved to the local Ordinary. (Can. 883 § 2.)

The faculties granted by Canon 883 become effective at the moment of boarding the ship or plane, and they remain in effect until the moment at which the priest definitively leaves the ship or plane at his destination.

The term "incidentally (*obiter*) go ashore" means that one is staying only a short time, with the intention of resuming the journey; it excludes the intention of remaining in a place. Faculties are given at these ports of call only during short interruptions of the *same* journey and *not for the time between two distinct journeys.* These faculties in the ports of call endure for three days, even in the case where the priest, in order to continue the same journey, has to leave one vessel and take another, and has to wait for the latter at the port for that length of time. In no case do the faculties in the ports of call last for more than three days except when the Ordinary of the place cannot be easily reached. (PCI, 20 May, 1923.)

Cases reserved to the Ordinary are, probably, both reserved sins and reserved censures (cf. Cappello, III, n. 490); probably also cases reserved either by the common law of the Church or by the local Ordinary himself. (Cf. *Periodica, XIX*, p. 119.)

The faculties granted by Canon 883 may be used in favor of women religious. (Abbo-Hannan, II, n. 883.)

3. *Supplied Jurisdiction:* confer above, p. 5.

IV. JURISDICTION FOR THE CONFESSIONS OF WOMEN RELIGIOUS

Both secular and religious priests, no matter what their rank or office, (except Cardinals) *need special jurisdiction* to hear validly and licitly the confessions of women religious and novices, except as provided in Canons 522 and 523. All contrary particular law or privilege is revoked. This special jurisdiction is granted by the Ordinary of the place in which the house of the religious is located. (Can. 876.)

1. *The ordinary confessor.* There must be assigned to the individual houses of women religious one ordinary confessor only, who shall hear the confessions of the entire community, unless, because of the number of religious or because of some other just cause, two or more confessors are required. (Can. 520 § 1.)

If only the pastor is available for the office of confessor, it certainly seems advisable that he be empowered and urged to delegate visiting priests to hear the entire community. Otherwise it is doubtful whether many of the sisters as feel the need of going to another confessor, would dare to avail themselves of the privilege accorded by Canon 522. In addition, it must not be forgotten that many superioresses are most unreasonable in this matter in spite of the regulations of the Church.

2. *The extraordinary confessor.* Each community of religious women shall be given an extraordinary confessor who shall go to the religious house at least four times a year; all the religious shall present themselves to him, at least to receive his blessing. (Can. 521 § 1.)

The extraordinary confessor usually presents himself during the four Ember Weeks. It is not necessary, however, that he go at these particular times. Hence, if he is impeded during Ember Week, he may go some other week.

3. *The supplementary confessors.* The local Ordinary should designate for the individual houses of women religious, several priests to whom the religious may recur in particular cases for the sacrament of penance, thus obviating the necessity of applying to the local Ordinary for faculties in each and every case. (Can. 521 § 2.)

The supplementary confessor's powers are not limited to the hearing of the confession of an individual sister. He may be summoned when the need is that of the house. Hence, the superioress may call him in to hear the confessions of the whole community in case, v.g., the ordinary confessor is sick, absent or otherwise impeded from making his weekly visit.

When a religious requests that the extraordinary or supplementary confessor be called, the superioress is not permitted to inquire the reason or to manifest opposition in word or manner, or to show herself in any way displeased. (Cf. Can. 521 § 3.)

4. *The occasional confessor.* If, notwithstanding the provisions already made above, a religious, for peace of conscience, goes to a confessor approved by the local Ordinary for the confessions of women, this confession, made in a church or an oratory even a semipublic oratory, is valid and licit, and every contrary privilege is revoked; the superioress may not forbid this or make inquiries regarding it; and the religious is not bound to report the matter to the superioress. (Can. 522.)

This confessor need have no special faculties for the confessions of women religious; it suffices that he have faculties for women's confessions.

This confessor may hear the confession of the sister, not only when she comes to him, but also when he is called to the convent. (PCI, 28 Dec. 1927.) The faculty granted in Canon 522 is distinctly granted in favor of individual religious. Therefore, the superioress cannot call in this priest to hear the confessions of the whole community. However, if he is summoned for an individual religious and other members of the community avail themselves of this opportunity, he may also hear their confessions. (V.C., I, n. 644.)

The reason necessary for the use of this faculty is that the religious make her confession to this priest for the sake of peace of conscience. This condition affects only the licitness, not the validity of the confession, and is present in any confession sincerely made, for the sacrament of penance by its very nature engenders peace of conscience.

The place where this confession must be heard is a church or oratory, even semipublic, or some other place legitimately destined for the confessions of women. If the confession is heard outside of these places by the confessor of Canon 522, the confession is invalid. (Cf. PCI, reply, 24 Nov., 1920; reply, 28 Dec., 1927.) A place legitimately destined for the confessions of women includes not only a place habitually designated, but also a place designated by way of act or chosen in accordance with Canon 910 § 1 which provides that the confessions of women may be heard outside of the confessional when this is required by reason of illness or some other real necessity. (PCI, 12 Feb., 1935.)

The place for women's confessions must as a rule be a confessional that has an irremovable grate with small perforations, placed generally in a church, a public or semipublic oratory (Can. 909), or in the sacristy or some other conspicuous place. In case of sickness or real necessity, however, women's confessions may be heard without a confessional. (Can. 910.) Hence, sisters' confessions may also, *in case of sickness or real necessity,* be heard validly and licitly outside of the confessional, in some other place, even in a private room, designated by the confessor for the hearing of this individual confession.

A general rule may be thus stated: A confessor can validly and licitly hear the confession of the sister concerned in Canon 522 in any place in which he may licitly hear the confessions of lay women according to the circumstances of the case.

If a priest *specially approved* for hearing sisters' confessions (ordinary, supplementary, extraordinary confessor), hears the confession of a sister in a place not designated for sisters' confessions, the confession may be *unlawful,* but it is *not invalid.*

If a priest happens to be hearing confessions in church and

sisters come to him of their own accord like the rest of the faithful, he hears their confessions validly and licitly. The number of sisters that come to him of their own accord does not alter the case.

5. *Confessors for the seriously ill.* When a woman religious is *seriously ill,* even though there be no danger of death, she may call any priest approved for women's confessions, even though not designated for the confessions of women religious, and may confess to him as often as she wishes during her serious illness; nor may the superioress prohibit her from doing so. (Can. 523.)

A serious illness includes any sickness which considerably lessens the strength of the sick person. Serious illness is usually present when a physician must be summoned or when the person is compelled to submit to a surgical operation. Merely being confined to one's room for a week by reason of a sprain is not sufficient, since the Code specifies a *serious* illness. In this latter case, however, the religious could avail herself of the privilege of Canon 521 § 3 by asking that the extraordinary or supplementary confessor be called in.

Note: To hear the confession of a cloistered nun who cannot leave her room, the ordinary, extraordinary, special and supplementary confessors, and any confessor called in by a nun who is *seriously* ill, may enter the papal enclosure. We may also include the occasional confessor of Canon 522 as one of those who may legitimately enter the enclosure to hear confessions. (Cf. S.C.Rel., instr., 25 March, 1956, n. 27.)

CHAPTER II

Reserved Sins

I. POWER TO RESERVE SINS

The local Ordinary (exclusive of the diocesan administrator and the vicar general without a special mandate), the superior general of a clerical exempt institute, and the abbot of an autonomous monastery of clerical exempt religious, may, with the advice of their respective consultors, reserve certain cases to their own judgment by limiting the power of their subordinates to absolve. (Cf. Canons 893-896.)

The only sin reserved as such (*ratione sui*) to the Holy See is the false accusation by which an innocent priest is charged before an ecclesiastical judge of the crime of solicitation. (Can. 894; explanation below under censures.)

All must absolutely abstain from reserving to themselves those sins which are already reserved to the Apostolic See, even by reason of censure (*ratione censurae*); all must regularly abstain from reserving those sins on which a censure, even though reserved to no one, is imposed by the law. (Can. 898.) Can an Ordinary validly reserve to himself a sin which is affected by a censure reserved to him by common law? It is doubtful. Probably he cannot do so, since there is a question of a reservation already made by the Holy See, and the new reservation made by the Ordinary would impede regulars from the use of privileges granted by the Holy See, in virtue of which they can absolve from cases reserved by common law to the Ordinary. An Ordinary cannot impede the use of privileges granted by the Holy See. (Thus Coronata, *De Sacr.,* I, n. 403; cf. also Abbo-Hannon, II, n. 898, and Cappello, III, n. 490, 4°.)

II. JUDGING A RESERVED CASE

1. That a sin be actually reserved, it is required:

a. That the sin be objectively and subjectively *mortal*.

b. That the sin be *external;* indeed, that it be a mortal sin externally also and not only internally, as v.g., if a sin against chastity is reserved, an impure touch that is only venially sinful is not reserved, even though one sin gravely by his internal intention and disposition.

c. That the sin be *consummated,* i.e., the words of the law stating the reservation must be fulfilled in their strict sense; thus, if incest is reserved, the reservation is not had unless intercourse actually take place. Likewise, an attempt at the sin would not be reserved, but the sin itself must take place.

d. That the sin be *certain;* hence, a doubtful sin is not reserved, whether the doubt be one of law (it is not certain that the sin committed is comprehended under the wording of the law), or of fact (was the sin really committed, was it really a grave sin?).

2. Ignorance of the fact that a sin is reserved does not excuse from the reservation, unless the one reserving the sin has either explicitly or implicitly excepted the ignorant from the reservation. (Genicot, II, n. 328; V.C., II, n. 174.)

III. ABSOLVING FROM RESERVED SINS

1. *Pastors and Missionaries.* By the law itself, pastors and others who are included by the law under the category of pastor (v.g., vicar econome, vicar substitute), are authorized to absolve from cases which Ordinaries have in any way reserved to themselves, during the whole time in which the paschal precept may be fulfilled; and missioners have the same power during the time they are giving missions to the faithful. (Can. 899 § 3.)

The time for fulfilling the paschal precept is, in the United States of America, from the first Sunday of lent to Trinity Sunday. Pastors may absolve during this entire time; it is not required that the confession in question be one's annual confession or one made in preparation for one's annual Communion. (V.C., II, n. 180.)

Equal to missions are retreats given to a group, even of clerics or religious. At the time of missions and retreats, other confessors who are designated to help the missioner or retreat master enjoy the faculty to absolve from cases which the Ordinary has reserved to himself. (Cappello, *De Sacr.,* II, n. 391.)

The faculties given in this canon extend to both sins and to censures which the Ordinary has reserved to himself, not however to censures reserved to the Ordinary by the common law. (Coronata, *De Sacr.,* I, n. 405.)

The power to absolve from reserved cases should be delegated habitually to deans, with the additional faculty of subdelegating confessors of their district as often as they may recur to them for some specific and more urgent case. (Can. 899 § 2.)

2. *Confessors*

a. According to Canon 900, any reservation of sin, even the reservation of the sin reserved to the Holy See (PCI, 10 Nov., 1925) ceases, and hence, any confessor can absolve:

1) When the confession is made by *the sick* who cannot leave their home, or by the parties who make it as a *preparation for marriage.*

2) When either the lawful superior *refuses to grant the faculty* which has been sought for a specific case, or when, in the prudent judgment of the confessor, the *faculty cannot be asked* from the lawful superior *without grave inconvenience for the penitent or without running the risk of violating the sacramental seal.*

A grave inconvenience for the penitent is the difficulty of returning, or the necessity of celebrating or receiving in order to avoid danger of infamy, or the fact that it is hard for him to remain in the state of sin till the faculties may be obtained to absolve from the reserved sin. The reservation also ceases if the confessor fears that by putting off the absolution until he can obtain the special faculty, the penitent will not return. (Genicot, II, n. 331.)

Danger to the seal is present when the confessor fears that the superior will suspect who the penitent is if he asks for the faculty. This can easily happen if the confessor is helping a pastor who is a rural dean with faculties to subdelegate in individual cases, and the confessor has no time to obtain the faculty from the bishop, since he (the confessor) will leave after a day or so

3) When the penitent confesses outside the territory of him who made the reservation, even though the penitent has gone outside the territory for the sole purpose of obtaining absolution.

Hence, when absolving a *peregrinus,* the reservation of sin in force in his own diocese means nothing in the diocese in which he confesses, even though the sin was committed in his own diocese. However, *peregrini* are bound to the reservations of the diocese in which they make their confession, even though they sinned elsewhere. (PCI, 24 Nov., 1920.)

One who receives faculties for confessions from the superior of an exempt clerical institute can absolve this superior's subjects (as well as those people mentioned in Canon 514 § 1) from sins reserved to the local Ordinary, since in this case, one's power over the sins is not restricted by the superior who grants faculties on his own authority. (Coronata, I, n. 544.)

The provision of paragraph 3 of Canon 900 which states that an episcopal reservation ceases if the penitent goes to confession outside the diocese where the case is reserved, does not hold if a Latin goes to a Ruthenian church in the diocese, or a Ruthenian to a Latin church, for confession. "Priests of the Latin rite cannot absolve the faithful of the Greek-Ruthenian rite from censures and reserved cases established by the Greek-Ruthenian Ordinary, without the latter's permission. The same thing, in turn, is true of Greek-Ruthenian priests regarding the censures and reservations established by the Ordinary of the Latin rite." (S.C.E.O., decr., *Cum data fuerit,* 1 March, 1929.)

Note: When the confessor absolves from reserved sins by virtue of Canon 900, recourse to the Ordinary or the Sacred Penitentiary for *mandata* etc. is *not* made. Such recourse is made only after the absolution of certain censures and vindicative penalties in more urgent cases or in danger of death.

b. In virtue of Canon 518, some confessors must be appointed for the individual houses of clerical institutes, and given power to absolve also from cases reserved in the institute; in virtue of Canon 519 a religious, even of an exempt institute, may for peace of conscience confess to any confessor approved by the local Ordinary, and be absolved by him also from sins and censures reserved in the institute.

CHAPTER III

Incurring Censures

I. IN ORDER THAT A CENSURE BE INCURRED, IT IS REQUIRED:

1. That the sin be objectively and subjectively *mortal.*

2. That the sin be *external,* even though secret. Hence,

although heresy in thought is a mortal sin, it does not fall under censure.

3. That the sin be *certain*.

4. That the sin be *consummated,* i.e., that the words of the law stating the crime and the punishment be fulfilled in their strict sense.

5. That the sin be *committed with obstinacy* toward the law, i.e., that the sin be committed with knowledge of the penalty imposed upon transgressions of the law. (Cf. Canons 2242, 2218, 2228.)

> In penal law, the benign interpretation is to be followed (Can. 2219 § 1), and the words of a law which define a crime or establish a penalty are to be strictly interpreted. (Cf. Can. 19.) Hence, the axiom: *censura dubia, censura nulla;* that is, there is no penalty contracted if the doubt concerns either the sin (whether it is grave, consummated, etc.), or the censure (whether it really exists, whether one knew of it, etc.). These doubts, of course, must be worthwhile, that is, one has good reason to say a doubt exists, even though one's reasons do not exclude prudent fear of error.

II. Co-Operators

Those who *co-operate* in a crime may also be censured. The *necessary co-operators* are those who by concerted physical action accomplish the crime, or those who command it, or those who by their physical or moral influence so concur in the crime that without their co-operation the crime would not have been committed; all these incur the same censure as the one who actually commits the crime unless the law expressly provides otherwise. The *accessory co-operators* are those who by their co-operation merely facilitate the crime; they do not ordinarily incur the same censure as the one committing the crime, but are to be punished according to the prudent judgment of the superior. (Cf. Canons 2209, 2231.)

Those who *culpably* neglect to hinder a crime when they are *bound in justice* (not merely in charity) to do so, are considered necessary co-operators, if the crime would not have been committed had they not been negligent.

In judging co-operators guilty of censure, it is necessary that their sin have the five requisites mentioned above. Since material co-operation may be permitted for grave reasons, the censure is not incurred thereby, if no mortal sin is committed.

III. CAUSES EXEMPTING OR EXCUSING ONE FROM CONTRACTING CENSURES

1. Those who have not yet reached the age of adolescence (the *impuberes*) are excused from all *ipso facto* (*latae sententiae*) penalties. (Can. 2230.)

In penal law, both boys and girls are considered *impuberes* until they are 14 years of age.

2. The habitually insane, even though they at times have lucid intervals, and even though they appear to be sane in certain types of action, are presumed to be incapable of crime. (Can. 2201.)

3. Whatever excuses from grave fault also excuses one from contracting a censure: involuntary complete drunkenness, very serious scrupulosity, physical force that cannot be physically resisted, uncontrollable passion if it precedes the action of the will and prevents full deliberation and consent, etc. (Cf. Canons 2201, 2203, 2205, 2206.)

4. Grave fear, necessity and grave inconvenience excuse from contracting *latae sententiae* penalties, unless the crime involves contempt of the Faith or of ecclesiastical authority or tends to the public harm of souls. (Canons 2205, 2229.)

Grave fear always excuses from *latae sententiae* penalties even though the crime be intrinsically wrong and gravely culpable, provided only that it does not fall to the contempt of the Faith, etc. (PCI, 20 Dec., 1937.)

5. Ignorance of the law or even only of the penalty excuses from censures even though the ignorance be

gravely culpable, provided only that it is not crass, supine or affected. (Cf. Can. 2229.)

6. If the law contains the words *praesumpserit, ausus fuerit, scienter, studiose, temerarie, consulto egerit,* or others similar to them which require full knowledge and deliberation, *any diminution of imputability* on the part of either the intellect or the will exempts the delinquent from *latae sententiae* penalties. (Can. 2229.)

> Hence, when the penal law contains such words, one is excused from contracting the penalty by ignorance (even crass), drunkenness, weakness of mind, passion (though not uncontrollable), grave fear (even in cases where the crime implies contempt of the Faith), minor age, etc. — provided that imputability is diminished in some way, and usually it is.

Note: If one recedes from contumacy before the time when the law places the penalty upon him, he is excused from contracting the penalty. One is understood to recede from contumacy if he truly repents of the crime, impedes the crime's effect in so far as he possibly can, and proposes to make satisfaction. (Cf. Canons 2209 § 5; 2242 §§ 2, 3.)

IV. EXCUSE FROM OBSERVING A PENALTY INCURRED

A *latae sententiae* penalty binds the delinquent in both the external and internal forum as soon as he is conscious of the crime; however, before a declaratory sentence is pronounced, the delinquent is excused from the observance of the penalty whenever he cannot observe it without defaming himself; and in the external forum no one can demand its observance of him until the declaratory sentence is pronounced or unless the crime is notorious. (Can. 2232 § 1.)

> Therefore, a pastor excommunicated *ipso facto* because of an occult crime, as long as no sentence intervenes, may say Mass and hear confessions etc., after he makes an act of perfect contrition (because of his sin), until he finds an opportunity to be absolved from his censure.

CHAPTER IV

Absolution from Censures

I. ABSOLUTION IN ORDINARY CASES

1. *Necessity of absolution.* Censures are taken away only by absolution. (Can. 2248 § 1.) If there is question of a censure which does not impede the reception of the sacraments (v.g., suspension), the person under censure may be absolved from his sins, the censure remaining. If, however, there is question of a censure which impedes the reception of the sacraments (excommunication and personal interdict), the censured person cannot be absolved from his sins, unless he is first absolved from the censure. (Can. 2250.)

> Censures may be *multiplied,* be it that the same crime is repeated, or that several crimes have been committed. In asking for absolution from the censures, the penitent must mention all the censures. If the penitent does not mention some sins (with censures) in his confession, then if the absolution was granted in general, the absolution is valid for censures concealed in good faith, with the exception of censures reserved *specialissimo modo* to the Holy See and censures *ab homine;* it is not valid for censures concealed in bad faith. (Cf. Can. 2249 § 2.)

2. *Author of the absolution*

a. Non-reserved censures may be absolved from by any confessor in the sacramental forum. (Can. 2253, 1°.)

> A *latae sententiae* censure is not reserved unless in the law or precept it is expressly stated that it is reserved; and in doubt either of law or of fact, the reservation does not bind. (Can. 2245 § 4.) Hence, when the reservation of absolution is doubtful, the reservation ceases. According to the common opinion, the reservation is doubtful when the doubt concerns the sin or the fact that a censure has been incurred as well as when the doubt touches the reservation only. In all these cases the reservation ceases and any confessor can absolve, so that if later, it became certain that a censure had been contracted, no new absolution would be needed. (Cf. Cloran, pp. 99-103; Cappello, *De Cens.,* n. 71.)

> The reservation of a *latae sententiae* censure in a *particular*

territory does not bind outside of the territory (Can. 2247 § 2); hence, a cleric excommunicated by diocesan statute, even though absolution be reserved to his Ordinary, when outside the diocese may be absolved by any confessor of the territory he is now in.

b. An *ab homine* censure is reserved to the one who inflicted it or who pronounced the sentence, as well as to his superior, his successor, or his delegate; hence, such a censure is reserved everywhere and no other person can absolve from it without having obtained the faculty from the competent superior. (Canons 2236, 2245, 2247, 2253.)

> An *ab homine* penalty is one directly inflicted without being contained in previous law or precept, *or* stated, indeed, in law or precept, but to be inflicted, and, indeed, actually inflicted by a condemnatory sentence of the superior.

c. From censures reserved by law to the Ordinary, any Ordinary can absolve his subjects, and a local Ordinary can also absolve *peregrini*. From censures reserved to the Holy See only they can absolve who have obtained special faculties either from the law or by indult. (Cf. Can. 2253, 3°.)

> All Ordinaries enjoy the faculty of absolving in occult cases from censures *latae sententiae* reserved *simpliciter* to the Holy See (Can. 2237 § 2.) Local Ordinaries usually obtain ample faculties from the Holy See to absolve from the same censures in public cases as well as from censures reserved *speciali modo* in both occult and public cases. Hence the pastor or confessor who needs special faculties for a particular case may often obtain them from his local Ordinary.

d. If a confessor, *unaware or ignorant of the reservation,* absolves a penitent from the censure and sin, the absolution from the censure is valid unless it is an *ab homine* censure or a censure *specialissimo modo* reserved to the Holy See. (Can. 2247 § 3.)

> The canon speaks of ignorance of the reservation, but we do not doubt that ignorance of the censure itself is included, so that the absolution from the censure is valid even though the confessor be ignorant of the fact that a censure has been con-

tracted (Ubach, II, n. 901; cf. also Coronata, IV, n. 1752 and Cappello, *De Sacr.,* II, n. 406bis.)

3. *Formula of absolution*

a. The formula for absolution from censures in the *sacramental forum* is contained in the usual form of absolution from sins: "ab omni vinculo excommunicationis, (suspensionis) et interdicti, in quantum possum et tu indiges."

b. In the *extrasacramental forum* or in the *external forum* absolution may be given in any manner, but ordinarily one should use the formula contained in the Roman Ritual, title III, chapter III for excommunication, and title III, chapter V for suspension and interdict.

> Practically the only ordinary censure absolved from *in foro externo* according to present practice is that of excommunication in the case of validly baptized heretics and schismatics upon their reception into the Church. In notorious cases, v.g., penalties contracted because of illicit or invalid marriages, it is good to have the penitent absolved in the external rather than in the internal forum.

4. *Effect of the absolution.* If absolution is granted in the internal forum only, the person thus absolved may conduct himself as absolved also in acts which pertain to the external forum, provided no scandal ensues; but unless the grant of absolution is proved or at least legitimately presumed in the external forum [v.g., by devoutly going to confession and Communion when many are present], the observance of the censure may be urged by the superiors of the external forum and the delinquent must obey until absolved also in the external forum. (Can. 2251.)

II. ABSOLUTION IN EXTRAORDINARY CASES

1. *In danger of death.*

a. In danger of death, whether it be from some internal cause (sickness) or from an external cause (dangerous voyage, difficult childbirth, dangerous operation), any priest, though not approved for confessions, and though censured, irregular, apostate, schismatic, heretical or degraded, can validly and licitly absolve any penitent from all sins and censures no matter in what manner reserved or notorious. (Cf. Can. 882.)

However, the absolution of one's accomplice in a sin of impurity, though valid in danger of death, is licit only in case of necessity. (Canons 882, 884.)

b. A person who was absolved in danger of death from an *ab homine* censure or a censure reserved *specialissimo modo* to the Holy See, must, after he recovers, have recourse under pain of relapsing into the same censure, to the one who imposed the censure if it be *ab homine,* or to the Sacred Penitentiary or someone else endowed with the proper faculty if the censure be *a iure*; and he must abide by the mandate thereupon given him. (Can. 2252.)

Recourse need not be made for censures reserved *speciali modo* or *simpliciter* to the Holy See, nor for censures reserved to the Ordinary. Recourse must, however, be made after one has absolved a priest in danger of death who has attempted marriage and for very grave reasons must continue to live under the same roof with the woman. (S.P., 18 April, 1936.)

The time for recourse is within a month after the person recovers or the danger of death ceases.

The Code places no special obligation upon the confessor to warn the penitent of the obligation of recourse. Hence, if the confessor sees that the person is *in extremis,* or also if the confessor prudently fears that the admonition will do no good, he may omit it. (V.C., II, n. 452; Brys, II, n. 975.)

2. *In urgent cases.*

a. In more urgent cases, that is, when *latae sententiae* censures cannot be externally observed without danger of grave scandal or infamy, or when it is hard for the penitent to remain in the state of mortal sin for the length of time needed for the competent superior to provide for the case, then every confessor can absolve, in the sacramental forum, from censures no matter how reserved; the confessor must, however, impose the obligation of having recourse within a month, and under the penalty of falling back into the censure, to the Sacred Penitentiary, or to the bishop or some other superior who has the faculty required, in order to obtain the *mandata*. (Can. 2254 § 1.)

> *Danger of infamy* is had if one must celebrate Mass or administer the sacraments, if one cannot abstain from Holy Communion without causing suspicion, etc. It is still *hard for the penitent* to remain in sin if it displeases him to defer reconciliation and sacramental absolution for such a time as is required to obtain special faculties from the competent superior, even though his sins be already deleted by perfect contrition.

> *Note well:* A priest, who after the crime of attempted marriage, is *unable to separate* from his partner, cannot be absolved at all under Canon 2254. The absolution is absolutely reserved to the Sacred Penitentiary, so that no one, except in danger of death, can absolve. (S.P., 4 May, 1937.) If, however, the priest has separated from the woman, he may be absolved by virtue of Canon 2254 if his case is urgent as explained in the canon.

> The object of the recourse is not to receive a supplementary jurisdiction for absolution, but to receive the *mandata, i.e.,* the penance to be imposed on the delinquent, etc. Recourse must be made after absolution from any reserved censures from which the confessor absolved by virtue of Canon 2254 § 1.

> Canon 2254 cannot be used for *ab homine* penalties, but only for *latae sententiae (ipso facto)* penalties, whether public or occult.

b. Nothing prevents the penitent, even after he has received absolution in the manner just described, and even after he has made recourse to the superior, from approaching another confessor who has the faculty to absolve from the censure in order to receive absolution from him after a repetition of his confession; after this absolution the penitent obtains the *mandata* from this confessor without any further obligation of abiding by later *mandata* coming from the superior to whom he had previously made recourse. (Can. 2254 §2.)

The penitent may, but is not bound to do this even if it is easy. If he wishes, therefore, he may always have recourse to the Sacred Penitentiary or to a competent superior.

c. If in some extraordinary case, recourse is morally impossible, the confessor can grant absolution from the censure without the obligation of recourse, except in the case of absolution from the censure incurred through unlawful absolution of an accomplice. In granting absolution without the obligation of recourse the confessor must impose a proportionate penance together with the obligation of making satisfaction; if the penitent fails to comply with these injunctions within the term fixed by the confessor he falls again into the same censure. (Can. 2254 § 3.)

Recourse is morally impossible if secret correspondence with the competent authority is impossible, or if the penitent cannot himself have recourse and cannot return to the same confessor for the purpose of receiving the mandata. The penitent is not obliged to give his name to the confessor so that the confessor can transmit the mandata to him by mail. To demand name and address in confession is something entirely out of the ordinary. To transmit mandata to a lay penitent by mail can easily lead to confusion. Nor need the penitent approach some other confessor to make recourse for him; there is no clear obligation for the penitent to make recourse through any other confessor than the one by whom he was absolved. (Moriarity, CUA, n. 113, p. 239.)

Note that one may not absolve a priest from the censure incurred because of unlawful absolution of an accomplice, unless he impose the obligation of recourse. Note also that one cannot absolve at all from the censure incurred by the priest who attempted marriage when the priest cannot separate from the woman.

III. Modus Agendi

When a confessor is confronted with a censure, he should first determine whether the penitent be guilty of grave sin, without which no censure can be incurred. Next he should consider if perhaps the delinquent be excused from contracting the censure because of ignorance, grave fear, passion, age, etc., as explained above. If it is certain that the penitent has incurred the censure, the confessor should ask himself whether by virtue of Canon Law, special delegation, or privilege, he may absolve the penitent out-right, without any obligation of recourse.

If the confessor has no faculty to absolve, he should instruct the penitent to come back and in the meantime he shall write for the special faculty needed. If, however, the confessor finds that the case is urgent by reason of danger of infamy or scandal, or be-cause it is hard for the penitent to wait for absolution from his sins for the time necessary to have recourse to the competent superior, then the confessor may absolve by virtue of Canon 2254 § 1. If the confessor finds it morally impossible to make recourse for the *mandata* after he has absolved someone in an urgent case, he may himself impose the *mandata* etc., as explained above, and with the exceptions mentioned above.

In letters written for the faculty to absolve, or for the *mandata* after absolution in an urgent case, fictitious names are to be used. The following may serve as an example:

Excellentissime Domine,

Titius ob crimen abortus excommunicationem Ordinario reser-vatam contraxit. Cum casus urgeret eum a censura absolvi. Nunc recurrit per me confessarium ut mandata recipiat. Respon-sum benigne dirigatur ad me infrascriptum confessarium.

Rev. John Jones
Reserve, Wisconsin

Recourse should ordinarily be made to the nearest authority having faculties to absolve from the censure in question. In many cases, one's Ordinary will have the required faculties either by law or by indult (the quinquennials), and hence, one may make re-course to him, excluding, however, danger to the seal. One may, if he prefers, make recourse to the Sacred Penitentiary, in which case, also, the letter may be written in English.

CHAPTER V

Excommunication

I. EFFECTS OF EXCOMMUNICATION

Excommunication is a censure by reason of which one is excluded from the community of the faithful, with the effects enumerated in the sacred canons.

A *vitandus* is one who has been excommunicated by name by the Apostolic See and the excommunication has been publicly announced, the decree also declaring that the person is to be avoided. All other excommunicates are *tolerati* and among them we may distinguish the *sententiati,* namely, those who have been excommunicated by a condemnatory sentence, or whose excommunication has been officially recognized and strengthened by a declaratory sentence, and the *non-sententiati,* namely, those whose excommunication has not been affected by any sentence of an ecclesiastical superior.

The main effects of excommunication are as follows:

1.   The excommunicate loses the right to assist at the divine services. A *toleratus* if he assists passively need not be expelled; a *vitandus,* however, is to be expelled. A *vitandus, sententiatus* or one whose excommunication is *notorious* must be excluded from active assistance at divine services, i.e., such assistance as involves some participation in the functions themselves. (Can. 2259.)

2.   The excommunicate is forbidden to receive sacraments. The *sententiatus* is, moreover, forbidden to receive the sacramentals, and, unless he gives signs of repentance before death, ecclesiastical burial is to be denied him. (Can. 2260.)

3.   The excommunicate is forbidden to celebrate Holy Mass and to confect or administer the sacraments or sacramentals. (Can. 2261 § 1.)

The faithful may for any good reason (frequent communion, spiritual solace etc.) ask an excommunicated priest for the sacraments and sacramentals, especially when there is no other minister at hand, and the excommunicate is not obliged to inquire as to the reason for the request. From a *sententiatus* the faithful may only in danger of death ask for sacramental absolution, and if there is no other minister at hand, then also the other sacraments and sacramentals. (Can. 2261 §§ 2, 3.)

The same is to be said of asking the sacraments of an *interdicted* or *suspended* priest. (Canons 2275 and 2284.)

4.   The excommunicate does not partake of the indulgences, suffrages, and public prayers of the Church; private prayers and private application of Mass for him are permitted provided scandal is avoided; but in regard to

the *vitandus,* Mass may be offered only for his conversion. (Can. 2262.)

5. An excommunicate is excluded from legitimate ecclesiastical acts (v.g., sponsorship at baptism or confirmation); he is forbidden to exercise any ecclesiastical office or post; he is forbidden to enjoy privileges granted him prior to his excommunication; he is forbidden to exercise the right to vote (the vote is invalid if the excommunicate is a *sententiatus*); he cannot acquire dignities, offices, benefices, pensions or any other post in the Church (the acquisition is invalid for the *sententiatus*). A *sententiatus* cannot validly obtain any pontifical favor unless in the rescript mention is made of the excommunication. A *sententiatus* is deprived of the revenue deriving from any dignity, office, benefice, pension or position that he has in the Church; a *vitandus* is deprived of the office, pension, etc. itself. (Canons 2263, 2265, 2266.)

> The privileges which the excommunicate cannot enjoy are not such as he may possess as a member of some community, v.g., as being a regular, but such as he may possess personally by special concession made to him, hence, privileges granted to him personally for his own convenience.

6. *An act of jurisdiction* of either the internal or the external forum performed by a *non-sententiatus* is valid but unlawful; it is also lawful if requested by the faithful as described above (n. 3). An act of jurisdiction performed by a *sententiatus* is not only unlawful but invalid as well, except when he absolves in danger of death. (Cf. Can. 2264.)

II. Excommunication Latae Sententiae Reserved Specialissimo Modo to the Holy See

The excommunication is incurred because of the following crimes:

1. *Desecration of the Sacred Species.* Excommunicated

are those who desecrate (throw away) the Sacred Species or carry it off or keep it with evil intent. They are also infamous by infamy of law. (Can. 2320.)

2. *Assault of the Roman Pontiff.* Excommunicated are those who lay violent hands on the person of the Roman Pontiff. (Can. 2343.)

3. *Illicit Consecration of Bishops.* A bishop of whatever rite or dignity *who confers* episcopal consecration upon a person who was not designated by the Holy See or whose election or presentation was not confirmed by the Holy See, as well as the person *who receives* episcopal consecration, even though they were under the influence of grave fear, incur, *ipso facto,* excommunication most specially reserved to the Holy See. (S.O., decr., 9 April, 1951.)

> The consecrating bishop, the co-consecrators and the bishop consecrated, if of the Latin rite, are also automatically *suspended* until the Holy See dispenses them. (Can. 2370.)

4. *Direct Violation of the Seal of Confession.* Excommunicated is the confessor who *presumes* to directly violate the seal of confession. (Can. 2369 § 1.)

Only the direct violation of the seal is punished with an *ipso facto* censure. Indirect violation is to be punished with *ferendae sententiae* penalties. Only the confessor is punished for the direct violation, not others who may perhaps be bound to the seal (v.g., an interpreter). The obligation of the seal arises only from a sacramental confession, i.e., one made with the purpose of receiving absolution. Hence, there is no obligation of the sacramental seal if one manifests his conscience to the confessor in order to obtain counsel but has no intention of receiving absolution.

Since the law uses the word "praesumpserit," *any diminution of imputability* excuses one from contracting the censure. (Can. 2229.)

The *sacramental seal* is the obligation to keep secret all those things known through sacramental confession, the revelation of which would betray both the sin and the sinner.

A *direct violation* of the seal consists in revealing both the person of the penitent and the sin of the penitent.

An *indirect violation* is had when from the things the confessor says or does there arises a danger that others will come to know a sin confessed and the identity of the penitent.

Prohibited use: use of sacramental knowledge, i.e., of matter which falls under the seal, to the detriment of the penitent is absolutely forbidden even if all danger of violating the seal is absent. (Can. 890 § 1.) This prohibited use occurs when the penitent suffers some detriment distinct from the suspicion of sin, as when a confessor dismisses his servant because from confession he knows the servant to be a thief. It is not a violation of the seal, however.

When *without the use of sacramental knowledge,* something is revealed that causes detriment to the penitent, i.e., when the confessor reveals a corporal or mental defect of the penitent, no violation of the seal is had, even though some authors speak of the case as a violation improperly so-called. One must be very careful, however, in mentioning, v.g., that such and such a one is scrupulous, since the scrupulosity may constitute matter of the seal, i.e., when the confessor knows of it not from the penitent's manner of confessing but because the penitent confessed his scruples as sins or manifested them in order to declare his sins the better.

5. *Absolution of one's accomplice in an impure sin.* The absolution of one's accomplice in a sin of impurity is invalid except in danger of death; and even in danger of death it is illicit, outside of the case of necessity, according to the norm of the Apostolic Constitutions, and especially the Constitution *Sacramentum Poenitentiae* of Benedict XIV, 1 June, 1741. (Can. 884.)

A priest who absolves or pretends to absolve his accomplice in a sin of impurity automatically incurs excommunication reserved in a most special manner to the Apostolic See. Even if the absolution is given in a case of danger of death, the priest incurs the penalty, if another priest, though not approved for confessions, can hear the dying person's confession without occasioning grave infamy or scandal. If the dying person refuses to confess to another priest, the priest accomplice may absolve his accomplice without incurring the excommunication. (Can. 2367 § 1.)

The same penalty is incurred by a priest absolving or pretending to absolve his accomplice, who indeed does not confess the sin of complicity from which he (or she) has not yet been absolved, but omits the sin of complicity because the confessor accomplice has directly or indirectly induced him (her) to do this. (Can. 2367 § 2.)

a. *Complicity*

1) In the first place it must be ascertained whether a grave sin against the sixth commandment (consummated, nonconsummated, touches, looks, words) was certainly committed by both parties.

It is necessary that both be accomplices immediately in the same act of impurity. An accomplice is to be understood as one who commits the same sin of impurity with another person. It does not suffice that one cooperate, even proximately, in the sin of another (v.g., by procuring the occasion), if both do not take pleasure in that same action.

2) An accomplice is to be understood as anyone with whom a priest has committed a sin of impurity, whether it be a woman, man, or child, even one who is not yet an adolescent, and even a person with whom the priest has sinned before receiving the priesthood. (S.P., 22 Jan., 1879.)

3) It is required that the sin, on the part of both persons, be certain, external and grave; moreover, it is required that it be grave both by reason of the internal act and by reason of the external act. Therefore, if there was present on the part of one person a sin externally only venial from the parvity of matter (e.g., holding hands, or other acts only venially illicit), even though because of one's impure feelings and desires there is internally a mortal sin; likewise, if one person resists the other at least externally; or if externally the act is mortally sinful, but internally it is not because of the imperfection of the act (e.g., in drunkenness): or if there is reasonable doubt concerning the gravity of either the internal or external act (e.g., with impure talk, one is often not certain)—in all these cases there is no foundation for the censure, since it is to be given a strict interpretation.

The crime, therefore, does not exist if a priest sins with an insane, drunken, or half-witted person, someone sleeping, a person who actually does not consent to the sin (oppression), or if the sin is committed with a person who resists externally, even though consenting internally, or if a doubt is had concerning the gravity of the committed sin. (Cappello, III, n. 525.)

b. *The Crime and Censure*

1) This censure is incurred by a priest who, knowing the person to be his accomplice, absolves the person from the sin of impurity which has not yet been confessed and remitted, or at least pretends to absolve, so that the penitent thinks himself to be truly absolved.

The censure is incurred even if the penitent, because he is influenced by the confessor accomplice, omits the sin of complicity which had to be confessed.

Moreover, the censure is incurred even if the penitent omits the sin of complicity, because the confessor, either inside or outside confession had persuaded the person that the act of impurity that they were *about to commit* together was no sin or certainly no grave sin. (S.O., decr., 16 Nov., 1934.) *A fortiori* the censure is incurred if the confessor persuades the person that the act of impurity they have *already committed* together is no sin. (These are examples of indirectly inducing the penitent not to confess the sin of complicity.)

2) In danger of death: When the priest prudently judges the penitent to be in danger of death, he can always validly absolve the accomplice, but he can do so licitly, i.e., without sinning and incurring the censure, only if there is no other priest present at the time, and another priest cannot be called, not even one without faculties; or if another priest refuses to hear the confession of the person about to die; or if the one who is about to die refuses to confess to another, so that a sacrilegious confession is to be feared; or if another priest cannot be called without danger of grave scandal or infamy to the accomplice priest. The priest, nevertheless, is bound to remove these difficulties in so far as he is able.

The probable suspicion of complicity which may be caused in the case by calling in another priest is in itself gravely infamous and scandalous. (V.C., II, n. 159; Coronata, IV, n. 2083.)

3) Outside of danger of death: The opinion of those who hold that the absolution is valid and licit and that the priest does not incur the censure, when he uses epikia in absolving the accomplice in a case which is truly most urgent, does not seem improbable; it may be reasonably presumed that the legislator does not wish these cases to be included by the law. Cases of this type are:

a) If the accomplice cannot omit annual confession and Communion or otherwise stay away from the sacraments for a long time without the danger of grave infamy or scandal, and at the same time there is no other priest present to whom the person can confess.

b) If an accomplice lives in a place where the only confessor is the accomplice, and the person cannot go to another place to seek a confessor, nor is another priest able to be called without infamy and scandal, nor is there hope that another priest will be coming so that the person would have to abstain from the sacraments even during the Paschal season. (V.C., II, n. 160; Genicot, II, nos. 335, 338; and others.)

V.C. say that in such cases it is better to warn the penitent not to confess the sin of complicity but to save it for the next confession to someone else. Cappello, *De Cens.*, n. 170, says that in practice it is better that the person be advised to make an act of perfect contrition and thus receive Holy Communion.

Outside of the danger of death, therefore, absolution can be given validly and licitly by the priest accomplice only because of the most grave danger of infamy, which in our country is rarely had since there are so many confessors available.

4) *He does not incur the excommunication:*

a) Who hears the confession of an accomplice, but does not absolve nor pretend to absolve.

b) Who dismisses an accomplice confessing before others with only the blessing in order to preserve the person's good name, even though others are led into error. The confessor must, however, inform the penitent what is being done.

c) Who absolves an accomplice concealing, even culpably, the sin of complicity, even though the confessor knows this, provided, however, that the confessor did not induce the person to act thus. Each, indeed, sins gravely; but the censure is not incurred.

d) Who absolves a penitent concerning whom he doubts whether the person is his accomplice, or by whom neither in the act of sinning nor afterwards was he known as a priest, because he is not bound to manifest his crime to the defamation of himself and the sacerdotal state, nor to inquire about the affair with equal danger of such defamation. If, however, it is only *now* when the confession is made that the penitent does not recognize the confessor as the accomplice, the censure is incurred if the confessor accomplice absolves.

e) Who absolves a penitent in a state of mental confusion or without advertence to the complicity, being greatly distracted.

f) Culpable ignorance, even if gravely sinful, but yet not crass, supine or affected, excuses from the censure. (Cappello, III, n. 524.) One who absolves out of crass or supine ignorance is punished by excommunication, provided he was in some way cognizant of his ignorance and absolved nevertheless.

g) Who absolves in a case in which the sin of complicity has already been directly absolved from by another confessor. The sin has already *been confessed* and *directly absolved from* in a former confession, but the penitent includes it again as a sin of his past life. (Cappello, III, n. 524; also Genicot, Noldin, V.C.)

Penitents are advised to abstain from such accusations and the confessor is advised not to hear the confession of such a penitent, or at least not to absolve from that particular sin. (S.P., resp., 29 Feb., 1904; cf. Cappello, *De Cens.,* n. 185.)

Note: Concerning the validity of a prohibited absolution, confer the controversies of the authors, v.g., Noldin, III, n. 371. In practice, the accomplice should repeat such confessions to another priest. The accomplice who is absolved incurs no censure.

c. *The Absolution from the Censure in an Urgent Case*

1) If the case is urgent any confessor can give absolution according to the norm of Canon 2254 § 1, with the obligation of recurring to the Sacred Penitentiary for the *mandata.* According to the norm of Canon 2254 § 3 the confessor cannot give absolution without imposing the obligation of recurring in cases of this kind.

The confessor should immediately impose upon the priest the obligation to refrain from hearing the confession of the accomplice; also to break off all relations with the person, or if he cannot do this entirely, at least to be on his guard against the danger of a new lapse.

2) In the letter of recourse sent to the Sacred Penitentiary these things must be indicated:

a) How many accomplices the confessor has absolved and how many times.

b) Whether he has contracted irregularities by violating the censures incurred.

c) Whether he has already obtained a favor of this nature before, i.e., whether he has applied for absolution from this censure or for the *mandata* on previous occasions.

3) The Sacred Penitentiary in granting the petitioned faculty (or the *mandata*), is wont to prescribe that a confessor thus absolved is in the future to refrain perpetually from hearing the confession of the accomplice.

But if the penitent priest commits the crime three times (by absolving the same person three times or three different persons once), the Sacred Penitentiary in granting the petitioned faculty (or the *mandata*) is wont to impose on the delinquent confessor that he give up the office of confessor as soon as he is able to within the time to be determined by the one absolving, not however beyond three months if there is question of a simple priest, and not beyond six months in case the priest is a pastor.

If a priest or a pastor cannot give up his office, recourse is to be made to the Sacred Penitentiary to obtain a dispensation from this obligation. Then generally the Sacred Penitentiary extends the obligation of giving up the office of confessor to a year, after which time if no relapse occurs, this obligation of giving up the office of confessor is no longer insisted on, and the delinquent is permitted to retain his office.

In asking the Sacred Penitentiary (for faculties or for the *mandata*) explain also the reasons why the penitent cannot give up the office of confessor, so that the Sacred Penitentiary will not demand that he leave this office within three months, etc.

d. *The Method of Recurring to the Sacred Penitentiary*

1) The confessor usually makes recourse for his penitent and explains the case as it has happened. In referring to his penitent or to anyone else involved in sin, he uses fictitious names, Titius, Caius, etc. The confessor indicates his own name and address so that the Sacred Penitentiary may communicate the *mandata* to him.

2) The rescript or answer of the Sacred Penitentiary is then sent to the confessor who has made the recourse. He opens the outside envelope and finds another envelope sealed and bearing the inscription *"confessario ab oratore eligendo"* or *"discreto viro confessario ex approbatis"* or some such similar inscription. The confessor who has made recourse does not open this envelope, but hands it sealed to his penitent. The penitent then hands it to a confessor of his choice as indicated by the inscription. This confessor opens it and communicates its contents to the penitent. The confessor then proceeds to execute the rescript by using the faculties, imposing the penances, etc. contained in the rescript. After the rescript is executed it is to be destroyed *statim*, i.e., within three days.

3) If the priest penitent cannot return to the confessor to whom he made his confession (and by whom he was perhaps absolved from the censure *in casu urgenti*), he should make the recourse to the Sacred Penitentiary himself. If the penitent does not care to do this, nor to reveal his case to another confessor who will make recourse for him, then the confessor to whom he confessed may make recourse for the *mandata* for him and request the Sacred Penitentiary to allow him to communicate the *mandata* to the penitent outside of confession. (Noldin, III, n. 372 *nota*.)

4) Formula for recourse:

Eminentissimo Principi Cardinali Poenitentiario Maiori
Piazza del S. Ufficio
Roma, Italia

Beatissime Pater:

Titius sacerdos, (parochus, vicarius co-operator) cum Anna (uxore, puella) his actibus . . . peccavit eamque in confessione . . . (quoties) absolvit. Nunc (exercitia peragens,) poenitentia ductus, rem confessus est; verum cum absolutio differri non potuerit (est enim in cura animarum constitutus, etc.) a me infrascripto confessario absolutionem a censura vi Canonis 2254 § 1 obtinuit. Quare pro eo mandata peto. Ipse quidem ad omnem poenam paratus est, sed officium confessarii (parochi, co-operatoris) dimittere non potest ob has causas . . . Ad me ad poenitentiam excipiendam in confessionale redire potest (vel non potest ob has rationes . . . Quare suppliciter peto, ut mihi liceat per litteras eum de poenitentia injuncta certiorem facere.) Responsio dirigatur quaeso ad me Josephum Jones confessarium, Reserve, Wisconsin, U.S.A.

N.B. Letters to the Sacred Penitentiary may be written in any language.

Note: The excommunications reserved *specialissimo modo* to the Holy See are incurred also by the faithful of the Oriental rite. (S.O., 21 July, 1934.)

III. EXCOMMUNICATION LATAE SENTENTIAE RESERVED SPECIALI MODO TO THE HOLY SEE

This excommunication is incurred because of the following crimes:

1. *Apostasy, Heresy, Schism.* Excommunicated are all apostates from the Christian faith as well as heretics and schismatics. (Can. 2314.)

a. *Apostates* are those who give up the Christian faith entirely.

The faithful who profess the materialistic and anti-Christian doctrine of Communism, and especially those who defend or propogate it are considered apostates. (S.O., decr., 1 July, 1949.)

b. *Heretics* are those who after baptism, although retaining the name of Christian, pertinaciously deny or doubt any of the truths which must be believed by divine and Catholic faith.

> The sin must be in some way external, not merely internal. The truth denied or doubted must be one to be believed by divine and Catholic faith (*fide divina et catholica*), i.e., contained in divine revelation and proposed by the Church through its universal *magisterium* or through the pope speaking *ex cathedra,* as revealed and, therefore, to be believed. The doubt must be a positive judgment that the truth is doubtful or uncertain, not merely a temptation or a difficulty in understanding the faith. Unwarranted communication in the sacred rites of heretics is an external denial of the faith, and the person is *suspect* of heresy, but is not yet considered heretical. (Cf. Can. 2316.)

c. *Schismatics* are Christians who refuse submission to the Supreme Pontiff or reject communion with the members of the Church subject to the Pontiff.

d. Other penalties: heretics and schismatics who join or publicly adhere to a non-Catholic sect or an atheistic sect are *ipso facto* infamous by infamy of law. (Can. 2314; PCI, 30 July, 1934.)

e. Absolving from the censure:

> By quinquennial faculties, local Ordinaries may absolve in the internal forum, whether the heresy be occult or public and may delegate this power to confessors in particular cases. (*Digest,* IV, p. 78.) If the case is urgent, the confessor may absolve by reason of Canon 2254 as with any other censure. (Confer explanation above.)

> In the external forum (especially with converts) faculties may be obtained from the local Ordinary. Before absolution the heretic or schismatic makes an abjuration of heresy and a profession of faith in the presence of two witnesses and the bishop's delegate (usually the one who is given the faculty to absolve).

2. *Reading Forbidden Books.* Excommunicated are *publishers* of the books of apostates, heretics, and schismatics defending or promoting apostasy, heresy, or schism; also those who defend or deliberately (*scienter*), without requisite permission, *read* or *retain* these books or other

books forbidden by name through Apostolic letters .(Can. 2318 § 1.)

Books: the term "book" must be taken strictly as meaning a published work of some quantity and of unity of theme. Manuscripts, even though mimeographed for one's students, are not books if not put on the market for sale or free distribution; the required quantity is 160 pages in 8°, hence, pamphlets, booklets, magazines do not fall under the censure; periodicals bound into a volume may very well constitute a book; because of lack of unity of theme, anthologies which contain parts of heretical works would not fall under the censure, nor would small booklets of diverse topics bound into one volume. (Cf. Cappello, *De Cens.,* n. 226.)

Promoting heresy: the book must not only contain heresy etc., but must professedly propound heresy, or apostasy or schism. Hence, a Protestant prayer book, although containing heresy would not fall under the censure if it did not teach or vindicate heresy. To fall under the censure, the book need not be on a religious topic.

Apostolic letters: by the Roman Pontiff himself, not by the Holy Office alone. Not all books in the Index are forbidden under censure.

Reading, etc.: a grave matter would be to read three or four pages of very dangerous material, or about thirty pages of material that is not very dangerous. A grave matter with regard to retaining a book would be to keep it for a notable time, i.e., about a month, unless perhaps one retains it longer while he is awaiting permission to read it or an opportunity to turn it over to the authorities, etc.

Note well: the law uses the word *scienter* with regard to those who *read* or *retain* such books. Hence, any diminution of imputability excuses them from the censure. (Can. 2229.) Note also that many books fall under the prohibition of the Church (cf. Can. 1399) and may not be read without permission; however, only such as are mentioned in the present Canon (2318) are forbidden under pain of excommunication.

Absolution: by the quinquennial faculties, the local Ordinary can absolve from the censure incurred by those who defend, read or retain forbidden books. The faculty is for the internal forum and can be delegated to confessors in particular cases. (*Digest,* IV, p. 79.)

3. *Simulation.* Excommunicated are those who, lacking the order of priesthood, simulate the celebration of

Mass or hear a sacramental confession. (Can. 2322.)

4. *Appeal to a Council.* Excommunicated are those who appeal from laws and mandates of the Roman Pontiff to an ecumenical council. (Can. 2332.)

5. *Appeal to Lay Authority, etc.*

a. Excommunicated are those who invoke the aid of the secular power to hinder the execution of letters or acts of the Holy See. (Can. 2333.)

b. Excommunicated are those who directly or indirectly impede the exercise of ecclesiastical jurisdiction by enlisting the aid of any secular power. (Can. 2334, 2°.)

c. Excommunicated are those who enact laws, mandates or decrees against the liberty or rights of the Church. (Can. 2334, 1°.)

> The crime would be, v.g., to forbid the Church to teach, to erect schools and churches, to control the contract of marriage of the baptized; to subject the clergy to military service, etc.
>
> Judges and magistrates who merely apply the laws made by others probably do not fall under the censure. (Coronata, IV, p. 383, note 6; V.C., III, n. 534 and others.)

d. Excommunicated are those who conspire against the legitimate ecclesiastical authorities or who in any way strive to undermine their authority. (S.C.Conc., decr., 29 June, 1950.)

e. Excommunicated are those who usurp an ecclesiastical office, benefice or dignity without canonical institution or provision; likewise, those who allow themselves to be unlawfully placed in the same or who unlawfully retain them. (S.C.Conc., 29 June, 1950.)

6. *Violation of the Privilegium Fori.* Excommunicated is he who, without the permission of the Holy See, dares (*ausus fuerit*) to summon before a lay judge, a cardinal, a legate of the Holy See, a major official of the Roman Curia because of business pertaining to his office, or one's

own Ordinary. (Can. 2341.)

7. *Violation of the Privilegium Canonis.* Excommunicated is he who lays violent hands on the person of a cardinal, papal legate, patriarch, archbishop, or bishop. (Can. 2343 §§ 2,3.)

8. Excommunicated is he who usurps or detains the property or the rights belonging to the Roman Church. (Can. 2345.)

> Outside of Vatican City this canon has little application.

9. Excommunicated are those who forge or falsify letters, decrees or rescripts of the Apostolic See, or who deliberately (*scienter*) use such forged or falsified documents. (Can. 2360 § 1.)

10. *False Denunciation.* Excommunicated are those who personally or through others falsely denounce a confessor to the ecclesiastical superiors as guilty of the crime of solicitation; and from this excommunication they cannot be absolved unless they formally retract the false denunciation and, in so far as they can, repair the damage they have occasioned; moreover, a grave and long penance is to be imposed. (Can. 2363.) This crime of false denunciation is also a sin reserved *ratione sui* to the Holy See. (Can. 894.)

> The crime punished here, as well as the reserved sin, is to falsely accuse to the bishop or the Holy Office a priest of having solicited to impure sins while he was acting in the capacity of a confessor. The nature of the crime of solicitation is explained in greater detail below. (Cf. p. 128 ff.)
>
> In order that the excommunication be incurred, and the sin reserved, it is necessary that the false denunciation be made juridically, i.e., that after taking an oath to tell the truth the person denounces the confessor to the bishop or his delegate. A private denunciation made to the bishop as a preparation for this juridic denunciation does not suffice to constitute the reserved sin or to incur the excommunication.
>
> Authors are in great disagreement as to whether one can be

absolved from this excommunication in an urgent case before formal (juridic) retraction has been made. We hold that in the urgent case (and of course in danger of death), if a formal retraction is impossible, either before the competent superior or by way of signed statement to be sent to the superior, a serious promise to retract the false accusation and to repair the harm will suffice for the granting of absolution according to Canon 2254. With regard to the reserved sin, the reservation ceases in danger of death, and whenever Canon 2254 can be used for the censure, the reservation of the sin ceases by Canon 900. (Cf. Moriarity, CUA, n. 113, pp. 268-272.)

11. *Forbidden Business*. Excommunicated are Latin rite clerics, religious, and members of societies of common life or of secular institutes, who engage, either personally or through others (agents) in commercial or mercantile trading, including currency exchange, whether for their own utility or for the utility of others, against the prescript of Canon 142. (S.C.Conc., 22 March, 1950.)

As the decree notes, it is forbidden to employ agents to manage a business being operated in the name of and at the risk of the cleric or religious. It is forbidden to operate a business even for the good of others as if one would turn over the profits to a pious or charitable undertaking.

It is required that one *engage* in the forbidden business. At least two, and probably three, grave violations morally united would be necessary before the term "engage in" (*exercere*) would be verified. Likewise, the decree would not affect those religious who according to their constitutions carry on some sort of business as their special apostolate, v.g., selling books of apologetics. If a member of a secular institute carries on a business as his proper position in the world, he does not fall under the prohibition.

The following kinds of business are distinguished:

a. Merchandising (*negotiatio quaestuosa seu mercatura*) is buying merchandise with the intention of selling it unchanged at a profit. All forms of merchandising are contrary to Canon 142.

b. Manufacturing (*negotiatio industrialis*) consists in buying materials, changing them and selling them for profit.

1) In the *strict sense* it is had when the change or improvement is done by hired labor, v.g., to buy grapes, make wine out of them through hired labor and then sell the wine. This is contrary to Canon 142.

2) In the *broad sense* it is had when the change in materials is effected by one's own or domestic labor, v.g., by members of a religious community, students of a trade school. Such business is not prohibited by Canon 142. Hence, it is licit to sell the products made by students in a trade school; the students may be paid a small wage, and the profit used to support the school.

c. Domestic business (*negotiatio oeconomica*) is the profitable handling of more or less permanent investments. This form of business is not forbidden by Canon 142. Hence, one may sell his home-made cheese, liqueur, etc.; a cleric may make investments in stocks and bonds (avoiding speculation, however, which is forbidden by Canon 142).

d. Factoring (*negotiatio politica*) is the purchasing of wholesale supplies necessary for some community, parish, school, and selling them at retail with profit or at cost plus expenses. To sell merely for the sake of profit makes the transaction *negotiatio quaestuosa* and hence it is forbidden by Canon 142; to sell at cost plus expenses, and, therefore, not for profit, or to sell because the public good renders it desirable that these goods be available, even though some profit is realized, is *not negotiatio* in the strict sense and is not forbidden by Canon 142. Hence, to sell pious articles at the rectory for the convenience of the faithful is allowed if it is reasonably conducted and is really for the convenience of the buyers.

e. *Varia:* holding charity sales, raising funds by way of selling chances, holding bingo parties, giving dinners and having bazaars, are simply not considered business in the sense of Canon 142.

IV. EXCOMMUNICATION LATAE SENTENTIAE RESERVED SIMPLICITER TO THE HOLY SEE

This excommunication is incurred because of the following crimes:

1. *Traffic in indulgences.* Those are excommunicated who traffic in indulgences (Can. 2327), i.e., who wrongfully obtain money or other temporal gain from the publication or concession of indulgences, who apply indulgences to a rosary for a price etc.

2. *Membership in Forbidden Societies.* Excommunicated are those who join the Masons or similar societies

which scheme against the Church or legitimate civil authority. (Can. 2335.)

a. Societies forbidden under censure are the Anarchists, Nihilists, Fenians.

b. Societies forbidden under pain of mortal sin but not under censure are: Knights of Pythias, the Odd Fellows, the Sons of Temperance, the Independent Order of Good Templars, Rebekas, Pythian Sisters.

c. Societies dubiously condemned, which, however, favor Masonry and occultism are: the Eastern Star, the Maccabees, the Royal Arcanum, the Harugari, the Sons of Hermann, the Rosicrucians, the Order of DeMolay, the Improved Order of Red Men, the Independent Order of Foresters, the Modern Woodmen, etc.

d. Societies which favor indifferentism: the Holy Office exhorts Ordinaries, pastors, and directors of youth groups to warn the faithful against societies which pave the way for naturalism, religious indifferentism and atheism. The Y.M.C.A. is mentioned by name. (S.O., 5 Nov., 1920.) Clerics are not allowed to join the Rotary Club nor to be present at its meetings; the laity should be urged to observe the prescription of Canon 684 in these matters. (S.O., decr., 11 Jan., 1951.) It seems that the ban on attending meetings refers to meetings which are for members only and treat of the private and professional affairs of the society, but not to meetings which are open to non-members, and conducted for purposes consonant with priestly activities, such as the promotion of works of charity.

e. Communists: those communists who belong to secret cells which scheme against the Church or civil authority fall under the censure of Canon 2335; those who embrace the anti-Christian doctrine of Communism are apostates and subject to the censure of Canon 2314; those who belong to Communist labor unions and political parties do not seem to fall under any censure however, those who knowingly and freely join such organizations and those who publish, disseminate or read periodicals, newspapers etc., which support the doctrine or action of Communists may not be admitted to the sacraments. (Cf. S.O., 1 July, 1949.)

f. Absolution from the censure: by the quinquennial faculties, local Ordinaries may absolve in the internal forum from the penalties incurred by those who have joined forbidden societies. This faculty may be delegated to confessors in particular cases. (*Digest*, IV, p. 79.)

g. Passive membership: if all relation with the condemned society cannot be abandoned without danger of most grave harm or inconvenience, passive membership may be permitted for a while, danger of scandal and spiritual detriment being excluded, until the danger can be avoided. This material communion with the society can be tolerated only in order to avoid great evils and *with the permission* of the Apostolic Delegate or the Metropolitan. (S.O., 27 June, 1913.)

3. *Unwarranted absolutions*. Excommunicated are those who, without the requisite faculty, presume (*praesumentes*) to absolve from an excommunication *latae sententiae* most specially or specially reserved to the Holy See. (Can. 2338 § 1.)

4. *Communication with a Vitandus*. Excommunicated are those who aid or favor an excommunicate *vitandus* in reference to the crime for which he was excommunicated; likewise, clerics who deliberately and voluntarily (*scienter et sponte*) participate with him in divine services and admit him to participation in divine services. (Can. 2338 § 3.)

5. *Violation of the Privilegium Fori*. Excommunicated is one who, without the requisite permission according to Canon 120, dares (*ausus fuerit*) to summon before a lay tribunal a bishop other than one's own Ordinary, an abbot or prelate *nullius* or the superior general of a religious institute of pontifical approval. (Can. 2341.)

6. *Violation of the Papal Enclosure*. Excommunicated are:

a. Persons of *either sex* who without due permission enter the *papal* enclosure of women religious; likewise, those who introduce them or admit them into the papal enclosure. (Can. 2342, 1°, Ap. Const. *Sponsa Christi,* 21 Nov., 1950; S.C.Rel., instr., 23 Nov., 1950.)

With regard to women religious having the *minor papal* enclosure, the excommunication refers only to a violation of that part of the house set aside exclusively for the community.

Those who may enter the enclosure, with due permission, are enumerated in Canon 600. The ordinary confessor or the one taking his place may enter the enclosure to administer the sacraments to the sick. If these are not at hand, another priest may enter the cloister. (S.C.Rel., instr., 25 March, 1956.) Hence, when the ordinary confessor and the chaplain are absent, the abbess may call into the cloister, to give Communion to the sick, the priest who celebrates the Mass.

By the quinquennial faculties, local Ordinaries may absolve in the internal forum from the penalties contracted by those who unlawfully entered the papal enclosure of religious of either sex, as well as those who introduced or admitted them. (*Digest,* IV, p. 79.)

b. Women who violate the enclosure of regulars (men with solemn vows); likewise, superiors and others who introduce them or admit them into the enclosure. (Can. 2342, 2°.)

The wife of the actual ruler of a country together with her retinue may be admitted into the enclosure of regulars. In an extensive interpretation of Canon 598 § 2 the Code Commission replied that the wives of governors of the individual states in the U.S.A., with their retinue, may be admitted within the enclosure of men regulars. (PCI, reply, 26 March, 1952.)

c. Nuns who without legitimate permission go outside of the papal enclosure. (Can. 2342, 3°.)

Nuns are allowed to leave the enclosure in case of danger of death or danger of some other very great evil. (Can. 601.) In virtue of the quinquennial faculties, the local Ordinary may permit nuns to leave the cloister to undergo surgical operation, even though there be no danger of death or of very great harm, for such time as may be strictly necessary. (*Digest,* IV, p. 76.)

7. *Usurpation of Ecclesiastical Goods.* Excommunicated is he who, either personally or through others, presumes (*praesumpserit*) to usurp and turn to his own use ecclesiastical goods of any kind, or presumes to impede revenues of ecclesiastical goods from accruing to those to whom they rightly belong. (Can. 2346.)

Simple theft of ecclesiastical goods probably does not fall under the excommunication for it seems that for crime to be verified it is necessary that one usurp the goods or impede the flow of revenue in an authoritative manner as if one had a right to do these things, taking them as belonging to himself, pretending to exercise an imagined right to them. (Genicot, II, n. 942; Coronata, IV, n. 2000 and others.)

8. *Duelling.* Excommunicated are those who fight a duel, who simply challenge to a duel, or accept a duel, who render service in arranging a duel, who show favor to a duel or who, of set purpose (*de industria*) watch, permit, or fail to prohibit it in so far as they can. (Can. 2351.)

Those who fight the duel, as well as their seconds, are also *ipso facto* infamous by infamy of law.

Those who challenge and those who accept a duel imposed by a so-called "tribunal of honor" by the very fact of such challenge or acceptance incur the penalties mentioned in Canon 2351 unless it is certain that the challengers and accepters did not have the intention of duelling. (PCI, reply, 26 June, 1947.)

9. *Attempted Marriage.* Excommunicated are clerics in sacred orders, regulars and nuns in solemn vows, who presume (*praesumentes*) to attempt marriage, even a merely civil marriage; likewise all who presume to attempt marriage with one of these persons. (Can. 2388 § 1.)

Absolution from the censure: those who commit this crime are irregular (Can. 985, 3°), clerics automatically lose any office they may have held (Can. 188, 5°), religious are automatically dismissed from their institute (Can. 646 § 1, 3°). Hence, if at all possible these people should be sent to their own ordinaries or superiors to seek reconciliation in the external forum. In a truly urgent case, however, Canon 2254 may be used to absolve the person from the excommunication. However, in the case of a *priest* who cannot separate from the woman, the censure is so reserved to the Sacred Penitentiary that no one, except in danger of death can ever absolve from it. (S.P., 4 May, 1937.)

10. *Simony.* Excommunicated are those who are guilty of simony in connection with ecclesiastical offices, benefices, or dignities. (Can. 2392.)

11. *Withdrawing documents.* Excommunicated are the diocesan administrator as well as other officials who withdraw from the episcopal curia a document belonging to it,

or who conceal, destroy, or substantially alter such documents. (Cf. Can. 2405.)

As is evident, the document must be of importance, before the actions enumerated can constitute a grave sin. The penal sanction of Canon 2405 probably arises only *sede vacante*. (Coronata, IV, n. 2227; Cappello, *De Cens.,* n. 365.)

V. EXCOMMUNICATION LATAE SENTENTIAE RESERVED TO THE ORDINARY

This excommunication is incurred because of the following crimes:

1. *Marriage before a Non-Catholic Minister.* Excommunicated are Catholics who contract marriage before a non-Catholic minister. (Can. 2319 § 1, 1°.)

This excommunication was subject to a variety of explanations and its application was further complicated by a similar penalty enacted by the III Plenary Council of Baltimore. Pope Pius XII decreed that the phrase referring to Canon 1063 was to be deleted from Canon 2319, and thereby ended a variety of opinions and disputes. (Pius XII, *motu proprio,* 25 Dec., 1953, promulgated 18 March, 1954.) The excommunication now certainly embraces not only marriages between a Catholic and a heretic, but also between a Catholic and an infidel, or between two Catholics. Likewise, it is not necessary that two ceremonies, a Catholic one and a non-Catholic one, take place. One ceremony before a non-Catholic minister suffices for the excommunication to be incurred. Every marriage entered into or attempted by a Catholic before a non-Catholic minister acting in his ministerial capacity, is punished with excommunication. As it now stands, the penal law of the Code is coextensive with decree 127 of the III Council of Baltimore and supplants it. In other words, the law of Baltimore is abrogated.

A non-Catholic minister is one who pertains to an heretical or schismatic sect. For the person contracting marriage to incur the excommunication, it is necessary that the minister assist at the marriage ceremony in his ministerial capacity (*uti sacris addictis*), i.e., that he use prayers or some sacred vestment or hold the ceremony in his church.

Marriage before a Justice of Peace or some other civil officer is not penalized by excommunication.

2. *Marriage after Divorce.* Excommunicated are those

who, after obtaining a civil divorce, dare (*ausi fuerint*) to attempt marriage. (Balt. III, n. 124.)

The excommunication is incurred only by the one who obtains the divorce and not by the person with whom he attempts marriage, unless this person acts as a necessary co-operator with the married party in procuring the divorce and then attemps marriage with him. (Slater-Martin, II, p. 195; Cloran, pp. 149-150.)

3. *Educating Children in Heresy.* Excommunicated are:

a. Catholics who enter marriage with an explicit or implicit agreement to educate all or some of their children outside the Catholic Church. (Can. 2319 § 1, 2°.)

The crime is the rearing of children in a non-Catholic religion, not merely rearing them in no religion. (Brys, II, n. 1012.)

b. Catholics who deliberately (*scienter*) presume to ask a non-Catholic minister to baptize their children. (Can. 2319 § 1, 3°.)

c. Catholic parents or guardians who deliberately (*scienter*) have their children educated or instructed in a non-Catholic sect. (Can. 2319 § 1, 4°.)

For example, to send to a Sunday-school, or to a Protestant boarding school or parochial school where religious instruction and training are given them besides the secular learning.

4. *Traffic in False Relics.* Excommunicated are those who make false relics, and those who deliberately (*scienter*) sell them, distribute them or exhibit them for the public veneration of the faithful. (Can. 2326.)

5. *Violation of the Privilege of the Canon.* Excommunicated are those who lay violent hands on the person of a cleric (of rank below a bishop), or of a religious of either sex. Absolution is reserved to one's own Ordinary. (Can. 2343 § 4.)

The crime punished here is an external and gravely sinful injury inflicted not by threats or words, but by facts, to the body, liberty or dignity of the privileged person. The gravity of the sin is measured not by the bodily harm inflicted, but by violation of one's honor and dignity, so that a grave sin is committed if one's honor or dignity are gravely violated in the estimation of prudent men.

Although novices in orders and congregations as well as members of communities living in common but without vows, enjoy the *privilegium canonis,* nevertheless, the violation of the privilege in regard to them does not fall under the penalty of Canon 2343. (Cappello, *De Cens.,* n. 382.)

6. *Abortion.* Excommunicated are those who effectively procure abortion, the mother not excepted. (Can. 2350.)

Abortion is the deliberate ejection from the womb of an unviable fetus. A fetus is unviable before the beginning of the seventh month of pregnancy. The abortion must be caused directly and deliberately. If it is caused by carelessness, striking, or other indirect causes, such as operations which indirectly, though foreseen, bring about the miscarriage, the censure is not incurred. (Cf. Cappello, *De Cens.,* n. 384.)

The procuring of abortion must be effective. If it is doubtful whether the effect was produced or not, there is no censure; likewise, if it is doubtful whether the means used caused the abortion or if rather it followed from some other cause. (Cappello, III, n. 652.)

The tube containing an ectopic fetus is in a diseased condition and its excision is only indirect killing of the fetus.

Ejection of the male seed by the woman after intercourse, if done within twenty-four hours of the intercourse is not abortion. (Coronata, IV, n. 2015.)

If the mother procures the abortion or consents to it she contracts the censure, unless she is under the influence of grave fear, in which case she is excused from the censure, even though the fear be *ab intrinseco,* and even though she be guilty of grave sin.

Those who co-operate in procuring an abortion are excommunicated if they are necessary co-operators, not, however, if their co-operation is merely accessory (confer above, p. 93.)

7. *Apostasy from Religion.* Excommunicated are religious who apostatize from their institute. The absolution is reserved to the major superior, or if the institute is lay or non-exempt to the Ordinary of the place where the

religious is staying. (Can. 2385.)

An apostate from religion is one professed of *perpetual* vows who unlawfully leaves the religious house and has the intention of not returning, or who after a lawful departure, does not return, having the intention of withdrawing himself from religious obedience. (Can. 644.) The excommunication is incurred at the moment when, having departed, the will of not returning or of withdrawing from obedience is externally manifested; if not otherwise manifested, this perverse will is presumed to exist if within a month of the departure the religious has neither returned nor manifested to his superior his intention of returning. (Can. 644.)

The apostate is also automatically excluded from legitimate ecclesiastical acts and loses all the privileges of his institute. In practice an apostate religious is to be sent back to his superior, with whom he may consult as to the advisability of returning to the institute or of seeking an indult of secularization. If, however, the conditions of the urgent case are verified, he may in the meantime be absolved from the excommunication by virtue of Canon 2254.

8. *Unlawful Marriage.* Excommunicated are religious in simple *perpetual* vows, both in orders and in congregations, who presume (*praesumentes*) to contract marriage, even a civil marriage, and all those presuming to contract marriage with them. (Can. 2388 § 2.)

If the form of marriage is observed and no diriment impediment is present, the marriage of one in simple vows is valid, except for members of the Society of Jesus whose simple vows are a diriment impediment to matrimony.

VI. EXCOMMUNICATION RESERVED TO NO ONE

This excommunication is incurred because of the following crimes:

1. *Publishing Books without Permission.* Excommunicated are authors and editors who, without the requisite permission (as demanded by Canons 1385 and 1391) provide for the publication of books of Sacred Scripture or annotations or commentaries on them. (Can. 2318 § 2.)

2. *Forcing the Grant of Burial.* Excommunicated are

those who dare (*ausi fuerint*) to command or force the Christian burial of infidels, public apostates, those who have publicly belonged to an heretical, schismatic or atheistic sect, those excommunicated or interdicted by condemnatory or declaratory sentence, against the prescription of Canon 1240. (Can. 2339.)

Because of various doubts of law the censure is not incurred unless the commanding or forcing is done by public authority and the command or force is effective, namely, that the corpse is actually buried in blessed ground.

3. *Unlawful Alienation.* Excommunicated are those who either by giving, receiving, or giving consent, deliberately (*scienter*) alienate ecclesiastical property without the requisite consent of the Holy See in cases where that consent is required by law. (Can. 2347, 3°.)

4. *Forcing One into the Clerical or Religious State.* Excommunicated are those who in any way force a person to embrace the clerical state, or to enter religion or to make religious profession whether solemn or simple, perpetual or temporary. (Can. 2352.)

The delict is not had if one forces a person to enter the seminary or the postulancy, provided that the force ceases before tonsure or entrance into the novitiate respectively.

5. *Omitting Denunciation of Solicitation.* The faithful who contrary to the prescript of Canon 904 knowingly (*scienter*) neglect to report within one month a priest guilty of the crime of solicitation, automatically incur excommunication *nemini reservata,* from which, however, they may not be absolved until they have satisfied their obligation, or have sincerely promised that they will satisfy it. (Can. 2368 § 2.)

According to the norm of the Apostolic Constitutions and especially of the Constitution of Benedict XIV, *Sacramentum Poenitentiae,* June 1, 1741, the penitent is obliged to report within a month to the local Ordinary or to the Sacred Congregation of the Holy Office, a priest guilty of the crime of solicitation in confession. The confessor is under grave obligation to warn the penitent of this duty. (Can. 904.)

Confessors must be reported who would attempt to solicit or incite a penitent (whoever that person may be) to indecencies and impurities either by words or signs or nods or touches, or by writing to be read either then or afterwards, or who would dare to carry on illicit and indecent conversation or discourse, doing these things either during the actual sacramental confession, or immediately before or after confession or on the occasion or pretext of confession or even outside the occasion of confession but in the confessional or in another place designated or selected for the hearing of confessions making pretense of hearing the confession there. (Benedict XIV, *Sacramentum Poenitentiae*, 1 June, 1741.)

APPENDIX

Solicitation

I. THE SOLICITATION ITSELF

1. *Nature of the Crime*

a. To solicit or incite is the same as to induce, and it suffices that it be attempted by the confessor even if the penitent does not consent or does not advert to it.

b. Any penitent, man, woman, or child, suffices to constitute the person involved. It need not be a woman.

c. Solicitation is made to indecencies or impurities: i.e., to a grave sin against the sixth commandment to be committed either with the confessor or with another or with oneself; also if the confessor wishes to sin with some third party and uses the penitent as an intermediary.

Confessors must be denounced who persuade women that they can, in the absence of their husbands, licitly procure sensual arousement and pollution. (S.P., 2 Sept., 1904.)

d. The sinful acts may be provocative of their very nature, so that one's evil intention is presumed (v.g., the confessor indulges in impure touches, obscene talk) or they may be indifferent in themselves, but gravely provocative from their purpose and the circumstances, as v.g., the confessor says, "Wait for me in my house," and when he meets the person in his house, begins impurities.

e. The illicit and indecent conversation or discourse may be a carrying on of impure talk or a planning of an impure sin to be committed later. In this conversation and talk, evil intention on the part of the priest is required. Thus, a confessor is not to be denounced if he is merely imprudent in interrogating or teaching, if it is evident that he has acted in good faith for the good of the penitent, or acted only out of inconsideration and thoughtlessness, even though he was in some way culpable.

2. *Relation to Confession*

In order that the crime be consummated it is required that the solicitation have relation to confession. There are, according to the papal constitutions, five circumstances in which solicitation has this relation to confession. We merely enumerate them here, referring the reader to standard works of moral theology for their explanation.

The solicitation must take place:

a. During the actual sacramental confession; or

b. Immediately before or immediately after confession; or

c. It is done on the occasion of confession even if the confession does not follow; or

d. It is done with the pretext of confession even if the confession does not follow; or

e. It is done outside the occasion of confession but in the confessional or in a place designated or chosen for hearing confession, with the pretense of confession.

II. DENUNCIATION TO BE MADE

1. *The Obligation.* In order that there be an obligation of denouncing, it is required that:

a. The sin be grave. The sin is grave, even if the act be in itself only venially sinful or indifferent, but is placed with an evil intention, trying to draw the person into a grave sin.

b. The sin be certain. If it is not certain, the right of the confessor to his good name prevails. No obligation of denouncing is present if the deed or the talk is not certain; or if the talk is indeed certain but the evil intention is not certain, and the talk is not provocative of its very nature; or if the relation to confession is not certain. Strictly speaking, by positive law, the confessor is not to be reported unless there is moral certitude of his evil dispositions at the time of the solicitation.

Note: The confessor who has solicited is not bound to report himself. However, if one of his own accord reports himself, he will be treated more leniently by the judge. For priests who freely confess their own crime are to be dismissed with a proper rebuke and the imposition of only a salutary penance, after being given the counsel or command to abstain from hearing the confessions of the person solicited. They are not to be punished with the ordinary penalties even though they are later denounced for the crime they have now of their own accord reported. (S.O., 20 Feb., 1867.)

2. *Causes Excusing from Making the Denunciation*

The precept of denouncing, although most grave, is nevertheless a precept of human law which does not oblige with a very grave inconvenience. If however, the denunciation must be made also because of the natural law, namely, when the solicitation leads to public scandal or common harm, not even a most grave private inconvenience will excuse one from making the denunciation.

a. The probable danger of very grave harm in goods of life, fame, or fortune excuses. One is not bound to report a very great benefactor from whom he receives extraordinary and necessary subsidy which he would lose because of the denunciation; nor is one bound to denounce a priest who is a most intimate friend or close relative unless the natural law demands it on account of the common good, i.e., if the ruination of many souls or grave scandal is feared from the omission of the denunciation, for the common good prevails over the private good.

b. Impossibility excuses. If the solicited person can neither go to the bishop nor write him a letter on account of inability, he is excused from making the report, for the confessor is not held to make the denunciation for the penitent unless grave public harm threatens.

c. Fear of incurring the indignation of the one who solicited does not excuse, nor does the obligation of gratitude, nor the shame which the person reporting undergoes in making the denunciation. In these cases, however, the confessor may recur to the Sacred Penitentiary to obtain a dispensation from the obligation of making the denunciation.

d. Even though one is not excused by the mere fact that the solicitation was made a long time ago, nevertheless, if the confessor who committed the crime has passed many years now in conspicuous virtue and there is *full certitude of his complete emendation,* the report may probably be omitted. (V.C., II, n. 191; Genicot, II, n. 395, and others.)

III. THE CONFESSOR'S OBLIGATION TO WARN THE PENITENT

1. *Obligation to Warn of the Report to Be Made.* The penitent has the obligation, under pain of excommunication, *nemini reservata,* to denounce the soliciting priest within a month after learning of the obligation. Therefore, if it is certain that solicitation took place, the confessor has a grave obligation to admonish the penitent of the duty of making the denunciation. (Can. 904.) The confessor is held *sub gravi* to make this admonition, even though the penitent be in good faith, and usually even if he foresees that

the penitent will not satisfy the obligation, excepting only in case of danger of death, lest the penitent be put into the danger of damnation. If the penitent cannot report here and now, the confessor should warn him that the obligation will bind when the impediment ceases.

Note: the soliciting confessor himself is never bound to warn the person solicited to make the denunciation even if later the person comes to him seeking to go to confession.

2. *Causes Excusing the Confessor from Warning the Penitent*

a. It is probable that the admonition may be omitted if the common good no longer demands it, as for instance in the case where the culprit no longer hears confessions, and the confessor foresees that the penitent would not comply with the obligation. (Noldin, III, n. 379.)

b. Although the authors teach that the penitent must be warned even though it is foreseen that he will refuse to denounce, nevertheless, if it is evident that the admonition will have *no other effect whatsoever* except the penitent's spiritual ruin, the natural law itself would seem to dispense from the positive law of making the admonition. (Coronata, IV, n. 2122.)

c. The admonition may also be omitted if the person is so simple that he did not understand what was going on when solicited. It is better to avoid scandalizing him.

IV. ABSOLVING FROM THE CENSURE

There is no *latae sententiae* penalty placed upon the confessor who has solicited. The penitent, however, who culpably does not report the solicitation incurs excommunication *nemini reservata*. If the penitent sincerely promises to make the report he may be absolved from the censure if he has incurred it. If later he fails to report, he does not fall back into the censure, but he still has the obligation of making the report.

V. MODUS AGENDI

1. Since it not rarely happens that women, out of hatred, envy, etc., calumniate innocent priests, the confessor should see if the person is trustworthy when solicitation is reported to him. If he doubts the good faith of the penitent, let him warn her of the grave penalty placed upon false accusation of an innocent confessor.

2. Let him examine whether all the conditions requisite to constitute the crime are present. For this purpose he should have the penitent come back at a later date and meanwhile *study the case in books of moral theology*.

3. If the penitent refuses to make the denunciation, let the con-

fessor see if perhaps an excusing cause is had. If not, let him have recourse to the Sacred Penitentiary for a dispensation from the obligation.

4. The denunciation is made in person to the local Ordinary or to the Holy Office. If this cannot be done, a delegate is appointed to take the denunciation, or at times the confessor himself is delegated to take the report. In the preliminary report which informs the Ordinary of the case, and which is usually done by letter, the one making the denunciation is not to include the name of the accused. The name is given only after it is asked for by the authorities. Likewise in cases where the confessor is deputed to take the denunciation he should have the penitent hand over the name of the accused in a sealed envelope, so that he will not learn the name of the accused.

5. If the penitent cannot personally contact the Ordinary and does not know how to write, the confessor is not bound to make the denunciation for him, unless a great public harm threatens, demanding that the confessor take this obligation upon himself.

CHAPTER VI

Interdict and Suspension

I. NOTION OF INTERDICT

1. Interdict is a censure by which the faithful, while remaining in communion with the Church, are forbidden certain sacred things as specified in the sacred canons. (Can. 2268 § 1.)

2. *Personal interdict* follows the person and hence must be observed everywhere. Its effects are similar to those of excommunication. The personally interdicted lose the right to assist at divine services, they cannot receive the sacraments nor confect or administer the sacraments or sacramentals, they cannot vote etc., nor obtain offices, benefices, etc. The *sententiati* are deprived of ecclesiastical burial. (Can. 2275.)

> The interdicted are not forbidden *per se* to exercise jurisdiction as are the excommunicated.

3. *Local interdict* does not urge outside of the interdicted place, but in the place it must be observed by all,

even *peregrini, vagi,* and exempt religious. (Can. 2269 §
2.) It forbids the celebration of the divine services or any
sacred rite in the interdicted place, with the exception of
those services and rites permitted by Canons 2270 and
2271, etc. According to these canons, unless the decree of
interdict specifies the opposite, some divine services may
be held daily in parish churches but in an altogether private manner. Likewise on some great feast days the interdict is suspended so that solemn services may be held.

4. *Interdict from entering the church* forbids one to
celebrate the divine services or assist at the divine services
in a church and carries with it the deprivation of ecclesiastical burial for such as are *sententiati.* (Can. 2277.)

II. INTERDICT LATAE SENTENTIAE

1. Those who deliberately (*scienter*) perform the divine services or arrange for the celebration of them in an
interdicted place, and those who deliberately (*scienter*)
admit the celebration of divine services forbidden to them,
clerics on whom there has been pronounced a declaratory
or condemnatory sentence of excommunication, suspension or interdict, contract automatically *interdict from entering a church,* binding until satisfaction is given according to the demands of the superior whose sentence they
have ignored. (Can. 2338 § 3.)

> The interdict of this law is a *vindicative penalty,* not a cen-
> sure. In regard to the removal of the penalty, see the general
> rules given below under the chapter on vindicative penalties.

2. Those who voluntarily (*sponte*) give Christian burial to infidels, public apostates, those who have publicly
belonged to an heretical, schismatic or atheistic sect, those
excommunicated or interdicted by condemnatory or declaratory sentence, contrary to the prescription of Canon
1240, contract *interdict from entering the church,* reserved
to the Ordinary. (Can. 2339.)

To give burial to others mentioned in Canon 1240 is sinful but is not penalized.

3. Those who have given the cause for the inflicting of a local interdict or of an interdict incurred by a community or collegiate body are automatically personally interdicted. (Can. 2338 § 4.)

The absolution is reserved to no one.

III. NOTION AND DIVISION OF SUSPENSION

1. Suspension is a censure by which a cleric is forbidden the use of his office, his benefice, or both. (Can. 2278 § 1.)

A suspended cleric is not forbidden to receive the sacraments (with the exception of holy orders). He may be absolved from his sins, the suspension remaining in force. (Cf. Can. 2250 § 1.)

2. *General suspension,* or suspension *simpliciter* without any further determination, forbids the use of one's office and benefice and of jurisdiction and prohibits the exercise of the power of orders. (Can. 2278 § 2.)

One under general suspension is forbidden to exercise the right to vote (the act is invalid if the one suspended is a *sententiatus*); he cannot acquire dignities, offices, benefices, pensions or any other post in the Church (the acquisition is invalid for the *sententiatus*); he cannot licitly be promoted to orders; if he is a *sententiatus* he cannot validly obtain any favor from the Holy See unless mention of the suspension is made in the pontifical rescript. (Canons 2283, 2265.)

3. *Partial suspensions* prohibit only the acts specifically mentioned; thus:

a. Suspension *from office* forbids any act of the power of orders or jurisdiction, as well as any act of administration attached to the office, except the administration of the property of one's own benefice. (Can. 2279 § 1.)

b. Suspension *from jurisdiction* forbids acts of the power of ordinary or delegated jurisdiction. (Can. 2279 § 2.)

c. Suspension from *divine acts* forbids all acts of the power of orders received by sacred ordination or by privilege. (Can. 2279 § 2.)

d. Suspension *from hearing confessions* simply forbids one to hear confessions.

e. Suspension *from benefice* deprives one of the fruits of the benefice, with the exception of the right of dwelling in the residence belonging to it, but not of the right of administering the property of the benefice unless the decree of suspension says otherwise. (Can. 2280 § 1.)

4. If one incurs a suspension which forbids the administration of the sacraments and sacramentals (v.g., general suspension, suspension from office, from divine acts, etc.), the prescription of Canon 2261 is to be observed. (Can. 2284.)

Hence the one suspended can licitly administer sacraments and sacramentals when he is asked to do so by the faithful. But from a *sententiatus* the faithful can ask only for sacramental absolution in danger of death, and if no other priest is available, then also for the other sacraments and sacramentals. (Can. 2261 §§ 2, 3.)

5. If one incurs a suspension which forbids the exercise of jurisdiction (v.g., general suspension, suspension from office) an act of jurisdiction placed in spite of this prohibition is valid but illicit; and if asked for by the faithful according to the norm of Canon 2261 § 2, it is also licit. If the suspended person is a *sententiatus,* the act is invalid, excepting absolution in danger of death. (Canons 2284, 882.)

IV. SUSPENSION LATAE SENTENTIAE

A. *Reserved to the Holy See*

1. A religious cleric in sacred orders dismissed for crimes not entailing a more severe penalty is *suspended* until he obtains absolution from the Holy See (Can. 671, 1°.)

2. Clerics who deliberately (*scienter*) have been promoted or have promoted to orders through simony, or have deliberately administered or received other sacraments through simony, incur *suspension* reserved to the

Holy See. (Can. 2371.)

> To exact a greater stole fee than is permitted by the schedule of taxes or by custom, is a sin against justice, but probably not simony. (Coronata, IV, n. 2153.)

> To accept an offering that is *altogether freely given* by the faithful on the occasion of the administration of a sacrament is not simony; indeed it is not even forbidden. (Cappello, *De Sacr.*, I, n. 81.)

3. Those who presume (*praesumentes*) to receive orders from one who is excommunicated, suspended or interdicted by declaratory or condemnatory sentence, or from a notorious apostate, heretic, or schismatic, incur *suspension from divine acts* reserved to the Holy See. (Can. 2372.)

B. *Reserved to the Ordinary*

1. A cleric who dares (*ausus fuerit*) to sue in a secular court, without the permission of the local Ordinary, any person enjoying the privilege of the forum (of rank lower than a bishop or of a superior general in an institute of pontifical approval) incurs *suspension from office* reserved to the Ordinary. (Can. 2341.)

> Hence, a layman or a religious who is not a cleric does not incur an automatic penalty by violating the *privilegium fori* in regard to a privileged person lower in rank than the above-named prelates.

2. A fugitive religious in major orders incurs a *suspension* reserved to his proper major superior. (Can. 2386.)

> A fugitive religious is also automatically deprived of any office or post he may hold in his institute. (Can. 2386.)

> A fugitive is one in temporary or perpetual vows who deserts the religious house without the permission of the superior, but with the intention of returning to the institute; or leaves with the proper permission but protracts his leave in order to withdraw himself from obedience to his superiors for a time. (Cf. Can. 644.) It is necessary that the absence last for two or three days before one is considered a fugitive, unless the constitutions of the institute determine a shorter time. He who leaves his

religious house without permission and goes to another house of his institute is not a fugitive and does not contract suspension. (Schaefer, n. 1565.) The crime implies that the religious withdraw himself from dependence upon his superiors. This element distinguishes flight from a simple unlawful absence.

The penalty of this canon applies also to societies of clerics living in common but without vows. (PCI, 2 June, 1918.)

Note: a fugitive is in no wise freed of his obligations as a religious. He has the duty of returning to his institute at once. The confessor should send such a one back to his superior, unless such a return be morally or psychologically impossible. In this case the confessor will contact the superior and provide for his penitent's needs. (Genicot, II, n. 967.)

C. *Reserved to No One*

1. A priest who, lacking the necessary jurisdiction, presumes (*praesumpserit*) to hear sacramental confessions is automatically *suspended from divine acts*. (Can. 2366.)

If one hears confessions by virtue of jurisdiction supplied in common error, but with no reason to make his act licit, he sins, but does not contract the censure. On the contrary, if common error does not exist and the priest provokes common error by hearing confessions and no grave cause exists to justify this course of action, he would sin gravely and also contract the censure. (Genicot, II, n. 968; Cappello, *De Cens.* n. 542.)

Since the law uses the word *praesumpserit,* any diminution of imputability such as crass ignorance, slight fear, hesitation, perplexity etc. excuses from contracting the censure. (Can. 2229.)

2. A priest who, lacking the necessary jurisdiction, presumes (*praesumpserit*) to absolve from reserved sins is automatically *suspended from the hearing of confessions*. (Can. 2366.)

Although the more common opinion includes under this penalty the unwarranted absolution from sins reserved either *ratione sui* or *ratione censurae,* nevertheless, because of a doubt of law, the penalty is contracted only if one thus absolves from reserved sins strictly so-called, not from sins reserved because of censure. (Cf. V.C., III, n. 569.)

3. Other non-reserved suspensions are the following:

a. Those who maliciously (*malitiose*) receive orders without dimissorial letters or with fraudulent dimissorials or before the canonical age or *per saltum* (cf. Can. 977), automatically incur *suspension from the order thus received.* (Can. 2374.)

This suspension also forbids the reception of a higher order. (Can. 2279.)

b.   A cleric who presumes (*praesumpserit*) to resign into the hands of a lay person an ecclesiastical office, benefice or dignity, is automatically *suspended from divine acts.* (Can. 2400.)

c.   An abbot *nullius* or a prelate *nullius* who, in the absence of a legitimate impediment, fails to receive the requisite blessing within three months of the receipt of the Apostolic letters is automatically *suspended from jurisdiction.* (Can. 2402.)

d.   A vicar capitular (diocesan administrator) who unlawfully, i.e., contrary to the prescription of Canon 958 § 1, 3°, grants dismissorial letters for ordination is automatically *suspended from divine acts.* (Can. 2409.)

D.   *Suspensions which are vindicative penalties*

1.   The Code of Canon Law contains several *latae sententiae* suspensions inflicted as vindicative penalties, the majority of which affect bishops unlawfully promoting to orders contrary to the prescriptions of the sacred canons. A list of such penalties may be found, for instance, in Genicot, II, nos. 974-978, or in Abbo-Hannan, II, pp. 870-871.

2.   Religious superiors who contrary to the prescription of Canons 965-967 presume (*praesumpserint*) to send their subjects to a bishop of another diocese for ordination are automatically *suspended* for a month *from the celebration of Mass.* (Can. 2410.)

This canon applies also to societies of clerics without vows who may have the privilege of granting dismissorial letters to their members. (PCI, 3 June, 1918.)

Canon 966 lists the occasions when religious may lawfully be sent to a bishop of another diocese for ordination.

CHAPTER VII

Vindicative Penalties

I.   NOTION

A.   *Definition.* A vindicative penalty is one which aims at the expiation of a crime in such a way that its remission does not depend on the mere termination of the delinquent's contumacy. It is terminated either by expiation, i.e., the fulfillment of the penalty, or by dispensation granted by a competent superior. (Canons 2286, 2289, 2290.)

B. *The more common vindicative penalties are:*

1. *Infamy of Law.* Infamy of law is that infamy which is imposed in cases determined by law. The law itself considers someone as having lost his good name and deprives him of various honors and rights.

> Those infamous by infamy of law are irregular; they are ineligible for ecclesiastical benefices, offices and dignities, and incapable of performing legitimate ecclesiastical acts and of exercising any ecclesiastical right or function (v.g., jurisdiction); they must be excluded from exercising any ministry in the celebration of sacred functions. (Can. 2294 § 1.) This infamy ceases only by dispensation from the Holy See. (Can. 2295.) In occult cases Ordinaries may dispense from it (Can. 2237 § 2), and in urgent occult cases any confessor can suspend the obligation of observing the penalty. (Can. 2290.)

2. *Infamy of Fact.* Infamy of fact is contracted when, because of a crime or immoral conduct, one has lost his reputation in the opinion of upright and conscientious Catholics; the judgment concerning this pertains to the Ordinary.

> Those infamous by infamy of fact must be excluded from the reception of orders, from appointment to benefices, dignities and offices, from the exercise of the sacred ministry and from legitimate ecclesiastical acts. (Can. 2294 § 2.) Infamy of fact ceases when the reputation of the delinquent has been restored in the opinion of upright men, a fact to be determined by the prudent judgment of the Ordinary. (Can. 2295.)

3. *Ineligibility.* Ineligibility can be for ecclesiastical favors, for promotion to positions in the Church, for obtaining offices, benefices, dignities. (Canons 2291, 9°; 2298, 5°.) Such ineligibility means that a person cannot validly obtain the favor, office, etc. in question.

4. *Exclusion.* Exclusion from the exercise of legitimate ecclesiastical acts (Can. 2291, 8°), excludes one

from being sponsor in baptism and confirmation, being the administrator of ecclesiastical goods, acting as judge, auditor, defender of bond, promoter of justice or faith, notary, advocate etc. in ecclesiastical court cases, voting in ecclesiastical elections. (Can. 2256, 2°.)

5. *Prohibition.* Clerics who hold an office can be forbidden to exercise some definite ministry connected with it, for a time, v.g., the prohibition to hear confessions. (Can. 2299 § 2.)

II. DISPENSATION FROM VINDICATIVE PENALTIES

1. In occult cases the Ordinary can dispense from *latae sententiae* vindicative penalties. (Can. 2237 § 2.)

2. In occult cases that are urgent because the observance of the *latae sententiae* penalty would result in infamy or scandal, every confessor can, in the sacramental forum, *suspend the obligation of observing it.* He imposes the obligation of having recourse, at least within a month by letter or through the confessor, to the Sacred Penitentiary or to a bishop endowed with the requisite faculty, and of abiding by the *mandata* they impose. (Can. 2290 § 1.)

> If, in some extraordinary case, recourse for the *mandata* is morally impossible, the confessor may himself grant the dispensation without imposing the obligation of recourse. In this case, the confessor imposes a suitable penance and satisfaction for the penalty in such a way that if the penitent fails to comply with these injunctions within the time fixed by the confessor, he falls back into the same penalty. (Can. 2290 § 2.)

Note: for a dispensation in public cases one must have recourse to the Holy See or to an Ordinary endowed with the necessary faculties.

III. VINDICATIVE PENALTIES LATAE SENTENTIAE

Besides such vindicative penalties as are placed on crimes already punished by censures (v.g., desecrating the Sacred Species is punished by both excommunication and infamy of law), the Code contains other vindicative penalties automatically incurred because of the commission of certain delicts. We list here only such as may be of some importance to one in pastoral work.

1. One who violates the bodies or the graves of the dead for the purpose of stealing or for any other evil purpose, is infamous by infamy of law. (Can. 2328.)

2. Whoever, for the purpose of marriage or of satisfying lust, abducts by force or fraud a woman who is unwilling, or a woman of minor age even though she be willing, but her parents or guardians are either ignorant of the fact or refuse their consent, is automatically excluded from legitimate ecclesiastical acts. (Can. 2353.)

3. A layman who has been legally found guilty of the crime of homicide, of abduction of a person of either sex who has not attained puberty, of selling human persons for slavery or for some other evil purpose, or of usury, robbery, theft accompanied by aggravating circumstance, or unqualified theft of a very grave matter, arson, malicious destruction of property in a notable degree, grave mutilation or wounding or assault, — is automatically excluded from legitimate ecclesiastical acts and from any position he may have in the Church. (Can. 2354 § 1.)

4. Bigamists, that is, those who in spite of the bond of an existing marriage attempt another marriage even though only a civil marriage, are automatically infamous by infamy of law. (Can. 2356.)

5. Laymen, and clerics in minor orders, who have been legally found guilty of a crime of sexual immorality committed with a minor under sixteen years of age, or of rape, sodomy, incest, pandering, are automatically infamous by infamy of law. (Canons 2357 § 1, 2358.)

6. A priest who has the faculty to confirm, if he presumes (*praesumpserit*) to exceed the limits of his mandate is automatically deprived of the faculty. (Can. 2365.)

7. Catholics who dare (*ausi fuerint*) to contract a mixed marriage, even though it be valid, without a dispensation from the Church, are automatically barred from legitimate ecclesiastical acts and from the sacramentals, until they have obtained a dispensation from the Ordinary. (Can. 2375.)

If the Catholic party is repentant and gives the promises to educate the children in the Church, he may be admitted to the sacraments, but not to legitimate acts (v.g., sponsorship at baptism) or to the sacramentals until dispensed by the Ordinary from the vindicative penalty. (V.C., III, n. 578.)

8. One who has an office, benefice or dignity with the obligation of residence (v.g., a pastor) and who is unlawfully absent,
is automatically deprived of the income of his office or benefice
in proportion to his unlawful absence, and must turn over this
income to the Ordinary. (Can. 2381.)

> If the delinquent cannot turn over this income to the Ordinary
> without defaming himself, he may return it to the funds of his
> church or give it to the poor.

CHAPTER VIII

Faculties to Dispense

I. FACULTIES TO DISPENSE FROM IRREGULARITIES

1. Any confessor can dispense from all irregularities
arising from an occult delict, with the exception of the
irregularities arising from voluntary homicide or effective
abortion, *in an occult urgent case* in which it is impossible
to reach the ordinary and imminent danger exists of serious harm or infamy. This faculty can be used only to permit the lawful exercise of orders already received; not,
however, the reception of new orders. (Can. 990 § 2.)

> The penitent is not bound to have recourse to the Sacred
> Penitentiary or to the Ordinary for *mandata* when thus dis-
> pensed from an irregularity.
>
> No special formula is prescribed for the dispensation; the
> following is appropriate: "Dispenso te ab irregularitate quam
> ob (. . . .) incurristi, in nomine Patris et Filii et Spiritus Sancti."
>
> For the privileges of regular confessors to dispense from
> irregularities, see p. 427.

2. Ordinaries can dispense their subjects from all
irregularities arising from occult delicts with the exception
of the irregularities arising from voluntary homicide and
effective abortion and of such as have been brought to the
judicial forum. This power can also be delegated. (Can.
990 § 1.)

> The power of the Ordinary can be used to permit one both
> to exercise orders and to receive orders. It can be used only for

irregularities *ex delicto,* not for irregularities *ex defectu,* nor for simple impediments.

In cases where recourse to the Holy See is difficult and there is danger of grave harm in delay, Ordinaries may dispense from irregularities *ex delicto* and *ex defectu* as well as from simple impediments to orders, provided there is question of an irregularity or impediment from which the Holy See is wont to grant dispensations. (Cf. Can. 81.)

If an irregularity or impediment is doubtful, no dispensation is needed if the doubt is a doubt of law. (Can. 15.) Likewise, strictly speaking, no dispensation is required if the doubt is one of fact, but in this case it is better to obtain the dispensation from the Ordinary *ad cautelam,* for in doubts of fact he has the power to dispense, as long as it is an irregularity from which the Holy See is wont to dispense. (Cf. Can. 15.)

By the quinquennial faculties, local Ordinaries may dispense from the irregularity arising from voluntary homicide or abortion, but only to allow the exercise of orders already received. (Cf. *Digest,* IV, p. 80 for details.)

3. Those irregular *ex delicto* are the following (Can. 985):

a. Apostates from the faith, heretics, schismatics;

b. Those who, outside the case of extreme necessity, have allowed themselves to be baptized by non-Catholics;

c. Those who have dared to attempt marriage or to perform only the civil act, while they were bound by the bond of matrimony, by sacred orders or by religious vows, even though the latter were but simple and temporary, or with a woman bound by these vows or by the bond of a valid marriage;

d. Those who have committed voluntary homicide or who have effectively procured abortion, as well as all who are necessary co-operators in these delicts;

e. Those who have mutilated themselves or others or who have attempted to take their own life;

f. Clerics who practice medicine or surgery forbidden them, if death results therefrom;

g. Those who perform an act of orders reserved to clerics in sacred orders, while either lacking that order or prohibited from its exercise by a canonical penalty whether local or personal, medicinal or vindicative.

In order that an irregularity arises from the above-mentioned delicts, it is necessary that the delict be a grave sin, subjectively and objectively, committed after baptism, and an external act, whether public or secret. (Can. 986.) Ignorance of the irregularity does not excuse one from incurring it. (Can. 988.)

4. *Excuse from observing an irregularity:* An irregularity forbids one both to receive orders and to exercise orders already received. If the irregularity is occult, the cleric would be excused from observing it when he cannot observe it without great infamy or scandal and he cannot recure to the Ordinary or confessor for a dispensation. In cases such as this the irregular person must make recourse to the Sacred Penitentiary or to a superior or confessor with the power to dispense. In the meantime he may place all such acts as he cannot omit without grave danger of manifesting his delict.

II. FACULTIES TO DISPENSE FROM VOWS AND OATHS

A. *Vows*

1. The confessor has no power from law to dispense from vows. To dispense from reserved vows, he should have recourse to the Sacred Penitentiary; from non-reserved vows, to the local Ordinary, or if the case warrants it, to the superior of a clerical exempt religion. For the privilege of regulars, see p. 426.

a. *A vow* is a deliberate promise freely made to God which has as its object something good, possible and better than its omission or its opposite. A vow made under the influence of serious and unjustly inflicted duress is automatically invalid. To invalidate a vow, the duress must be grave, unjust, inflicted by a free external cause (i.e., not by a storm, shipwreck, one's imagination), and must be the reason why one made the vow. (Cf. Can. 1307.)

b. A *public* vow is one that is accepted by a lawful ecclesiastical superior in the name of the Church; otherwise the vow is *private*. (Can. 1308.)

c. *Reserved* vows are such as can be dispensed from only by the Holy See. (Can. 1308.) Reserved vows are: 1) Public vows; 2) Two private vows, namely, a) The vow of perfect and perpetual chastity and b) The vow of entering an institute of solemn vows, the members of which actually take solemn vows.

In order that these two private vows be reserved it is necessary that they are made *absolutely* (i.e., without a condition), and after the completion of the *eighteenth year of age* (after midnight following one's eighteenth birthday), and with the *intention of assuming a serious obligation* to fulfill them. (Cf. Can. 1309.)

The vow of perfect chastity exists only if the person wished to bind himself under pain of mortal sin always to avoid every sin against chastity and never to marry. The vow simply not to marry, or to preserve one's virginity is not the vow of perfect chastity.

The vow to enter a convent, to become a priest, to become a religious brother or sister is not reserved unless the person includes in his vow an institute in which solemn vows are taken.

d. *Formula for recourse* to the Sacred Penitentiary requesting a dispensation from a reserved vow:

Beatissime Pater:

Caia annos viginti nata vovit castitatem perfectam et perpetuam (vel ingressum in ordinem regularem). At cum in gravi incontinentiae periculo versetur (vel . . . 3, humillime supplicat pro dispensatione voti, (ut inde valeat matrimonium inire, cuius opportuna occasio sese illi offert).

This letter may be written in any language.

2. *Cessation.* A vow *ceases* by the lapse of time specified for the fulfillment of the obligation, by a substantial change in the subject matter of the vow, by non-fulfillment of a condition on which the obligation of the vow depends, or the (complete) cessation of the purpose (*causa finalis*) for which the vow was made; finally, by annulment, dispensation and commutation. (Can. 1311.)

3. *Dispensation.* The following may, for a just cause, *dispense* from *non-reserved vows,* provided that the dispensation does not infringe upon the vested rights of others:

a. The local Ordinary in regard to his subjects (everywhere), and to *peregrini* (who are in his diocese);

b. The superior (even local) of an exempt clerical institute in regard to all the persons enumerated in Canon 514 § 1 (professed, novices, and others who stay at the religious house day and night as servants, pupils, guests or patients);

c. Those to whom the power to dispense has been granted by the Apostolic See. (Can. 1313.)

The above-mentioned may dispense only if the dispensation does not injure the vested rights of others; thus, v.g., one could not dispense from private vows made in institutes of men or women living in common but without public vows, because the vested right of the institute would be injured.

The just cause requisite for a valid dispensation from (or commutation of) a vow may be the good of the Church or the state, or the good of a family, a notable difficulty in fulfilling the vow, notable scruples in its observance, frequent doubts on the part of the person who has made the vow, inconsideration and hastiness in the making of the vow.

In doubt as to the sufficiency of the reason the dispensation may be lawfully petitioned and lawfully and validly granted; the dispensation remains valid even though one would subsequently discover that the reason was insufficient, provided that the dispensation had been granted in good faith.

4. *Annulment.* One who legitimately exercises dominative power over the will of the person who made a vow may validly, and for a just cause also lawfully, annul the vow in such a way that its obligation never revives. (Can. 1312 § 1.)

The power of annulment belongs to a father, mother (with the consent of the father) or guardian, in regard to the vow of a minor not yet emancipated. This paternal authority is not unlimited, but is restricted to matters in which children are subject to their parents. A private vow made after religious profession, with the exception of the vow to enter an institute of stricter observance, may be annulled by one's superior or superioress. It is not certain that a husband has the power to annul vows made by his wife.

Annulment can be effected only by one who had dominative power over the will of the person who made the vow at the time when the vow was made.

5. *Suspension.* One who has power, not over the will of the person making a vow, but over the matter of the vow, may suspend the obligation of the vow for such time as its fulfillment is prejudicial to him. (Can. 1312 § 2.)

Thus, a superior or superioress can suspend the vows of a novice which interfere with the discipline of the novitiate; a husband or wife can suspend the vows of the other party which interfere with the full use of the marital rights, whether these vows were made before marriage or after it.

Vows made prior to religious profession are suspended as long as the one who made them remains in religion. (Can. 1315.)

6. *Commutation.* A work promised by a *non-reserved* vow may be commuted by the one who made the vow into a better or equally good work; and can be commuted into a less good work by one who has the power to dispense according to Canon 1313. (Can. 1314.)

B. *Oaths*

1. *Concept.* An oath is an invocation of God as a witness to the truth of an assertion or to the honesty or fidelity of a promise. For a valid oath it is required that the person have at least a virtual intention of calling God to witness and that this intention be externally manifested by some accepted formula of words.

An oath is to be interpreted strictly according to law and the intention of the person to whom the oath is made. (Can. 1321.)

2. *Obligation*

a. One who freely swears that he will do something is under a special obligation of religion to do what he affirmed by oath that he would do. If an oath is extorted by violence or grave fear, it is valid, but it may be rescinded by an ecclesiastical superior. (Can. 1317 §§ 1, 2.)

An oath, taken without compulsion or fraud, by which one renounces a *private* benefit or favor granted him by law must be kept, provided it does not involve the loss of eternal salvation. (Can. 1317 § 3.)

b. A promissory oath is one that affirms the sincerity of a promise. Such an oath follows the nature and the conditions of the act to which it is attached. (Can. 1318 § 1.) Thus, an oath to keep a secret obliges only as far as the secret itself.

If an oath is attached to an act which directly tends to harm other persons, the public welfare or the salvation of one's own soul, the act receives no strength or confirmation from the oath. (Can. 1318 § 3.)

3. *Cessation.* An obligation imposed by a promissory oath cases:

a. If it is remitted by the person in whose favor the oath was taken;

b. If the thing promised is substantially changed, or on account of changed circumstances becomes morally wrong or entirely indifferent or impedes a greater good;

c. On default of the purpose (final cause) or of a condition under which the oath was made;

d. By annulment, dispensation, commutation. (Can. 1319.)

Those who have power to annul, dispense from, or commute a vow, have the same power, and in the same way, in regard to a promissory oath; but if the dispensation from an oath tends to the prejudice of other persons who refuse to remit the obligation, the Holy See alone can dispense from it, for the need or advantage of the Church. (Can. 1320.) For the privilege of regulars, see p. 426.

CHAPTER IX

The Place for the Hearing of Confessions

1. The proper place for sacramental confession is a church, a public oratory, or a semipublic oratory. (Can. 908.)

2. The confessional for the confessions of women must always be located in an open and conspicuous place, and generally in a church, a public oratory, or semipublic oratory designated for women. The confessional should have a fixed and narrowly perforated grating between the confessor and the penitent. (Can. 909.)

For a just cause the local Ordinary may permit the hearing of women's confessions outside a church or oratory, but with the use of a confessional set up in an open conspicuous place. The Ordinary may even designate such a confessional as the habitual place for the hearing of women's confessions; he may do this also for the confessions of women religious. (Cf. Coronata, *De Sacr.,* I, n. 463.)

A confessor or a religious superioress could also designate a place outside of the church or oratory, but with a confessional, for the hearing of women's confessions; they may not, however, designate such a place for habitual use but only for single occasions, v.g., during a girls' retreat, on the occasion of a feast day when many confessions are to be heard etc. (Cf. Cappello, *De Sacr.,* II, n. 632.)

By custom the confessions of the hard of hearing are heard in the sacristy or some other such place even though hidden but with a confessional. (Genicot, II, n. 231.)

3. *The confessions of women* are not to be heard outside the confessional unless an exception is required by reason of illness or some other true necessity, and in these cases the safeguards which the local Ordinary has judged opportune are to be observed. (Can. 910 § 1.)

A true necessity is had if because of danger of infamy the woman cannot go to a confessional in a church or in some other public place; also, in case of the hard of hearing, if no special confessional is at hand for such persons; also, great timidity on the part of the woman; likewise, in the case of a woman making the first Fridays who will not have the opportunity to confess if she must go to a church and to a confessional.

If one, without necessity, hears a woman's confession outside of a confessional only *once or twice,* no grave sin is committed if, considering the circumstances of place and persons, danger of scandal is precluded. (Genicot, II, n. 231, and others.)

4. The confessions of men may be heard even in a private house. (Can. 910 § 2.)

The ordinary place for the confessions of men is the confessional in the church or public or semipublic oratory (PCI, 24 Nov., 1920); however, for any reasonable cause whatsoever the confessions of men may be heard outside of a church and confessional.

5. When hearing sacramental confessions the priest is to be vested in surplice and violet stole as the custom of the times and places direct. (*Rit. Rom.*, Tit. III, Cap. 1.) This rubric is directive and not preceptive, yet it should not be neglected. (Cf. S.R.C., reply, 31 Aug., 1867.)

Religious use the stole only, without the surplice; and in some places they do not even use the stole according to a custom peaceably possessed. (Coronata, *De. Sacr.*, I, n. 465.)

PART VI

EXTREME UNCTION

I. THE MINISTER OF EXTREME UNCTION

1. The ordinary minister of the sacrament of extreme unction is the pastor of the place in which the sick person is staying; however, in case of necessity, or with at least the reasonably presumed permission of the pastor or the local Ordinary, any other priest may administer this sacrament. (Cf. Can. 938 § 2.)

In every *clerical religious institute* the right and duty to administer Holy Viaticum and extreme unction to the professed, the novices, and to those who stay at the religious house day and night as servants, pupils, guests, or patients, belong to the religious superior. (Can. 514.) When one of these persons becomes seriously ill outside of the religious house, the superior has the right to administer to the professed and novices; all others (postulants, boarders, etc.) should receive the sacraments from the local parish priest. (PCI, reply, 16 June, 1931.)

In *houses of nuns* the same right pertains to the ordinary confessor or to the one taking his place. (Can. 514.) In the absence of the ordinary confessor or the one appointed by him to take his place, the chaplain exercises this right. If these priests are not at hand, any other priest may be called into the enclosure to administer the last rites. (Cf. S.C.Rel., instr., 25 March, 1957, n. 27.)

In *other lay institutes* (houses of brothers, convents of sisters) this right and duty belong to the local parish priest or to the chaplain appointed by the local Ordinary to take the place of the parish priest with regard to that house or convent in accordance with the provision of Canon 464 § 2. (Can. 514.)

The rector of *the seminary* has the right and duty to administer the last sacraments to all who are living in the seminary (Can. 1368.)

151

2. A pastor must carefully keep the oil of the sick (placed in a silver or nickel vessel) under key in a safe and fitting place in the church, but not at home except in case of necessity or for some other just reason, with the permission of the Ordinary. (Cf. Canons 946, 735.)

> Just reasons for keeping the oil of the sick at home are many, v.g., frequent necessity of assisting the dying at night which is often the case in large cities, hospitals, and the like. Moreover, the tacit or reasonably presumed permission of the Ordinary suffices. (Coronata, *De Sacr.*, I, n. 559.)

II.   THE SUBJECT OF EXTREME UNCTION

1. Extreme unction can be administered only to one of the faithful who, after attaining the use of reason is in danger of death because of sickness or old age. (Can. 940 § 1.)

> The person must be in danger of death because of some *intrinsic* cause such as a disease, wound, accident, the infirmity of old age etc. One in danger of death because of some *extrinsic* cause cannot be anointed, v.g., a soldier before battle, a criminal awaiting execution.
>
> The sickness must put one in the danger of death. The danger of death is judged to be present as soon as it becomes probable that the sick person will die from his present sickness or danger, even though it may be more probable that he will recover. (Genicot, II, n. 425.) It is not necessary that the danger of death be proximate, but it is sufficient if it is remote. Thus, one may anoint a person dying of cancer even though it is evident that the person will live for several months. (Cf. Noldin, III, n. 444.)

2. When there is doubt whether the sick person has attained the use of reason, whether he is truly in danger of death, or whether he is already dead, the sacrament is to be conferred conditionally. (Can. 941.)

> If there is doubt whether one is in danger of death, the sacrament can always be licitly conferred conditionally as long as the person is sick. (V.C., II, n. 225.)
>
> Doubt as to actual death may arise in cases where the priest arrives shortly after the sick person has ceased to give signs of life. It is generally held that some time intervenes between the

last apparent signs of life and the actual separation of soul and body. In cases of previous illness and gradual weakening of vitality it is generally believed that the time between apparent death and actual death is quite short, i.e., half an hour. In cases of sudden collapse, accidents, strokes of apoplexy, the time between apparent and actual death is thought to be quite long, i.e., two hours or perhaps longer.

If the sacrament is administered conditionally, the condition should be *si vivis* if one doubts whether the person is still alive, and this condition should be expressed in the formula. If one administers the sacrament conditionally for any other reason the conditions *si capax es* or *si sacramentum valet* are used, and these need not be mentioned in the formula but it suffices that they be conceived mentally.

3. *The required intention*

a. The sacrament is to be conferred absolutely (i.e., without any condition) on those sick persons who, while they were conscious asked for the sacrament at least implicitly, or very likely would have asked for it, even though they have now become unconscious or have lost the use of reason. (Can. 943.)

One asks for the sacrament *implicitly* if he asks that a priest be summoned, or declares that he wishes to die as a Christian, or gives some other sign of repentance. One very likely *would have asked* for the sacrament, if in life he had faithfully fulfilled the duties of a Christian, or even if he had not always been faithful in these duties, nevertheless, did not altogether neglect them. In practice, the intention of receiving the sacrament of extreme unction is presupposed in all Catholics until the contrary is proved. (Genicot, II, n. 427.)

In these cases, the sacrament is to be conferred *absolutely, not conditionally*. (Can. 943.)

b. This sacrament is not to be administered to those who contumaciously remain impenitent in manifest mortal sin; but if there is doubt in regard to this it is to be conferred conditionally. (Can. 942.)

The sacrament may probably be administered conditionally to an unconscious person who had lived in the state of mortal sin (v.g., in concubinage), or who had died in the act of sin, (v.g., adultery, duelling) if, while he lived in sin, he did not entirely neglect the duties of a Christian, for instance, he attended Mass occasionally, was known to say daily prayers, attended novenas, etc., for it can be hoped that he breathed an internal act of contrition and hence had an implicit intention to receive the sacrament as well as the requisite disposition. If such a one had neglected his religion entirely, however, and had refused the administrations of the priest, if he gave no sign of repentance before becoming unconscious, he cannot be anointed because he lacks the intention which is absolutely requisite for the validity of the sacrament. Nevertheless, some authors permit conditional administration of the sacrament even in this case. (Genicot, II, n. 427.)

The reason why the Code speaks of a conditional administration of the sacrament in doubtful cases is because there is a doubt about the person's *intention to receive the sacrament,* and at least an habitual implicit intention is necessary for the valid reception of the sacrament. When the minister doubts the presence of such an intention, he administers the sacrament conditionally, the condition being *si capax es* and never *si dispositus es.*

c. When the minister has no doubts about the recipient's intention to receive the sacrament, but doubts the person's disposition so that it is doubtful whether the sacrament will be fruitful, the sacrament is administered *absolutely and not conditionally.*

The reason for this is that the sacrament thus administered is valid and if the recipient is in fact not disposed at the time of reception, but becomes disposed later, the sacrament will revive and produce its fruits. If on the contrary, one used the conditional administration *si dispositus es,* and in fact the person was not disposed, the administration would be invalid and it would be impossible for the sacrament to revive later. Hence also, when administering the sacrament of extreme unction conditionally, because of doubt about the person's intention to receive it, never use the condition *si dispositus es,* but always *si capax es.*

III. REPETITION OF THE SACRAMENT

The sacrament of extreme unction cannot be administered a second time during the same illness unless the sick person has recovered after he was anointed and then fell again into the danger of death. (Can. 940 § 2.)

If in a protracted illness the patient has rallied and felt appreciably better for a considerable time (about a month) and then has a relapse, extreme unction may be repeated. In doubt whether the same danger continues or a new crisis has arisen one should decide in favor of repeating the sacrament, since repetition in that case is more in conformity with the ancient practice of the Church.

If it is certain that the patient has, after being anointed, rallied from the danger, as often happens with those who have asthma, consumption or pneumonia, he may be anointed again after a short period of time, v.g., one week, if new danger of death sets in. If it is not certain whether the former danger ceased and a new danger has arisen, the person should not be anointed again unless a notable time (about a month) has elapsed. (Noldin, III, n. 448.)

IV. RITES AND CEREMONIES

1. The anointings are to be made exactly with the words, and in the order and manner prescribed in the Ritual. The anointing of the loins is always omitted. The anointing of the feet may be omitted for any reasonable cause. Except in cases of grave necessity the minister shall perform the anointings with his hand, and shall use no instrument. (Can. 947 §§ 1, 2, 3, 4.)

The unctions are made with the right thumb, in the form of a cross, on both organs beginning with the right, and observing the order of senses prescribed in the Ritual. In case of danger of contagion the minister may attach a ball of cotton to a small stick and use this instrument to make the anointings.

The oil used for the unction is the oil of the sick (oleum infimorum). For the lawful administration of the sacrament it is required that it be oil blessed in that year, that is, on the Holy Thursday most recently celebrated. However, if the new oils are not at hand, it is licit to use the old oils.

The sacred chrism and the oil of the catechumens are probably valid matter for the sacrament of extreme unction. Hence, in case of necessity, when one does not have oil of the sick, he may confer the sacrament with one of these other oils. In such a case the sacrament is to be conferred conditionally (si sacramentum valet) and should later be repeated again conditionally using the oil of the sick. (Noldin, III, n. 433.)

2. In case of necessity one anointing on only one of the senses, or better on the forehead, with the short form

suffices; there is an obligation to supply the individual anointings when the danger has passed. (Can. 947 § 1.)

Cases of necessity are: fear that the patient will die before the rite can be completed; danger of contagion; surgical operation brooking no delay; throes of parturition making it advisable for the minister to retire from the scene.

The short form is: Per istam sanctam unctionem indulgeat tibi Dominus quidquid deliquisti. Amen.

When the individual anointings are supplied they are to be performed absolutely and not conditionally. (S.O., 9 March, 1917.)

The individual anointings *may* be supplied as long as the identical danger of death continues; however, the *obligation* to supply them ceases with the lapse of a notable time, a half-hour in the opinion of Genicot. In any case, the obligation of supplying the omitted unctions does not seem to be grave. (Genicot, II, n. 421.)

When the single unction is used in case of apparent death, the other unctions are not to be supplied unless the patient gives signs of life.

3.   In administering the sacrament of extreme unction, the prayers may be said in the English language, with the exception of the following which must be said in the Latin language only, namely: the oration for the imposition of the hands upon the infirm person, the words of the anointings, the orations which follow the anointing. (S.R.C., decr., 3 June, 1954.)

APPENDIX

Administering Sacraments to Dying Non-Catholics

1.   If a dying Protestant or schismatic is unconscious (*sensibus destitutus*) he may be given absolution and extreme unction conditionally (*si sacramentum valet* or *si capax es*) if one has reason to think that the person lived in good faith and would welcome the help of the priest if

he knew it to be necessary. (Genicot, II, n. 264.) Arregui allows the same to be done for formal heretics, namely, such as are not in good faith, but being unconscious, are about to die. (Arregui, n. 589.)

2. If a dying Protestant or schismatic is conscious (*sensibus non destitutus*), he is first to be instructed to renounce his errors and make a formal profession of the Catholic faith. If, however, the priest foresees that because of his instructions on the matter and his admonition to return to Catholic unity, the dying person's good faith will be destroyed and his eternal salvation endangered, the priest should see ot it that the person at least makes an act of contrition. He may then grant absolution and extreme unction conditionally (*si capax es* or *si sacramentum valet*). (Genicot, II, n. 264; cf. also Noldin, III, n. 297 and Arregui, n. 589.)

Modus agendi. The dying Protestant should be asked if he wishes to be helped in preparing for death; then he should be asked if he wishes to do all that *Christ our Lord* wishes him to do in order to gain eternal salvation; let the priest make acts of faith, hope, love and perfect contrition with the dying person and have him declare he is a sinner who asks God's pardon. Then the priest may absolve him conditionally (and secretly if necessary to avoid scandal or admiration of any sort), and may also grant extreme unction conditionally. *If there is doubt about the validity of the person's baptism, he should first be re-baptized conditionally.*

The reason why the priest should have the person declare that *he wishes to do all that Our Lord wants him to do to be saved,* is to make sure that the person has at least an implicit intention to receive the sacraments. This declaration is also considered by the authors as being an implicit retraction of heresy and a profession of the true faith, both of which the Holy Office requires before a priest may licitly grant the sacraments to baptized non-Catholics. (Cf. S.O., reply, 17 May, 1916.)

PART VII

CHRISTIAN BURIAL

I. GENERAL PRINCIPLES

1. The bodies of the faithful are to be buried in a cemetery which, in accordance with the rites prescribed in the liturgical books, has been blessed or consecrated. (Can. 1205 § 1.) In places where it is not possible to have Catholic cemeteries the local Ordinaries shall see to it that the public cemeteries are blessed if the majority of persons who are buried there are Catholics, or at least that Catholics have in these cemeteries a special section for their own exclusive use and that this section be blessed. If even this cannot be done, then the individual graves are to be blessed in each particular burial. (Cf. Can. 1206.)

> The rite for the blessing of an individual grave can be found in the Ritual (Tit. VI, cap. 3, n. 12); the blessing is not reserved, hence, the priest who accompanies the body to the grave can also bless the grave.
>
> *Amputed limbs* of Catholics are to be buried in blessed ground if this is not too difficult; otherwise they may be buried in profane ground or cremated at the order of the physician. The amputated limbs of non-Catholics are to be buried in profane ground or cremated upon the advice of the physician. (S.O., decr., 3 Aug., 1897.)
>
> *A dead fetus,* if it had been baptized, is to be buried in blessed ground, preferably in a blessed cemetery rather than on the hospital grounds.

2. Those who have died without baptism are not to be admitted to Christian burial. However, catechumens who, through no fault of their own, died without baptism, are to be treated as the baptized [and hence given Christian

burial]. Finally, all [Catholic] baptized persons are to be given Christian burial unless they are expressly deprived of it by law. (Can. 1239.)

> The baptized expressly deprived of Christian burial are enumerated immediately below in Canon 1240.
>
> If the funeral is to be held on a feast when the funeral Mass is forbidden by the rubrics, the obsequies shall take place after the vespers of the feast, at an hour free from any sacred function; and it is not permitted to toll the funeral bells as on other days. The days on which funeral Masses are forbidden are listed in the Directory.

II. PRIVATION OF ECCLESIASTICAL BURIAL

1. Unless before death they shall have manifested some signs of repentance, the following are deprived of ecclesiastical burial (Can. 1240 § 1):

a. Notorious apostates from the Christian faith, or persons who are notoriously adherents of an heretical, schismatic or atheistic sect or of the Masonic order or of other societies of the same kind.

> For societies similar to the Masonic order, membership in which deprives one of Christian burial, confer our commentary above under the excommunication inflicted on those who join such societies, p. 118ff.

b. Persons under excommunication or interdict following a condemnatory or a declaratory sentence.

c. Those who, with full deliberation, have committed suicide.

> If there exists a reasonable doubt as to full deliberation, the person is not to be denied ecclesiastical burial. Scandal will be unlikely where it is commonly known that the suicide probably resulted from nervous or mental disorders. Publicity and solemnity should, in as far as possible, be avoided.

d. Those who have died in a duel or from a wound received in a duel.

e. Those who have ordered the cremation of their body.

> The penalty is incurred even though the command is not car-

ried out by the family or heirs. (PCI, 10 Nov., 1925.) If there was no such command, but the body is actually cremated by the family or heirs, ecclesiastical burial is still prohibited except in as far as scandal can be efficaciously prevented. (S.O., 19 June, 1926.)

The ashes of those who were cremated are not to be buried in a blessed cemetery but are to be buried in a separate place, i.e., in unconsecrated ground according to the norm of Canon 1212. (S.O., 19 June, 1926.)

f.   Other public and manifest [i.e., notorious] sinners.

As such must be considered: those living in public concubinage or in an invalid marriage; those who bring up their children in heresy; prostitutes; "gangsters"; those who habitually fail to make their Easter duty. If a person neglected his Easter Communion one or the other time, he is not to be excluded from Christian burial unless his culpable neglect be certainly and publicly known.

2.   The above-mentioned are not excluded from ecclesiastical burial if before they died they gave signs of repentance. If doubt should arise in any of these cases, the Ordinary is to be consulted, if time permits; if the doubt cannot be resolved, the body of the deceased is to be given Christian burial, in such wise, however, that scandal is prevented (Can. 1240 § 2), v.g., by divulging the fact that the person showed signs of repentance before death, etc.

3.   When a person has been deprived of ecclesiastical burial, any kind of funeral Mass, even an anniversary Mass, as well as other public funeral services must also be denied. (Can. 1241.)

Priests may say Mass privately, and the faithful may pray for such a person.

The priest is not forbidden to visit the funeral parlor privately and to recite a few informal prayers together with the faithful gathered there.

III.   SPECIAL QUESTIONS

1.   *Burial of non-Catholics in a Catholic Cemetery*

In consideration of a bond of consanguinity or of marriage, may non-Catholics be buried in the family vault or plot of Catholic families? Where this practice exists and it cannot be discontinued without causing scandal, alienation of souls, or other disturbances and inconveniences, it may be tolerated. (Cf. S.O., 30 March, 1895; 4 Jan., 1888.)

> Hence, the burial of non-Catholics in the family plot of a blessed cemetery may be passively tolerated (not positively approved as a privilege or favor) by the bishops in particular cases where such action seems necessary to avoid greater evils. The pastor should confer the diocesan statutes or regulations on this matter. In these cases, no ecclesiastical service is permitted. However, the priest may say prayers of a private and non-liturgical nature at the home and at the grave. (Cf. S.O., 15 Nov., 1941, *Digest*, III, p. 300.)

2. *Burial of Catholics in non-Catholic Cemeteries*

According to the decrees of the Second and Third Plenary Councils of Baltimore, when there is question of the burial of *converts* whose surviving non-Catholic relatives have a private plot in a non-Catholic cemetery, or even of *Catholics* who before the First Plenary Council (anno 1853) had their own burial plots, or afterwards acquired such plots in good faith, it is permitted to perform ecclesiastical rites, whether at the home or at the church, whenever the bishop has not forbidden it. With the exception of these cases, pastors may never perform the aforesaid rites in the burial of the faithful in a non-Catholic cemetery unless with the express permission of the Ordinary. (Balt. II, n. 391; Balt. III, n. 318.) These provisions may still be followed in the United States as being sanctioned by immemorial custom. (Cf. Bouscaren-Ellis, p. 672.)

> When Catholics are lawfully buried in non-Catholic cemeteries, the grave is blessed.

> If a Catholic chooses to be buried in a non-Catholic cemetery in a place where a Catholic cemetery exists and outside the provisions mentioned above, the granting or refusal of

Church services and services at the grave depend upon the prudent judgment of the Ordinary. Note, however, that by Canon 1206, in places where no Catholic cemetery is available and where it is impossible to have a section of the public cemetery set aside for the use of Catholics, the faithful are lawfully buried in non-Catholic cemeteries, and the single graves are blessed in each particular case of burial.

3. Burial of Infants Who Die without Baptism

Infants of Catholic parents who die without baptism are not granted ecclesiastical burial; however, they may and should be buried in an unblessed portion of the blessed cemetery. (Balt. II, n. 390.) In particular:

a.   If the mother and fetus die together: the unbaptized fetus, which has remained in the mother's womb, and the mother are buried together in consecrated ground. (Coronata, II, n. 815; cf. also Balt. II, n. 390.)

b.   If the baby is born but both mother and child die: If the baby had not been baptized through no fault of the parents, it is probable that both mother and child may be buried together in consecrated ground. (Bouscaren-Ellis, p. 666; Arregui, n. 913, note 1.)

c.   In doubt as to whether the infant had been baptized or had been validly baptized, ecclesiastical burial is to be granted. (Cf. Canon 19 collated with Canon 1239 § 3.)

IV.   THE CHURCH, CEMETERY AND MINISTER OF BURIAL

A.   The Church

1.   The church for the funeral is that of the proper parish of the deceased *unless he had chosen another church*. If the deceased had several proper parishes (v.g., by reason of domicile and quasi-domicile), the church for the funeral is the church of the parish in which the person died. (Can. 1216.)

If the person died outside all of his proper parishes, the body is to be transferred to his nearest parish church, if it can be done easily by foot, otherwise it is to be buried from the church of the parish in which the person died. The family, however, may transfer the body to any of the deceased's proper parishes if they wish. (Cf. Can. 1218.)

In regard to those who stay at a religious house or at a college as students, guests or patients, and to those who have died in a hospital, the same provisions hold, namely, they are to be buried from their parish church. (Can. 1222.) If however, the local Ordinary exempts certain places (colleges, hospitals, institutions) from the jurisdiction of the pastor according to the norm of Canon 464 § 2, it seems that those who die in these places may be buried from the chapel and by the rector or the chaplain. (Beste, p. 592; confer Canons 1230 §§ 3, 4; 1231.)

Details concerning *the choice* of church or cemetery of burial may be found in Canons 1223-1228.

2. If a person (student, professor, servant) dies in the diocesan seminary he is to be buried from the seminary chapel by the rector of the seminary. (Cf. Canons 1222, 1368.)

3. *Men religious,* clerical or lay, exempt or non-exempt, are buried from the church or oratory of their own house or at least of their own institute; if this cannot be done because they died far away from their house, they are buried from the church of the parish in which they died unless the superior wishes to transfer the body to a church of the institute. (Cf. Can. 1221.)

Servants who actually live in the religious house, follow the same rules as the religious if they die within the house; if they die outside the house, they are buried as any other lay person. (Can. 1221.) The ruling of Canon 1221 has nothing to do with the funerals of postulants or students in religious houses (PCI, 20 July, 1929), and hence these persons are buried according to the norms stated above in n. 1 for the laity in general.

4. *Women religious* who die in the religious house are buried from the church or oratory of the institute if the religious house is not subject to the jurisdiction of the pastor, and the funeral service is conducted by the chaplain; women religious not exempted from the parochial jurisdiction are buried from the parochial church by the pastor. (Can. 1230 §§ 1, 5.)

The law contains no special provision for the case of a woman religious who dies outside of the religious house. It seems that the body may be taken to the convent and buried from the oratory by the chaplain or from the parish church by the pastor according to whether the house is exempted from parochial jurisdiction or not. (Cf. V.C., II, n. 538.) If the body is not taken back to the convent it should be buried from the parochial church of the place where the sister died.

Servants, students, guests, etc. if they die in houses of women religious are buried by the pastor according to the rules laid down for the rest of the faithful.

B. *The Cemetery*

1. The cemetery which the deceased has lawfully chosen receives preference over all others. (Cf. Canons 1228, 1223.)

2. If no choice of cemetery has been made by the deceased, the body is to be buried in the family cemetery or the family plot. A wife follows the cemetery of her husband. (Cf. Can. 1229.)

3. If no such family plot exists, the body is to be buried in the cemetery of the church from which it was buried. (Cf. Can. 1231.)

Note: Religious usually possess cemeteries of their own (cf. Can. 1208), and deceased religious are usually buried there by their superiors.

C. *The Minister of Burial*

1. When the pastor lawfully buries a person from his church, he is the lawful minister of the service. (Can. 1230 §§ 1, 2.) Hence, in the cases mentioned above, when the parish church is the lawful place of the funeral, the pastor is the lawful minister of the service.

2. If the place of the funeral services is a church of regulars or some other church exempted from the parochial jurisdiction (v.g., the chapel of the diocesan seminary) the service is conducted by the rector of that church or chapel. (Can. 1230 § 3.)

If the church of the funeral is not exempt from the pastor's jurisdiction, the conducting of the funeral service does not pertain to the rector of the church, but to the pastor of the territory in which the church is located, provided that the deceased was subject to him (Can. 1230 § 4), that is, provided that the deceased was his parishioner by reason of domicile or quasi-domicile; otherwise the minister of the funeral services is the rector of the church. (Abbo-Hannan, II, n. 1230.)

3. The minister for the funeral services of *woman religious:* confer above under A, 4.

4. The minister of the funeral services of *men religious:*

a. In clerical institutes: when burial is from the church of the institute, the religious superior is the minister of the services. If burial is from the parish church of the place where the religious died, the pastor of the church is the minister of the funeral.

b. In lay institutes: when burial is from the church of the institute, the chaplain or the pastor is the minister of the service depending on whether the religious are exempted from the pastor's jurisdiction or not. If the burial is from the parish church, the pastor is the lawful minister of the service. (Beste, p. 597; confer Canons 1221 §§ 1, 2; 1230 §§ 3, 4.)

Concerning lay persons who live in the houses of men religious day and night, only the servants *if they die within the house* are buried from the chapel by the superior. All others (pupils, patients, etc.) whether they die within the religious house or not are buried according to the norms laid down for the rest of the laity.

5. *In the transfer of a body for reburial* after exhumation (v.g., in the case of a soldier buried on foreign shores), if the burial ceremonies were observed in the first burial, none are prescribed in the second. If they are held, they are not reserved as of right to any particular pastor. If the due ceremonies were not observed in the first burial,

they are to be performed in the second by the pastor of the deceased's domicile according to Canon 1216, i.e., according to the ordinary norms of law. (Cf. S.C.Conc., 12 Jan., 1924.)

PART VIII

MATRIMONY

CHAPTER I

Introduction

I. JURISDICTION OVER MARRIAGE

1. Marriage of *baptized persons* is governed not only by the divine law but also by Canon Law, without prejudice to the competence of the civil power in relation to merely the civil effects of marriage. (Can. 1016.)

a. It is the exclusive competence of the Church to legislate concerning those things that pertain to the essence of the marriage of a baptized person, v.g., the form, the impediments, cohabitation, legitimacy of children, etc. The State may legislate concerning the social status of wife and children, the right of inheritance, the distribution of temporal goods etc. The State has no right to establish impediments for the baptized and cannot make the marriage of the baptized either invalid or illicit. (Noldin, III, n. 515.)

b. The Church claims control of the contract of marriage involving a baptized person even though that contract be not a sacrament, as is the case when only one person to the marriage is baptized.

c. *Heretics* also if validly baptized *are subject to the exclusive jurisdiction of the Church* and *their marriages are ruled by Canon Law* (cf. Canons 12, 87, 1038 § 2), unless exceptions are made in their favor as is the case concerning the form (Can. 1099) and the impediment of disparity of cult (Can. 1070). Hence the validity of marriages of two heretics or of a heretic and an infidel is judged according to the canons of the Code.

d. With regard to the *doubtfully baptized:* If the validity of the baptism is doubtful there is a general presumption at least in the external forum, in favor of the validity of the baptism, and hence in favor of the obligation of the person to obey the

167

laws of the Church; but if the doubt persists after the marriage the presumption in favor of the marriage would prevail (Can. 1014), except where the privilege of the faith is involved. (Can. 1127.) (Cf. Payen, I, n. 538.)

2. The marriage of *two non-baptized* persons is subject to the competence of the State. Hence the civil power may enact laws requiring formalities to be observed for the validity of the marriage contract and may also establish impediments to the valid celebration of marriage. One must consult the laws of the various States to ascertain which laws affect the validity and which only the licitness of the marriage. As is evident, a civil law contrary to divine law is invalid.

Hence the validity of a marriage of two non-baptized persons is judged according to the civil law under which it was contracted. If the marriage of infidels is invalid because of impediments of civil law, when the infidels enter the Church they are allowed to enter entirely new marriages with different parties. (Gasparri, I, n. 285.)

According to a general principle of law, *a contract* is governed by the laws of the place where the contract is made; however, some exceptions may be made to this principle for matrimonial contracts. Some states demand that the stranger be qualified to marry by the laws of his own country or of his own state; likewise that residents of the state intending to remain residents may not marry in another state if their marriage would be illegal in the home state. Other states recognize the general principle of contracts, i.e., if the contract is valid in the place where it was made, it is valid everywhere, and if invalid in the place where made, it is invalid everywhere. (Cf. Woywood, n. 1938.)

If a non-baptized person marries a baptized person is the former bound by the impediments of the civil law? Cappello, Wernz-Vidal, Coronata, Sipos etc. say that the person is not bound by the civil law impediments; Gasparri, D'Annibale, Vermeersch-Creusen say the person is bound by such impediments. The first opinion seems to be more probable. *Post factum,* even in the second opinion, one would hold for the validity of the marriage because of the presumption of Canon 1014 namely, marriage enjoys the favor of the law; hence in doubt as to its validity the marriage is to be considered valid until the contrary is proved.

3. *Oriental Catholics.* The matrimonial legislation of the Oriental Church is codified in the *motu proprio, Crebrae allatae,* of Pope Pius XII, 22 Feb., 1949. The obliging force of this legislation began on 2 May, 1949. Hence marriages of Oriental Catholics are judged by the law of the *Crebrae allatae,* if celebrated on or after 2 May, 1949. Marriages celebrated before that date are judged by the discipline in force at the time of the celebration of the marriage; before 2 May, 1949, there was no uniform discipline among the various Oriental rites and hence one must consult the discipline in force in the rites to which the spouses belonged.

> *Oriental Dissidents* are subject to the laws of *Crebrae allatae,* unless they are expressly exempted in some particular canon. (Herman, *Periodica,* XXXVIII, p. 95; Coussa, III, nos. 5, 7-9; Pospishil, p. 111.)

II. Presumption in Favor of Marriage

1. Marriage enjoys the favor of law; hence in doubt one is to hold for the validity of the marriage until the contrary is proved, without prejudice however to the prescription of Canon 1127. (Can. 1014.)

> Hence when there is doubt concerning the validity of marriage that was certainly celebrated, the marriage is considered valid until the contrary is proved with moral certainty. If the very fact of the celebration of the marriage is doubtful, but it is favored by the fact that the parties are in possession of a decent public reputation as man and wife, the marriage is likewise considered as valid until the opposite is proved.

2. When there is a positive and insoluble doubt concerning the validity of a first marriage, a second marriage is to be declared invalid in virtue of Canon 1014; the case is however to be handled according to the norms of law, i.e., not merely in a summary and administrative manner. (PCI, 26 June, 1947.) Hence a second marriage is to be declared invalid if a former marriage existed that was doubtfully valid.

3. The presumption of Canon 1014 holds not only for the marriages of the baptized but also for the marriages of the non-baptized. (V.C., II, n. 279.) But the presumption of Canon 1127 takes precedence over the presumption of Canon 1014, and since the privilege of the faith enjoys the favor of law, if there is doubt as to the validity of a marriage contracted by the non-baptized, the doubt is to be resolved in favor of the faith, i.e., in favor of the convert.

CHAPTER II

Engagement

I. NATURE OF ENGAGEMENT

A promise of marriage may be unilateral, in which case it will be binding either by the virtue of fidelity or by that of justice according to the intention of the one promising; or it may be bilateral and binding in justice. In this latter case it is called an engagement, which may be defined as a contract whereby two persons who are capable, mutually promise that they will marry each other in the future.

A conditional engagement made by persons who are bound by some impediment to marriage is valid if the impediment will cease of its very nature (v.g., age) or will cease by action of the parties themselves (v.g., mixed religion ceases when the non-Catholic enters the Church). If the impediment is one from which the Holy See cannot or is not accustomed to dispense, the engagement is invalid; even when there is question of an impediment from which a dispensation is usually granted, the more common opinion holds that the engagement is invalid. (Cf. V.C., II, n. 280.)

Minors cannot enter an engagement licitly if their parents are ignorant of the engagement or are reasonably opposed to it for in this case their marriage would be illicit. (Coronata, *De Sacr.*, III, n. 45.)

II. FORMALITIES OF THE CONTRACT

1. The promise of marriage, whether unilateral or bilateral (engagement), *is invalid in both the internal and*

external forum unless it is made in writing, signed by the parties, and by either the pastor or local Ordinary or by at least two witnesses. (Can. 1017 § 1.)

> The contract may be typewritten, but must be signed by the parties and witnesses; the signatures must be affixed at one and the same time, i.e., the parties and the witnesses must sign in each other's presence. (S.C.Conc., decr., 27 July, 1908.)

> If the pastor or Ordinary act as witness they must act personally and cannot delegate this function to others. (V.C., II, n. 281.)

> The more probable opinion requires that the day, the month, and the year be inserted for the validity of the document; some authors, however, deny this.

2. If either or both of the parties do not know how to write or cannot write, it is required for validity that this be noted in the document itself and that an additional witness sign the document together with the pastor or local Ordinary or the two witnesses mentioned in paragraph one of this canon. (Can. 1017 § 2.)

III. EFFECT OF ENGAGEMENT

1. The parties to the contract of engagement have the following obligations:

a. An obligation in justice to contract marriage at the time specified or if no time is specified, at a reasonable time according to custom and usage.

b. An obligation of not entering into marriage with a third party.

c. An obligation of fidelity to the other party.

> A sin of fornication with a third party would be a sin of injustice, but probably the injustice would be venial not mortal.

2. Even though a promise of marriage be valid and though no sound reason excuses from not fulfilling it, nevertheless it does not give rise to legal action compelling the celebration of the marriage; but it does give one the

right to action for damages if any are due. (Can. 1017 § 3.)

> Hence although one may be bound to celebrate the marriage, nevertheless the law does not recognize any legal action forcing the person to fulfill his obligation. Since marriages rarely have a happy issue when enforced under the terms of an engagement the law refuses judicial aid to such an enforcement. (Abbo-Hannan, II, n. 1017.)

> If, however, one suffers harm from the non-fulfilment of an engagement, he may sue for damages. One may sue for damages in either the ecclesiastical court or before a secular tribunal. (PCI, 2 June, 1918.)

IV. DISSOLUTION OF THE CONTRACT

1. The contract of engagement is automatically dissolved by the mutual consent of the parties, by papal dispensation, by the subsequent occurrence of an invalidating impediment which cannot be dispensed from, by entrance into a religious institute or by the reception of sacred orders.

2. Each party has the right to break the engagement because of a notable change in the object of the contract. (V.C., II, n. 283.)

> Thus one may break the engagement if the other has become a heretic, a gambler, a drunkard; also if the other has commited fornication with a third party; if the spouse has become incapable of supporting a family or has become involved in heavy debts; if the other has suffered a notable mutilation or deformity, fallen into mental illness etc. (Cf. Genicot, II, n. 513.)

ORIENTAL LAW

1. The promise of marriage, also bilateral (engagement), is invalid in both the internal and external forum unless it is made before the pastor or the local Hierarch or the priest delegated by one of these to assist at the marriage. Only that pastor, Hierarch, or delegated priest is competent who can validly assist at the marriage itself. The promise of marriage does not give rise to legal action

compelling the celebration of the marriage; it does give rise to action for damages if any are due. (Mp, Can. 6.)

A written contract is not demanded.

2. If the parties are of diverse rites (one a Latin, the other an Oriental) it would seem that they could make their engagement either according to the Code or according to the Oriental legislation, as it may please them. (Sipos, § 101, n. 9.)

CHAPTER III

Preparations for the Celebration of Marriage

I. PRE-MARITAL INVESTIGATION

1. The pastor who has the right of assisting at the marriage shall first, and in due time, diligently investigate whether there exists any obstacle to the contracting of the marriage. (Can. 1020 § 1.)

The obligation therefore is generally imposed on the pastor of the bride (Can. 1097); he may request the pastor of the groom to conduct the investigation of the groom's freedom to marry. (S.C.Sacr., instr., 29 June, 1941.)

2. He shall ask the bride and groom separately whether they are under any impediment, whether they give consent freely (especially the woman), and whether they are sufficiently instructed in Christian doctrine, unless in view of the character of the parties, this last question should seem superfluous. (Can. 1020 § 2.)

According to the instruction of the Sacred Congregation of the Sacraments, 29 June, 1941, the following points are to be covered in the investigation:

a. Name of parents; place of birth; age; religious affiliation; proof of identity; record of baptism.

b. Possible previous marriage; if any suspicion of previous marriage, reliable and sworn witnesses are to be questioned. Possible dissolved marriage; document of death of former spouse or definite sentence of court declaring former marriage invalid.

c.   Domicile and quasi-domicile of the parties.

d.   Dioceses in which parties have lived for at least six months after attaining puberty; parishes in which the parties lived.

e.   Has there been a civil marriage? With each other? With a third party? Has such marriage been terminated?

f.   The pastor now goes through the various impediments to ascertain whether either of the parties is bound by one or more of them. (See the list of impediments in Chapter IV.)

g.   Is either party an apostate, heretic, member of a forbidden society etc.? Is either party under censure?

h.   Each party is to be asked if he or she is under duress to celebrate the marriage; each party should be asked if the other party is under duress.

i.   If the parties are minors; are their parents opposed to the marriage? If so, why?

j.   Do the parties know the principal points of Christian doctrine? The pastor must ask the parties if they know the purpose and ends of marriage, its rights and obligations. He should ask them if they wish to contract one indissoluble union whose purpose is the procreation of children with no contrary intention or condition in their minds. If the parties wish to enter the marriage with intentions or conditions contrary to the validity of the marriage, e.g., excluding the right to the marital act, excluding fidelity or indissolubility, the pastor must inform them that such a marriage is invalid.

k.   Have the parties attached to their marriage any lawful and acceptable conditions, present, past or future? How do they intend to ascertain whether the condition has been fulfilled?

1.   Is there any obstacle to the marriage arising from civil law?

3.   If there are suspicions concerning a party's freedom to marry, or if a party has lived after puberty in many places, the following canons give norms to be followed in collecting additional evidence and proofs to ascertain the party's freedom. *In danger of death,* however, if other proofs cannot be had, and in the absence of indications to the contrary, the sworn statement of the contracting parties that they have been baptized and are under no impedi-

ment is considered sufficient proof of freedom to marry. (Can. 1019 § 2.)

4. *Vagi*. Except in case of necessity a pastor shall never assist at the marriage of *vagi* (those who have no domicile or quasi-domicile anywhere) unless he shall have first brought the matter to the attention of the local Ordinary or a priest delegated by him and obtained permission to assist at the marriage. (Can. 1032.)

> The permission of the Ordinary is required even if only one of the parties is a *vagus*. (Abbo-Hannan, II, n. 1032.) Pastors may not assist at the marriage of imigrants from Europe, even though perhaps they are not *vagi*, without first consulting the Ordinary. (S.C.Sacr., instr., 4 July, 1921.)

5. *Minors*. The pastor shall earnestly warn minor sons and daughters not to contract marriage without the knowledge or against the reasonable wishes of their parents. If they refuse to obey, he shall not assist at their marriage without previous consultation with the local Ordinary. (Can. 1034.)

> Minor sons and daughters are those who have not completed their twenty-first year and who are not legally emancipated from parental authority.
>
> The pastor should also consult civil law, for some States require the permission of the parents for the marriage of minors.

5. *Oriental Law*. The same things are prescribed as in the Latin Code for the pre-nuptial investigations, the marriages of minors and *vagi*. (Mp, Canons 9-11, 22, 24.)

II. PUBLICATION OF THE BANNS

A. *Obligation*

1. The pastor must publicly announce the parties between whom a marriage is to be contracted. (Can. 1022.) The proclamation of marriage must be made by one's *proper* pastor. (Can. 1023 § 1.)

> The proper pastor is the pastor of the parties' domicile and/ or quasi-domicile. For *vagi*, the proper pastor is the pastor of

the place in which they are actually staying. The proclamations must be made in each parish where the bride and groom have a domicile or a quasi-domicile. For minors, the domicile is that of their parents or guardians. Minors may have their own quasi-domicile and hence may have a second proper pastor and parish.

2. If after reaching the age of puberty (fourteen for boys, twelve for girls), a party has dwelt for six months in another place, the pastor shall explain the matter to the Ordinary, who shall demand that the publications be made there or shall prescribe the collection of other proof and evidence in regard to the freedom of the party to marry. (Can. 1023 § 2.)

> In these cases, as well as in cases in which the pastor has doubts about the answers given by the parties in the pre-marital investigation, several witnesses who know the parties well are examined under oath as to the free state of the parties. The witnesses are asked especially if the parties are free from all impediments, if they are entering the marriage freely, and if they intend to contract an indissoluble union, proper for the procreation of children, without any contrary intention or condition. (Cf. S.C.Sacr., instr., 29 June, 1941.)

> In cases falling under Canon 1023 § 2, when the parties cannot furnish witnesses or other proofs as to their free state, they are made to take a supplementary oath stating that they contracted no impediments in the places in which they lived and that they are free to carry.

3. The publications are not made in the case of marriages contracted with a dispensation from the impediment of disparity of cult or of mixed religion, unless the local Ordinary deems it advisable to have them made, scandal being excluded, and provided that a dispensation from the impediment shall have been granted beforehand. No mention is made of the religion of the non-Catholic party. (Cf. Can. 1026.)

B. *Manner*

The proclamations shall be made in church on three successive Sundays or Holydays of Obligation during the parochial Mass or during other sacred functions [vespers, missions, benediction] attended by a large number of the faithful. (Can. 1024.)

> *If a doubt arises* regarding the existence of an impediment, the pastor shall make or complete the publications if the doubt arose before they were begun or completed. If the doubt persists, he is not to assist at the marriage without consulting the local Ordinary. (Can. 1031 § 1.)

> *If a certain impediment* has been detected: if the impediment is occult the pastor shall make or complete the publications and, without mentioning the names of the parties, refer the matter to the local Ordinary or the Sacred Penitentiary; if the impediment is public and it is detected before the publications have been begun, the pastor shall not proceed further until the impediment has been removed, even though a dispensation has already been obtained from the forum of conscience; if the impediment is discovered after the publications have been begun, the pastor shall continue the publications and refer the matter to the Ordinary (Can. 1031 § 2), who will either himself dispense if he has special faculties or if the case is urgent (Can. 1045), or will ask a dispensation of the Holy See.

C. *The Manifestation of Impediments*

If they know of any impediments to the marriage, all the faithful are obliged to reveal them to the pastor or to the local Ordinary before the celebration of the marriage. (Can. 1027.)

> A natural, promised or committed secret does not excuse from making this revelation; the secret of the sacramental seal excuses as does also a secret committed by reason of office (professional secret). Hence if the knowledge is had as a strictly professional secret by a priest, doctor, lawyer, it should not be revealed.

> Grave personal hardship or harm excuses one from manifesting a known impediment. (Cf. V.C., II, n. 292.)

D. *Dispensation from the Proclamations*

1. The proper local Ordinary can for a just cause dispense from the publications, even from those which should be made in another diocese. If there are several proper Ordinaries, the right of dispensing belongs to the one in

whose territory the marriage is to be celebrated; if the marriage is to be celebrated outside the territory of all, the right belongs to any of the proper Ordinaries. (Can. 1028.)

> *Peregrini* are therefore dispensed not by the Ordinary of the place in which they are, but by the Ordinary of their place of domicile or quasi-domicile.
>
> The power to dispense is ordinary and hence may be delegated to others, v.g., to rural deans with the power also to subdelegate in individual cases. (Cf. Can. 199 §§ 1, 4.)
>
> A grave cause is necessary to dispense from all three publications, v.g., the pregnancy of the woman, danger of incontinence in those who have attempted a civil marriage, the danger that the parties will be satisfied with a civil ceremony, etc.

2. If the law of the proclamations cannot be observed without grave harm the law does not bind. Hence in cases where it is not possible to obtain a dispensation from the Ordinary in time to avert danger of grave harm the proclamations may be omitted. (Cf. Genicot, II, n. 516.)

E. *Oriental Law*

The same provisions are made in the Oriental Code as in the Latin Code for the obligation, person, place, time, manner of publishing the banns, as well as for the obligation of manifesting impediments, and for the power to dispense from the banns. According to the Oriental Code however, the banns are to be published only in those rites and disciplines in which particular law demands it. Otherwise they are not published. (Cf. Mp, Canons 12-18, 20 § 2, 21.) The banns are published amongst the Italo-Albanians, the Malabars, Malenkars, Maronites, Romanians, Ruthenians, and Russians. (Coussa, III, n. 32.)

> The local Hierarch in whose territory a marriage is celebrated can dispense from the banns of marriage parties who are bound by that law although belonging to a different rite, provided that the local Hierarch is the proper Hierarch of the one needing the dispensation. If the local Hierarch in whose territory the marriage is being celebrated is not the proper Hierarch of the

parties he cannot dispense them from the banns even though he be of the same rite as the parties. (PC Or., 3 May, 1953.)

III. DOCUMENTS

1. Unless the baptism was conferred in his own territory, the pastor shall demand a testimonial of the baptism of both parties, or, in marriages contracted with a dispensation from the impediment of disparity of cult, of the Catholic party only. (Can. 1021 § 1.)

> Proof of a Protestant's baptism must also be obtained in case of mixed marriages; if a doubt exists as to the baptism or the validity of baptism of such a person, a dispensation from disparity of cult should be obtained *ad cautelam.*
>
> A recent baptismal certificate is necessary, i.e., not more than six months old.
>
> If it is impossible to obtain a certificate of baptism because the records have perished, Canon 779 is to be applied, namely, the fact of the baptism of a party may be established by the sworn evidence of one thoroughly reliable witness or of the party himself if he was baptized in adult age.

2. If another pastor has conducted an investigation or has announced the banns he shall immediately send an authentic notification of the outcome of the investigations and publications to the pastor who is to assist at the marriage. (Can. 1029.)

> When the pastors belong to *different* dioceses, the transmission of parish records and the results of investigations shall be made through the Episcopal Curia of the pastor who transmits the documents to the pastor who is to assist at the marriage. (Cf. S.C.Sacr., instr., 29 June, 1941.)

3. At the conclusion of the investigation and of the publications, the pastor shall not assist at the marriage until he has received all the required documents, and, unless a reasonable cause suggests contrary action, until three days have elapsed from the last publication. (Can. 1030 § 1.)

> The necessary documents are:
>
> a. Testimonial of baptism.

b. Reports of pastors who have conducted investigations or made publications.

c. Document of dispensation from an impediment (if necessary).

d. Document certifying death of former spouse, or attesting the declaration of nullity of a previous marriage, etc. (if necessary).

e. Document of proper pastor granting permission to assist at the marriage (if needed).

f. The *nihil obstat* of the local Ordinary for interdiocesan marriages.

g. The civil marriage license should also be had.

If the pastors of the parties belong to *different* dioceses, the pastor assisting at the marriage must send all the pre-nuptial documents and the proof of freedom to marry to his Episcopal Curia and from it obtain a permission or *nihil obstat* to proceed with the marriage. (S.C.Sacr., instr., 29 June, 1941.)

4. *Oriental Law*. The Oriental Code contains the same prescriptions concerning the documents to be gathered and the proceeding to the celebration of the marriage. (Mp, Canons 11, 19, 20 § 1.)

IV. PRE-MARITAL INSTRUCTION

The pastor shall not fail to instruct the parties on the sanctity of the sacrament of matrimony, the mutual obligations of the spouses and the obligations of parents toward their children; he shall also urge them strongly to confess their sins before the celebration of the marriage and to worthily receive Holy Communion. (Can. 1033.)

The subjects to be treated in the pre-marital instruction are:

1. *The nature of marriage:*
a. Divine origin of the marriage contract.
b. Marriage a sacrament: matter and form; ministers of the sacrament; graces of the sacrament.
c. Unity and indissolubility.
d. Primary and secondary aims of marriage.

2. *Duties of parents toward children:*
a. Bodily welfare before and after birth. (Malice of abortion.)
b. Spiritual welfare: reception of sacraments; moral and

religious training; baptism of fetus in case of miscarriage.

3. *Rights and duties of the spouses toward each other:*

a. Conjugal love, fidelity; indissolubility of the contract.

b. Acts permitted in the married state:

1) Licitness of the marriage act; duty to render the debt when it is rightly, reasonably and seriously demanded; circumstances in which intercourse is unlawful.

2) Thoughts, desires, touches, etc. that are sexually stimulating are lawful in connection with the marriage act, whether as a preparation for or as a completion of the act.

3) Mutual acts performed apart from intercourse for a just cause, v.g., showing of mutual love, are licit, if there is no danger of voluntary pollution or orgasm.

4) Solitary acts which are sexually exciting (thoughts, desires, touches) are not gravely sinful if there is no danger of consent to orgasm or pollution which might result. Desires or thoughts of intercourse with one's spouse are not sinful, unless they lead to pollution. (Cf. Genicot, II, n. 663.)

c. Acts which are unlawful in the married state:

1) Thoughts and desires about a third party are mortal sins.

2) Adultery.

3) Masturbation.

4) Onanism.

The pastor will do well to purchase a book that has these instructions worked out. Pastors have a *serious* obligation to instruct the bride and groom in these matters, especially in our day when so many immoral notions on the use of matrimony are flouted about.

CHAPTER IV

Impediments to Matrimony

I. IMPEDIMENTS IN GENERAL

A. *Division*

1. Impediments may be of *divine law* (v.g., impotence) or of *human law* (v.g., public decency).

2. Impediments are said to be *absolute* if they prohibit marriage with any person (v.g., age) and *relative* if they prohibit marriage with some particular person only (v.g., consanguinity).

3. An *impediment* (prohibiting) impediment imposes a grave prohibition against the contracting of marriage but it does not render invalid a marriage contracted in spite of the impediment. A *diriment* impediment both gravely prohibits the contracting of marriage and prevents it from being contracted validly. (Can. 1036.)

Although an impediment exists on the part of only one of the contracting parties, it nevertheless renders the marriage either illicit or invalid as the case may be. (Cf. Can. 1036 § 3.) The reason is that matrimony is a bilateral contract and hence both parties must be capable of making the contract.

4. An impediment is regarded as *public* when it can be proved in the external forum; otherwise it is *occult*. (Can. 1037.)

Possibility of proof in the external forum is had when the impediment can be proved by an authentic document or by two witnesses giving concordant testimony of things of which they have personal knowledge, or by the testimony of an official in reference to matters pertaining to his office, v.g., a pastor asserting he assisted at a certain marriage; also by the testimony of experts or by the confession of the party made in court. Note however that proof in the external forum must be possible not theoretically only but also practically, i.e., in the concrete case the impediment can be proved. (V.C., II, 297.)

When there is question of dispensing from impediments, the Code speaks of public *cases* and occult *cases*. (Cf. Can. 1045.) Indeed a case is still to be considered occult if the impediment is by nature public but is in fact occult. (PCI, 28 Dec., 1927.) Thus an impediment which is public by nature (because it arises from a fact which is in itself public), v.g., consanguinity, age, sacred orders, affinity, etc., can be in fact occult because it is not known and not likely to become known. A public case is one in which the impediment is known or very likely will become known. In the use of his faculties and in the granting of dispensations an Ordinary may accept this distinction of public and occult or the distinction given in Canon 1037. (Gasparri, I, n. 210.)

5. An impediment may be *doubtful* either by doubt of law or by doubt of fact.

If the impediment is one of merely *ecclesiastical law*, the impediment does not bind if the doubt is a positive doubt of law; if it is a doubt of fact the Ordinary can dispense if there is question of an impediment from which the Roman Pontiff is **wont to dispense. (Cf. Can. 15.)** If the doubt of fact is reducible to a doubt of law, probabilism would allow the marriage, if after due inquiry it is still positively probable that the im**pediment does not exist.**

If the impediment is one of *divine law,* ordinarily it is illicit to proceed to the marriage, whether the doubt be of law or of fact, for probabilities will not make the sacrament valid. Exceptional cases will be treated under the individual impediments. In cases where the divine law does not invalidate but simply prohibits a marriage, a doubt of law would *ordinarily* excuse one from the impediment. (Cf. Bouscaren-Ellis, p. 475 for details.)

6.   Impediments are of *minor* or of *major* degree.

The impediments of minor degree, namely, such as are more easily dispensed from, are enumerated in Canon 1042:

   a.   Consanguinity in the third degree of the collateral line;
   b.   Affinity in the second degree of the collateral line;
   c.   Public propriety in the second degree;
   d.   Spiritual relationship;
   e.   Crime resulting from adultery with the promise of marriage or an attempted marriage made through even a civil ceremony.

All other impediments are of major degree. (Can. 1042 § 3.)

B.   *Establishment of Impediments and Persons Subject To Impediments*

1.   It belongs exclusively to the supreme ecclesiastical authority to declare authentically when the divine law forbids or invalidates marriage. It also belongs as an exclusive right to the same supreme authority to establish, by either universal or particular law, other impedient or diriment matrimonial impediments for the baptized. (Can. 1038.)

Heretics are bound to the impediments of ecclesiastical law. Confer above p. 167.

Infidels, when marrying amongst themselves are not bound to impediments of purely ecclesiastical law. They are bound to the impediments of civil law. Confer above, p.   . When an infidel marries a baptized person, the infidel is indirectly affected by all diriment and impedient impediments to which the baptized party is subject. (Cf. Can. 1036 § 3.) Hence an infidel could not validly marry a baptized person who is not of age or who is the subject of grave fear etc. However, the infidel party is not himself bound by impediments of purely ecclesiastical law, v.g., age, even when he marries a baptized person. (De Smet, n. 438bis.) When an infidel marries a baptized person, is the infidel bound by the impediments of civil law? Confer above p. 168.

2. Local Ordinaries are authorized, in regard to all actually dwelling within the limits of their territory and to their subjects even when outside their territory, to prohibit marriages in a particular case, but only temporarily and for a just cause, and only for as long as the just cause lasts. Only the Apostolic See can attach to the prohibition an invalidating clause. (Can. 1039.)

The Ordinary therefore can forbid marriages for a time and because of a just cause, but this prohibition affects only the licitness, and not the validity of the marriage.

C. Cessation of Impediments

1. A diriment impediment of merely ecclesiastical law can cease in some circumstances without a dispensation, namely, through the application of epikia. The common opinion holds that if the matrimony is necessary to avoid great evils, especially spiritual evils, and the possibility of obtaining a dispensation is excluded for a long time, epikia may be used. (V.C., II, n. 300.) This opinion is confirmed by a response of the Holy Office which asserts that the faithful in China, since they can either not at all or only with the greatest difficulty ask for a dispensation, are freed from all impediments of ecclesiastical law from which the Church usually dispenses as well as from the canonical form. (S.O., reply, 27 Jan., 1949.)

2. Dispensations from impediments are treated in Chapter V.

D. Oriental Law

The Oriental discipline in regard to the impediments in

general is essentially the same as that given in the Code of Canon Law. (Mp, Canons 25-31.)

With regard to the impediments of minor degree, however, there is a difference. For Orientals, the impediments of minor degree are:

1. Public propriety, spiritual relationship, crime—just as in the Code.

2. Legal relationship.

3. Consanguinity in the *sixth* degree of the collateral line.

4. Affinity *ex digeneia* in the *fourth* degree of the collateral line; affinity *ex digeneia* arising from particular law and affinity *ex trigeneia* arising from particular law, in any degree. (Mp, Can. 31 § 1.)

II. THE IMPEDIENT IMPEDIMENTS

An impedient or prohibiting impediment imposes a grave prohibition against the contracting of marriage but it does not invalidate a marriage contracted in spite of the impediment.

A. *Simple Vows*

1. Marriage is rendered illicit by the simple vows of virginity, of perfect chastity, of not marrying, of receiving sacred orders, and of embracing the religious state. (Can. 1058 § 1.)

The vow of virginity in the sense of Canon 1058 is the vow to abstain from the first act by which virginity is lost; virginity is lost and the object of the vow becomes impossible by the first consummated solitary sin or by the first voluntary sexual intercourse. (V.C., II, n. 326.) It is rare that this vow alone is taken; in the mind of the one making such a vow it usually includes the obligation not to marry or of observing perfect chastity.

The vow of perfect chastity is a vow to abstain either perpetually or for a time from every sexual pleasure, whether complete or incomplete.

The vow not to marry simply means that one will not enter wedlock. In the mind of the person making the vow it may also include the obligation of perfect chastity.

The vow to embrace the religious state is the vow to enter an institute of either solemn or simple vows.

2. The obligations of those who make one of these

vows and illicitly contract marriage may be defined as follows:

a. One who enters marriage in spite of the vow of virginity sins gravely, but once married, can licitly ask and render the marriage act as well as all other acts proper to conjugal life according to the norm of Canon 1111. (Gasparri, I, n. 429; Sipos, § 111.)

b. One who validly but illicitly contracts marriage while bound by the simple vow of perfect chastity may, on the force of Canon 1111, seek marital relations as well as all the usual acts of conjugal love; but any act that is unlawful for married persons (v.g., onanism, adultery) is also a sin against the vow, and if the marriage is dissolved the vow would forbid a further marriage. (Gasparri, I, nos. 429-430; Sipos, § 111.)

c. The vow not to marry excludes only the celebration of marriage. It does not render the use of marriage illicit once a person has contracted marriage in spite of the vow. According to some authors the vow would however forbid a second marriage in case the first is dissolved. This may be doubted. (Gasparri, I, n. 432.)

d. If one marries validly but illicitly in spite of a vow to embrace the religious state or to receive sacred orders, he sins; but these vows do not render the use of marriage illicit once the marriage has been validly contracted. If the marriage is dissolved the person is *per se* bound to fulfill the vow. (Genicot, II, n. 533.)

3. *Dispensation*

a. Since it is the vow that constitutes the impediment, the impediment ceases in all those ways in which a vow may cease. (Cappello, *De Sacr.,* V, n. 305.)

Confer p. 145 for the cessation of a vow.

b. Non-reserved vows are dispensed from by the Ordinary according to the norm of Canon 1313 (confer p. 145) and by regular confessors in virtue of papal privilege (confer p. 426).

c. Local Ordinaries may also, by reason of their quinquennial faculties, dispense from all the impediments of Canon 1058 (hence also from private reserved vows) but only for marriages to be contracted. (Cf. *Digest,* IV, p. 74.)

> Local Ordinaries may also, by the quinquennial faculties, dispense for the purpose of enabling him or her to ask for the conjugal rights, a person who has violated a vow of perfect and perpetual chastity made privately after completing the age of eighteen, when the person contracted marriage while bound by the vow. The person is bound to observe the vow however outside the lawful use of marriage, and in case he or she survives the other party to the marriage. (*Digest,* IV, p. 80.)

d. Canons 1043-1045 may be used to dispense in danger of death and in the urgent case.

4. *Oriental Law*

Marriage is forbidden because of a public vow of perfect chastity taken in simple or minor profession, or a private vow of virginity, of perfect chastity, of not marrying, of embracing the religious life, and in those rites where clerics after the reception of the order of subdiaconate are obliged to observe sacred celibacy, the vow of receiving the subdiaconate or a major order. (Mp, Can. 48.)

> The local Hierarch, but not the Vicar General without a special mandate, may dispense his own subjects for canonical reasons from these impediments with the exception of public vows taken in a religion of papal or patriarchal right. (Mp, Can. 32 § 1.)

B. *Legal Relationship*

1. In those countries in which legal relationship arising from adoption renders marriage illicit according to the civil law, marriage is illicit also according to Canon Law. (Can. 1059.)

2. *Dispensation:* by the Apostolic Delgate by reason of special faculties. Canons 1043-1045 may be used to dispense in urgent cases.

3. *Oriental Law.* In those countries in which by civil law marriage is forbidden on account of guardianship or legal relationship resulting from adoption, marriage is

illicit according to Canon Law. (Mp, Can. 49.) The local Hierarch has power to dispense from this impediment. (Mp, Can. 32 § 1.)

C. *Mixed Religion*

1.   The Church most severely prohibits everywhere the contracting of marriage between baptized persons one of whom is a Catholic while the other is affiliated with a heretical or a schismatic sect; moreover, if there is danger of perversion of the Catholic spouse and the offspring, the marriage is forbidden by the divine law itself. (Can. 1060.)

> Baptism in a heretical or schismatic sect is sufficient affiliation to give rise to this impediment. Moreover, persons who belong or have belonged to an *atheistic sect* are to be considered as to all legal effects, even those which concern marriage, the same as persons who belong or have belonged to a non-Catholic sect. (PCI, 30 July, 1934.)

2.   The Church does not dispense from the impediment of mixed religion unless:

a.   Just and grave reasons require it;

b.   The non-Catholic party gives a guaranty to remove from the Catholic party the danger of perversion, and both parties give a guaranty that all offspring will be baptized and reared only in the Catholic Faith;

c.   There is moral certainty that these guaranties will be fulfilled. (Can. 1061 § 1.)

> 1) The guaranties shall ordinarily be required in writing. (Can. 1061 § 2.)
>
> 2) *Grave causes* for a dispensation from the impediment are, v.g., the hope of conversion of the non-Catholic, the avoiding of public discord, the fear of a mere civil marriage, the paucity of Catholics in the district, etc. A dispensation given by the Ordinary or by any one else inferior to the Holy See where no grave cause exists would be invalid. (Can. 84 § 1.)
>
> 3) *The guaranties* in regard to the baptism and education of the children refer only to those children to be born; yet the parties should be warned of their grave obligation under the

divine law to see to the Catholic education also of children who are already born. (S.O., 16 Jan., 1942.)

The Holy Office admonishes Ordinaries as well as all pastors and other persons mentioned in Canon 1044 who are empowered to dispense from the impediments of mixed religion and disparity of cult, never to grant a dispensation of this sort unless the parties to the marriage have given guaranties whose faithful execution no one can prevent, even in virtue of civil law; otherwise the dispensation itself is to be entirely null and void. (S.O., decr., 14 Jan., 1932.) In countries in which the civil laws do not recognize the binding power of promises in relation to the future religious education of children, this restriction is not applicable, and Ordinaries may dispense provided that they themselves judge that there exists in each case a moral certainty that the promises will be lived up to. (S.O., reply, 4 Aug., 1932.) Indeed in a later decision the Holy Office states that the mind of the Sacred Congregation is this: Although the Holy See has from time immemorial required, and now strictly requires, that in all mixed marriages the fulfillment of the conditions be safeguarded by a formal promise explicitly demanded and given by both parties, still the use of the faculty to dispense, whether it be ordinary or delegated, cannot be called invalid if both parties at least implicitly gave the *cautiones,* that is, if they placed acts from which it must be concluded and can be proved in the external forum that they were conscious of their duty to fulfill the conditions and that they manifested a firm purpose to perform that duty. (S.O., 10 May, 1941.)

Note well: The guaranties regarding the children must be given *by both parties,* not only by the non-Catholic party, and this *for the validity* of the dispensation. (S.O., 10 May, 1941.)

4) *The Ordinary must have moral certainty* that the guaranties will be fulfilled, and this too is a condition for the valid granting of the dispensation. The parties who give the guaranties must be sincere, so that if they are not sincere but merely go through the external formalities and have no intention of keeping the promise, the dispensation *is invalid.* (Cf. S.R.R., decr., 4 April, 1951; cf. *Digest,* IV, pp. 323-329.)

3. Even though a dispensation from the impediment of mixed religion has been obtained from the Church, the spouses are not permitted, either before or after the marriage contracted before the Church, to go also either in person or by proxy to a non-Catholic minister acting in his

ministerial capacity, for the purpose of giving or renewing their matrimonial consent. (Can. 1063 § 1.)

> For the excommunication placed on Catholics who marry before a non-Catholic minister, see p. 123.

> If a pastor knows with certainty that the spouses are about to violate or have already violated this law, he shall not assist at their marriage except for the gravest of reasons, and only if danger of scandal is removed and the Ordinary has been previously consulted. (Can. 1063 § 2.)

If, however, the civil law requires it, it is not forbidden the spouses to even go to a non-Catholic minister acting merely in the role of a civil official for the sole purpose of performing the civil act of marriage for the sake of the civil effects. (Can. 1063 § 3.)

4. Mixed marriages are to be celebrated without any sacred rite and outside of a church or oratory, unless the local Ordinary makes an exception to the contrary. (Can. 1064, 4°.) Confer our commentary below, pp. 262, 267.

5. *Dispensation*

Local Ordinaries may dispense from the impediment of mixed religion in virtue of the quinquennial faculties. (*Digest,* IV, pp. 70-71.) Canons 1043-1045 may be used in urgent cases.

> *Pastoral notes.* a. If a mixed marriage was contracted *illicitly and invalidly* (for instance, if the canonical form was not observed) and the parties wish to convalidate the marriage, this can be done by a simple convalidation in which both parties give the guaranties, a dispensation is obtained from the impediment and both renew matrimonial consent before the pastor and two witnesses. (Sipos, § 113.) If the matrimonial consent cannot be thus renewed either because the non-Catholic party cannot be informed of the invalidity of the marriage without danger of grave inconvenience to the Catholic party, or because the non-Catholic party can by no means be induced to renew consent before the Church or to give the guaranties required by Canon 1061 § 2, the local Ordinary may, in virtue of the quinquennial faculties grant a *sanatio in radice* under certain specified conditions. One of the conditions is that it is morally certain the non-Catholic party will not impede the baptism and

the Catholic education of all children who may thereafter be born. (*Digest,* IV, pp. 72-73.)

   b. If the marriage was contracted *illicitly* because the guaranties were not given or were not given with sincerity, the marriage is valid if there is question only of the impediment of mixed religion and not of the impediment of disparity of cult. If the non-Catholic party cannot be induced to make the guaranties, the Catholic party, if repentant, may be admitted to the sacraments if he or she sincerely promises to see to the Catholic baptism and education of the children. (Genicot, II, n. 536.)

6. *Oriental Law*

The same prescriptions concerning the impediment of mixed religion are had amongst the Orientals (Mp, Canons 50-54); however the prohibition of a sacred rite is not contained in the Oriental legislation. The sacred rite allowed in mixed marriages amongst Orientals is considered in the chapter on the canonical form of marriage.

D. *Marriage with (or of) Unworthy Catholics*

1. The faithful shall likewise be deterred from contracting marriage with those who have either *notoriously abandoned the Catholic Faith,* even though they have not become affiliated with a non-Catholic sect, or with those who have *notoriously become members of societies condemned by the Church.* (Can. 1065 § 1.)

   One has abandoned the Catholic Faith if he publicly and notoriously states that he is no longer a Catholic, if he boasts that he is a freethinker, a materialist, a rationalist, etc.

   Condemned societies are not only such as fall under censure, but any society, membership in which is forbidden by the Church. (Cappello, II, n. 349.)

A pastor shall not assist at marriages of this kind without consulting the Ordinary, who after an examination of all the circumstances, may permit him to assist at the marriage, provided a serious reason exists for this, and provided the Ordinary judges that there is sufficient guaranty of the Catholic education of all the children and of the removal of the danger of perversion of the other spouse. (Can. 1065 § 2.)

> If the marriage is permitted, it is *per se* celebrated in church and with sacred rites, unless perhaps the Ordinary decides otherwise in order to avoid scandal. (Abbo-Hannan, II, n. 1065.)

2. If *a public sinner* or one who is *notoriously under censure* refuses to make a sacramental confession or to be reconciled with the Church before marriage, the pastor shall not assist at his marriage unless a serious reason demand it, regarding which he should, if possible, consult the Ordinary. (Can. 1066.)

> The canon speaks only of a *public* sinner, and of one *notoriously* censured. The former is bound first to confess his sins; the latter to be reconciled to the Church by being absolved from his censure. In most cases if the latter is absolved from his censure in the sacramental forum, there is sufficient reconciliation to permit the pastor's assistance at the marriage. If these people refuse to confess or to be reconciled respectively, the pastor needs a serious reason to proceed with the marriage (such as danger of complete defection from the faith, danger of concubinage, danger of an attempted civil marriage, etc.). The Ordinary should be consulted if time permits.

> *Per se* the marriage, if it can be permitted, is celebrated in church and with sacred rites, scandal however must be avoided.

3. *Communists:* With regard to the marriage of one who professes the materialistic and anti-Christian doctrine of communism, and especially of one who defends or propagates it, Canon 1061 (guaranties), 1102 and 1109 § 3 (no sacred rite nor church) are to be observed. With regard to the marriage of a communist who does not profess such doctrine but who has joined the party or who helps communism by editing, reading, propagating its papers, periodicals, etc., Canons 1065 and 1066 are to be observed. (S.O., decl., 11 Aug., 1949.)

4. *Oriental Law.* Concerning marriage with (or of) the unworthy, the Oriental law contains the same prescriptions as does the Latin Code. (Mp, Canons 55, 56.)

III. The Diriment Impediments

A diriment impediment both gravely prohibits the contracting of marriage and prevents it from being contracted validly.

A. *Age*

1. A valid marriage cannot be contracted by a man before he has completed the sixteenth year of his age, by a woman before she has completed the fourteenth year. (Can. 1067 § 1.)

Although a marriage contracted after the completion of the aforesaid ages is valid, nevertheless pastors of souls should endeavor to deter young people from marrying before the age at which, according to accepted usage of the country, marriage is usually contracted. (Can. 1067 § 2.)

Natural Law requires for the validity of the marriage that the parties have a sufficient understanding of the obligations of the matrimonial contract to be able to oblige themselves to these obligations. Puberty and present physical ability to have intercourse is not demanded by natural law. (V.C., II, n. 337.)

Pre-Code law demanded the completion of the fourteenth year for males, the completion of the twelfth year for girls, *nisi malitia suppleat aetatem:* i.e., if a girl attained puberty before being twelve years old or a boy before being fourteen years old, matrimonial capacity was also acquired.

The present law states a canonical age which admits of no exceptions. Note that the day of birth is not computed in the age and hence one completes the sixteenth or fourteenth year *at the close* of the day on which he celebrates his birthday (cf. Can. 34 § 3, 3°); likewise, a marriage contracted invalidly by reason of lack of age is not convalidated by the mere running of time, but the consent must be renewed. (Canons 1133-1135.) The law states the canonical age irrespective of actual puberty. Hence the marriage is valid even though the parties are not yet physically adolescent and capable of the marriage act. (Genicot, II, n. 548.)

2. *Civil Law.* Practically all the States of the Union have the impediment of nonage; however, there is variation as to its effect. One must consult the laws of the state in which he exercises the ministry, for the impediment may be only impedient or also diriment; in some states the

marriage may be validated upon the cessation of the impediment by mere cohabitation freely accepted and granted; in some states the judge or other public official is authorized to grant a dispensation from the impediment especially in cases of pregnancy. Practically all the States have, besides the age at which the impediment of nonage is established, another and higher age under which parental consent is required. This latter form of impediment however is usually only a conditional prohibition in reference to the issuance of the marriage license and does not affect the validity of the marriage. (Cf. Abbo-Hannan, II, n. 1067.)

> Knowledge of the impediments of civil law is important for the pastor when he is faced with the necessity of investigating the validity of marriages contracted by two *un*baptized persons.

3. *Dispensation:* must be obtained from the Apostolic Delegate. It is dispensable also under the terms of Canons 1043-1045.

4. *Oriental Law.* The same impediment of defect of age exists amongst the Orientals as amongst the Latins. (Mp, Can. 57.)

B. *Impotence*

1. *Antecedent* and *perpetual* impotence, whether on the part of the man or woman, whether known to the other party or not, whether absolute or relative, invalidates marriage by the law itself. (Can. 1068 § 1.)

> *Impotence.* The classical definition of impotence is: Incapacity for intercourse which is in itself suitable for generation. Authors dispute the explanation of the conditions requisite to make the marital act suitable for generation. According to the jurisprudence of the Rota there is required for potency, not only the *capacitas coeundi,* but also a capacity to inject true semen into the vagina, true semen being understood as semen *elaborated in the testicles* even though it does not contain spermatozoa. True semen is not that produced only in the vesicles and glands. Hence, impotence is the incapacity to have normal

intercourse, which is had by the penetration of the penis into
the vagina with the injection of true semen. (S.R.R., case, 25
April, 1941; case, 25 Oct., 1945.) According to a contrary
opinion, impotence is the impossibility of having normal intercourse, but normal intercourse is defined as the penetration of
the vagina by the male organ with the ejection of male seed
into the vagina. It is not required that the seed contain anything
elaborated in the testicles. Today, it is safe to follow this opinion in practice. (Cf. *Theological Studies,* XVI, pp. 533-557;
XX, p. 625; *The Jurist,* XIX, pp. 29, 187, 309, 465; S.O., 28
Sept., 1957.)

The impediment. Note that it is only *antecedent* and *perpetual* impotence that renders marriage invalid, not subsequent or
temporary impotence. Impotence is antecedent if it existed before marriage; subsequent, if it arises after the marriage; it is
perpetual if it cannot be cured by means which are licit and
not dangerous to life; temporary, if it disappears naturally, or
can be cured by means licit and not dangerous to life. (Genicot,
II, n. 560.)

Absolute impotence prevents marital intercourse with all
persons; relative impotence prevents it with a certain person or
persons, v.g., because of disproportionate size of the sex organs,
aversion for a certain person causing frigidity (*vaginismus*).
Absolute impotence renders marriage invalid with regard to
anyone; relative impotence is an impediment only in regard to
the persons with which the person affected cannot have intercourse.

Cases. A man is impotent if he is deprived of both testicles;
if his penis is so deformed that he cannot inject semen into the
vagina; if he cannot have an erection. In case of a double
vasectomy, if the condition is temporary in the canonical sense
(cf. above), the man is not under the impediment; if the condition is permanent, the impediment is doubtful and the marriage is not to be prevented, according to the norm of Canon
1068 § 2.

A woman is impotent if she does not have a vagina; if the
vagina is so small, or is so closed up, that no penetration whatever is possible. A woman is not impotent but merely sterile, if
she has no ovaries; if she has suffered a double fallectomy;
generally also if the uterus has been excised, or if the opening
between the vagina and uterus is entirely occluded. (Cf. Bouscaren-Ellis, pp. 517-518 for important details.)

2.   If the impediment of impotence is doubtful either
by doubt of law or by doubt of fact, the marriage is not

to be prevented. (Can. 1068 § 2.)

The reason for this rule is the extreme difficulty of directly solving doubts of law or fact regarding this impediment. To settle the consciences of the faithful in these cases, the Church declares that in all probable and prudent doubts, the natural law to marry prevails, even though this impediment is of natural law.

If one doubts about the impediment of impotence *before marriage,* he cannot licitly contract marriage until he investigates and dispels the doubt; if the doubt remains, he may enter marriage provided he informs the other party; during the marriage he may enjoy conjugal acts until the impediment would become certain. If the marriage *has already been contracted* and a doubt arises concerning the presence of impotence and whether it was antecedent and perpetual and therefore whether the marriage is invalid, the parties may try to have marital relations. If every serious hope of potency vanishes and it becomes morally certain that antecedent and perpetual impotence is present, they should petition the local Ordinary to begin the process for a declaration of nullity. (Cf. Genicot, II, n. 561.) Special circumstances may suggest to the confessor that he leave the parties in good faith or that he counsel them to obtain permission to live as brother and sister. (Sipos, § 117.) If people are validly married and *subsequent impotence* arises, they may use the marital rights as long as there is reasonable hope of a substantial fulfillment of the marriage act; if there is no hope of this, the parties must abstain from acts which would expose them to the proximate danger of pollution. (Bouscaren-Ellis, p. 519.)

3.   Sterility neither invalidates marriage nor renders it illicit. (Can. 1068 § 3.)

Sterility is incapacity for generation. People who are sterile are capable of having intercourse (*capaces coeundi*) but are not capable of propagating offspring. Thus, young people before they attain puberty, old people, women after they have reached the menopause and ovulation ceases, women who have no ovaries, no uterus, who have suffered a double fallectomy, etc.

4.   *Dispensation*: none

5.   *Oriental Law:* same as that of the Code. (Mp, Can. 58.)

C. *Prior Marriage*

1.   One who is bound by the bond of a prior marriage, even though the marriage was not consummated, invalidly attempts another marriage, without prejudice, however, to the privilege of the faith. (Can. 1069 § 1.)

This impediment is of divine law and hence binds also infidels.

2.   Even though a former marriage be invalid or dissolved for any reason whatever, it is not therefore allowed to contract another marriage until the nullity or dissolution of the former shall have been legally and certainly established. (Can. 1069 § 2.)

a.   *Death of a former spouse* can be proved from an authentic document, either ecclesiastical or civil, stating the fact of this person's death. If the death can be proved by an authentic document, the pastor may allow the living spouse to enter a new marriage. In many dioceses particular law requires that the Ordinary be first consulted. If, however, such a document is not available, the Ordinary shall collect proof by hearing witnesses, and in case witnesses are not available, he shall have recourse to the various presumptions mentioned in an instruction of the Sacred Congregation of the Holy Office, 13 May, 1868. (The gist of this instruction can be found in the *Digest,* I, p. 510.)

b.   With regard to *declarations of nullity* of previous marriages:

1) In cases in which it is certainly known that the marriage is invalid because of defect of canonical form, the Ordinary, or even the pastor after he consults the Ordinary, can without any process declare the marriage invalid. (PCI, 16 Oct., 1919.)

Chanceries usually demand the following documents for a declaration of nullity: document of baptism; document of first Communion and/or confirmation; civil marriage record (obtained from the county clerk); civil divorce record (obtained from the clerk of the circuit court); sworn statement that the marriage has never been celebrated in the form prescribed by the Church.

2) In cases in which the invalidity of a previous marriage is based on one of these diriment impediments, namely, disparity of cult, holy orders, solemn vows, bond, consanguinity, affinity or spiritual relationship, and the impediment can be proved by

a certain and authentic document, and it is equally certain that no dispensation had been obtained, the Ordinary may declare the marriage invalid without the formalities of a trial but using a simple summary judicial process with the intervention of the defender of the bond. (Can. 1990.)

3) If the invalidity of a previous marriage is said to arise from some other cause (v.g., impotence, defective consent, etc.) a formal judicial trial is necessary, and two concordant sentences to the effect that the invalidity of the former marriage has been proved. (Canons 1986, 1987; S.C.Sacr., instr., 15 Aug., 1936, art. 220.)

c. If a person bound by the bond of previous marriage attempts another marriage and sins by adultery with this other party either before or after the attempted marriage, he contracts the further impediment of crime. (Can. 1075.) A person attempting a second marriage is also automatically infamous by infamy of law (Can. 2356); he is to be regarded as a public sinner and hence denied admission to the sacraments (Can. 855) as well as Christian burial, unless he gives signs of repentance. (Can. 1240 § 1, 6°.) If after obtaining a civil divorce from a valid marriage, a Catholic attempts a second marriage he is automatically excommunicated, the absolution being reserved to the Ordinary. (Balt. III, n. 124.)

3. *Oriental Law.* The impediment of the bond is the same here as in the Latin Code. (Mp, Can. 59.)

D. *Disparity of Cult*

1. A marriage is invalid if contracted by an unbaptized person with a person baptized in the Catholic Church or converted to the Church from heresy or schism. (Can. 1070 § 1.) Bound by the impediment of disparity of cult is anyone who has been baptized in the Catholic Church or converted ot it, even though he later fall away from the Church and even if he join a non-Catholic sect. (Sipos, § 119.)

a. *Who is baptized in the Catholic Church?* Properly speaking, all who are validly baptized are baptized into the Catholic Church and become subjects of the Church because baptism as instituted by Our Lord aggregates a person only to the true Church. However in the sense of Canon 1070 not only the fact and rite of baptism are considered but also the external profession of the Catholic Faith whereby one adheres to the external communion of the faithful, for baptism may be received or administered with an intention that will signify and effect adherence to the true Church or to an heretical or schismatical sect. The Church or sect to which one belongs depends on the intention *of the person* being baptized if he is baptized in adult age; on the will of the *parents or guardians,* if a child is subject to them, except when in case of danger of death, the child is baptized by a Catholic minister; on the will of the *minister of baptism,* as long as he does not confer baptism against the will of the parents or guardians or the person baptized according to the norms of Canons 750 and 752. (V.C., II, n. 344.)

Considered baptized in the Catholic Church are:

1) Adults who enter it by baptism;

2) All children whose parents or guardians have them baptized with the intention of aggregating them to the Catholic Church;

3) All children, adults who are unconscious, who are baptized by a Catholic minister in danger of death;

4) Children baptized by a Catholic minister in the case where the parents do not wish or are not able to exercise parental rights over the child.

Baptized outside of the Catholic Church are:

1) All adults baptized in an heretical or schismatic sect;

2) Children whose parents or guardians have them baptized with the intention of aggregating them to their sect;

3) Children who are baptized by a non-Catholic minister with the intention of aggregating them to his sect, the parents not objecting when it is possible for them to do so. (V.C., II, n. 344.)

b. *Conversion to the Catholic Faith* is ordinarily effected by formal admission to the Church and its sacraments. Infant children of converts are aggregated to the Church. Children of converts over the age of seven, if they accept Catholic education until the age of fourteen, are presumed to belong to the Catholic Church; and their conversion would be certain if they have permitted the supplying of the ceremonies of baptism, and especially if they have received the sacraments of the Church. (Abbo-Hannan, II, n. 1070.) Children who have been baptized outside of the Church, but who have been reared and educated in the Church by their parents are considered converts to the Church. (V.C., II, n. 344.)

c. The impediment of disparity of cult affects those who, being born of non-Catholic parents, were nevertheless baptized in the Catholic Church, even though from infancy they have been reared in heresy, schism, or infidelity. (PCI, reply, 29 April, 1940.)

d. Before the Code the impediment of disparity of cult invalidated marriages between an unbaptized person and any person validly baptized. Hence before 19 May, 1918, the marriage of a heretic validly baptized in a non-Catholic sect and an unbaptized person was invalid. Pre-Code marriages must be judged, therefore, according to the impediment as it existed at the time the marriage was contracted.

2. If at the time the marriage was contracted a party was commonly regarded as baptized, or his baptism was doubtful, the marriage must be held valid according to the norm of Canon 1014, until it is certainly established that one of the parties was baptized and that the other was not. (Can. 1070 § 2.)

a. If a doubt arises concerning the fact of baptism or the validity of a baptism *before the marriage,* the case is to be handled in this way:

1) If the doubtfully baptized person wishes to live as a Catholic he should be baptized conditionally.

2) If a non-Catholic who is doubtfully baptized does not wish to convert to the Church, he may not be re-baptized, but the pastor is to apply for a dispensation from the impediment of mixed religion and, *ad cautelam,* from the impediment of disparity of cult. (V.C., II, n. 345.)

b. If a doubt arises *after the marriage,* a universal presumption in favor of the validity of the marriage is stated by Canon 1070 § 2, and hence the marriage is presumed valid until the opposite is proved. If it can be proved with moral certainty that one person was baptized and the baptism of the other was invalid, the presumption falls and the marriage is held as invalid if no dispensation from the impediment of disparity of cult had been obtained.

3. *Dispensation.* The prescriptions laid down in Canons 1060-1064 in regard to mixed marriages must be applied also to marriages affected by the impediment of disparity of cult. (Can. 1071.)

a. Confer our commentary above (under mixed religion) on Canons 1060-1064. Note the importance of the prescriptions of Canon 1061 for the validity of these marriages. Before a dispensation from the impediment can be given validly, there must exist *grave causes* for the dispensation, *both* parties must give *sincere* guaranties, the superior dispensing must be *morally certain* that the guaranties will be fulfilled. If these conditions for the dispensation do not exist the dispensation is *invalid* and hence also *the marriage is invalid.*

b. Local Ordinaries, by virtue of the quinquennial faculties, may dispense from the impediment of disparity of cult when the unbaptized party is an infidel or Jew. (*Digest,* IV, pp. 71, 62.) If the unbaptized party is a Moslem the dispensation must come from the Apostolic Delegate.

c. Canons 1043-1045 may be used to dispense in danger of death and in urgent cases.

d. Convalidating an invalid marriage: confer what has been said above under the impediment of mixed religion (n. 5, *Dispensation, Pastoral Notes,* a.), p. 190.

4. *Oriental Law*

a. The prescriptions of the Latin Code regarding the impediment of disparity of cult are found also in the Oriental legislation (Mp, Canons 60, 61), with one notable difference, namely, the form of the impediment reads: *the marriage contracted by an unbaptized person with a baptized person is null.* (Mp, Can. 60 § 1.) Hence, although the Latin Code exempts non-Catholic baptized persons from the impediment, the Oriental legislation does not. The impediment is therefore more comprehensive than in the Latin Code, in so far as Oriental schismatics are also comprehended under its terms.

The reason for this difference is that since many schismatics retain the impediment of disparity of cult, it would have been imprudent to exempt them from the impediment; hence the impediment is retained according to the ancient discipline.

Oriental schismatics are bound by the law of the *motu proprio, Crebrae allatae* and hence by the impediment of disparity of cult. The Holy Office declared in two private decisions (18 May, 1949; 17 April, 1950), that a marriage can be declared null on the ground of disparity of cult if it can be juridically proven that one party is not baptized and the other party is validly baptized in an Oriental schismatic sect. (Cf. *Digest,* III, pp. 422-424, 427.)

b. According to Oriental law, a marriage celebrated

with a dispensation from the impediment of disparity of cult is celebrated with sacred rites, otherwise than in the Latin discipline. (Mp, Can. 85.)

E. *Sacred Orders*

1. Clerics in sacred orders attempt marriage invalidly. (Can. 1072.)

a. A cleric who received a sacred order under the influence of grave fear and who did not afterward ratify the ordination at least tacitly when coercion ceased, by the exercise of the functions of the order, with the intention in so doing, of submitting to the clerical obligations, shall be reduced to the lay state by a sentence of the judge after proof of the coercion and the absence of ratification; and he shall be thus freed from the obligations of celibacy and of the divine office. However, the duress and the absence of ratification must be proved according to the norms set down in Canons 1993-1998. (Can. 214.)

b. A cleric would not be bound by the impediment if he were ignorant of the obligation of celibacy attached to sacred orders. (V.C., II, n. 347.) Such ignorance must be proved, and it can hardly be proved where the instruction of the Sacred Congregation of the Sacraments, 27 Dec., 1930, concerning the examination before ordinations, has been observed.

c. A cleric in minor orders may marry, but unless the marriage is null by reason of force or fear suffered by him, he is automatically reduced to lay state. (Can. 132 § 2.)

d. Clerics in sacred orders who attempt even a civil marriage incur excommunication reserved simply to the Holy See (Can. 2388 § 1), they become irregular *ex delicto* (Can. 985, 3°), and automatically lose all ecclesiastical offices. (Can. 188, 5°.) If they refuse to amend, they are to be degraded. (Can. 2388 § 1.)

2. *Dispensation:* From the Holy See. The Holy See practically never dispenses from the priesthood. In danger of death and in urgent cases a subdeacon or deacon may be dispensed according to the norms of Canons 1043-1045. Ordinaries may *not* dispense subdeacons and deacons in virtue of Canon 81. (PCI, 26 Jan., 1949.)

3. *Oriental Law.* Clerics in major orders or in the subdiaconate attempt marriage invalidly. (Mp, Can. 62.)

F. Solemn Vows

1. Marriage is invalidly attempted by religious who have taken either solemn vows, or simple vows which by special provision of the Holy See are endowed with the power of invalidating marriage. (Can. 1073.)

> Only in the Society of Jesus do simple vows invalidate the contracting of marriage.
>
> Attempted marriage (even only a civil attempt) in spite of this impediment results in an excommunication simply reserved to the Holy See (Can. 2388 § 1), irregularity *ex delicto* (Can. 985, 3°), and automatic dismissal from the religious institute. (Can. 646 § 1, 3°.)

2. *Dispensation:* From the Holy See. In danger of death and in the urgent case Canons 1043-1045 may be used. The impediment ceases by an indult of secularization. (Cf. Can. 640.)

3. *Oriental Law.* Religious bound by solemn or major profession as well as those who have taken the vow of chastity outside of major profession with which is connected the power of invalidating marriage by a special prescription of the Holy See, attempt marriage invalidly. (Mp, Can. 63.)

G. Abduction

1. Between an abducted woman and the man who has abducted her with a view to marriage there can be no marriage as long as the woman remains in the power of the abducter. (Can. 1074 § 1.)

As regards the nullity of marriage, the violent detention of a woman is regarded as equivalent to abduction, *i.e.,* when with a view to marriage, a man violently detains a woman in the place where she is staying or to which she has freely come. (Can. 1074 § 3.)

> a. Abduction is the forceful removal of a woman from a safe place to a place that is not safe. Abduction is *violent* if the woman is carried off by force or deceit; abduction is *seductive*

if the woman is a minor and consents to go, but against the will of her parents or guardians or these being ignorant of the fact. Seductive abduction is not an impediment to marriage. (V.C., II, n. 350.)

b.   If a woman is detained in a place through force or deceit the marriage is likewise invalidly attempted. The purpose of the detention must be marriage, not only the satisfying of lust; hence, if a man detains a woman or if he abducts her for purposes of lust and not for marriage and the woman freely consents to marry him, the impediment does not arise. (V.C., II, n. 350.) If, however, the woman is abducted for purposes of lust, and is later detained for the purpose of forcing her to marry, the impediment arises.

c.   The impediment of abduction is of ecclesiastical law and hence does not affect infidels when marrying amongst themselves. If, however, the abductor is a baptized person and the person abducted unbaptized, or vice versa, the baptized person is bound directly, the unbaptized person indirectly by the impediment and the marriage is invalid. (Sipos, § 122.)

2.   If the woman abducted, upon being separated from the abductor and placed in a safe place, consents to have him for her husband, the impediment ceases. (Can. 1074 § 2.)

Note that the impediment does not cease simply by the fact that the woman consents to marry; she must first be placed outside the power of the abductor.

Dispensation from the impediment is granted by the Apostolic Delegate; it is rarely granted, however, for ordinarily it is demanded that the woman be first placed in a free and safe place, and this being done, the impediment ceases if the woman wishes to marry the man. Canons 1043-1045 may be used to dispense in urgent cases and in danger of death.

3.   *Oriental Law*. The impediment of abduction is the same in the Oriental legislation as in the Latin Code. (Mp, Can. 64.)

H.   *Crime*

1.   They cannot contract a valid marriage who during the term of the same lawful marriage, commit adultery with each other and either give each other a mutual promise of marriage or actually attempt marriage, even though

by a merely civil act. (Can. 1075, 1°.)

a. This impediment is verified by the following conditions: true *adultery*, i.e., at least one of the parties is bound by a valid marriage; *consummated*, i.e., sexual intercourse with the depositing of the male seed into the vagina, hence, onanistic intercourse is not sufficient, but once adultery has taken place it is presumed consummated until the opposite is proved; *formal*, i.e., both parties know that at least one of them is married. Ignorance, not gravely culpable, on the part of one of the adulterers that the other party is married excuses from the impediment. Crass ignorance of this fact that the other party is married probably excuses and hence the impediment is doubtful and in practice does not bind. (Genicot, II, n. 574.)

b. To verify the impediment the following conditions are also required: a *true* promise, i.e., not merely an intention or resolution; *absolute*, i.e., not conditional; *serious*, i.e., not fictitious; *mutual*, i.e., given and accepted doubly, i.e., by both parties; finally it must be a promise of marriage upon the dissolution of the present marriage by the death of the present spouse, not by divorce. (Sipos, § 123.)

c. The impediment also arises without a promise of marriage, if two people commit adultery and attempt a marriage while one is still bound by a previous valid marriage. *Note that a person validly married but legally divorced, who marries again during the life of the former spouse and consummates this second "marriage" incurs the impediment of crime.* Hence if after the death of the former partner a validation of the second marriage is to be effected, a dispensation from the impediment of crime is required.

2. They cannot contract a valid marriage who, during the term of the same lawful marriage, commit adultery with each other and one of them commits conjugicide. (Can. 1075, 2°.)

Two conditions are required for the impediment, namely, adultery (as described above) and murder, namely, one of the adulterers kills either his own spouse or the spouse of the other party or both spouses.

The adultery must precede the killing of the lawful spouse and the murder must be perpetrated with the intention of making marriage possible with one's accomplice in adultery, though it is not required that the accomplice know of this intention. If one kills his spouse for other reasons, v.g., collecting insurance, the impediment is not contracted; in law, however, the intention of murdering for the purpose of contracting a new marriage is presumed unless the contrary is very evident. (Sipos, § 123.)

3. They cannot contract a valid marriage who, even without committing adultery, have by mutual cooperation, physical or moral, killed the lawful spouse. (Can. 1075, 3°.)

a. For cooperation here, both delinquents must be efficacious accomplices in murder. If one party manifests his intention to commit the murder and the other party merely consents or approves of the plan, the impediment arises if the consent or approbation efficaciously influences the main agent, i.e., if the crime would not have been committed without the consent or approbation. If the approbation is not efficacious, namely, the crime would have been committed anyway, the impediment does not arise. (Cappello, II, n. 365.)

b. It is required that the murder be perpetrated with the intention of celebrating marriage with one's accomplice. It is sufficient that this intention be had by one of the conspirators, but probably it must be manifested to the other party. In the external forum these requisites on the part of the intention are presumed. (Sipos, § 123.)

4. *Multiplication of the impediment.* The impediment is multiplied if adultery with the promise of marriage or an attempt at marriage is accompanied by the murder of a legitimate spouse; if adultery with the promise or attempt is injurious to two marriages, v.g., *both* adulterers are already married; if *two* spouses are killed, etc. In practice, when applying for a dispensation simply give all the details and circumstances of the persons and the case so that the authority dispensing may judge how many dispensations are necessary.

5. *Infidels.* The impediment of crime is of ecclesiastical law and hence infidels are not affected when marrying amongst themselves. But if one party is baptized and is guilty of adultery with a promise or an attempt at marriage with an unbaptized person, the impediment arises. If one party is baptized and is guilty of murder of the lawful spouse (either alone or with the other), the impediment is incurred. But if the baptized party is guilty only of adultery but not of murder, no impediment arises because the baptized party is innocent of the murder and the unbaptized party is not directly subject to ecclesiastical law. (Cf. Sipos, § 123, 3°.)

6. *Dispensation*

a. From the impediment of crime arising from adultery

with a promise of, or attempt at, marriage, the Ordinary dispenses in virtue of the quinquennial faculties. (*Digest,* IV, p. 74.)

A dispensation from this impediment is also granted by the very fact that the Holy See or the local Ordinary permits one to remarry because of the presumed death of a former consort; also if the Holy See issues a dispensation from the bond of a ratified but unconsummated marriage. (Can. 1053; PCI, 26 March, 1952.)

b. From crime arising from adultery with conjugicide, the Apostolic Delegate dispenses. The Ordinary may in virtue of the quinquennial faculties dispense if the crime is occult, provided the impediment incurred without the mutual cooperation of the parties. (*Digest,* IV, p. 80.)

c. From crime arising from conjugicide committed by both parties together, the Apostolic Delegate dispenses. However, the Church does not dispense if the murder has been public.

Canons 1043-1045 may be used in dispensing from all three forms of the impediment of crime in danger of death and in the urgent case.

7. *Oriental Law.* The impediment is the same as in the Latin Code. (Mp, Can. 65.)

I. *Consanguinity*

1. In the *direct line* of consanguinity marriage is invalid between all in the ascending and the descending line, whether of legitimate birth or not. In the *collateral line* marriage is invalid to the third degree inclusively, but the impediment is multiplied only as often as the common ancestor is multiplied. (Can. 1076 §§ 1, 2.)

a. Consanguinity or blood relationship exists in the *direct line,* if one person is the direct ancestor of the other, v.g., grandfather, father, son; in the *collateral or oblique line,* if neither person is the direct ancestor of the other but both are descended from a common ancestor, v.g. brother and sister, cousins, aunt and nephew.

Since carnal generation is the basis of consanguinity, the

relationship arises from both legitimate and illegitimate generation.

Consanguinity is of the *full blood* if the parties related have two ancestors in common; of the *half blood* if they have only one ancestor in common. Thus, brothers who have the same father but not the same mother are relations of the half blood. Canonically there is no practical difference between relationship of full blood and of half blood.

b. A degree of relationship indicates the measure of distance of two related persons from their common ancestor in the collateral line or the measure of distance of one person from his ancestor in the direct line.

In the *direct line* there are as many degrees as there are generations, or as there are persons not counting the ancestor. (Can. 96 § 2.) Thus grandfather and grandson are related in the second degree.

In the *collateral line,* if the distance of both relatives from the common ancestor is equal, that is, if both lines are of *equal length,* there are as many degrees as there are generations in one line or as there are persons in one line not counting the common ancestor. Thus brother and sister are related in the first degree. If the lines are *not equal* then there are as many degrees as there are generations in the longer line or as there are persons in the longer line not counting the common ancestor. (Can. 96 § 3.)

Thus:

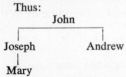

                    John
        ┌────────────────┐
    Joseph   Andrew
        │
    Mary

Mary and Andrew (niece and uncle) are related in the second degree of the collateral line; or expressed more accurately, in the second degree touching the first, or the second degree mixed with the first.

c. Pre-Code law: Before 19 May, 1918, marriage was invalid in the collateral line of consanguinity up to the fourth degree inclusive.

d. The impediment is multiplied as often as the common ancestor is multiplied. This can happen:

1) If someone marry a person who is his blood relative. Their children will be related multiply to cousins, etc.

2) If two persons who are related (v.g., two brothers) marry two persons who are related (v.g., two sisters). The children

of these marriages will be multiply related.

3) If one person successively marries two persons who are related, v.g., a man marries a woman and upon her death marries the woman's cousin. The children of these marriages will be multiply related to cousins, etc.

(Schematic examples of multiply relationships can be found in Bouscaren-Ellis, p. 535; also in V.C., II, pp. 254-255, and in many textbooks of Canon Law.)

2. Marriage shall never be permitted as long as there remains some doubt whether the parties are blood relatives in any degree of the direct line or in the first degree of the collateral line. (Can. 1076 § 3.)

In the direct line, consanguinity is an impediment of the divine law certainly in the first degree, more probably in the other degrees; in the collateral line it is more probably an impediment of divine law in the first degree, although some weighty authors doubt it; in all other degrees of the collateral line it is certainly an impediment of ecclesiastical law only.

Infidels when marrying amongst themselves are not bound by the impediment in the degrees in which it is certainly of ecclesiastical law only; if the impediment exists in a degree in which it is not certainly an impediment by divine law, the marriage is to be considered valid. However, infidels are bound by the impediment of consanguinity established by the civil law and hence the validity of the marriage must be judged according to the laws of the State in which the marriage was contracted.

If an infidel wishes to marry a relative who is baptized, the impediment of ecclesiastical law affects both parties.

3. *Civil law.* In almost all of the States the impediment of consanguinity is an invalidating one and it extends to all degrees of the *direct line* and to the second degree touching the first of the *collateral line,* (including, therefore, uncle-niece, aunt-nephew). In about half the states the invalidating impediment extends to first cousins; in a few states it extends to the third degree of the collateral line touching the first or second; in Oklahoma, to second cousins. (Alford, nos. 135-145.)

4. *Dispensation*

a. In the direct line — none.

b. In the collateral line:

1) First degree — none.

2) Second degree — from the Ordinary in virtue of the quinquennial faculties, but only for grave and urgent reasons when there is danger in delay and the marriage cannot be postponed until a dispensation be obtained from the Holy See. (*Digest,* IV, p. 74.)

3) Second or third degree touching the first (uncle-niece or grandniece; aunt-nephew or grandnephew) — from the Ordinary in virtue of the quinquennial faculties, under the same limitations as mentioned in 2), and provided no *admiratio* results from the dispensation. (*Digest,* IV, p. 74.)

4) Third degree — from the Ordinary in virtue of the quinquennial faculties. (*Digest,* IV, p. 74.)

The faculties of Canons 1043-1045 for urgent cases and for the danger of death extend to all degrees of the impediment that are *certainly* of ecclesiastical law *only.*

If a dispensation from the impediment of consanguinity or affinity is granted in some degree of the respective impediment, it is valid in spite of an error regarding the degree made in the petition for the dispensation or in the grant of the dispensation, provided the degree that actually exists is lower than the one mentioned; the dispensation is also valid in spite of a failure to mention another impediment of the same kind in the same or in lower degree. (Can. 1052.) The dispensation is valid also for this other impediment of the same kind in an equal or lower degree, even when it was omitted in bad faith. (PCI, 8 July, 1948.)

In the case of a mixed degree (v.g., third degree touching the second), though both degrees are to be mentioned, the failure to mention one does not invalidate the dispensation even though it be the closer degree that is not mentioned, *unless the latter be the first degree,* for in this case the practice of the Roman Curia seems to require, for validity, that the closer degree be named. Hence, if one ask for a dispensation from the second degree of consanguinity or affinity when in fact the impediment which alone existed or exists together with the one mentioned is consanguinity or affinity in the second degree touching the first, the dispensation is most probably invalid. Note, finally, that a dispensation erroneously given from the impediment of affinity in a case involving the impediment of consanguinity, or vice versa, is invalid.

5. *Oriental Law*

a. In the direct line of consanguinity, marriage is invalid between all in the ascending and the descending line, whether of legitimate birth or not. (Mp, Can. 66 § 1.)

In the direct line there are as many degrees as there are persons, not counting the ancestor. (Mp, Can. 66 § 4, 2°.)

b. In the collateral line marriage is invalid to the sixth degree inclusively, and the impediment is multiplied as often as the common ancestor is multiplied. (Mp, Can. 66 § 2.)

In the collateral line there are as many degrees *as there are persons in both lines, not counting the common ancestor.* (Mp, Can. 66 § 4, 3°.)

This method of computation makes the impediment a little more comprehensive than it is in the Latin Code. In the Latin computation persons related in the fourth degree touching the second would be allowed to marry because the longer line and not the shorter line determines the degree of consanguinity, but in the Oriental legislation this same case would constitute a relationship in the sixth degree and hence the parties would be bound by the impediment.

c. Marriage shall never be permitted as long as some doubt remains whether the parties are blood relatives in any degree of the direct line or in the *second* degree of the collateral line. (Mp, Can. 66 § 3.)

Related in the second degree of collateral line, according to Oriental computation, are brother and sister.

Note: When one party to a marriage is a Latin and the other party an Oriental, they must be free to marry according to *both* the Latin and the Oriental legislation. This holds not only for consanguinity, but is a general principle applicable to all points of marriage legislation.

J. *Affinity*

1. Affinity in the direct line invalidates marriage in all

degrees; in the collateral line, to the second degree inclusively.

The impediment of affinity is multiplied as often as the impediment of consanguinity on which it is based is multiplied, or through a subsequent marriage with a blood relative of one's deceased spouse. (Can. 1077.)

a. Affinity arises from valid marriage, whether ratified only or both ratified and consummated. It exists only between the husband and the blood relatives of the wife, and between the wife and the blood relatives of the husband. Affinity is computed as follows: The blood relatives of the husband become *affines* of the wife in the same line and degree as they are related by consanguinity to the husband, and *vice versa.* (Can. 97.) Thus the husband's brother is *affinis* to the wife in the first degree of the collateral line; the wife's first cousin is *affinis* to the husband in the second degree of the collateral line.

Affinity arises from any valid marriage, and affinity contracted in infidelity becomes an impediment after the baptism of one or both parties. (S.O., resp., 31 Jan. 1957.)

b. The impediment is one of ecclesiastical law only, hence it does not bind infidels when marrying amongst themselves. If an infidel wishes to marry a baptized person he becomes subject to the impediment if it exists in the case.

c. Before the Code affinity arose from sexual intercourse, whether legitimate (within marriage, at least a putative marriage, or a union having the appearance of marriage) or illegitimate (outside of marriage). It existed between the man and the blood relatives of the woman and *vice versa.* It invalidated marriage in all degrees of the direct line; to the fourth degree of the collateral line inclusive if it arose from licit intercourse, to the second degree if it arose from illicit intercourse. (V.C., II, nos. 359-360.)

d. Examples of multiple affinity:

John and Thomas are related by consanguinity in both the first and second degrees of the collateral line. Mary marries John. She is related to Thomas by affinity in both the first and second degrees.

Eve and Ann are sisters; they are cousins to Bess and Joan, also sisters. Andy marries Eve and after her death marries Bess; Andy is related by affinity to Ann and Joan in both the first and second degrees of the collateral line, i.e., each girl is both his sister-in-law and his cousin-in-law.

2. *Civil Law.* In more than half the States of the Union the impediment of affinity does not exist in the civil law. In States where the impediment exists one must study the laws of the respective State to ascertain whether it is a diriment or impedient impediment. In some States, also, the impediment ceases upon the death of one's spouse. Only in a few States does it extend to the collateral line, for usually the impediment is restricted to the direct line and extends to the mother- and father-in-law, the daughter- and son-in-law, the stepmother or stepfather, the stepson or stepdaughter. (Cf. Alford, nos. 151-160 for details.)

3. *Dispensation:*

a. In the direct line:

1) After the marriage from which affinity arose is consummated — from the Holy See, and it is rarely given.

2) When the marriage is not consummated — from the Apostolic Delegate.

b. In the collateral line:

1) In the first degree, or in the first degree touching the second degree — from the Ordinary by reason of the quinquennial faculties, but only for grave and urgent reason, whenever there is danger in delay and the marriage cannot be postponed until a dispensation can be obtained from the Holy See. (*Digest,* IV, p. 74.)

2) In the second degree — from the Ordinary by reason of the quinquennial faculties. (*Digest,* IV, p. 74.)

> Canons 1043-1045 may be used to dispense from affinity except when the impediment exists in the direct line, and the matrimony from which it arose has been consummated.

4. *Oriental Law.* In Oriental law affinity, which arises *from any valid marriage,* invalidates marriage in all degrees of the direct line, to the fourth degree inclusive of

the collateral line. The computation of degrees is made in the manner proper to Orientals, i.e., by counting the number of persons in both lines, not counting the common ancestor. The blood relatives of the wife are *affines* of the husband in the same degree in which they are related by consanguinity to the wife, and *vice versa*. The impediment is multiplied the same as amongst the Latins. (Mp, Canons 67 § 1, 1°; 67 § 2; 68 § 1.) Note that the method of computation makes the impediment a little more extensive in the Oriental legislation. Thus, the Latin affinity of the third degree touching the first is in Oriental law, affinity of the fourth degree. Such affinity is a diriment impediment in Oriental law, it is not an impediment in Latin law.

By particular law two other kinds of affinity exist amongst the Orientals.

a. By particular law affinity from *digeneia* arises also between the blood relatives of the husband and the blood relatives of the wife. It is to be reckoned in such a manner that there are as many degrees of affinity as result from the *sum of degrees* of consanguinity by which both *affines* are distant from the spouses from whose marriage the affinity arose. This affinity invalidates marriage to the fourth degree inclusively. (Mp, Canons 67 § 1, 2°; 68 § 2.) Example: John and Alice are married. John's brother and Alice's sister are *affines* in the fourth degree of the collateral line because John's brother is related to John by consanguinity in the second degree of the collateral line and Alice's sister is related to Alice in the same degree.

This impediment exists amongst the Chaldeans, Melkites, Rumanians, Bulgarians, Russians, Greeks from Greece and Turkey, Ethiopians. It is never a multiple impediment. The local Hierarch has ordinary power (Mp, Canon 32 § 1, 2°) to dispense from this kind of affinity in any degree. (Pospishil, p. 110.)

b. By particular law affinity also results from *trigeneia,* that is, from two valid marriages, although not consummated, when two persons contracted marriage 1) with the same third person, after the previous marriage had been dissolved, or 2) with two persons who were blood relatives. This affinity exists between each of the spouses and those who are *affines ex digeneia* of the other spouse by way of the other marriage. This affinity between one spouse and the *affines* of the other spouse is computed in such a way that those who are *affines* of the husband *ex digeneia* because of the other marriage are in the same degree *affines* of the wife *in trigeneia,* and *vice versa.* This affinity invalidates marriage in the first degree only. (Mp, Canons 67 § 1, 3°; 68 § 3.)

This impediment exists only among Catholic Russians, Bulgarians, and Greeks from Greece and Turkey; also amongst many dissidents. The impediment is never multiplied and the local Hierarch has ordinary power to dispense from it. (Pospishil, p. 111.)

K. *Public Propriety*

1. The impediment of public propriety arises from an invalid marriage, whether consummated or non-consummated, and from public or notorious concubinage; it invalidates marriage in the first and second degree of the direct line between the man and the blood relatives of the woman and *vice versa.* (Can. 1078.)

a. An invalid marriage is one which has at least the appearance of marriage but is invalid on the score of some diriment impediment, defective consent, etc.

Concubinage is had when two persons live as husband and wife for the purpose of habitually having sexual intercourse, the union however not having even the appearance of marriage. For the impediment to arise it is necessary that the concubinage be public; hence, occult concubinage does not induce the impediment. If two persons are living in concubinage but are commonly thought to be man and wife, the crime is not public and does not give rise to the impediment. (Sipos, § 126.)

b. The impediment does not arise from a mere civil marriage between persons bound by the canonical form, independently of the fact of cohabitation. (PCI, reply, 12 March, 1929.) If, however, the parties live together they are considered as living in notorious concubinage and the impediment arises. (V.C., II, n. 361.)

c. The impediment is one of ecclesiastical law only and hence does not bind infidels when marrying amongst themselves; infidels may be bound indirectly, i.e., by reason of the baptized party with whom they wish to contract marriage.

Infidels living in public concubinage or in an invalid marriage are not bound by the impediment upon their conversion if they do not continue the concubinage or invalid marriage after their baptism; if, however, after the baptism of one or both parties, they continue in the invalid marriage or public concubinage the impediment arises. (Coronata, *De Sacr.*, III, n. 416.)

d. Pre-Code impediment: before the Code the impediment arose from a valid contract of engagement and extended to the first degree of both the direct and the collateral line; it also arose from a non-consummated marriage, whether valid or invalid (provided the invalidity did not arise from defective consent or lack of canonical form), and invalidated marriage in all degrees of the direct line, up to the fourth degree inclusive of the collateral line. (Sipos, § 126.)

2. *Dispensation.* First note that the impediment extends to the direct line only, not to the collateral line; it invalidates marriage up to the second degree inclusively.

From the first degree, Ordinaries may dispense by reason of the quinquennial faculties, for grave causes whenever there is danger in delay and the marriage cannot be postponed until a dispensation is obtained from the Holy See, and provided there be no possibility that one of the parties is the offspring of the other. (*Digest,* IV, p. 74.)

From the second degree, Ordinaries may dispense by reason of the quinquennial faculties. (*Digest,* IV, p. 74.)

The impediment is of itself perpetual and hence even if the invalid marriage or concubinage has been dissolved, the impediment still exists and must be dispensed from. Whether or not the impediment remains or is rather absorbed by the impediment of affinity in case the invalid marriage is validated or those living in concubinage contract marriage, is doubtful; a dispensation should be obtained *ad cautelam.*

A dispensation from the impediment may, if the case warrants it, be granted in virtue of Canons 1043-1045.

3. *Oriental Law.* The impediment is the same as in the Latin Code. (Mp, Can. 69.)

L. *Spiritual Relationship*

1. Only spiritual relationship arising from baptism invalidates marriage. This relationship exists between the one baptizing and the person baptized as well as between the sponsors and the person baptized. (Canons 1079; 768.)

a. For spiritual relationship to arise it is required that the baptism be certainly valid; it arises both from private as well as from solemn baptism.

b. It is also required for spiritual relationship between the baptized and the person baptizing that the latter be himself baptized. For spiritual relationship between the person baptized and the sponsors it is required that the latter be themselves baptized, be designated as sponsors, touch the person in the act of baptism etc., in a word, that they are valid sponsors according to the norm of Canon 765. If one is sponsor by proxy, it is the sponsor and not the proxy who contracts the spiritual relationship and the impediment.

c. If one is baptized conditionally, spiritual relationship arises only if the same sponsor is used in both the first (dubious) baptism and the second (conditional) baptism; likewise in regard to the minister, if he is the same in both baptisms, spiritual relationship arises, otherwise not.

d. Pre-Code law: the impediment arose from both baptism and confirmation and in each case it existed between the person receiving the sacrament and the minister of the sacrament as well as the sponsors, and also between the parents of the person receiving the sacrament and the minister and the sponsors. (V.C., II, n. 365.)

2. *Dispensation:* from the Ordinary by virtue of the quinquennial faculties. (*Digest,* IV, p. 74.) This impediment is also dispensable under the terms of Canons 1043-1045.

3. *Oriental Law.* In Oriental law the sponsor contracts spiritual relationship with the person baptized *and with this person's parents.* Spiritual relationship *does not arise* between the minister and the person baptized. When baptism is repeated conditionally, the sponsor does not contract spiritual relationship, unless the same sponsor is employed for both baptisms.

Spiritual relationship as just described is a diriment impediment to marriage. (Mp, Can. 70.)

M. *Legal Relationship*

1. Those who are disqualified for marriage by the civil law because of legal relationship arising from adoption,

cannot validly marry under Canon Law either. (Can. 1080.)

a. An invalidating impediment because of adoption exists only in Puerto Rico, according to most authors. (Cf. Alford, n. 163.) According to Bouscaren-Ellis (p. 474, footnote n. 58), the impediment exists also in Massachusetts, Rhode Island and Connecticut.

b. Persons who come to the United States from other countries, if they intend to stay here only temporarily, still remain subject to the laws of their own country. According to a general principle of law, *a contract* is governed by the laws of the place where the contract is made, however, some exceptions may be made to this principle for matrimonial contracts. Some states demand that the stranger be qualified to marry by the laws of his own country or of his own state; likewise that residents of the state intending to remain residents may not marry in another state if their marriage would be illegal in the home state. Other states recognize the general principle of contracts, i.e., if the contract is valid in the place where it was made, it is valid everywhere, and if invalid in the place where made, it is invalid everywhere. (Cf. Woywod, n. 1038.)

2. *Dispensation:* from the Apostolic Delegate. The impediment is also dispensable under the terms of Canons 1043-1045.

3. *Oriental Law.* Those who are considered incapable of marriage by civil law on account of guardianship or on account of legal relationship arising from adoption cannot under Canon Law validly contract marriage. (Mp, Can. 71.)

CHAPTER V

Dispensations from Impediments

I. GENERAL NORMS

A. *Distinctions*

1. The impediments are of major or of minor degree, public or occult, etc. Confer above, pp. 181-183.

2. A dispensation is given in the external forum if the impediment is public; in the internal forum if the impediment is occult.

3. A dispensation *in forma gratiosa* is granted directly to the parties by the dispensing authority; *in forma commissoria* by an executor, i.e., by an inferior delegated by the dispensing authority, and the inferior may be charged with the simple duty of granting the dispensation (*executor necessarius*), or he may be given the freedom to decide whether or not the dispensation is to be granted (*executor voluntarius*).

B. *Petition for a Dispensation*

1. Dispensations from the impediments of mixed religion and disparity of cult are granted by the Holy Office; from the impediment of public vows by the Sacred Congregation of Religious; from the other impediments by the Sacred Congregation of the Sacraments if the parties are Latins, and by the Sacred Congregation for the Oriental Church if the petitioners are Orientals; and from this same congregation even if only one of the petitioners is an Oriental.

Dispensations from all impediments, however, for either Latins or Orientals, for *the internal forum* (whether sacramental or extra-sacramental) are granted by the Sacred Penitentiary.

2. When the pastor asks for a dispensation in the *external forum* the petition is to be sent to the chancery office; if the bishop has not faculties to handle the case, the chancery forwards the petition to the proper congregation in Rome.

If the pastor asks for a dispensation in the *internal* forum, he may write directly to the Sacred Penitentiary; however, since the local Ordinary has special powers by virtue of his quinquennial faculties, the pastor may find that his bishop can dispense from the impediment in question. He then writes directly to the chancery, *provided that the sacramental seal is not thereby endangered.*

a. Dispensations in the *external* forum, (obtained for a public impediment): Apply to the chancery of the diocese where the bride has a domicile or quasi-domicile if both parties are affected by the impediment (v.g., crime, consanguinity). If only one party is affected by the impediment (v.g., age, vow) apply to the chancery of this person's diocese. If the impediment is that of mixed religion or disparity of cult apply to the chancery of the diocese of the Catholic party. Include in the letters of petition: Full name of both parties; their ages, domicile, quasi-domicile, place of actual residence; the impediment in its exact kind and degree; the number of impediments, including multiple consanguinity or affinity; the religion of both parties; the fact whether the marriage is to be contracted or convalidated; canonical causes for the dispensation.

b. Dispensation in the *internal* forum, (obtained for an occult impediment): Same information regarding the impediment, the canonical causes etc. as above. Fictitious names are used and all circumstances which might betray the parties' identity are omitted.

If the dispensation is sought in the *internal extra-sacramental* forum, (obtained for an occult impediment known outside of confession): The names and residences of the parties are given, for the dispensation must be recorded (though secretly) in the archives according to Canon 1047.

c. If both a public and occult impediment occur in the same case: The dispensations are asked for separately, from the chancery or proper Congregation for the public impediment, without mentioning the other impediment; from the Sacred Penitentiary for the occult impediment, mentioning that a public impediment also exists and that a dispensation has been asked for from the proper authority. (Bouscaren-Ellis, p. 483.)

Note: Per se whenever the impediment is public in the sense of Canon 1037 (confer above, p. 182) a dispensation should be obtained in the external forum. If the case is *de facto* occult, even if the impediment is public by nature and even though it is public according to the definition given in Canon 1037, one may still petition for the dispensation in the internal forum. (V.C., II, n. 304.)

C. *Use of Faculties*

1. The Ordinary may use his power to dispense (whether ordinary or delegated) on his own subjects everywhere. (Can. 201 § 3.) The laws and indults granting the Ordinary various faculties to dispense usually also explicitly include the power to dispense *peregrini,* or all persons actually in his territory. If such a clause is not contained in the grant of faculties, we believe that the Ordinary may nevertheless use his faculties (whether ordinary or delegated) in favor of *peregrini* actually in his territory. (Cf. Beste, p. 218.)

2. The Latin Ordinary may use his ordinary powers to dispense, as well as the powers granted him by the quinquennial faculties, in favor of Orientals subject to him, in places where Orientals have not an Ordinary of their own, but are subject to the Latin Ordinary. (S.C.E.O., private reply, 24 July, 1948.) In the United States and Canada

all Oriental Catholics, *except Ruthenians,* are subject to the Latin rite Ordinaries. (Pospishil, p. 20.)

The Latin Ordinary cannot dispense Ruthenians who are in his diocese unless the other party to the marriage is a baptized Latin, i.e., the Ruthenian is not considered a *peregrinus* and is in no wise subject to the jurisdiction of the Latin Ordinary. (Cf. Pospishil, pp. 95-96.)

3. If one party to the marriage is an Oriental, the other a Latin, or if both are Orientals, but belong to different rites, or to different dioceses of the same rite, or to dioceses of different rites, the dispensation is to be petitioned from the Ordinary of the man, but if the man is a non-Catholic, from the Ordinary of the woman. (Cf. Mp, Can. 32 § 5; PC Or., 3 May, 1953.)

This prescription affects only the licitness of the dispensation, for the Ordinary of the woman can also dispense validly (PC Or., 3 May, 1953), not only from relative impediments (v.g., consanguinity) but also from absolute impediments which directly bind the man (e.g., vow, age). (Sipos, § 107; Coussa, III, n. 58; Herman in *Mon. Eccl.*, 1953, p. 577.)

II. DISPENSATION IN ORDINARY CIRCUMSTANCES

1. The Ordinary may dispense from impediments which are doubtful because of a doubt of fact provided there is question of an impediment from which the Holy See is wont to dispense. (Can. 15.) He may also dispense from non-reserved vows. (Can. 1313.)

The Holy See never dispenses from consanguinity in the first degree of the collateral line, from the order of episcopate, from the impediment of crime arising from public conjucicide; it very rarely dispenses from affinity in the first degree of the direct line after the marriage has been consummated from which affinity arose, from the order of priesthood. (V.C., II, n. 310.)

2. By the quinquennial faculties the Ordinary may dispense from a number of matrimonial impediments as well as grant a *sanatio in radice* for certain invalid marriages. These powers are treated in the *Pastoral Companion* under each of the impediments and under the various

types of convalidations of invalid marriages.

> In Oriental Law the *motu proprio, Crebrae allatae,* grants to the local Hierarch, as well as to the Patriarch, special faculties to dispense from some of the more ordinary impediments. (Mp, Can. 32 — AAS, XLI, pp. 89ss., or Pospishil, pp. 166ss.). These faculties are not enjoyed by Ordinaries of the Latin rite even if they have subjects of the Oriental rite. (Coussa, III, n. 60; Sipos, § 107.)

III.   DISPENSATION IN DANGER OF DEATH
   A.   *Powers of the Local Ordinary.* (Can. 1043.)

In danger of death, local Ordinaries, for the purpose of quieting conscience and, in a proper case, of effecting the legitimation of children, both as to the form to be observed in the celebration of marriage, and as to each and every impediment of ecclesiastical law, public as well as occult, even though multiple, except the impediments arising from the sacred order of the priesthood and from affinity in the direct line based on a consummated marriage, can dispense their own subjects wherever they may dwell, and all persons actually staying in their territory, provided that scandal be removed and that, if a dispensation is granted from disparity of cult or mixed religion, the usual promises be given. (Can. 1043.)

> 1. *Nature and extent of the power:* the local Ordinary's power is ordinary power and hence may be delegated to others, even habitually; it may be used even if recourse to the Holy See is possible; it may be used on one's subjects everywhere and on non-subjects when in the Ordinary's territory; it extends to all impediments that are certainly of ecclesiastical law only, with the two exceptions mentioned in the Canon; it extends to impediments from which the Holy See only rarely dispenses, v.g., diaconate, conjugicide; it does not extend to impediments which are certainly or most probably of divine law, i.e., consanguinity in the direct line and in the first degree of the collateral line, previous bond, certain impotence; it extends to the form of marriage, *but not to the renewal of consent.* (V.C., II, n. 307.) (*As to the necessary renewal of consent* confer pp. 293-296.)
>
> 2. *Conditions for the use of the faculty:*

a. For the valid use of the faculties, it is necessary that danger of death probably exists; it need not be the *articulum mortis*, i.e., the last moment, but the danger of death suffices, provided that the danger is certain or seriously probable; the danger may affect only one of the parties, the party directly dispensed or the other party, the Catholic or the non-Catholic party; the danger may arise from intrinsic causes (v.g., sickness) or extrinsic causes (v.g., impending air raid, floods, impending serious surgical operation; the case of one going to the front lines, or being held in prison for proximate execution, etc.).

b. The reason for the dispensation must be either the quieting of conscience or the legitimation of the children. The first is had if the dispensation and consequent marriage or convalidation remove the parties from proximate danger of incontinence, if sins against charity or justice are prevented, or the marriage makes amends for former sins.

The second reason, legitimation of children, is had if a child has been conceived out of wedlock, or has already been born. If the child is conceived but not yet born, it is born legitimate if the parents marry before its birth; if the child is already born it is legitimated by a dispensation from a diriment impediment if the child is not adulterine (conceived when one of the parents was bound by another marriage) or sacrilegious (conceived when one of the parties was bound by sacred orders or solemn vows), (Can. 1051); a child already born is also legitimated by the subsequent marriage of the parents or the convalidation of an invalid marriage, if the parents were capable for marriage (i.e., could have validly married) either at the time of the child's conception or the pregnancy or the child's birth. (Can. 1116.)

Note: According to a probable opinion, neither of the reasons (peace of conscience, legitimation of children) is necessary for the valid or even licit use of the faculty to dispense. It suffices that danger of death be present and that some reason be had to render the celebration of the marriage useful. (Thus Vlaming, p. 300.)

c. In granting dispensations from disparity of cult or mixed religion the guaranties must be given first. They are required for the validity of the dispensation. (S.O., 14 Jan., 1932.)

d. The removal of scandal spoken of in the canon is a condition for the licit use but not for the valid use of the faculty.

B. *Powers of the Pastor, Assisting Priest, Confessor.* (Can. 1044.)

1. In the same circumstances as those mentioned in

Canon 1043 but only *for cases in which not even the local Ordinary can be reached,* the same faculty of dispensing is enjoyed by the pastor, the priest who assists at the marriage in accordance with Canon 1098, 2°, and the confessor, but the latter enjoys the faculty only for the internal forum in the course of a sacramental confession. (Can. 1044.)

Hence, in danger of death, for the purpose of peace of conscience, of legitimation of children, these priests may dispense from the form (but not from renewal of consent) and from impediments of ecclesiastical law, two impediments being excepted. Scandal must be avoided, and the *cautiones* given in the proper case. *(Details on these points in A,* 1 *and* 2 *above.)* The Ordinary cannot be reached (a requirement for the valid use of the faculty) if he cannot be reached in the normal way, i.e., by writing or by personal visit; the use of telephone or telegraph is extraordinary in law and is not to be considered. (Cf. PCI, reply, 12 Nov., 1922.) The Ordinary is also considered out of reach, if he cannot be approached without danger of violating the sacramental seal or a secret. (Genicot, II, n. 593.)

a. *The Pastor.* His power is ordinary jurisdiction and hence may be delegated to others even habitually; it may be used for the internal or external forum; the impediment may be occult or public; the pastor may use the faculty in favor of his subjects everywhere and in favor of all others who are actually within the confines of his parish. (V.C., II, n. 311.)

b. *The Assisting Priest.* The power to dispense from the form and the impediments in danger of death is granted to the priest who is present at a marriage celebrated in danger of death before only two witnesses because the pastor or a priest delegated by him is absent or impeded from witnessing the marriage. (Cf. p. 256 for further details.)

This faculty is given to every priest who assists at a marriage celebrated under such circumstances; it may be used for the external forum and for either occult or public impediments. For the validity of the dispensation it is required that there be danger of death, that the *cautiones* be given in mixed marriages, that it is not possible to contact the Ordinary in time to take care of the case, and according to some that the dispensation be given for peace of conscience or legitimation of children.

It is probable that an assistant pastor delegated by the pastor to assist at marriages enjoys the same power as the assisting priest of Canon 1098, 2°. Hence, he too may dispense according to the norms of Canon 1044. (Genicot, II, n. 593; V.C., II, n. 311.)

c. *The Confessor.* The confessor has the same power as the others mentioned in Canon 1044 but may use it only in the sacramental forum. Many authors restrict the use of this power to cases which are, at least in fact, occult. However, it is probable that the power may be used even over impediments which are by nature and in fact public; but the confessor is advised in such cases to get the matter outside of the sacramental forum and obtain faculties from the pastor to handle the case in the external forum, or if time does not allow for this, to take the matter outside of the sacramental forum and then assist at the marriage as the assisting priest of Canon 1098, 2°. (Payen, I, n. 673.)

2. Recording dispensations granted in danger of death: if the pastor or the assisting priest grant a dispensation for the external forum they are to inform the Ordinary, and to record the dispensation in the matrimonial register, (Can. 1046); if they dispense from occult impediments in the internal extra-sacramental forum, they are to inform the Ordinary so that the dispensation can be recorded in the secret archives of the Episcopal Curia. (Can. 1047.) The confessor does not record the dispensation since he can give it in the sacramental forum only.

C. *Oriental Law*

1. The local Hierarch has the same power as is given the local Ordinary by the Latin Code. (Mp, Can. 33.)

2. The pastor, *assistant pastor,* assisting priest, and confessor enjoy the same faculties in danger of death as are described in Canon 1044 of the Latin Code. (Mp, Can. 34.)

IV. DISPENSATION IN URGENT CASES

A. *Powers of the Local Ordinary.* (Can. 1045 §§ 1,2.)

Local Ordinaries may dispense from all impediments of ecclesiastical law, public as well as occult, even though multiple, except the impediments arising from the sacred order of the priesthood and from affinity in the direct line based on a consummated marriage, whenever the impediment is discovered only when everything is already prepared for the marriage and the marriage cannot, without probable danger of grave harm, be deferred until a dispensation is obtained from the Holy See. They may dispense their own subjects wherever they may be staying, and all others actually staying in their territory, provided that scandal be removed and that, if a dispensation is granted from disparity of cult or mixed religion, the usual promises be given. (Can. 1045 § 1.)

This faculty holds also for the convalidation of a marriage already contracted, if there is the same danger in delay and there is not sufficient time for recourse to the Holy See. (Can. 1045 § 2.)

1. For the use of the faculties it is required that there be probable danger of grave harm in a delay. Examples are the loss of reputation owing to the fact that a child has been conceived, scandal, the danger of incontinence, danger of a merely civil marriage, notable financial loss.

To obtain a dispensation from the Holy See the ordinary time consumed is from six to eight weeks. Means such as telephone or cable, etc., need not be used, since these are considered extraordinary in law. (Cf. PCI, 12 Nov., 1922.)

2. It is also required that preparations have already been made for the marriage. This condition is usually verified as soon as the proclamation of the banns has been begun even though not all the material preparations have been completed. The fact that the invitations have not been issued does not necessarily exclude the use of the faculties (S.R.R., case, 25 May, 1925.)

3. The existence of the impediment is discovered only after preparations have been made and it is too late to defer the marriage; that is, it is only then that the impediment is discovered

by the pastor or Ordinary, even though the parties knew about it beforehand (cf. PCI, 1 March, 1921), so that to avoid grave harm the wedding must be celebrated within a shorter time than that which is required to obtain a dispensation from the Holy See.

4. The power granted by Canon 1045 enables the Ordinary to dispense from the impediments but not from the canonical form. Some authors teach that the power includes also the faculty to dispense from the form, and, although the arguments they adduce are not convincing, out of respect for the learning of the authors who hold this opinion we may admit that the opinion is probable. (Cf. Payen, I, n. 648.)

5. When the Ordinary uses Canon 1045 to convalidate a marriage already contracted, it is not necessary that the impediment be just now discovered. Danger in delay is had if the parties cannot be separated without grave harm (v.g., because all think them to be husband and wife, because there are children to care for, etc.) nor can they live together without danger of incontinence.

6. By virtue of Canon 81 the Ordinary may dispense from impediments from which the Holy See is wont to dispense, even in cases where all things are not prepared for the wedding, but it is difficult to make recourse to the Holy See and at the same time there is danger of grave harm in delay. (PCI, 27 July, 1942.) For example, no preparations have been made for a wedding but the girl is pregnant.

The faculties granted by Canon 81 do not extend to impediments arising from reserved vows or from the subdiaconate and diaconate. (PCI, reply, 26 Jan., 1949.) These impediments may be dispensed from by the Ordinary only in urgent cases falling under Canon 1045 and in danger of death, Canon 1043.

B. *Powers of the Pastor, Assisting Priest, Confessor.* (Can. 1045 § 3.)

1. In the same circumstances as described in paragraphs 1 and 2 of Canon 1045, the pastor, the priest who assists at the marriage in accordance with Canon 1098, and the confessor (but the latter only for the internal forum in the course of a sacramental confession), enjoy the same faculty (as the Ordinary) *but only for occult cases* in which not even the local Ordinary can be reached or in which he cannot be reached without the danger of the

violation of a secret, provided that scandal is removed and that if a dispensation is granted from disparity of cult or mixed religion, the usual promises are given. (Can. 1045 § 3.) Hence the faculties granted here may be used only:

a.   if preparations have been made for the marriage and there is probable danger of grave harm in delay;

b.   if the local Ordinary cannot be reached by the ordinary means of letter or personal visit in time to avoid the danger of grave harm, or cannot be reached without the danger of the violation of a secret, certainly the secret of the seal of confession and also any professional secret;

c.   to dispense from all impediments of ecclesiastical law, with two exceptions, and according to some from the canonical form also;

d.   *only for occult impediments;* however, the faculties may be used over impediments that are by nature public (v.g., consanguinity, age) as long as they are in fact occult (PCI, 28 Dec., 1927);

e.   if there is danger of harm in delaying until a dispensation can be obtained from the Ordinary, the faculties may be used also for the *convalidation* of an invalid marriage.

> *The pastor.* The pastor's power is ordinary and hence may be delegated even habitually; he may dispense his own subjects anywhere, and all others who are actually within his territory.
>
> *The assisting priest.* This priest assists at a marriage celebrated before only two witnesses in the case where the Ordinary or pastor or a priest delegated by them cannot without grave inconvenience assist at the marriage, and it is prudently judged that this state of affairs will last for a month or more. (Can. 1098.)
>
> *The confessor.* The confessor has power for the sacramental forum only. The power may be used to dispense from impediments which are by nature public, provided that they are in fact occult. Whenever possible the confessor should get the case outside of the sacramental forum, and either send the parties

to the pastor or obtain faculties from the pastor to handle the case.

2. Recording the dispensation: according to the norm of Canon 1047, the pastor and the assisting priest who dispense in the extra-sacramental forum from occult impediments in the urgent case, should record the dispensation in the secret archives of the diocesan curia. (Abbo-Hannan, II, n. 1047.) Should the occult impediment later become public, no further dispensation for the external forum is necessary. (Can. 1047.) The confessor, since he dispenses only in the sacramental forum, does not record the dispensation anywhere; however, if the impediment later becomes public, since the dispensation was given only in the sacramental forum, it will now become necessary to obtain a dispensation also for the external forum. (Can. 1047.) It is for this reason that the confessor should, if possible, get the case out of the sacramental forum in the first place and handle it in the external or at least in the extra-sacramental forum.

C. *Oriental Law*

1. The local Hierarch has the same powers in the urgent case when all is prepared for the marriage, or for convalidation, as does the Latin Ordinary. However, recourse in due time to avoid the danger must be impossible both to the Holy See and to the Patriarch. (Mp, Can. 35 § 1.)

The local Hierarch also enjoys the same powers over matrimonial impediments and the form of marriage as does the Latin Ordinary by Canon 81, when recourse to the Holy See or to a legate of the Roman Pontiff, endowed with the necessary faculty, is difficult, and at the same time there is danger of serious harm in delay. (Mp, Can. 35 § 4.)

2. The pastor, *assistant pastor,* assisting priest and con-

fessor enjoy the same faculties in the urgent case as are described in Canon 1045 of the Latin Code. (Mp, Can. 35 § 3.)

V. REASONS FOR DISPENSATIONS

A. *Distinctions*

1. *Motive causes* for dispensations are such reasons as are sufficient to move the superior to grant a dispensation; *persuasive causes (causae impulsivae)* are such as are not in themselves weighty enough for the granting of a dispensation, but they aid the motive cause in so far as they persuade the superior to grant the dispensation more easily or more readily. Several persuasive causes grouped together in the same case may amount to a motive cause which is sufficient for the granting of the dispensation.

2. *Canonical causes* are such as are accepted by the Roman Curia; all others are *uncanonical*. Usually canonical causes are motive causes, but with regard to dispensations from certain impediments not all but only some of the canonical causes are considered as motive and the others are merely persuasive. On the other hand, causes which are not canonical are in themselves merely persuasive, and of themselves do not suffice for dispensations from any impediment. They can, however, induce a final or motive cause if several coalesce and are taken collectively.

B. *Enumeration of Reasons*

According to various instructions of the Holy See issued before the Code, the authors make the following distinctions of causes:

1. *Canonical causes which are motive causes:*

a. *Affecting the public good:* intercourse, especially if publicly known; pregnancy and hence the legitimation of children; the convalidation of an invalid marriage, even though the marriage had been entered into before a civil official or before an heretical minister; the fear of a merely civil marriage or of a marriage before an heretical minister; the danger of public concubinage; the removal of grave scandals (arising from concubinage, hatred, enmity); public peace (v.g., extinction of enmity between families); litigation over inheritance; the well-founded hope of the conversion of the non-Catholic party to a mixed marriage; the danger of apostasy on the part of the Catholic party; the good of children already born (their Catholic education).

b. *Affecting only the private good of individuals* (which reasons therefore do not suffice for the dispensations from the impediments of mixed religion and disparity of cult, cf. Abbo-Hannan,

II, p. 233; Quigley, p. 11): the poverty of a widow who has a large family or who is young and in danger of incontinence; the limitations of the neighborhood (*angustia loci*); the advanced age of the woman (*aetas superadulta,* 24) which does not hold if the woman is a widow; the lack of inadequacy of the dowry.

2. *Canonical causes which are only persuasive (impulsivae):* secret intercourse; suspected intimacy with cohabitation; the loss of a woman's reputation because of suspected intercourse with one related by consanguinity or affinity; the excellence of the petitioner's merits because of his great services to the Church.

3. *Non-canonical causes,* all of which are persuasive and not motive: the loss of a woman's parents; illegitimacy, infirmity or deformity on the part of the woman; the man is a widower with children; both petitioners are very good people, they are very generous towards the poor; also mutual aid in advanced age; the help which one of their parents will obtain from the marriage, etc.

The explanation of these reasons may be found in Abbo-Hannan, II, pp. 233-238; Genicot, II, n. 596; Quigley, pp. 10-13. When the pastor applies for a dispensation he will find the various reasons listed on the form sent him by the Chancery. He must decide which reasons can be found in the case and report them to the Chancery with the petition for the dispensation.

C. *Importance of the Reasons*

1. No dispensation from an ecclesiastical law can be granted without a just and reasonable cause proportionate to the gravity of the law from which a dispensation is given; otherwise a dispensation granted by a subordinate is illicit and invalid. (Can. 84 § 1.)

Hence, when the pastor applies for a dispensation, he has a grave obligation to certify to the existence and the truth of the reasons alleged, for the local Ordinary cannot grant a dispensation from a law of the Code validly without a proportionate cause. If the cause is false the dispensation will ordinarily be invalid.

2. When there is doubt about the sufficiency of the cause, the dispensation may be licitly asked for and licitly and validly granted. (Can. 84 § 2.)

According to the common opinion, the same rule applies also when there is doubt as to the very existence of the cause. (Coronata, I, n. 115); and if after the dispensation is granted it should become evident that the reason for the dispensation was not sufficient or was non-existent, it is probable that the dispensation is still valid, provided that all concerned acted in good faith. (Coronata, I, n. 115.)

CHAPTER VI

Matrimonial Consent

I. NATURE OF MATRIMONIAL CONSENT

1. *Definition and Effect*

Matrimonial consent is an act of the will by which each party gives and accepts a perpetual and exclusive right over the body, for acts which are by their nature suitable for the generation of children. (Can. 1081 § 2.) Marriage is effected by consent legally expressed between persons who are capable according to law; and this consent no human power can supply. (Can. 1081 § 1.)

2. *Perseverance*

Even though a marriage has been contracted invalidly because of an impediment, the consent which has been given is presumed to persevere until its revocation shall have been proved. (Can. 1093.)

> The most important application of the presumption stated in this canon takes place in a *santio in radice* where an invalid marriage is validated without the renewal of consent. Consent must exist at the time when the *sanatio* takes place, but the presumption of this canon is sufficient to show that the consent once given still exists, unless it can be proved that it was revoked.

3. *Oriental Law:* Canons 72 and 84 of *Crebrae allatae* contain the same principles as do Canons 1081 and 1093 of the Latin Code.

II. DEFECTIVE CONSENT

A. *Ignorance and Error*

1. *Ignorance of the nature of marriage.* In order that matrimonial consent be possible, it is necessary that the contracting parties shall not be ignorant at least of the fact that marriage is a permanent society between a man and a woman for the procreation of children. Lack of this knowl-

edge is not presumed after the age of puberty. (Can. 1082.)

> For a valid matrimonial consent the parties must know at least:

> a. That marriage is a permanent union, not merely a transient companionship. As will be pointed out in the next canon, it is not necessary to know that the union is indissoluble.

> b. That marriage is a society for the procreation of children. It is not necessary to know the way in which children are procreated, provided *that the parties know that it is done by their own mutual and bodily cooperation.* (Rota case, 20, Jan., 1926). Hence distinct and explicit knowledge, either of the sexual act or of the way in which, or the organs by which, it is exercised, is not required. (Rota case, 30 July, 1927.) But if a girl thinks that offspring is born as a result of kisses, and lacks even a confused and vague knowledge that some other sort of bodily union is required, it would seem that she lacks sufficient knowledge for a valid matrimonial consent. (Abbo-Hannan, II, n. 1082.) For a valid consent, one must have at least a vague knowledge that some sort of carnal familiarity is required for the birth of offspring and one must surrender whatever right is necessary for that familiarity and accept a similar right from the other party.

2. *Error in regard to the person*

a. Error regarding the person makes marriage invalid. (Can. 1083 § 1.)

b. Error regarding a quality of the person, even though it is the cause of the contract, invalidates marriage in the following cases only:

If the error regarding the quality amounts to an error regarding the person.

If a free person contracts marriage with a person whom he or she believes to be free, but who is on the contrary a slave, in strictly servile bondage. (Can. 1083 § 2.)

> A person may be identified not only by personal appearance and by name but also by a certain quality which distinguishes him from others. Hence, it may happen that an error as to a quality of the person in reality results in an error concerning the identity of the person, namely, in the case where the person

is identified in the mind of the other party by a certain personal quality.

In other cases an error of quality does not invalidate the contract. If a man marries, thinking the bride to be healthy, rich, a virgin, etc., and later finds out he was in error, the contract is valid even though he would not have married had he known the truth. The only way in which such an error would invalidate the contract is in the case where the quality is made a *conditio sine qua non* of the contract, for in that case the error is substantial, not accidental. (Cf. Can. 104.)

3. *Error in regard to the essential properties of marriage.* Simple error regarding the unity or the indissolubility or the sacramental dignity of marriage, even though it be the motivating reason for making the contract, does not invalidate matrimonial consent. (Can. 1084.)

Error is *simple* if it remains in the mind without passing over to the will. It exists when error in the mind remains speculative and is not actually incorporated in the choice made by the will. Despite this error concerning the indissolubility, unity, or sacramental dignity of the marriage, the will wishes to contract a marriage that is valid, a marriage as it has been instituted by' the law of nature. The fact that one would not have chosen marriage in the absence of the error is an hypothetical fact; the *actual* fact is that the will has chosen marriage, without making any explicit modification or reservation.

On the other hand, if the error modifies the act of the will, so that the consent is explicitly directed to, v.g., a dissoluble marriage, it is no longer simple error; it is then an error explicitly incorporated as a condition or reservation in the contract and hence the matrimonial consent is vitiated (Cf. Vlaming, p. 385.) It is one thing to contract a marriage which one thinks is soluble, or even to contract *because* one thinks it is soluble, and another thing not to intend to contract *unless* it is soluble. Thus, if one wishes to contract a trial marriage the consent is invalid because indissolubility is positively excluded.

4. *Error in regard to the validity of the marriage.* The knowledge or belief that the marriage is null does not necessarily exclude matrimonial consent. (Can. 1085.)

The reason for this is that together with the knowledge or the opinion of nullity there can exist a will to enter marriage in so far as one can; true matrimonial consent can easily exist even though the marriage itself is invalid, v.g., because of the impediment of previous bond.

B.   *Lack of True Consent*

1.   *Simulation*. Simulation is had when one does not have the intention to contract marriage even though he go through the formalities. Simulation invalides marriage since matrimonial consent is lacking. There is no intention to contract a marriage. However, simulation must be proved, since "the internal consent of the mind is always presumed to be in conformity with the words or signs used in the celebration of marriage." (Can. 1086 § 1.)

2.   *Exclusion of the bona matrimonii*

a.   If either party or both parties by a positive act of the will exclude marriage itself, or all right to the conjugal act, or any essential property of marriage, the marriage contract is invalid. (Can. 1086 § 2.)

> *Exclude marriage itself:* the case of total simulation treated above under n. 1.

> *All right to the conjugal act:* this right is the essential object of the contract, and if the *right* to conjugal act is excluded only for a specified time, v.g., during the fertile periods, the contract is invalid. (Pius XII, allocution, 29 Oct., 1951.)

> *Any essential property:* i.e., unity and indissolubility.

b.   In cases involving intentions contrary to the *bona matrimonii* one must be careful to distinguish *the intention not to grant the right or not to assume the obligation* from *the intention merely of not fulfilling the obligations* imposed by the marriage contract. Thus if a person enter marriage by a consent which excludes the right or obligation to normal intercourse, to perpetuity of the bond, or of fidelity, the marriage is invalid. In marriages of this kind one intends to contract only with the reservation that onanism be practiced (*contra bonum prolis*) or that one be permitted to have affairs with others (*contra bonum fidei*) or that divorce be permitted (*contra bonum sacramenti*).

On the other hand, one may enter marriage with the intention merely not to fulfill the obligation assumed. Thus, if the parties intend to practice birth-control or intend to commit adultery, the marriage is valid. But if they contract marriage with the intention to divorce if the marriage is unhappy, the marriage is invalid, because in this case the exclusion of the obligation itself cannot be distinguished from the intention not to fulfill the obligation. The intention to obtain a divorce must be understood as an intention to contract a dissoluble union, for the presumption in this case is that the person reserves to himself the right to depart and contract another marriage. In this case, the bond is assumed without indissolubility and hence invalidly.

> In practice it is most difficult to ascertain whether there is a true reservation or condition contrary to the substance of marriage, i.e., excluding the *bonum prolis, fidei* or *sacramenti,* or merely an intention or agreement to abuse the marriage. Cases of this type must be handled in the ecclesiastical courts according to the norms of procedure established in law.

3. *Force and Fear.* That marriage is invalid which has been contracted under the influence of coercion or grave intimidation unjustly induced from without, to free oneself from which, one is compelled to choose marriage. No other kind of intimidation, even though it is the motivating reason for the contract entails the nullity of the marriage. (Can. 1087.)

> To invalidate marriage consent, the fear must be:
>
> a. *Grave,* in so far as the evil threatened is serious and imminent, or at least that the one suffering the fear so conceives the situation.
>
> b. *Inspired from without,* that is, by another person. Reverential fear may be internal to oneself and not at all inspired by one's parents, for it may arise from one's imagination rather than from the action of the parents. However, it may also be true fear applied by one's parents, and it can be grave if it

consists in excessive and prolonged indignation on the part of one's parents, accompanied by annoying importunities, even when there are no threats of physical punishment or of loss of inheritance or of ejection from the parental dwelling. (Abbo-Hannan, II, n. 1087.)

c. *Unjust,* that is, the evil threatened is unjust either in itself or in the manner in which it is applied. The threat of prison for a seducer is *unjust in itself* because the payment of compensation or damages is a choice to which the culprit is justly entitled. The threat of punishment without due process of law is *unjustly applied* even though the punishment itself be justly merited. (Bouscaren-Ellis, p. 555.)

d. *Forcing one to contract marriage,* i.e., in order to escape the fear the person is compelled to choose marriage. The person is convinced that he cannot free himself from the fear except by contracting marriage. There is no alternative.

Special questions:

a. Must the fear be applied precisely with the purpose of compelling assent to the marriage? The question is disputed; more probably it is not required that the fear be applied with this intention in mind, but it is sufficient that the one undergoing the fear cannot free himself from it unless he choose marriage. (Gasparri, II, n. 856; V.C., II, n. 376; thus also S.R. R., case, 20 April, 1956; applies also when one party is a Latin, the other an Oriental, cf. S.R.R., case, 23 March, 1956; *Periodica,* XLV, pp. 30ss.)

b. Does grave fear invalidate marriage by natural law or merely by ecclesiastical law? The question is disputed. Coronata, Wernz-Vidal, Cappello, hold that the consent is invalid by virtue of the natural law; Vermeersch-Creusen, Gasparri, Genicot, claim that the consent is invalid only by ecclesiastical law. Hence, marriage entered into because of grave fear unjustly applied will be of doubtful validity if both parties are infidels. If one party is an infidel and the other party is baptized, Genicot and Gasparri hold that the marriage is invalid if the baptized party suffers the fear; Bouscaren and Cappello hold that the marriage is invalid even if it is the infidel party who suffers the fear. As is evident, these cases will, of necessity, be adjudged by the ecclesiastical courts.

C. *Oriental Law*

In Oriental law the same norms hold for defective consent (ignorance, error of person, error of essential properties, error concerning validity, simulation, exclusion of the

bona matrimonii, force and fear) as in the Latin Code.
(Mp, Canons 73-78.) One difference exists, however,
namely, in order to invalidate marriage, grave fear unjustly
caused must be applied *with the purpose of compelling
assent to the marriage.* (Mp, Can. 78.)

III. MANIFESTATION OF CONSENT

A. *Presence*

1. In order that marriage be contracted validly it is
necessary that the contracting parties be present either in
person or by proxy. (Can. 1088 § 1.)

> In virtue of this canon marriage is not contracted validly if
> the parties are only morally present, i.e., by telephone, radio,
> letter, etc. (Vlaming, p. 377.) The prescription of this canon is
> of ecclesiastical law only and hence does not bind infidels. How-
> ever, baptized non-Catholics are bound by this canon. (S.O.,
> reply, 30 June, 1949.)
>
> The marriage of a baptized non-Catholic contracted *in ab-
> sentia* without a proxy, can be declared null by the Ordinary
> after a simple investigation to ascertain the certainty of the
> fact; no procedure, not even summary is required. (S.O., 16
> Nov., 1949.)

2. The parties must express matrimonial consent in
words; and they may not use equivalent signs if they are
able to speak. (Can. 1088 § 2.)

> The use of the faculty of speech, as well as the use of the
> words of the Roman Ritual concern the licitness, not the va-
> lidity of the marriage ceremony.
>
> *Oriental Law:* the Oriental legislation regarding the presence
> of the parties and the use of the faculty of speech is the same
> as the Latin legislation. (Mp, Can. 79.)

B. *Marriage by Proxy*

1. Without prejudice to diocesan statutes containing
further regulations, in order that a marriage may be validly
contracted by proxy, a special mandate is required for the
contracting of marriage with a specific person, signed by
the person giving the mandate, and either by the pastor or

the Ordinary of the place in which the mandate is given, or by a priest delegated by either of these, or by at least two witnesses. (Can. 1089 § 1.)

A special mandate is required, i.e., one for contracting marriage; it is not sufficient that one give a general mandate for the placing of all legal acts in one's name.

The mandate must be to contract marriage with a *specific* person; hence, one cannot give a mandate which would allow the proxy to choose a spouse and marry her in the name of the one giving the mandate.

The proxy must be designated by the one giving the mandate and this designation may not be committed to others. (S.O., reply, 31 May, 1948.)

Probably the date must be affixed to the mandate for its validity. (Sipos, § 132.)

In some States, proxy marriages are not legally permitted, and the priest is advised to familiarize himself with the laws of his own State before proceeding with a proxy marriage.

2. If the principal does not know how to write, this shall be noted in the mandate and another witness shall be added, and the latter shall also sign the document; otherwise the mandate is invalid. (Can. 1089 § 2.)

3. If, before the proxy has contracted in the name of the principal, the latter has revoked the mandate or become insane, the marriage is invalid, even though these facts were unknown to the proxy or to the other contracting party. (Can. 1089 § 3.)

4. That the marriage be valid the proxy must perform his function in person. (Can. 1089 § 4.)

The authors commonly teach that the principal cannot, in the mandate, authorize the proxy to substitute another for himself. (Sipos, § 132.)

Oriental Law. Canon 81 of the *motu proprio* is practically the same as Canon 1089 of the Latin Code. But Canon 80 of the Oriental legislation states that marriage cannot be contracted by proxy unless in a certain case the local Hierarch grants permission in writing; and Canon 82 adds that in order to contract marriage by proxy validly, it is necessary to observe the contractual formalities stated in Canons 85 and 86. (These canons will be treated under the canonical form of marriage for Orientals.)

C. *Marriage Through an Interpreter*

Marriage can be contracted through an interpreter. (Can. 1090.)

> *Oriental Law.* The Oriental legislation says nothing about the use of an interpreter.

D. *Permission for Lawful Use of Interpreter or Proxy*

A pastor shall not assist at a marriage that is to be contracted with the use of a proxy or an interpreter unless there be a just cause for doing so and the authenticity of the mandate and the trustworthiness of the interpreter are beyond all question of doubt, and even then, if time permits, he needs the permission of the Ordinary. (Can. 1091.)

IV. CONDITIONAL CONSENT

1. A condition once placed and not revoked:

a. If it is a condition regarding a future event which is necessary, or impossible, or immoral but not contrary to the substance of marriage, it is to be considered as not having been made. (Can. 1092, 1°.)

> Future necessary: I marry you if the sun rises tomorrow.
>
> Future impossible: I marry you if you learn ten languages in a week.
>
> Future immoral: I marry you if you give up the Catholic Faith.
>
> If any such conditions are attached to the matrimonial consent they are presumed not to be serious or not to have been meant; however, the presumption is overcome by the opposite truth. Hence, if one seriously attaches an impossible condition, the marriage is invalid; if a necessary condition, the marriage is suspended until the condition is verified.
>
> In regard to an immoral condition seriously meant, if the validity of the consent is made to depend on the assumption of an obligation to do evil, the contract is null, for no one can be obliged to do evil. Thus: I marry you if you oblige yourself to educate the children in Protestantism; the marriage is invalid

since no such obligation can be imposed. If however the validity of the consent is made to depend on whether one here and now has the intention to do evil, v.g., I marry you if here and now you have the intention to educate the children in Protestantism, if the other party has such an intention, the marriage is valid, invalid if the party has no such intention. Intentions such as these, however, are usually not added as a *conditio sine qua non* so that the party does not wish to contract marriage unless the other actually intends to do the evil, but these intentions are added as an accessory obligation, as an *onus* added to the contract, which indeed the other must fulfill, but which is not intended to affect in any way the main clauses of the contract, i.e., is not intended to condition the validity of the marriage contract. In law such an attached *onus* is called a *mode*. (Cf. Genicot, II, n. 623.)

b. If the condition concerns the future and is contrary to the substance of marriage, it makes the marriage invalid. (Can. 1092, 2°.)

Conditions contrary to the substance of marriage are such as are *contra bonum prolis, fidei et sacramenti.* Confer our commentary above under Canon 1086 where the doctrine is explained under the aspect of intentions contrary to the three *bona* of matrimony.

A marriage of heretics celebrated according to a formula containing a condition opposed to indissolubility (v.g., permitting divorce because of adultery, "I take you as wife unless you commit adultery, when the bond shall cease") would be invalid; for the spouses are considered as giving a mere rescindible consent in conformity with the formula according to which the marriage is being celebrated. (V.C., II, n. 381; cf. also Abbo-Hannan, II, p. 332.)

Some authors consider conditions contrary to the physical rearing of the child as being *contra bonum prolis,* v.g., if you procure abortion, if you kill the babies, etc. These conditions, however, are not *contra bonum prolis,* for abortion and the killing of a new born child do not exclude the right to acts which are in themselves suitable for the generation of children. (Sipos, § 133.)

c. If the condition concerns the future and is licit, it suspends the validity of the marriage. (Can. 1092, 3°.)

Licit future condition: I marry you on condition that you give up excessive drinking within a month. Here we have *a true* matrimonial consent but its efficacy is suspended for a time —

until the condition is fulfilled. Here and now no marriage is effected, but once the condition is fulfilled the marriage materializes without a renewal of consent. If, however, one withdraws his consent before the condition is fulfilled, the marriage will never materialize, i.e., there is no marriage.

If the condition is: "Provided a dispensation is granted from a diriment impediment which binds us," the marriage is valid upon the granting of the dispensation. (Timlin, CUA, n. 89, pp. 101, 180.) Others hold that in virtue of Canon 1133 the consent must be renewed after the dispensation is granted. (V.C., II, n. 381.)

d. If the condition concerns the past or the present, the marriage will be valid or not according as the matter concerning which the condition is made exists or not. (Can. 1092, 4°.)

Past condition: I marry provided you have never had sex relations with other men.

Present condition: I marry provided you are sincere in your promise to have the children baptized and reared in the Catholic Church.

In such marriages the marriage is valid at once if the condition is verified, otherwise it is null from the beginning since the consent is attached to the fulfillment or existence of the condition.

2. In the pre-nuptial interrogation the pastor must ask the parties if they are placing any conditions on their matrimonial consent. If they are, he must ask them to explain how they intend to ascertain whether the condition is verified. The pastor *must consult the local Ordinary* before allowing parties to impose even lawful conditions on their consent. (S.C.Sacr., instr., 29 June, 1941.)

3. *Oriental Law*. Canon 83 of *Crebrae allatae* states that marriage cannot be contracted on condition. This prohibition affects the licitness and not the validity of the marriage and, hence, if a condition is actually placed we may judge the validity of the marriage according to the rules stated in Canon 1092 of the Latin Code, applying them to these Oriental marriages. We do this since we consider

the rules of Canon 1092 declarations of obscure points of the natural law itself. Hence, with ordinary licit conditions, the marriage is suspended until the condition is fulfilled; if the condition is contrary to the substance of the contract the marriage is invalid, etc. (Sipos, § 133; Pospishil, pp. 120-121; Coussa, III, n. 158.)

CHAPTER VII

The Form of Marriage

I. PRE-CODE LAW

1. According to *the natural law* alone a clandestine marriage (without formality and without witnesses but with a mutual, external expression of matrimonial consent) is valid. However, both ecclesiastical and civil law can demand certain formalities to be observed for the validity of the contract.

2. *The Tametsi*

a. The form demanded for the validity of marriage by the Council of Trent is contained in the decree *Tametsi*. It states that marriage is invalid unless contracted in the presence of *one's own pastor,* or another priest delegated by one's pastor or Ordinary, and at least two witnesses.

b. This law was to be promulgated by command of the bishop in the individual parishes, in the vernacular, and as a law made by the Council, and in these parishes the law would oblige (not in others). In the course of time it was generally admitted that the promulgation was supplied by the observance of the decree for a long time as being imposed by the Council. (V.C., II, n. 385.)

c. Bound to this form were *all baptized persons (even heretics)* who married in the place where the decree was promulgated, even though they were *peregrini* or *vagi*. If one had a domicile or quasi-domicile in a place where the decree was promulgated he was bound to observe the decree even if he married in a place where it was not promulgated; but if the other party had a domicile or quasi-domicile in the place where the decree was not promulgated then both were exempted from the form if they married in the place where the decree was not promulgated.

d. The competent pastor was the pastor of the domicile or quasi-domicile of either of the spouses, and this pastor could validly assist at the marriage of his subjects anywhere, i.e., even outside his own territory. He could also delegate any other priest to assist at the marriage.

3. *Relaxations of the Tametsi*

a. *Declaratio Benedictina.* In 1741 Benedict XIV modified the force of the *Tametsi* for Holland in so far as he exempted heretics from the form when they married among themselves or with Catholics. Later this exemption was extended to some other countries where Protestants and Catholics lived side by side.

b. *Constitutio Provida.* From April 15, 1906 mixed marriages in Germany were exempted from the observance of the form; this exemption was extended to Hungary on Feb. 27, 1909. The rule of the *Provida* obtained until May 19, 1918 when the Code went into force. (Cf. details given in V.C., II, n. 388 and Sipos, § 134 in reference to the validity of mixed marriages celebrated in Germany and Hungary between 1906-1918.)

c. In the United States: the *Tametsi* and the *Declaratio Benedictina* were in force in the province of New Orleans, the province of San Francisco and the territory of Utah, with the exception of the section of Utah east of the Colorado River, the diocese of Vincennes (in Indiana); the cities and towns of St. Louis, St. Genevieve, Florissant, St. Charles, Kaskaskia, French Village, Cahokia, Prairie du Rocher.

The *Tametsi* but not the *Benedictina* was in force in the province of Santa Fe with the exception of the northern part of the territory of Colorado.

In all other places in the United States the *Tametsi* was not operative. (Balt. III, pp. cvii-cix.) In these places neither Catholics nor heretics were bound to observe a form of marriage for the validity of the contract.

4. The *Ne Temere*

a. From the 19th April, 1908, the form of the *Tametsi* was supplanted by the new form of the decree of Pius X, *Ne Temere*. Marriage can be contracted validly only before the pastor *of the place* or the Ordinary of the place, or their delegate, and two witnesses. Therefore, pastors and Ordinaries are competent only in their territory, but they can there assist at anyone's marriage. *Heretics are not bound to this form;* but a mixed marriage, i.e., between a Catholic and a heretic is subject to this form, except in Germany and Hungary, where the *Provida* remains in force until the Code.

b. Since most of the points of the *Ne Temere* have been incorporated into the Code, we shall indicate points of difference between the form of the Code and the form of the *Ne Temere* in the commentary on the individual canons of the Code which refer to the form of marriage.

II. THE FORM ACCORDING TO THE CODE

A. *Pastor and Witnesses*

1. Only those marriages are valid which are contracted in the presence of the pastor or the local Ordinary, or a priest delegated by either, and at least two witnesses, in accordance, however, with the rules given in the Canons which follow, and with the exceptions stated in Canons 1098, 1099. (Can. 1094.)

> Assistance at marriages is not an act of jurisdiction nor an act of the power of orders. It is very similar, however, to jurisdiction for the right and power to assist at marriages is had by reason of one's office, it can be delegated, and the act of assistance is requisite for the validity of the marriage. A reply of the Code Commission states that the prescription of Canon 209 (supplying of jurisdiction in common error and in positive and probable doubt) is to be applied in the case of a priest who, lacking delegation, assists at a marriage. (PCI, 26 March, 1952.)

> *Oriental Law*. The substantial form of matrimony is the same as in the Latin Code, but with this difference: the marriage must be contracted with a sacred rite, i.e., with the blessing of the priest who witnesses the marriage. (Mp, Can. 85.) The sacred rite required for the validity of the marriage is not a certain liturgical rite, but a simple blessing (PC Or., reply, 3 May, 1953); the orations and ceremonies are only *ad liceitatem*.

2. Besides pastors strictly so called, the following also enjoy the right of witnessing marriages:

a. The vicar of a moral person (v.g., religious pastor);

b. The administrator of a vacant parish;

c. The vicar substitute, i.e., the priest who takes the place of a pastor who must be absent from his parish for over a week; this priest has power to assist at marriages *after he has been approved by the Ordinary,* unless the pastor or Ordinary have excepted this power from his faculties. In case the pastor must leave suddenly and will be

absent for over a week, the priest he designated as his substitute has power to assist at marriages even *before* the
approval of the Ordinary, provided the Ordinary has been
notified of the designation of the supplying priest and has
not provided otherwise. (Canons 465 §§ 4, 5; PCI, reply,
14 July, 1922.)

    d. The vicar coadjutor (of Canon 475) *if* he is given
complete parochial authority;

    The *vicarius cooperator,* i.e., the assistant pastor, has no
power by reason of his office to assist at marriages (PCI, reply,
31 Jan., 1942), and hence can assist validly only if he is delegated by the pastor or the Ordinary.

    e. Missionaries to emigrants who have been given the care of
souls according to article 39 of the Apostolic Constitution *Exsul
Familiae* can validly assist at the marriage of their subjects within
the boundaries of the territory assigned to them. For licit assistance
Canon 1097 § 2 is to be observed. (S.C.Consist., decl., 7 Oct.,
1953.) Hence if one of the parties is his subject, the missionary
assists validly but only within the confines of the territory assigned
to him.

    f. Military chaplains usually receive faculties to assist at the
marriages of people who are subject to them; the faculty is cumulative with the faculty of the pastor of the place (cf. S.C.Consist.,
instr., 23 April, 1951), so that the subjects of the military chaplain
may contract marriage validly either in the presence of the competent chaplain or of the local pastor. (Cf. *Digest,* II, pp. 587-605.)

    g. Chaplains or rectors of hospitals and other pious institutions
which have been withdrawn from the jurisdiction of the local
pastor in accordance with Canon 464 § 2, can assist at the marriages of their *own subjects* and *only in the place* where they exercise their jurisdiction, provided they have been given the *full
parochial powers* in these places. (S.C.Conc., 1 Feb., 1908.)

    h. A putative pastor, namely, one who really is not the pastor
but who is commonly thought to be the pastor, assists validly at
marriages because the requisite power is supplied by Canon 209.

    3. The two witnesses who must assist at the marriage
with the pastor or local Ordinary must be present physically, and indeed simultaneously with the pastor. They
must be present morally so that they can testify to what is
taking place. They must be used as witnesses, but for va-

lidity it seems sufficient that they be implicitly designated by the parties, as they are whenever the parties in any way at all wish to contract in the presence of the persons who are watching the celebration of the marriage. (Genicot, II, n. 627.)

> Anyone capable of being a witness by natural law acts as a valid witness in a Catholic marriage, whether he be a minor, an infidel, a heretic, an excommunicated person, etc. Non-Catholics may not be used as witnesses licitly; the Ordinary, however, may tolerate the use of non-Catholic witnesses for a grave cause and provided scandal is avoided. (S.O., decr., 19 Aug., 1891.)

B. *Conditions for Valid Assistance*

1.   The pastor and local Ordinary validly assist at marriage (Can. 1095 § 1):

a.   Only from the day on which they took canonical possession of their benefice in accordance with Canons 334 and 1444, or entered their office, unless by sentence they have been excommunicated or interdicted or suspended from office, or by sentence it has been declared that they have incurred these penalties.

> Pastors take canonical possession of their parish by installation; the method of installation is determined by particular law or custom, and if the Ordinary dispenses from the installation, this dispensation is equivalent to canonical possession. (Can. 1444.)

> Those who have no benefice (v.g., the vicar substitute, military chaplain, etc.) enter their office by an appointment made according to the norms of law.

> The censured pastor must be a *sententiatus* before his act of assistance is invalid; the interdict spoken of in the canon is *personal* interdict; it is only suspension *ab officio* or a *suspensio generalis* which affects the valid assistance, and suspension from benefice, from orders, from divine acts, from jurisdiction would not invalidate the pastor's assistance. (Cappello, *De Sacr.*, V, n. 662.)

b.   Only within the limits of their territory; in which they validly assist at the marriages not only of their subjects but also of those who are not their subjects.

Hence the pastor cannot validly assist at the marriages of even his own subjects outside of his territory; but within his territory he may validly assist at the marriages of people who are not his subjects. Exceptions with regard to Orientals are listed below.

A church belonging to exempt religious is considered within the territory of the parish in which the pastor can validly assist at marriages. (S.C.Sacr., 12 March, 1910.)

A pastor who does not have a territory exclusively his own but who holds a territory cumulatively with another or with other pastors may validly assist at the marriage of subjects and non-subjects in the entire territory he holds cumulatively with other pastors. (S.C.Conc., 1 Feb., 1908.) This is the case with pastors of national parishes.

c. Only if, unconstrained by coercion or grave fear, they ask and receive the consent of the contracting parties.

Note the importance of an active assistance on the part of the pastor. Although the exact words of the Roman Ritual are not required for the validity of the marriage, nevertheless the pastor must in some positive way ask and receive the consent of the parties. Any way of acting (words, signs, nods) which signifies the asking and receiving of the consent of the parties is sufficient and is required for the validity of the assistance.

If the pastor is constrained to assist by threats of the parties to report him to the local Ordinary, or by threats of penalties made by the Ordinary against those who unjustly refuse to assist, the assistance at the marriage would be valid. (Abbo-Hannan, II, n. 1095, and others.) Likewise, fraud and deceit do not invalidate the pastor's assistance.

2. *Oriental Law.* What is stated concerning the valid assistance of the pastor or local Ordinary in Canon 1095 of the Code, is stated also in Canon 86 of *Crebrae allatae*. The following points, however, must be added:

a. The pastor and local Hierarch assist validly at a marriage only within the limits of their territory, whether the contracting parties are their subjects or not, *provided the parties belong to the same rite* as the pastor or the Hierarch. (Can. 86 § 1, 2°.) Hence at least one of the contracting parties must belong to the rite of the pastor who assists. The pastor of an Oriental rite cannot validly assist at a marriage of two Latins, and a pastor of the Latin rite cannot assist validly at a marriage of two Orientals. (PC Or., reply, 3 May, 1953.) However, a Latin pastor assists validly at the marriage of a Latin Catholic to an Oriental. (Sipos, § 134; Herman, *Periodica,* XXXVIII, p. 112.)

b. Exceptions to the rule stated in a: at a marriage of the faithful of a different rite (i.e., the parties are of a different rite than the pastor or Ordinary) that local Hierarch and that pastor can validly assist who according to the rules given here become the proper pastor or Hierarch:

1) In the territory (diocese) of their own rite, if the faithful of a certain rite do not have a pastor, their Hierarch shall assign the pastor of another rite who is to assume their care after the same Hierarch has obtained the consent of the Hierarch of the pastor so assigned. This pastor can then assist validly at the marriages of the people assigned to his care even though they belong to a different rite. (Can. 86 § 2; § 3, 2°.) Thus, Ruthenians in the United States are within the territory of their own Ruthenian diocese; if a Latin pastor in some place is charged with the care of the Ruthenian faithful by one of the Ruthenian Bishops or Exarchs in the United States, the pastor can validly assist at the marriages of these people.

2) Outside the territory (diocese) of one's rite, since there is no Hierarch of that rite, the local Hierarch is to be considered as the proper one. If there are several, he shall be considered the proper Hierarch who has been assigned to the Apostolic See. (Can. 86 § 2; § 3, 3°.)

In the United States there are several co-existent territorial jurisdictions; the jurisdiction of the Latin Ordinary, the jurisdiction of the Ruthenian Archbishop of Philadelphia, the jurisdiction of the Ruthenian Apostolic Exarch of Pittsburg, the jurisdiction of the Ruthenian Bishop of Stamford. Since there are no dioceses and no Hierarchs for Orientals who are not Ruthenians, the Holy See has designated the Latin Ordinaries as the proper Ordinaries of all non-Ruthenian Orientals in their respective dioceses. (Pospishil, p. 128.) Hence a pastor of the Latin rite who is put in charge of Oriental faithful by his own Ordinary can validly assist at the marriages of these people. (Cf. Can. 86 § 2; § 3, 3°.)

3) The proper pastor or Hierarch of a *vagus* is the pastor or Hierarch of his own rite having jurisdiction in the place where the *vagus* is actually staying; in case there is no pastor or Hierarch of this rite, the rules given in 1) and 2) are to be observed. (Can. 86 § 3, 4°.)

c. The pastor and local Hierarch, to assist validly at marriages of faithful of their own rite within the boundaries of their territory, *but in places which are exclusively of another rite,* must have the express consent either of the Ordinary or the pastor or the rector of the aforesaid places. (Cf. PC Or., reply, 8 July, 1952.) Hence in the United States, a Latin pastor cannot validly assist at a marriage of his subjects in places within his territory which are under the exclusive jurisdiction of a Ruthenian Bishop or Exarch, and a Ruthenian pastor cannot validly assist at a marriage of his subjects in a place under the exclusive jurisdiction of the Latin Ordinary, unless they have the express consent of the Ordinary, pastor or rector of that respective place. Such places are churches, rectories, hospitals, sanitoria, etc. Even though these places be within the territory of the pastor of another rite, the required consent of the Ordinary, pastor or rector is an essential condition stipulated by law for the validity of the marriage. (Pospishil, pp. 124-125.)

C. *Delegation for Marriage*

1. The pastor and the local Ordinary who can validly assist at a marriage can also grant to another priest the permission to validly assist at a marriage within the limits of their respective territories. (Can. 1095 § 2.)

Hence besides pastors strictly so called, the following can also delegate another priest to assist at marriages: the religious pastor; the administrator of a vacant parish; the vicar substitute mentioned in Canon 465 § 4 after the approval of the Ordinary if the latter placed no limitation; the vicar or supplying priest of Canon 465 § 5 even before the approval of the Ordinary provided the Ordinary has been notified of the designation of the supplying priest and has not provided otherwise; the vicar coadjutor if he has been given the full parochial authority according to Canon 475 § 2. (Cf. PCI, reply, 20 May, 1923.)

2. The permission to assist at a marriage, granted in accordance with Canon 1095 § 2, must be given expressly to a definite priest for a determinate marriage, all general delegations being excluded, except in the case of parochial assistants for the parish to which they are attached; otherwise it is invalid. (Can. 1096 § 1.)

For the delegation *to be valid:*

a. *A definite priest must be delegated;* the priest must be determined by name, by office, etc. The priest is not sufficiently designated when the pastor notifies the superior of a monastery that he delegates as the priest to assist at a marriage whatever priest the superior shall select to send to the parish. (PCI, reply, 20 May, 1923.) However, several priests may be delegated for one and the same marriage, provided that each priest is determined by name, office, etc., i.e., is specifically designated. (Sipos, § 134.)

b. *The marriage must be determinate;* the marriage is specified by the names of the contracting parties, or by the hour and
place of marriage, etc. However delegation can be given to one
priest for several determinate marriages, provided each marriage is specifically designated. (Cappello, *De Sacr.,* V, n. 674.)

Under the law of the *Ne Temere,* a definite priest had to be
delegated but he could be given general delegation to assist at
marriages, i.e., the marriages did not have to be specifically
designated. Now only the assistant pastor can be given such
general delegation and only for the parish to which he is attached.

c. *The delegation must be express;* i.e., given explicitly by
words or in writing, or implicitly by signs or facts. A tacit or
presumed delegation is invalid. Hence the mere silence of the
pastor who knows another priest is assisting at a marriage in
his parish is only tacit delegation and not sufficient; it is invalid.

d. *The marriage must take place in the territory of the delegating pastor.*

3. *Subdelegation*

a. One who is delegated for a marriage can subdelegate another priest to assist at the marriage only if this
power of subdelegating is expressly conceded to him by
the one delegating. (Cf. Can. 199 § 4.)

Thus a pastor or local Ordinary can delegate a certain priest
to assist at a certain marriage and can also give him power to
subdelegate another priest to assist at that marriage. (PCI,
reply, 28 Dec., 1927.)

b. One who has received general delegation for marriages can subdelegate another priest in single cases. (Cf.
Can. 199 § 3; V.C., II, n. 396.)

Thus an assistant who has received general delegation to
assist at marriages from the pastor or local Ordinary, can subdelegate another priest to assist at a definite marriage. (PCI,
reply, 28 Dec., 1927.)

Assistants can receive such general delegation either from
diocesan statutes, from letters of their Ordinary or from the
pastor himself.

In Latin law, an assistant pastor who receives general delegation cannot grant his subdelegate the power to again subdelegate, unless this power was expressly granted to him by the
pastor or Ordinary who delegated him. (Cf. Can. 199 § 5.)

4. *Oriental Law* (Mp, Canon 87.)

a. The pastor and the local Hierarch who can validly assist at a marriage can grant to another priest the faculty to assist at a determinate marriage within the limits of their territory, provided they do it expressly and the priest is specifically determined. They can also grant to this priest the power to subdelegate another determinate priest to assist at that marriage. (Can. 87 § 1, 1°.)

b. The vicar cooperator (assistant pastor) can be given the general faculty to assist at marriages by the pastor or local Hierarch; and after this general faculty has been obtained, he enjoys the same faculty to subdelegate as in a. (Can. 87 § 1, 2°.)

c. Local Hierarchs who according to law have the administration of faithful of a different rite, can grant to rectors of churches of any Oriental rite or to other priests who have the care of the faithful deprived of a pastor of their own rite, the *general* faculty to assist at marriages of faithful of the Oriental rite, though it is a different rite than that of the rector or priest. (Can. 87 § 3.)

Hence the Latin local Ordinary in the United States can delegate a Latin priest to assist at the marriages of any non-Ruthenian Orientals.

Note: When *a pastor* has power to delegate another priest, he must be careful to delegate the priest for a place that is under his jurisdiction. In a case decided by the S.C.E.O., 11 July, 1952, it was stated that for validity a Latin pastor who wished to delegate an Oriental priest for the marriage of a Latin Catholic to an Oriental schismatic, must grant the faculty for a Latin church or a place under his jurisdiction. (*Digest,* III, p. 452.) However, in another case, decided 27 Nov., 1952, the Sacred Congregation of the Oriental Church stated that a Maronite pastor could delegate the local Latin rite pastor to assist at the marriage of a Maronite man to a baptized non-Catholic woman [presumably a Latin] in the Latin parish church, for what he can do personally he can, with the express consent of the rector of the Latin rite church in the territory, also do through another. (Cf. *Digest,* IV, pp. 13-14.) In another case decided on the 11 July, 1952, the Sacred Congregation stated that a Latin pastor who wishes to assist at the marriage of two Orientals in a Latin church, in a place where there is a canonically erected parish of the rite of the contracting parties, but the parties are subject to the local Ordinary of the Latin rite, that the Latin pastor cannot validly assist without delegation from this local Ordinary. If there is in the same territory a local Hierarch of the parties, the faculty to celebrate the marriage before a Latin pastor and in a Latin church is to be granted by the Holy See. (*Digest,* III, p. 453.)

D. *Conditions for Licit Assistance*

1. The pastor and the local Ordinary lawfully assist at marriage:

a. After they have satisfied themselves according to law regarding the free state of the contracting parties;

b. After they have moreover satisfied themselves that one of the contracting parties has a domicile or quasi-domicile or a month's residence in the place of the marriage or, in the case of a *vagus,* that one of the parties has actual residence there;

c. Provided that, if the conditions mentioned in b are wanting, they have the permission of the pastor or Ordinary of the domicile or quasi-domicile or place of month's residence of one of the contracting parties, except in the case of *vagi,* who are actually traveling and have no dwelling place anywhere, or unless some grave necessity occur which excuses from asking the permission. (Can. 1097 § 1.)

> *Month's residence* means an actual living for a month in a diocese or parish; the residence must be continued up to the time of the marriage. The month is computed as it stands in the calendar and the first day is not counted (Can. 34 § 3, 3°); if it began on Feb. 12, the pastor cannot assist lawfully until March 13. Absence for a day or two would not interfere with the continuity of the residence; nor need these days be made up to fill out a certain number of days. (Gasparri, n. 986.)

> *Vagi* who are actually traveling are such as are merely through a place on their way to some other place without settling down for a time. Note that to be a *vagus* it is necessary that one have no domicile or quasi-domicile, and in this case, no month's stay, anywhere.

> *Grave necessity* excusing from asking permission from the proper pastor is a notable inconvenience on the part of the pastor or parties; v.g., necessity of incurring great expenses, danger of merely civil marriage, etc. In cases of grave necessity one is excused from asking the permission, i.e., one need not ask the permission even though it is possible to ask for it. (V.C., II, n. 400.)

2. In every case let it be taken as the rule that the marriage be celebrated before the pastor of the bride, unless a just reason excuses; however, marriages of Catholics of different rites shall be celebrated in the rite of the groom and in the presence of his pastor. (Can. 1097 § 2.)

Just reason: any just cause, v.g., utility, convenience, the bride is not a Catholic, etc., excuses from the observance of this rule; in fact, it seems that the Code does not give the pastor of the bride a strict right to have the wedding. Hence the pastor of the groom who assists at the wedding contrary to this rule, and even without a just cause, would not be strictly bound to ask the permission of the pastor of the bride. (Sipos, § 134.)

Catholics of different rites: confer commentary below, under Oriental law.

3. A pastor who assists at marriage without the permission required by law is not entitled to the stole fee and he must remit it to the proper pastor of the contracting parties. (Can. 1097 § 3.)

The fee should be remitted to the pastor of the bride; if she has several pastors, the fee should be divided among them. If permission was obtained according to law, the stole fee belongs to the pastor of the place where the marriage was celebrated and not to the pastor of the parties; diocesan law, however, can assign the fee to the pastor of the parties even in cases where permission is given to have the wedding elsewhere.

The pastor of the groom who assists at a marriage without a just cause is not bound to remit the stole fee, since he does not need the permission of the pastor of the bride. (Sipos, § 134.) The same should be said of one who assists with the permission of the pastor of the groom instead of with the permission of the pastor of the bride.

4. *Oriental Law*

a. In Oriental law the conditions of lawful assistance are the same as in the Latin Code, but with this notable difference that marriages are to be celebrated in the presence of *the pastor of the groom,* unless either legal custom provides otherwise or a just reason excuses. (Mp, Can. 88.)

A just reason would be utility, convenience, etc.

Contrary custom exists among the Ruthenians, who celebrate marriage before the pastor of the bride.

b. Another point to note: marriages of Catholics of mixed rite are to be celebrated in the rite of the man and before his pastor, unless the man, having his domicile or quasi-domicile in an Oriental region, consents to have the marriage celebrated in the rite of the bride and before her pastor.

This rule applies in the marriage of a Latin with an Oriental as well as in the marriage of two Catholics of different Oriental rites. If an Oriental man has no pastor of his own rite, and therefore cannot have the marriage witnessed according to the ceremonies of his own rite, he may still have his own pastor, i.e., the Latin pastor who is in charge of Orientals; hence this pastor alone assists licitly at the marriage. (Cf. Pospishil, pp. 142-145.)

There is *only one reason* which the law allows as an excuse from the rule stated here: namely, where the man having a domicile or quasi-domicile in an Oriental region, consents to have the marriage celebrated before the pastor of the bride. An Oriental region is one in which the Oriental rite has been in existence from ancient times, v.g., the Near East, Greece, Egypt, etc. The law does not allow the pastor or Ordinary of the groom to grant permission to the pastor of the bride to assist at these marriages of mixed rite. Nevertheless, note that Canon 88 § 1, 3° of *Crebrae allatae* states that for a grave reason a marriage may take place licitly before even a *parochus non proprius* without anyone's permission.

c. The phrase of Canon 1097 § 2 of the Latin Code stating that a marriage of mixed rite is to be celebrated in the rite and before the pastor of the bride when particular law so demands, is abrogated by Canon 88 § 3 of *Crebrae allatae*. (PC. Or., 3 May, 1953.)

E. *Mixed Marriage and Mixed Rite*

When a Latin Catholic marries an Oriental Dissident, or an Oriental Catholic a Latin Protestant: the Sacred Congregation of the Oriental Church seems to teach that it is the pastor of the rite of the Catholic party alone who is competent to validly assist at the marriage or validly delegate another priest to assist. (Cf. cases decided on 11 July, 1952 — *Digest,* III, pp. 452-453.)

III.   THE EXTRAORDINARY FORM

If it is impossible, without serious inconvenience, to have or to approach a pastor, Ordinary or delegated priest who can assist at marriage in accordance with Canons 1095 and 1096:

1. In danger of death a marriage is valid and lawful when contracted in the presence of witnesses only; and also outside the danger of death, provided it is prudently foreseen that this situation is to last for a month;

2. In both cases, if there is at hand another priest who can be present he must be summoned, and together with the witnesses, assist at the marriage, without prejudice to the validity of the marriage before the witnesses alone. (Can. 1098.)

1. *In danger of death*

To contract marriage before witnesses only, it must be a case of *true danger of death,* either from an intrinsic cause (sickness) or an extrinsic cause (war, flood, etc.). The *articulum mortis* is not required, i.e., death need not be imminent.

It is also necessary that it be either *absolutely or morally impossible* to have or to approach an authorized witness. It is absolutely impossible when there is simply no time to approach the authorized witness or to obtain from him delegation to assist at the marriage. It is morally impossible when this cannot be done without grave inconvenience, v.g., a dangerous journey during time of war, persecution, floods, etc.

It is also morally impossible to have or to approach the authorized witness when the pastor or Ordinary, although materially present in the place, is unable by reason of grave inconvenience to assist at the marriage asking and receiving the consent of the contracting parties. (PCI, reply, 25 July, 1931.) Thus, if the pastor is forbidden by civil law to assist at the marriage of certain parties under penalties to be inflicted either on the pastor or on the parties, the pastor can be considered absent and unavailable in the sense of Canon 1098. (S.C.Sacr., private response, 24 April, 1935.) Note that the grave inconvenience mentioned in the canon is not only one which threatens the pastor, Ordinary or delegated priest, but also one which threatens both parties or either party to the marriage. (PCI, reply, 3 May, 1945.)

2. *Outside the danger of death*

To contract marriage before witnesses only, it is required that it be either absolutely or morally impossible to have or to approach an authorized witness. It is also necessary that it be prudently foreseen that this situation is to last for a month.

The impossibility of having or approaching an authorized witness has been explained above. This is the case especially in mission countries, and also in other places during time of war and persecution.

It must be foreseen that *this situation will last for a month.* Hence a past month's absence does not suffice, but it is required that one prudently judge that the situation will last for a month yet. For the valid and licit use of Canon 1098 the mere fact of the pastor's absence does not suffice, but it is required that there exist moral certainty, based either on common knowledge or on inquiry, that for one month the pastor will be neither available nor accessible without grave inconvenience. (PCI, reply, 10 Nov., 1925.) The marriage would not, however, be invalid if the assistance of a competent priest became possible before the month elapsed, provided that at the time of the marriage there was little hope of this. (Sipos, § 134.)

3. *The priest of Canon* 1098, 2°

If there is a priest at hand, he is to be called to the wedding to assist together with the witnesses. The priest of Canon 1098, 2° is one who has no delegation or authorization to assist at marriages as the official witness. However, he is given ample faculties to dispense from matrimonial impediments and from the form of marriage according to the norms of Canons 1043-1045. (Confer above, pp. 223-230.)

This priest is to be called both in danger of death and also outside the danger of death for marriages legally celebrated before two witnesses alone.

Canon 1098 speaks of a priest who is at hand; hence if there is none at hand, a priest need not be sought out. (V.C., II, n. 406.) Even if he is at hand, the marriage is celebrated validly without him, provided two witnesses are used.

4. *Pre-Code law*

According to the *Ne Temere* when death was imminent and the pastor or his delegate could not be had, a marriage taking place for peace of conscience or to legitimate offspring was valid before *any priest and two witnesses.* Some priest had to be present for validity. A decree of the Sacred Congregation of the Sacraments, 14 May, 1909, permitted this priest to dispense from the necessity of the two witnesses.

Likewise, according to the *Ne Temere,* when in any region the competent priest could not be had without grave inconvenience and the parties had *already waited* for a month, the marriage could be celebrated validly before two witnesses alone. In this case no priest was required but the two witnesses were required for the validity of the marriage. In 1912 the Sacred Congregation of the Sacraments declared that personal impossibility sufficed, i.e., that the impossibility need not affect a region or district. (S.C.Sacr., 12

March, 1912.)

5. *Oriental Law*. In Oriental law the form to be observed in these extraordinary cases is the same as in the Latin Code. It is further stated that the priest who is at hand and who should be called to assist together with the witnesses, may be *any Catholic* priest. (Mp, Can. 89, 2°.)

IV. SUBJECTS OF THE LAW

1. The following persons are obliged to observe the canonical form:

a. All who are baptized in the Catholic Church and all who are converted to it from heresy or schism (even though the former or the latter may have later fallen away from the Church) — whenever they contract marriage with each other;

b. The persons just mentioned when they contract marriage with non-Catholics, either baptized or not baptized, even after obtaining a dispensation from the impediment of mixed religion or disparity of cult;

c. Orientals when they contract with Latins who are bound to the form. (Can. 1099 § 1.)

a. *Persons baptized in the Catholic Church or converted to it:* confer the enumeration of persons belonging to the Church, above, under the impediment of disparity of cult, p. 199.

b. *Mixed marriages.* Mixed marriages are subject to the form. They were thus subject under the *Ne Temere* already except in Germany and in Hungary where the *Provida* exempted them from the form. This exemption for Germany and Hungary was abrogated by the Code, so that now mixed marriages everywhere are subject to the form. (Concerning the validity of mixed marriages celebrated in Germany and Hungary between 1906-1918, confer Sipos, § 134, pp. 519-520.)

c. *Orientals.* The reason why the Code states that Orientals are subject to the form when they marry Latins is because at that time of the Code and until the publication of *Crebrae allatae* not all Orientals were subject to a canonical form of marriage, or at least in some Oriental disciplines the law was doubtful. Hence to make things more certain the legislator subjected them to the Latin form when they married Latins. Now all Orientals are bound to the form of marriage demanded by

Crebrae allatae. The only difference between the Oriental and the Latin form is that the blessing of the priest is required for the validity of the marriage in the Oriental form. Even in the Latin ceremony such a blessing is contained, and hence no difficulty is had. A mixed rite marriage between two Catholics would be contracted validly either in the rite of the woman or of the man; licitly, however, in the rite of the man as explained above, pp. 254-255.

2. Without prejudice to the provision of § 1, 1°, non-Catholics whether baptized or unbaptized, when they contract with each other, are nowhere bound to observe the Catholic form of marriage. (Can. 1099 § 2.)

a. Canon 1099 § 2 of the Code also exempted from the law of the form *persons born of non-Catholic parents,* even though they had been *baptized in the Catholic Church,* who *had grown up from infancy* in heresy, schism, or infidelity, or without any religion, when they contracted with a non-Catholic party. This exemption was *abrogated* by the *motu proprio* of Pius XII, 1 Aug., 1948; the abrogation took effect on 1 Jan., 1949. Hence, such people are now bound to the Catholic form of marriage.

Marriages celebrated between 19 May, 1918 and 31 Dec., 1948 must be judged by the exemption contained in the code. *Born of non-Catholic parents were* children whose parents at the time of their birth were infidels or who belonged to an heretical or schismatic sect; also children born of parents one only of whom was a non-Catholic, even when the *cautiones* were given in accordance with Canons 1061 and 1071 (PCI, 20 July, 1929); also children born of apostates (PCI, 17 Feb., 1930), i.e., at the time of the child's birth at least one of the parents was an apostate; also children both or one of whose parents at the time of birth had become heretics or schismatics. (Sipos, § 134.)

Note that with all these children born of non-Catholic parents, but baptized in the Catholic Church, it was necessary that they had grown up from infancy in heresy, schism or in no religion. If they had been baptized and *reared* in the Catholic Church, no exemption from the law of the form was granted.

Children of *Catholic parents,* who were baptized in the Church but because of the death, neglect, or sin of their parents had not been reared in the Church, were not exempted from the form. (Cf. S.O., case, 7 Jan., 1947 in the *Digest,* III, p. 462.)

From 1 Jan., 1949, anyone baptized in the Catholic Church is subject to the Catholic form, irrespective of his training and of the religious status of his parents.

b. *Under the Ne Temere*. Non-Catholics were not bound to the form when they married among themselves. It was doubtful whether children born of non-Catholic parents, baptized in the Catholic Church, but educated in heresy, etc., were subject to the Catholic form of marriage or not. The Holy Office replied that when there was question of the validity of the marriage of such a person with a non-Catholic, recourse should be made in each case to the Holy See. (S.O., 31 March, 1911.)

3. *Oriental Law*. Canon 90 of the Oriental legislation is the same as the Latin legislation as it now is in force: All baptized in or converted to the Church are bound to the form; mixed marriages are bound to the form; all non-Catholics when they marry among themselves are not bound to the Catholic form.

The Ruthenians in the United States were bound to the form of the *Ne Temere* before the time of *Crebrae allatae;* (S.C.P.F., 17 Aug., 1914; S.C.E.O., 1 March, 1929); non-Ruthenians in the United States had no prescribed form of marriage before *Crebrae allatae*. (Cf. Pospishil, pp. 156-157.)

V. CEREMONIES OF MARRIAGE

Except in case of necessity, the rites prescribed in the approved liturgical books or sanctioned by praiseworthy custom should be observed in the celebration of marriage. (Can. 1100.) The rites consist in the asking and receiving of the consent of the parties by the pastor (*ad validitatem*), the blessing of the ring(s), the simple blessing, "Ego vos coniungo," the Mass with the nuptial blessing.

A. *The Nuptial Blessing*

1. The pastor should see to it that the parties receive the solemn blessing, which may be given them even after they have lived a long time in the married state, but only at Mass, with the observance of the special rubric, and except during the forbidden seasons. (Can. 1101 § 1.)

a. *The nuptial blessing may not be given:* outside of Mass, except by apostolic indult (Can. 1101); during the closed seasons except by permission of the Ordinary (Canons 1101, 1108); if the bride has already received it in a former marriage

(Can. 1143); on All Souls' Day; in mixed marriages (Can. 1102); in marriages of the excommunicated or interdicted; in marriages celebrated through a proxy or with a suspensive condition. (Abbo-Hannan, II, n. 1101.)

b. The nuptial blessing may be given outside of Mass only by apostolic indult. This indult is contained in the quinquennial faculties and may therefore be delegated to pastors and others who assist at marriage. The form of this blessing is found in the Ritual, appendix, *De Matr.,* I.

When the nuptial blessing cannot be given in any form, neither in the Mass nor outside of Mass, a substitute for the nuptial blessing may be given by apostolic indult. This indult is contained in the quinquennial faculties and may be delegated to others. The form of this blessing is found in the Ritual, appendix, *De Matr.,* II.

c. *The votive Mass pro sponsis*

1) If the blessing cannot be given, the votive Mass for the spouses cannot be said nor can a commemoration be inserted in the Mass of the day. (S.R.C., decr., 23 June, 1853; decr., 14 Aug., 1858.)

2) The votive Mass cannot be said during the closed seasons, except with special permission of the Ordinary. (Can. 1108; S.R.C., 14 June, 1918.)

3) On days when the rubrics forbid the votive Mass (cf. the Ordo or Directory), the Mass of the day is said, with the commemoration from the Mass *pro sponsis* (*sub unica conclusione*), and the three prayers of the blessing (which are said in the same way as in the *Missa pro sponsis*). However, on All Souls' Day the commemoration and the prayers of the blessing may not be said during the Mass.

2. Only the priest who can validly and licitly assist at the marriage can give the solemn nuptial blessing; this he can do either in person or through another. (Can. 1101 § 2.)

Hence the pastor may assist at the marriage and have another priest read the Mass and impart the solemn blessing. (Coronata, *De Sacr.,* III, n. 576.)

B. *Mixed Marriages*

1. In marriages between a Catholic and a non-Catholic party, the questions requiring an expression of consent

must be made in accordance with the requirement of Canon 1095 § 1, 3°. (Can. 1102 § 1.)

> As is evident from Canon 1095 *the asking of the consent by the pastor* is necessary for the *validity* of the marriage. The faculty of assisting passively at illicit mixed marriages which was granted by the Holy See, for some places, is revoked by Canon 1102 § 1. (PCI, 10 March, 1928.)

2. But all sacred rites are forbidden; if it is foreseen however, that from this prohibition greater evils will result, the Ordinary may permit some of the usual ecclesiastical ceremonies, excluding always the celebration of Mass. (Can. 1102 § 2.)

> Not only the Mass *pro sponsis* but also any other Mass is forbidden if this Mass may from the circumstances be regarded as a complement to the marriage ceremony. (PCI, 10 Nov., 1925.)

> *Greater evils:* hatred of non-Catholics for the Church and its laws; danger of a non-Catholic marriage; danger that the *cautiones* will not be kept; danger of defection on the part of the Catholic spouse.

> *Usual ceremonies:* v.g., use of surplice and stole; the blessing, "ego vos coniungo"; blessing of the ring; giving of a sermon; use of music and flowers, etc. (Coronata, *De Sacr.,* III, n. 281.)

C. Oriental Law

1. In Oriental law the simple blessing of the priest assisting is required for the *validity* of the marriage (Mp, Can. 85), and this *also in mixed marriages.* (Sipos, § 135.) The other liturgical ceremonies are required for the licit celebration of the marriage only (Mp, Can. 91), and they are used also in mixed marriages in order to avoid scandal and greater evils. (Sipos, § 135; Coussa, III, nos. 92, 173.) Hence the prescription of Canon 1102 § 2 of the Latin Code is not found in the Oriental legislation.

2. However, a priest of the Latin rite who lawfully assists at a marriage of an Oriental Catholic and a non-Catholic (baptized or not baptized), observes the prescriptions of Canon 1102 § 2 of the Latin Code and not

the prescription of Canon 85 of *Crebrae allatae*; a priest of the Oriental rite who lawfully assists at the marriage of a Latin Catholic and a non-Catholic (baptized or not baptized), observes the prescription of Canon 85 of *Crebrae allatae* and not the prescription of Canon 1102 § 2 of the Latin Code. (PC Or., 8 Jan., 1953.)

D. *Recording the Marriage*

1. A record of the marriage must be kept in the matrimonial register of the parish in which the marriage was celebrated, and the fact of the marriage must be recorded in the baptismal register of the parishes where the parties who contracted the marriage were baptized. The obligation of recording the marriage and of sending notice to the pastors of baptism is incumbent on the pastor of the place where the marriage was celebrated or on the priest taking his place, even though another priest delegated by the pastor or by the Ordinary assisted at the marriage; this obligation must be fulfilled as soon as possible. (Can. 1103 §§ 1, 2.)

If one of the contracting parties is an immigrant, the notification to the pastor of baptism should be made through one's episcopal curia. (S.C.Sacr., instr., 4 July, 1921.)

2. Whenever marriage is contracted in accordance with the norm of Canon 1098, the priest, if there was one present, otherwise the witnesses are bound *in solidum* with the contracting parties to see to it that the marriage is recorded as soon as possible in the prescribed registers (Can. 1103 § 3), i.e., in the register of the parish in which the marriage took place.

3. *Oriental law* contains the same prescriptions with regard to the recording of the marriage in the prescribed registers of marriage and baptism. (Mp, Can. 92.)

VI. COMMON LAW MARRIAGE

1.   Common law marriage, i.e., one in which a man and woman contract marriage by the expression of true matrimonial consent but without any ceremony, i.e., without the intervention of a civil or religious official and of witnesses, is considered valid in about sixteen states of the Union. In the other states it is required by law that marriage be celebrated before a qualified civil or religious offi-

cial, and common law marriages are considered invalid.

> Since the laws of the states change in this matter, we do not attempt an enumeration of states in which common law marriages are considered valid. In marriage cases involving common law marriages, the pastor must ascertain the date of the marriage, the domicile of the parties, the place of the marriage, and the law of the states involved as the law existed at the time the marriage was celebrated. Investigations may also be necessary to ascertain the competence of the civil or religious official who assisted at a marriage in states which do not recognize common law marriages. As is evident a civil lawyer should be consulted in these matters.

2. Common law marriage between two *baptized* non-Catholics or between a baptized non-Catholic and an unbaptized person is valid, even in states which do not recognize common law marriage, provided there is no direment impediment. The reason for this is that marriages involving the baptized are not subject to the civil authority.

3. Common law marriage between *two unbaptized persons* is valid only in the manner recognized by the civil law to which the parties are bound. If the civil law recognizes the validity of such a marriage, the marriage is valid; if the civil law does not recognize the validity of common law marriage, such a union is invalid, even though the parties give a consent that by the law of nature would suffice.

> *Note:* Clandestine marriages contracted before the *Ne Temere* (19 April, 1908):
>
> a. Where the *Tametsi* was in full force (Province of Santa Fe) a clandestine marriage between two Catholics, or between a Catholic and a non-Catholic or between two baptized Protestants was invalid.
>
> b. In places where the *Tametsi* and the *Benedictina* were in force (cf. above, p. 243), a clandestine marriage between two Catholics was invalid; between a Catholic and a baptized non-Catholic, and between two baptized Protestants, was valid.
>
> c. In places where the *Tametsi* was not in force a clandestine marriage between two Catholics or between a Catholic and

a baptized non-Catholic or between two baptized Protestants, was valid.

VII. MARRIAGE OF CONSCIENCE

1. *When permitted.* Only for an extremely grave and urgent reason and only with permission granted by the local Ordinary himself, to the exclusion of the Vicar General unless he has a special mandate, is it allowed to enter a marriage of conscience, that is, to celebrate marriage secretly and without the proclamation of the banns. (Can. 1104.)

2. *The obligation of secrecy*

a. Permission for the celebration of a marriage of conscience carries with it the promise and the grave obligation of secrecy on the part of the priest assisting, of the witnesses, of the Ordinary and his successors, and even of each of the spouses as long as the other does not consent to the revelation of the marriage. (Can. 1105.)

b. The obligation of this promise on the part of the Ordinary does not extend to the case in which scandal or grave harm to the sanctity of marriage impends from the observance of the secret, or in which the parents neglect the baptism of the children born of such a marriage, or provide that they are baptized under fictitious names, (unless in the meantime, and within thirty days, they notify the Ordinary of the birth and baptism of a child giving also the correct identification of the parents) or in which the parents neglect the Christian education of the children. (Can. 1106.)

3. *Recording the marriage.* A marriage of conscience is not to be recorded in the usual matrimonial and baptismal registers, but in a special book to be kept in the secret archives of the episcopal curia, of which mention is made in Canon 379. (Can. 1107.)

4. *Record of baptism of the children.* If the pastor knows that the child was born of a marriage of conscience or if he is told so by the parents, he should not enter the record of baptism into the parish register, but should send the record to the Ordinary for entry into the secret register of the curia. If the pastor does not know about the marriage of conscience and is not told about it, he will enter the record into the register of the parish in the same manner as for an illegitimate child, and hence the parents should be careful to send notice to the Ordinary of the baptism of the child, indicating that it is a legitimate child of a marriage of conscience. (Cf. Sipos, § 137.)

5. *Oriental Law* is the same as the law of the Latin Code. (Mp, Canons 93-96.)

CHAPTER VIII

The Time and Place for the Celebration
of Marriage

I. THE TIME

Marriage can be contracted at any time of the year. It is only the solemn blessing of marriage that is forbidden from the first Sunday of Advent to Christmas inclusive and from Ash Wednesday to Easter inclusive. But local Ordinaries may, without prejudice to liturgical laws, permit this solemn blessing for a just cause even during the forbidden seasons, with an admonition to the spouses, however, that they abstain from excessive festivity. (Can. 1108.)

> *The marriage contract* may be celebrated on any day of the year and any restriction of this right by diocesan law would seem to be opposed to the Code and therefore of no force. Restrictions as to the hour of the day (v.g., not in the evening) do not seem to be opposed to the Code and could be the object of particular legislation.
>
> *During the closed seasons* it is the solemn blessing of marriage, i.e., the Mass *pro sponsis* and the nuptial blessing that is forbidden. The Ordinary can, for a just cause, permit the Mass and the nuptial blessing. Hence with the Ordinary's permission the Mass *pro sponsis* may be said even during the closed season, provided it is permitted by the rubrics on the day chosen for the celebration of the marriage. (Cf. S.R.C., reply, 14 June, 1918.)
>
> *Excessive festivity.* The obligation to abstain from excessive display extends to the ornament of the church and altar, the number of couples attending the bride and groom, the fashion of the wedding dress, etc., but probably does not extend to the banquet, etc. (V.C., II, n. 412.)

II. THE PLACE

1. *Catholic Marriages*

a. A marriage between Catholics shall be celebrated in the *parochial church;* only with the permission of the local

Ordinary or of the pastor can it be celebrated in another church or semi-public oratory. (Can. 1109 § 1.)

b. Only in an extraordinary case and then only for a just and reasonable cause, can the local Ordinary permit a marriage to be celebrated *in private dwellings;* but the Ordinary shall not permit it in the churches or oratories of the Seminary or of women religious, except in a case of urgent need and with the observance of appropriate safeguards. (Can. 1109 § 2.)

> A just cause for celebrating marriage in a private home may be the illness of one of the spouses, the inequality of social rank, the fact that the spouses are of the nobility, etc.

2. *Mixed Marriages*

But marriages between a Catholic party and a non-Catholic party shall be celebrated outside of the church; but if the Ordinary shall prudently judge that this provision cannot be observed without giving rise to greater evils, it is committed to his prudent discretion to dispense from this restriction, without prejudice, however, to the provision of Canon 1102 § 2. (Can. 1109 § 3.)

> Mixed marriages may be celebrated in the sacristy, the rectory, or also in a private oratory. It does not seem permissible to celebrate mixed marriages in private homes except with the permission of the Ordinary. (V.C., II, n. 413; Sipos, § 138.)
>
> According to Canons 1102 and 1109, therefore, Ordinaries may permit the celebration of a mixed marriage in a church and with the use of some of the customary ecclesiastical ceremonies; the Ordinary may never permit the celebration of Mass in connection with a mixed marriage.

ORIENTAL LAW

1. *The time.* Marriage may be contracted at any time of the year; during the sacred time before Christmas and during the Great Lent, as well as during other times determined by particular law, the celebration of the marriage itself, or the solemn blessing alone, is forbidden in accordance with particular law. (Mp, Can. 97 §§ 1, 2.)

Hence particular law may add other closed seasons during which the solemn blessing may not be given and also forbid the marriage contract itself during the closed seasons prescribed by the common law or during other closed seasons introduced by particular law.

The local Hierarch may, however, for a just cause, permit either the celebration of marriage or the solemn blessing during the closed seasons. (Mp, Can. 97 § 3.)

2. *The place.* For Catholic marriages the same prescriptions are given as in the Latin Code except that permission to celebrate marriages in private dwellings can be given simply for a just and reasonable cause, i.e., the Hierarch's faculty is not restricted to extraordinary cases only (Mp, Can. 98); but nothing is said concerning mixed marriages, for church weddings are tolerated in order to avoid scandal and greater evils.

CHAPTER IX

Legitimacy and Legitimation

I. LEGITIMACY

A. *Definition*

Legitimacy is a juridical quality conferred on a child born of lawful wedlock, producing definite effects in law, as, v.g., capacity for offices, dignities, etc.

B. *Who are Legitimate*

1. Those children are legitimate who are conceived or born of a valid or a putative marriage, unless, at the time of conception, the use of a marriage previously contracted was forbidden the parents on account of solemn religious profession or of the reception of a sacred order. (Can. 1114.)

Hence the child need not be both conceived and born of a valid marriage in order to be legitimate; it suffices, v.g., that the child, although conceived outside of marriage, is born only after his parents contracted marriage.

A putative marriage is an invalid marriage that was celebrated in good faith by at least one of the parties; it remains putative until both parties become aware of its invalidity. (Can. 1015 § 4.) That an invalid marriage be considered putative, it is required that it shall have been contracted before the Church, i.e., with the form to which the spouses were bound. (Cf. PCI, reply, 26 Jan., 1949.)

Illegitimates are children not conceived or born of a valid or putative marriage. They are called *natural* if the parents could have been married, i.e., no diriment impediment existed, either at the time of conception, or of pregnancy or of birth; *spurious* if the parents could not have contracted marriage at any time from the conception to the birth of the child because of a diriment impediment; the spurious are further divided into the *adulterine* if the impediment separating the parties was the impediment of previous bond; *sacrilegious* if the impediment disqualifying the parents was the impediment of solemn vows or sacred orders (or if solemn vows or sacred orders existed as an obstacle to the licit use of a valid marriage previously contracted); *incestuous* if the parents were bound by the impediment of consanguinity or affinity; *nefarious,* if the parents were bound by the impediment of consanguinity in the direct line.

The effects of illegitimacy. Illegitimates may not be admitted to the seminary (Can. 1363); they are irregular (Can. 984, 1°); they cannot obtain certain ecclesiastical offices or benefices. (Cf. Can. 991 § 3.)

2. The father is he who is shown to be such by the existence of a recognized marriage unless the contrary is demonstrated by evident proof. (Can. 1115 § 1.) They are presumed legitimate who were born at least six months after the day on which the marriage was celebrated or within ten months from the day on which conjugal life was dissolved. (Can. 1115 § 2.)

Canon 1114 states that a child is legitimate even though it was conceived outside of marriage but was born in marriage; the canon presupposes, however, that the mother married the man with whom she had relations. However, according to Canon 1115, if the child is born before six months from the beginning of the marriage, one cannot say it was conceived of the married couple unless one presupposes that the husband committed fornication before he married. This supposition one is not allowed to make unless the husband admits it by his silence. Hence if the child is born before six months after the day of the marriage (or after ten months from the dissolution of conjugal life), the husband or heirs may at once declare the child illegitimate and the burden of proof of legitimacy would rest with the child and its mother. (V.C., II, n. 420; Sipos, § 139.)

On the other hand if the child is born after the six months or before the ten months mentioned in the canon there exists a strict presumption that the husband is the father of the child, and only very stringent proofs to the contrary can overcome this presumption. *Breviter:* If the child is born a day after the marriage it is generally considered legitimate. (Can. 1114), unless the husband immediately repudiates the child (Can. 1115); when a child is born after the sixth month from the date of the marriage or before the tenth month from the date of dissolution of conjugal life, only very convincing proof can destroy the presumption that it is legitimate. (Can. 1115 § 2.)

The six and ten months may be computed as 180 and 300 days, the day of the marriage and the day of the dissolution of conjugal life not being counted according to Canon 34 § 3, 3°. (Genicot, II, n. 651.)

II. LEGITIMATION

A. *Definition*

Legitimation is a favor by which a child born out of wedlock is granted by the law rights and honors of legitimacy, either in whole or in part.

B. *How Granted*

1. *By the subsequent* valid or putative *marriage of the parents,* whether the marriage is only now contracted, or was contracted before (invalidly) and is now convalidated, even if it is not consummated, the children are made legitimate, provided the parents were legally capable of contracting marriage with each other at the time of the child's conception, or of the pregnancy, or of the child's birth. (Can. 1116.)

Canon 1116 speaks of children born before the marriage of the parents. Legitimation is granted only for *natural* illegitimate children, *not for the spurious,* for it is said that the parents must have been capable of contracting marriage with each other at some time from the conception to the birth of the child.

It is not necessary that the parents were capable of marriage (i.e., that no diriment impediment existed) during this whole period of time, but it is sufficient if they were capable of marriage *either* at the time of conception, *or* at some time during the pregnancy, *or* at the time of birth.

2. The legitimation of illegitimate children, even of spurious illegitimates, can be effected by *a rescript of the Holy See* when legitimation is impossible by subsequent marriage. Such a rescript is appended to certain matrimonial dispensations issued by the Sacred Congregation of the Sacraments and by the Sacred Penitentiary. Legitimation is also granted by a *sanatio in radice* according to the norm of Canon 1138. (Cf. below, p. 297.)

3. By a dispensation granted from a diriment impediment in virtue of either ordinary power, or of power delegated by a general indult but not by a rescript in a particular case, there is automatically granted the legitimation of offspring already born or conceived by the persons receiving the dispensation, with the exception, however, of adulterine and sacrilegious offspring. (Can. 1051.)

Ordinary power: v.g., by the bishop or pastor in virtue of Canons 1043-1045.

General indult: v.g., by the bishop in virtue of powers contained in the quinquennial faculties; by the pastor in virtue of powers subdelegated to him by the diocesan pagella; by the confessor in virtue of powers given him by Canons 1044-1045 (Sipos, § 107; cf. Bouscaren-Ellis, pp. 496-497.)

Rescript in a particular case. If a dispensation is granted by the Holy See *in forma gratiosa* it seems that the legitimation of children is effected according to the norm of Canon 1051; but if the rescript is *in forma commissoria,* i.e., it grants someone the power to grant the dispensation in the particular case, the legitimation is not effected since we have here a case of delegated power granted by rescript in a particular case. (Cf. Bouscaren-Ellis, pp. 496-497.)

Note: The method of legitimation mentioned in Canon 1051 is important in the case where the child, provided it is not adulterine or sacrilegious, cannot be legitimated through the subsequent marriage of the parents because a diriment impediment made them incapable of marriage during the whole time from the child's conception to its birth. On the other hand, if the impediment ceased or did not exist at any time during the mother's pregnancy or at the time of the child's birth, *legitimation* could be effected through the subsequent marriage of the parents, even if the child was adulterine or sacrilegious in its conception. (Can. 1116; Abbo-Hannan, II, n. 1051.) Indeed, if the impediment ceased and the parents married before the child's birth, the child would be born legitimate. (Sipos, § 109, footnote 16.)

C. *Effects of Legitimation*

1. In reference to canonical effects, children legitimated *by a subsequent marriage* are regarded as equivalent to legitimate children, unless the contrary is expressly provided. (Can. 1117.)

> Hence they can be admitted into the seminary (PCI, 13 July, 1930); they are not irregular and hence can be promoted to orders, offices and benefices, even to the post of major superior in a religious institute, but they cannot be raised to the dignity of cardinal (Can. 232), bishop (Can. 331), abbot or prelate *nullius* (Can. 320.)

2. The effects of legitimation *granted by rescript* must be judged from the tenor of the indult granting the legitimation. A dispensation from the irregularity of illegitimacy for the reception of orders also makes one a fit subject for non-consistorial benefices, even *curata,* but does not make one a fit subject for the dignity of cardinal, bishop, abbot or prelate *nullius,* or major superior in an exempt clerical institute. (Can. 991 § 3.) It seems that the same should be said of the effects of legitimation by solemn vows. (Cf. Can. 984, 1°; Sipos, § 139.)

ORIENTAL LAW

In Oriental law, legitimacy and legitimation are treated in the same manner as in the Code; Canons 103-106 of *Crebrae allatae* are the equivalent of Canons 1114-1117 of the Code, Canon 41 of the Oriental legislation is the equivalent of Canon 1051 of the Code. The *nisi . . . Contracti* clause, however, of 1114 is not found in Canon 103 of *Crebrae allatae* since the discipline of the Oriental church is different than that of the Latin with regard to the celibacy of the clergy.

CHAPTER X

The Dissolution of the Bond

I. RATIFIED-CONSUMMATED MARRIAGE

A valid ratified and consummated marriage cannot be dissolved by any human power or by any other cause except death. (Can. 1118.)

A ratified marriage (*matrimonium ratum*) is a valid marriage between baptized persons that is not yet consummated; ratified and consummated (*matrimonium ratum et consummatum*) is a valid marriage between baptized persons after there occurs the conjugal act toward which the matrimonial contract is by its nature directed, and by which the spouses become one flesh. (Can. 1015 § 1.) Once the spouses have lived together after the celebration of the marriage, the consummation is presumed until the contrary is proved. (Can. 1015 § 2.)

The principle enunciated in Canon 1118 obtains for the marriage of *all* the baptized, even of non-Catholics provided both parties are validly baptized. No authority, civil or ecclesiastical, can dissolve such marriages after they have been consummated. The civil authority has no power to dissolve any kind of valid marriage, even the marriage of infidels. (Cf. Pius IX, *Syllabus*, prop. 67.)

II. NON-CONSUMMATED MARRIAGES

A *non-consummated* marriage between baptized persons or between a baptized and an unbaptized person is dissolved both by the law itself through solemn religious profession and by a dispensation granted by the Holy See for a just cause on the petition of both parties or of one of the parties, even though the other be unwilling. (Can. 1119.)

A. *Dissolution by solemn religious profession*

It is only solemn profession, not simple profession (not

even in the Society of Jesus) that produces this effect. It is necessary that the marriage be non-consummated. The marriage is dissolved only at the moment when one of the parties actually makes solemn vows, not when the party enters the novitiate or when he or she makes the simple vows prior to the solemn vows.

B.   *Dissolution by dispensation of the Holy See*

1.   Before the Holy See dispenses, a thorough investigation of the marriage is made. The procedure to be followed in this investigation is governed by the decree of the Sacred Congregation of the Sacraments, 7 May, 1923. The process has a double objective, namely, to prove that the marriage was not consummated, and to prove that there exists a just cause for the dispensation. Both points must be proved with moral certainty before a dispensation can be granted.

A summary of the procedure to be followed may be found in Bouscaren-Ellis, pp. 593-594, or Abbo-Hannon, II pp. 379-381.

2.   Just causes for the granting of the dispensation are: subsequent impotence; possible existence of antecedent impotence; irreconcilable discord; contagious disease contracted or discovered after the marriage; danger of perversion; desertion; partial proof that the marriage was invalid for want of consent, etc. Often in impotence cases, the impediment cannot be proved with certainty, but it can be proved that the marriage was not consummated and hence a dispensation from a *non-consummatum* is asked.

3.   When a non-consummated marriage is dissolved by a dispensation of the Holy See, the parties (if they are otherwise free to marry) may contract new marriages unless the Holy See forbids it. This prohibition, if made, is generally only prohibitive and not invalidating.

A dispensation granted by the Holy See from a ratified but

non-consummated marriage carries with it a dispensation from the impediment arising from adultery with the promise or attempt of marriage (crime in the lowest degree) but not from the impediment of crime in the two higher degrees. (Can. 1053.)

4. The papal power spoken of in Canon 1119 extends to the following marriages: 1) ratified non-consummated marriage (between two baptized persons); 2) non-consummated marriage between a baptized and non-baptized person; 3) a legitimate consummated marriage which becomes a ratified non-consummated marriage, i.e., the marriage is contracted in infidelity and consummated in infidelity, both parties are baptized but the marriage is not consummated again after the baptism; 4) the same marriage as in 3) if only one party receives baptism and the marriage is not again consummated after baptism. (Gasparri, II, n. 1131.)

III. THE PAULINE PRIVILEGE

A. *Introduction*

1. The *privilege of the faith* may be defined as the right to act in a way that is favorable to the acquiring or preserving of the faith. In reference to marriage the term privilege of the faith is used to designate the following:

a. *The Pauline privilege.* The right promulgated (according to some, introduced) by the Apostle, in virtue of which a spouse who had contracted a marriage in infidelity with another infidel, even if the marriage had been consummated, may, upon receiving baptism, enter a new marriage if the infidel party departs. When the new marriage is contracted, the former marriage is automatically dissolved.

b. *The extension of the Pauline privilege* by the apostolic constitutions mentioned in Canon 1125.

c. *The Petrine privilege,* namely, the power of the Roman Pontiff to dissolve a legitimate consummated marriage between a baptized party and an unbaptized party, in favor of the faith.

2. *In doubtful matters, the privilege of the faith enjoys the favor of law.* (Can. 1127.)

The privilege of the faith is the faculty given to the convert to liberate himself from the servitude of a marriage contracted in infidelity. According to the principle of law enunciated in Canon 1127, in doubtful matters the case is to be decided in favor of the convert, namely, that decision is to be given which favors the liberty of the party converted from infidelity, so that he may contract a new marriage with a Catholic party. Hence whenever there is doubt as to whether all the conditions for the application of the Pauline privilege or the privileges granted by Canon 1125, are fulfilled, this doubt is to be settled in favor of the use of the privileges so that the converted person may enter a new marriage if this favors his conversion to the Catholic faith or his perseverance in the faith. (Vlaming, p. 507.)

A matter is doubtful when every effort has been made to ascertain the truth but the doubt remains insoluble, i.e., certitude cannot be obtained either by evidence or by presumptions. The doubt may concern the validity of the former marriage, the identity of the first spouse, the sincerity of the answers to the interpellations, the cause for the desertion of the infidel party, the sufficiency of the reasons for a dispensation from the interpellations, in general, the existence of any condition requisite for the use of the Pauline privilege or privileges of Canon 1125. (Cf. Sipos, § 140; Bouscaren-Ellis, pp. 608-610.) However:

a. In the marriage of two non-Catholics whose baptisms are doubtful, where the doubt regarding the baptism is insoluble, the use of the Pauline privilege cannot be permitted to either of the parties, upon his or her conversion to the faith, in virtue of Canon 1127; and

b. In a marriage contracted between a party who is not baptized and a non-Catholic party who is doubtfully baptized, in case of an insoluble doubt regarding baptism, the Ordinaries cannot allow to either party upon conversion the use of the Pauline privilege in virtue of Canon 1127, but recourse must be made to the Holy Office for each case. (S.O., decr., 10 June, 1937.)

B. *The Privilege*

1. A legitimate marriage between unbaptized persons, even though it be consummated, is dissolved in favor of the faith by virtue of the Pauline privilege. (Can. 1120 § 1.)

The privilege may be used by any infidel who had married another infidel and now receives valid baptism either in the Catholic Church or in an heretical sect. (V.C., II, n. 428; Vlaming, p. 497; Genicot, II, n. 679.) The reason why baptism in an heretical sect suffices is because the foundation of the privilege is not the reception of the true faith but the reception of the sacrament of faith, i.e., valid baptism.

The Pauline privilege is promulgated in I Cor., 7, 8-15.

2. This privilege is not available in the case of a marriage between a baptized person and an unbaptized person contracted with a dispensation from the impediment of disparity of cult. (Can. 1120 § 3.)

Can the privilege be used by one who was validly baptized *in a sect* and who contracted a valid marriage with an unbaptized person? This case is certainly excluded from the use of the privilege since the privilege is given only to those who contract marriage in infidelity. Canon 1120 § 1 says that a legitimate marriage between *unbaptized persons* is dissolved by the Pauline privilege. (Sipos, § 140; V.C., II, n. 428.) In brief: the privilege can be used only if both parties were unbaptized at the time of the marriage.

The case of a marriage contracted between a non-baptized person and a non-Catholic whose *baptism is doubtful:* if the doubt concerning the baptism is insoluble, the Ordinaries cannot allow either party, upon conversion, the use of the Pauline privilege in virtue of Canon 1127, but recourse must be made to the Holy Office in each case. (S.O., 10 June, 1937.)

C. *The Interpellations*

1. *Nature and Necessity*

Before the party who has been converted and baptized can validly contract a new marriage, he or she must, except as provided in Canon 1125, interpellate the non-baptized party:

1°. Whether he (or she) also desires to be converted and receive baptism;

2°. Whether he (or she) at least wishes to cohabit peacefully without offense to the Creator. (Can. 1121 § 1.)

These interpellations must always be made unless the Apostolic See shall have declared otherwise. (Can. 1121 § 2.)

a. *Necessity of the interpellations.* The divine law itself requires the interpellations whenever the departure or the intentions of the infidel party are not known with certainty. If certitude is had on these points, the interpellations are nevertheless required by ecclesiastical law. If therefore, the interpellations were omitted without a dispensation, would the new marriage be valid? We must distinguish. If the departure, or intentions of the infidel spouse are not certain from other sources, then the interpellations are necessary for the valid use of the privilege and the new marriage entered into without them is invalid. (Cf. S.R.R., case, 5 Dec., 1925; *Digest,* II, p. 341.) If, however, the departure of the infidel party is certain from other sources, the matter is altogether doubtful. The interpellations are necessary for the valid use of the privilege and hence the new marriage is invalid without them according to Gasparri, Genicot, Cappello, Vlaming-Bender, Creusen; the interpellations are not necessary for the valid but only for the licit use of the privilege and hence the new marriage is valid according to Wernz-Vidal, Vermeersch, Sipos, Chelodi, Coronata. Since the whole matter is doubtful, *after a marriage has been contracted* it should be considered valid (Can. 1014) until referred to and decided on by the Holy Office; if there is question of *a marriage to be contracted* the case should be referred to the Holy Office or a dispensation obtained from the making of the interpellations. (Cf. Sipos, § 140.)

b. *Departure of the infidel party* is had if he does not wish to be converted and either has no intention of cohabiting with the convert at all (physical departure), or will not cohabit peacefully without offense to the Creator (moral departure). One will not cohabit peacefully if he intends to afflict the convert with beatings or to deprive the convert of support, or by other means to make life miserable for the convert. One will not cohabit without offense to the Creator if he will be a source of scandal to the convert. If, therefore, cohabitation places the convert in danger of perversion, i.e., of losing the faith, of committing sins of onanism, or of committing any grave sin, the Pauline privilege may be used. *Note that if the infidel party is willing to cohabit peacefully and without offense to the Creator, the convert cannot use the Pauline privilege even though the infidel does not wish to be baptized.*

If the infidel party is *willing to be baptized* but is *unwilling to cohabit* with the convert, this would seem to amount to a physical departure. Hence the convert may use the privilege before the baptism of the infidel party. (Thus Bouscaren-Ellis, p. 597, Genicot, II, n. 680, Sipos, § 140, V.C., II, n. 433; contra Abbo-Hannan, II, n. 1121.)

A physical departure is also had in the case where the infidel party *is ready to cohabit peacefully but finds it impossible to do so,* provided that the convert did not place the cause of this impossibility after his conversion. Thus the infidel party may be impeded from cohabitation by her second husband or because of a long prison term or by some similar prolonged and enforced restraint. (Cf. Sipos, § 140; Abbo-Hannan, II, n. 1121; V.C., II, n. 343.)

c. *Dispensation from the interpellations.* Dispensations from making the interpellations are sometimes granted by the Holy See when it is impossible or very difficult to make them. The faculty to dispense from interpellations is not contained in the quinquennial faculties of Ordinaries; however, in certain cases the law itself grants to Ordinaries, pastors and certain confessors the faculty to dispense, as will be explained under Canon 1125.

Mission Ordinaries subject to the Sacred Congregation for the Propagation of the Faith obtain more ample faculties to dispense. A gist of these faculties may be found in V.C., II, n. 435 and in Genicot, II, n. 691. Note that several complete commentaries (v.g., by Winslow, Vermeersch, Peeters) have been written on the apostolic faculties given to missionaries.

2. *When the interpellations are to be made*

The interpellations are to be made *after the baptism* of the convert and before the conversion of the other party. If, however, the interpellations were made before the baptism of the convert they would be valid provided they establish the fact that the infidel's departure will persevere after the convert's baptism. (Genicot, II, n. 681.)

The interpellations need be made only once. The plural is used because there are two questions to be asked.

3. *The manner of making the interpellations*

The interpellations are to be made regularly in at least a summary and extra-judicial form, by the authority of the Ordinary of the converted party, and this Ordinary shall grant to the infidel party, if he or she ask for it, a period of grace in which to deliberate, warning the said party, however, that if this period of grace elapse without reply, a negative response will be presumed. (Can. 1122 § 1.)

Interpellations, even when made privately by the converted party himself, are valid, and indeed even licit in case the above prescribed form cannot be observed; but in this case proof that they were made must be had for the external forum through the use of at least two witnesses, or by some other legitimate form of proof. (Can. 1122 § 2.)

> The various forms (judicial and extrajudicial) the Ordinary may use in making the interpellations are described in Bouscaren-Ellis, p. 599 and Abbo-Hannan, II, n. 1122.

> It is *licit* for the party to make the interpellations on his own authority only when they cannot be made on the authority of the Ordinary. In this case the party should see to it that several witnesses can testify to the answers given by the infidel party, or to the fact that letters have been sent to him and negative answers received. In the absence of witnesses, letters signed by the infidel party or the sworn testimony of a good Catholic would be sufficient proof. (V.C., II, n. 432.)

> It is not necessary, though advisable, to tell the unbaptized party that the convert intends to enter another marriage.

D. *Proceeding to the New Marriage*

1. If the interpellations were omitted in virtue of a declaration of the Apostolic See, or if the unbaptized party tacitly or expressly replied to them in the negative, the baptized party has the right to contract a new marriage with a Catholic party, unless he himself has, after his baptism, given the unbaptized party a just cause for departure. (Can. 1123.)

> a. *A negative response* would be long delays on the part of the infidel party; his obstinate silence; his subterfuges to impede the serving of the interpellations, etc., if from these acts moral certitude is had that he does not wish to convert or to at least cohabit peacefully without offense to the Creator.

> b. *A just cause for departure* would be adultery or some other crime, provided it is not condoned by the infidel party. Thus adultery on the part of the convert would cease to be the cause of the desertion if the infidel party has also been guilty of that sin, if he has condoned it, if he was unaware of it so that it did not influence his departure. Note that the offense must have been committed *after* the baptism of the convert; if committed before the baptism it does not stand in the way of the use of the privilege, unless it is continued or perdures after

the conversion. (Cf. S.C.P.F., instr., 16 Jan., 1797; S.O., 6 Aug., 1759; Sipos, § 140, footnote 24; Cappello, *De Sacr.,* V, n. 771.)

Since the right to use the Pauline privilege is lost if the departure of the infidel party is justified by a cause placed by the convert after the baptism, *the non-existence of such a cause should be established by an inquiry* to ascertain the reason for non-willingness to cohabit peacefully. (Winslow, in *The Jurist,* X (1950), p. 312.) However, in doubts as to the cause of departure, the judgment is to be rendered in favor of the convert according to Canon 1127. (Cf. S.O., decr., 5 Aug., 1759; S.C. P.F., instr., 16 Jan., 1797; S.O., reply, 19 April, 1899.)

c.   In Pauline privilege cases, as is evident, *an investigation must also be made to establish with moral certainty the non-baptism of both spouses* who contracted marriage in infidelity. The investigations concerning the fact of non-baptism are carried out under the direction and by the authority of the Ordinary. (Cf. *The Jurist,* X, pp. 307-309 for details concerning this investigation.)

d.   Canon 1123 allows the convert to contract *a new marriage with a Catholic party.* However, this requirement would not affect the validity of a marriage to be contracted with a baptized non-Catholic or, after a dispensation from the impediment of disparity of cult is obtained, with an unbaptized person. Ordinaries do not have faculties to dispense from the impediment of disparity of cult or of mixed religion when the Pauline privilege is used, hence the dispensations must come from the Holy See. However it seems that Ordinaries could dispense by reason of Canons 1043-1045 in the circumstances and under the conditions mentioned in these canons.

2.   Even though after receiving baptism, the baptized party may have again lived in matrimonial relations with the infidel party, the former does not lose the right of contracting a new marriage with a Catholic party, and therefore he (or she) can use this right if the infidel party later changes his mind and departs without just cause or ceases to cohabit peacefully without offense to the Creator. (Can. 1124.)

In this case it is not necessary to repeat the interpellations if they were once made, since the canon does not mention them. However, the new departure must be proved with moral certainty. (Cf. Woeber, CUA, n. 172, p. 71.)

If, however, the infidel party had also received baptism before the first convert contracted a new marriage, the Pauline privilege could no longer be used.

3. The bond of the former marriage which was contracted in infidelity is dissolved only at the time when the baptized party validly contracts a new marriage. (Can. 1126.)

After the new marriage is contracted, the bond of the former is dissolved and hence the unbaptized party is also free to enter a new marriage; this he could do even if later on he himself converts.

IV. EXTENSION OF THE PAULINE PRIVILEGE (Can. 1125)

A. Those provisions which concern marriage in the Constitutions *Altitudo* of Paul III, 1 June, 1537, *Romani Pontificis* of St. Pius V, 2 Aug., 1571, and *Populis* of Gregory XIII, 25 Jan., 1585, which were written for particular places, are extended to other regions also in the same circumstances.

Concerning these Constitutions, note the following:

1. The Constitutions, which were originally given for particular regions, are now *extended to the whole world,* and the concessions granted by them may be used in favor of people who find themselves in the same circumstances as are envisioned by the Constitutions.

2. The concessions given to men by the Constitutions *are applicable also to women* in the same circumstances.

3. All the marriages spoken of in the three Constitutions are marriages between *non-baptized parties*.

B. *The Constitution Altitudo of Paul III*

One who, before his conversion, had several wives, [either simultaneously or successively], and who does not remember which of them he married first, may, after his conversion to the faith, choose any one of them and marry her by present expression of consent and keep her [to the exclusion of all the others]. If, however, one remembers which wife he married first, he must keep her and dismiss the others. The privilege herein granted contains also a dispensation from the impediment of consanguinity or affinity in the third degree of the collateral line.

> Hence if a man does not remember which wife he took first he may marry any one of his wives, even if the one chosen remains an infidel; no dispensation from the impediment of disparity of cult is necessary, but the requirements of the divine law which are referred to in the *cautiones* of Canons 1061 and 1071 are to be imposed. (S.O., 30 June, 1937.)

> In the use of this privilege, no interpellations are necessary. The desire to receive baptism or even the actual baptism of anyone of the uncertain spouses in no wise affects the use of the privilege. (Winslow, in *The Jurist,* X (1950), p. 320.)

> If the man remembers which wife he took first, the privilege may not be used; however, he may use the Pauline privilege if she is unbaptized and refuses to cohabit peacefully without offense to the Creator.

C. The Constitution Romani Pontificis of St. Pius V

If a man had several wives, [either simultaneously or successively], he may, upon conversion, choose the wife who is willing to receive baptism with him, and keep her to the exclusion of the others, even though she was not the first one whom he lawfully married. This is granted because it is often very hard for the man to dismiss the wife who received baptism with him and because it is often very difficult to find the first and legitimate wife.

> This privilege applies to a man or woman who, after a valid marriage contracted in infidelity with an unbaptized party, obtains a divorce and marries another or other unbaptized parties. The authors consider two conditions necessary for the valid use of this privilege, namely that it is hard for the convert to separate from the wife with whom he is now living (or has lived), and that this wife is willing to be baptized with him. Strictly speaking, however, only one condition is necessary for the valid use of the privilege, namely that the wife chosen also converts and is baptized. (Coronata, *De Sacr.,* III, n. 648.)

> The difficulty of finding the first wife is not looked upon as a condition on which the use of the privilege depends but rather as the general motive why the favor was granted in the first place. (Vlaming, p. 506.)

> Note that the Constitution of Pius V simply dispenses from the obligation of making any interpellations whatsoever. (Vlam-

ing, p. 507.) Hence the privilege can be used even though the first and legitimate wife expresses of her own accord the desire to receive baptism. (Thus Coronata, *De Sacr.,* III, n. 648; V.C., II, n. 436; Genicot, II, n. 689; Cappello, *De Sacr.,* V, n. 787; Winslow, in *The Jurist,* X, p. 329; contra: Payen, Vromant and others, who contend that no interpellations need be made, but restrict the use of the privilege to the case in which the first and true spouse does not express her desire to receive baptism.) To us it seems that the convert is given the privilege of choosing either his present partner or any of his former partners who is willing to become a Catholic with him, irrespective of the intentions of his first wife.

What if the first wife is already baptized? According to the text of the Constitution it seems that the privilege may still be used; however, *pro praxi,* the case should be referred to the Holy See. (Cf. V.C., II, n. 436; Genicot, II, n. 689.)

D. *The Constitution Populis of Gregory XIII*

1. Local Ordinaries, pastors, and priests of the Society of Jesus approved for confession [by the local Ordinary], can dispense from the interpellations in Pauline privilege cases, provided that by an at least summary and extra-judicial investigation it has been established that the absent spouse cannot be interpellated, or that the absent spouse was interpellated and has not made known his intentions within the time specified.

Cases in which the absent spouse cannot be legally interpellated according to the Constitution *Populis:* a. when the absent spouse has moved to other parts and his whereabouts are entirely unknown; b. when the absent spouse lives in a place that is entirely inaccessible because of the hostility of the people, wars, etc.; c. when the absent spouse may be reached only by a long and arduous journey; d. finally when interpellations have been made but no answer has been forthcoming. Authors hold as a general rule that the interpellations may be dispensed from when moral impossibility of making them exists; however, the evident uselessness of the interpellations (v.g., infidel party has remarried) is not considered sufficient reason to dispense in virtue of the faculties given by this Constitution. (Cf. Bouscaren-Ellis, pp. 604-605.)

It seems that the Ordinary or the pastor can use this faculty in favor of his own subjects anywhere and in favor of *peregrini* within the territory of the diocese or parish respectively. It is also ordinary power and hence it may be delegated, even habitually. (V.C., II, n. 434.) Confessors of the Orders which enjoyed the communication of privileges with the Jesuits would seem to enjoy the same faculty. The faculty of the confessors is not limited to the sacramental forum.

2. Once the new convert obtains the dispensation from the interpellations, he is allowed, by the Constitution, to contract a new marriage with a Catholic of any rite; and this marriage will remain valid even though it afterward becomes known that the former spouse was justly prevented from declaring his will, or that at the time of the second marriage the absent spouse had already been converted to the Faith.

Hence the Constitution also contains a dispensation from a legitimate consummated marriage between two infidels, which later became a ratified marriage but was not consummated after being ratified.

V. THE PETRINE PRIVILEGE

A. It is generally admitted that the Supreme Pontiff can dissolve, for a just cause, any marriage that is not both ratified and consummated, provided that at least one of the parties is subject to the Church at the time the dissolution is given. (Sipos, § 140.) This power reaches over and beyond the favors granted by the Pauline privilege and by the Constitutions of Canon 1125 (in which the marriages of infidels are alone considered), for it includes the power to dissolve marriages involving a baptized person. This power may be called the *Petrine privilege,* and although it extends to any marriage that is not at the same time ratified and consummated, the term Petrine privilege usually refers to the power of the Pontiff to dissolve in favor of the faith a marriage between a baptized person and an unbaptized person even though the marriage has been consummated.

Thus, in recent years, the Roman Pontiff has dissolved the following types of marriages in favor of the faith:

1. Marriage of a baptized Protestant and an unbaptized person; presumably consummated; unbaptized person converted, a dissolution of the marriage was given and the convert was allowed to remarry. (S.O., 6 Nov., 1924; *Digest,* I, p. 553 — The Helena case.)

2. Marriage of a baptized Protestant and an unbaptized person; presumably consummated; Protestant party converted, a dissolution of the marriage was granted, and the convert allowed to remarry. (S.O., 10 July, 1924, Ayrinhac, p. 324; another case of the same kind, S.O., 25 May, 1933, *Digest,* III, p. 479.)

3. Baptized Catholic married, with a dispensation from disparity of cult, an unbaptized person; presumably consummated; unbaptized person converted; marriage dissolved and convert allowed to remarry. (S.O., 30 Jan., 1950, *Digest,* III, p. 486.) The Catholic party was also allowed to remarry. (S.O., 10 April, 1950, *Digest,* III, p. 488.)

4. Baptized Catholic woman married, with a dispensation from disparity of cult, an unbaptized man; presumably consummated; civil divorce; the marriage was dissolved in favor of the faith by the Roman Pontiff and the Catholic party allowed to enter a new marriage with a Catholic man. (S.O., 8 Aug., 1955, *Digest,* IV, pp. 350-352.)

For other examples of Petrine privilege cases, confer *The Jurist,* XX, pp. 71-74, 106.

B. The canonical procedure in Petrine privilege cases is regulated by a document of the Holy Office communicated privately to local Ordinaries. (S.O., *Normae,* 1 May, 1934.) The process of investigation must prove:

1. The existence of two essential conditions, namely, a. lack of baptism in one of the spouses during the whole time of the conjugal life; and b. the non-use of the marriage after the baptism of the previously unbaptized spouse.

2. The existence of two further conditions, namely, a. moral impossibility of the restoration of conjugal life; and b. the absence of scandal or admiration from the eventual granting of the favor.

All the acts of the case are sent to the Holy Office with the petition for a pontifical dispensation from the natural bond of the marriage in favor of the faith.

ORIENTAL LAW

Canons 107-116 of *Crebrae allatae,* concerning the dissolution of the bond, are the same as Canons 1118-1127 of the Code of Canon Law.

CHAPTER XI

Separation from Bed and Board

I. OBLIGATION OF COMMON LIFE

Husband and wife are obliged to observe community of conjugal life unless a just reason excuses them. (Can. 1128.)

Community of conjugal life includes the sharing of bedroom, table and home. The spouses are obliged to this community of life because it is the ordinary means of providing for the fulfillment of the marital debt and for the education and rearing of the children. Temporary cessation of common life may be permitted for a just cause, and by the mutual consent of the spouses themselves, v.g., for the undertaking of a long journey by the husband, for the making of retreats, etc. Perpetual cessation of common life, however, especially of cohabitation, by the mere mutual consent of the parties themselves is almost never licit; for this, the intervention of public authority, i.e., of the local Ordinary is necessary.

> By mutual consent the spouses may establish separation from bed alone, even perpetually, for a grave cause, v.g., great difficulty in supporting children, danger of communicating a disease, the observance of perfect chastity, etc. Indeed, separation from bed would be obligatory when the marital debt cannot be fulfilled and the common bed would be a proximate danger of sin for the parties. Separation from bed alone would be lawful even without mutual consent if one of the parties is lawfully not obliged to render the marriage debt. Since these cases pertain to the internal forum, they may be decided by the parties themselves; however, the advice of a prudent confessor should be sought lest the parties place themselves in danger of incontinence. (Cf. V.C., II, nos. 442, 445.)

II. PERPETUAL SEPARATION

1. *Reason for perpetual separation*

Because of the adultery of one spouse, the other spouse has the right to terminate community of life, even perpetually, unless he consented to the crime or was the cause of it, or expressly or tacitly condoned it, or has himself committed the same crime; the marriage bond itself remains intact. (Can. 1129 § 1.)

a. *The adultery must be:*

1) *Consummated.* It must consist of sexual intercourse; touches, embraces, etc. do not suffice. With regard to onanistic intercourse, it is for practical purposes certain that such intercourse is sufficient reason for perpetual separation. The same may be said of sodomy committed with a third party, and of bestiality.

2) *Formally sinful.* Hence the husband cannot separate from a wife who was raped; likewise, the right to separate would be uncertain if the wife was compelled to adultery by grave fear.

3) *Morally certain.* Demonstrated by weighty and urgent presumptions; presumptions which force one to prudently judge that adultery has been committed are sufficient (Genicot, II, n. 695), as, for instance, when it is known that the persons shared the same hotel room, or that they went off alone to a private cabin for the week-end.

b. *Adultery is not sufficient reason* for separation if the other spouse consented to the crime, or has also committed adultery, or has been the cause of the partner's adultery. One is not considered the cause of the crime if he (or she) causes it only indirectly, v.g., by quarrelling, for it is necessary that one be the direct cause of the crime, v.g., by refusing marital relations frequently or for a long time, by desertion, etc. (V.C., II, n. 440.)

c. *Adultery is not sufficient reason* for separation if the innocent spouse expressly or tacitly condones the adultery. Tacit condonation is had if the innocent spouse, after learning of the commission of the adultery, voluntarily lives with the other and shows him conjugal affection; condonation is presumed if within six months the innocent party does not expel or desert the delinquent spouse, or does not lodge a legal complaint against him. (Can. 1129 § 2.)

It does not seem that sexual intercourse is a requisite condition for tacit condonation, for marital affection is also displayed by kissing, embracing, etc. Note that condonation can be given tacitly only *after* one learns of the crime of the delinquent spouse. Marital affection shown before the innocent party comes to that knowledge cannot be construed as tacit condonation. The showing of marital affection must be entirely voluntary; hence if it is shown because of fear or some other grave inconvenience it does not constitute tacit condonation.

2. *The authority competent to effect a perpetual separation; effects of separation*

The innocent party who has departed legally, whether in pursuance of a judicial sentence or on his own authority, is never bound to admit the adulterous partner to conjugal life again; but he may either receive or recall the party, unless the latter has, in virtue of consent given by the innocent spouse, adopted a state of life incompatible with marriage. (Can. 1130.)

a. *If the adultery is both certain and public* (commonly known, or committed under such circumstances that it must easily become known), the innocent party may separate on his own authority. *If the crime is certain, but occult,* strictly speaking the innocent party may still separate on his own authority, however, the necessity of avoiding scandal will almost always oblige the party to seek a decree of separation from the ecclesiastical authorities. (Genicot, II, n. 698; Gasparri, II, n. 1175; Sipos, § 141.) *If the adultery is not certain* the intervention of ecclesiastical authority is absolutely required for the separation.

b. *A state incompatible with marriage* is the religious state or the clerical state. The delinquent party cannot enter such a state without the permission of the innocent party; the innocent party can enter these states without the other party's permission; both, however, would need a papal dispensation. (Cf. Canons 542, 987.)

III. TEMPORARY SEPARATION

1. *Reasons for temporary separation; the competent authority*

If one of the parties has joined a non-Catholic sect; or educated the children as non-Catholics; or is living a criminal or disgraceful life; or is causing grave spiritual or

corporal harm to the other; or makes the common life
intolerable because of his cruelty — these and other grievances of the same kind are all lawful reasons for the other
party to depart, on the authority of the local Ordinary,
and even on one's own authority if the grievances are certain and there is danger in delay. (Can. 1131 § 1.)

> The reasons are not enumerated taxatively; the ones given
> here are only examples. Other reasons are malicious desertion;
> implacable hatred, insanity, contagious disease. If the danger of
> infection is restricted to the occasion of carnal intercourse,
> separation is not justified, though one may refuse the marital
> debt. (Abbo-Hannan, II, n. 1131.)

> One must have recourse to the local Ordinary in all cases of
> temporary separation unless the reason is certain and at the
> same time there is danger in delay. Such cases can occur when
> grave corporal harm is imminent from the insanity of the other
> spouse, or when grave spiritual harm is imminent as when one
> spouse is attempting to lead the other into grave sin, v.g.,
> onanism.

2. *Effect of temporary separation.* In all cases of temporary separation, when the cause of the separation has
ceased to exist, the common life is to be restored; but if
the separation was decreed by the Ordinary for a definite
or indefinite time, the innocent spouse is not obliged to
restore the common life unless by decree of the Ordinary
or upon expiration of the time. (Can. 1131 § 2.)

> When a separation has been effected, the children shall be
> reared by the innocent spouse or, if one of the spouses is a non-
> Catholic, by the Catholic spouse, unless in either case the Ordi-
> nary shall have decreed otherwise for the good of the children
> themselves, without prejudice, in any case, to their Catholic
> education. (Can. 1132.)

IV. CIVIL DIVORCE IN SEPARATION CASES

1. The Third Plenary Council of Baltimore states that
those who sue before a civil magistrate for a dissolution
of marriage are guilty of grave sin, and it forbids the faithful to sue in civil court for a separation from bed and
board unless they first consult the ecclesiastical authorities,

otherwise they also are guilty of grave sin. (Balt. III, nos. 124, 126.) Hence, the faithful have a grave obligation to obtain the local Ordinary's permission before suing in civil court for separation (in States permitting this) or divorce (in States not granting legal action for separation, or when it is only divorce that will fully protect the innocent spouse according to the laws of the State in question).

> Since people are sometimes hesitant about entering into direct communication with diocesan officials in these matters, the confessor must be very prudent in insisting on this obligation; at times it will be best for him to remain silent, namely, in cases in which the parties have sufficient reason for a separation and he foresees that his admonition will serve no other purpose but to disturb the good faith of the penitent. This is all the more true when the separation has already been effected and there is no great scandal connected with it; and this is especially the case when the parties have not been living together for a very long time so that now people just take them and their status for granted. (Cf. Genicot, II, n. 698; Bouscaren-Ellis, p. 616.)

2. It seems that the defendant in a civil divorce case has no special obligation placed on him by the Council of Baltimore to contest the divorce. Hence no canonical obligation. But a moral obligation to contest the divorce can arise from many sources: e.g., the protection of the children; the cooperation in the sin of the plaintiff; scandal (to neighbors); negative aid given to the plans of the plaintiff to enter a new marriage; therefore in general from our duty to avoid scandal and cooperation in the sins of others on the one hand, and to promote the bodily and spiritual welfare of our children on the other. On the other hand, note that grave inconvenience, v.g., long journeys, large fees for lawyers, nervous breakdown, etc. may excuse from the obligation to contest the divorce. The *causae excusantes* are to be weighed against the good effects flowing from the contesting of the divorce and then a prudent decision is to be made.

ORIENTAL LAW

Canons 117-121 of *Crebrae allatae* contain the same provisions concerning separation from bed and board as do Canons 1128-1132 of the Code of Canon Law. The Oriental law also mentions malicious desertion as a reason for obtaining from the local Hierarch a decree of separation for a definite or indefinite time. (Mp, Can. 120 § 2.)

CHAPTER XII

Convalidation of Marriage

When the pastor or confessor discovers that persons are living in an invalid marriage, *per se* he should try to have the marriage convalidated, but prudently, i.e., he should be careful not to be in haste in convalidating unions which were entered into hastily and which will probably be repented of in due time, as for instance when a young girl runs off with a man she has known for only a short time. In cases such as these it may be better to wait in order to see how things develop.

If the marriage cannot be convalidated, *per se* a declaration of nullity is to be sought from the ecclesiastical authorities. If one or both of the parties know of the invalidity of their marriage, and grave reasons stand in the way of their separation, v.g., the care of small children, the pastor may investigate the possibility of having the parties live as brother and sister.

Finally, if both parties are in good faith, i.e., they are inculpably ignorant of the invalidity of their marriage, and the case is such that the marriage cannot be convalidated, the confessor should ordinarily leave them in good faith if he foresees that they can in no wise be induced to separate, or that grave harm would come to the children in case of a separation of the parents. (Cf. Sipos, § 142; Genicot, II, nos. 703, 706.)

I. SIMPLE CONVALIDATION

A. *Convalidation of Marriage Invalid Because of a Diriment Impediment*

1. To validate a marriage that is invalid because of a diriment impediment, it is required that *the impediment cease or be dispensed from,* and that *consent be renewed* at least by the party who is aware of the impediment. This renewal of consent is required by ecclesiastical law for the validity of the marriage, even though both parties gave consent in the beginning and have not since revoked it. (Can. 1133.)

> *The impediment* may cease automatically (v.g., the bond, by the death of the former spouse; disparity of cult, by the conversion of the infidel; age, by mere lapse of time), or by dispensation. In danger of death or in the urgent case Canons 1043-1045 may be used to dispense. (Cf. above, p. 222 ff.)
>
> *The renewal of consent* is required by ecclesiastical law only. However, this law is binding also for baptized Protestants (PCI, 3 Dec., 1919, *Digest,* II, p. 336-338.) This renewal of consent is *not required by natural law,* for after the removal of the impediment, the consent given in the beginning and not since revoked would now take effect and effect the validation of the marriage. Hence an invalid marriage of two infidels would be validated upon the cessation of the impediment by mere continuation of conjugal life. (Genicot, II, n. 706.) This rule is generally recognized also in civil law especially when the impediment was non-age or defective consent; however, in some states limitations are placed, so that marriages invalid because of certain types of impediments are not convalidated by mere marital cohabitation upon the cessation of the impediment. Hence marriages involving infidels only, call for special investigation in the individual cases.

2. The renewal of consent must be a new act of the will directed to a marriage *which is known to have been invalid from the beginning.* (Can. 1134.)

> Knowledge of the invalidity of the marriage must be had before the renewal of consent will effect the convalidation of the marriage. This also is a requirement of ecclesiastical law (Sipos, § 142), and hence would affect the marriage of Protestants but not the marriage of two infidels.

3. a. *If the impediment is public,* consent must be renewed by both parties in the form prescribed by law. (Can. 1135 § 1.)

The impediment is public when it can be proved in the external forum (v.g., consanguinity, age, previous bond); otherwise it is *occult.* (Cf. Canon 1037.) Note, however, that the possibility of proof must be practical, i.e., one can find witnesses who are able and willing to testify, documents are available to prove the existence of the impediment, etc. Theoretic possibility of proof, v.g., the impediment is of its nature public and therefore should be able to be proved, does not suffice. (Cf. V.C., II, n. 297.) Hence if the parties are related but the fact cannot be proved, the impediment is occult.

The form required by law is the presence of the pastor or delegated priest and two witnesses. However, if the impediment is by law public but in fact occult, the form can be observed quietly and secretly; if the impediment is also factually public, the form is to be observed publicly and openly. (Sipos, § 142.) Since Protestants are not bound by the canonical form when marrying each other or infidels, they would not be obliged to renew consent in this way, but it suffices that they renew their consent by an *external act,* provided that they are conscious of the invalidity of the marriage. (Cf. Can. 1134.)

The consent must be renewed by both parties. If the impediment is public by law but nevertheless unknown to one of the parties, he should be told and the marriage consent renewed with the observance of the canonical form; and if this cannot be done, a *sanatio in radice* should be obtained. (Genicot, II, n. 707.)

b. If the impediment is *occult and known to both parties,* it suffices that the consent be renewed by both parties privately and secretly. (Can. 1135 § 2.)

Hence in this case the canonical form need not be observed and the consent is renewed without the intervention of pastor and witnesses. If, however, the marriage is also invalid because the canonical form was not observed in the first place, it is now necessary to renew consent in the presence of pastor and witnesses. (Can. 1137.)

Whenever consent may be renewed without observing the canonical form it may be renewed implicitly, v.g., by sexual intercourse with marital affection, i.e., the intercourse is meant as an expression of marital consent, as a giving of oneself in marriage. (Gasparri, II, n. 1200.)

c. If the impediment is *occult and unknown to one of the parties,* it suffices that only the party who is aware of the impediment privately and secretly renew consent, provided that the other's consent perseveres. (Can. 1135 § 3.)

> Hence, in this case also the canonical form need not be observed, unless it had not been observed in the first giving of consent. (Can. 1137.) The other party's consent is presumed to persevere until its revocation shall have been proved. (Can. 1093.) The fact that this party would wish to break off the marriage if he knew of its invalidity does not destroy the perseverance of the consent actually given. (Genicot, II, n. 704.)

B. *Convalidation of Marriage Invalid Because of Defective Consent*

1. A marriage that is invalid because of defective consent is validated if the party who did not consent, now consents, provided that the consent given by the other party perseveres. (Can. 1136 § 1.)

> *Defective consent:* A positive act of the will excluding conjugal rights, indissolubility, or fidelity; error of person; force and fear.

> For the convalidation of this type of invalid marriage it is necessary that a new and valid consent be given. According to the norm of Canon 1134 this renewal of consent must be a new act of the will directed to a marriage which is *known to have been invalid from the beginning. Hence if the party was unaware of the invalidity of the marriage, subsequent consent or the granting of marital rights would not convalidate the marriage.* (Cf. S.R.R., case, 29 July, 1926, *Digest,* I, p. 523.)

2. If the defect of consent was *merely internal,* it suffices that the party who did not consent now consents internally. (Can. 1136 § 2.)

3. If the defect of consent was *also external,* it is necessary to manifest the consent also externally either in the form prescribed by law, if the defect was *public,* or in some private and secret manner, if it was *occult.* (Can. 1136 § 3.)

> *External defect:* An agreement between the parties to allow

divorce; the application of force and fear.

Public defect: In the sense of Canon 1037, i.e., it can be proved in the external forum, as is often the case with force and fear. In these cases the canonical form (pastor and witnesses) is necessary for a valid convalidation. (Cf. Sipos, § 142.) Although baptized Protestants are bound by the canons on the convalidation of marriage, they are not bound by the canonical form; hence for them the convalidation is effected in this case by renewing consent with an external act. (Cf. Abbo-Hannan, II n. 1135.) However, the party renewing consent would have to know the marriage was invalid from the beginning. (Cf. Can. 1134.)

Occult defect: The defect cannot be proved in the external forum, v.g., if witnesses refuse to testify, if there are no witnesses, if witnesses can prove nothing (as is often the case with intentions contrary to the substance of marriage). In these cases the consent must be renewed externally but without the observance of the canonical form. It can be renewed implicitly, v.g., by sexual intercourse with marital affection. However the person renewing consent must know that the marriage was invalid from the beginning.

C. *Convalidation of Marriage Invalid for Want of Form*

In order that a marriage which is invalid for want of form be made valid, it must be contracted anew in the form prescribed by law. (Can. 1137.)

If the nullity is occult, the marriage may be contracted before the pastor and witnesses secretly; if the nullity is publicly known the form should be observed publicly.

If one of the parties refuses to renew consent before a priest, apply for a dispensation from the form and have the parties renew consent privately, i.e., amongst themselves. If one of the parties will not renew consent at all, v.g., because he is convinced that his civil marriage is sufficient, apply for a *sanatio in radice.*

D. *Oriental law:* Canons 122-126 of *Crebrae allatae* are the same as Canons 1133-1137 of the Code.

II. RADICAL SANATION

1. *Nature and Effects of Radical Sanation*

a. The radical sanation of a marriage is the validation

of the marriage effecting, besides a dispensation from or a cessation of the impediment, a dispensation from the law requiring renewal of consent and, by a fiction of law, a retroaction as regards canonical effects to the past. The validation is effected at the moment when the favor is granted; the retroactive effect is understood to date from the beginning of the marriage unless a contrary provision is expressly made. (Can. 1138 §§ 1, 2.)

Hence the marriage is convalidated without a renewal of consent; once the impediment is removed, the consent previously given, which was naturally valid but juridically invalid, becomes efficacious and produces its effect, namely, a valid marriage. Sometimes a renewal of consent is demanded in the rescript granting the sanation, the reason being to make sure that the consent previously given still perseveres, but this does not change the nature of the sanation, even if the renewal is required for the validity of the marriage, and it does not deprive the sanation of its retroactive power. (Sipos, § 142; Coronata, *De Sacr.*, III, n. 683; cf. also, Abbo-Hannan, II, n. 1138.)

As regards canonical effects, a marriage radically sanated is equivalent to a marriage valid from the beginning, and hence the children are not merely legitimated but are legitimate, just as if they had been born of a valid marriage, provided that they were born after the date when the parents gave the marital consent which the radical sanation validates. Hence these children are eligible also for the cardinalate, episcopate, abbacy and prelacy *nullius,* and the position of major superior in a religious institute. (Sipos, § 142; Abbo-Hannan, II, n. 1138.) If the children were born before the date when the parents gave the marital consent which the sanation validates, they would be legitimated by the sanation according to the norm of Canon 1116 which states that children are legitimated by the subsequent marriage of their parents, provided, however, that the parents were capable of marrying each other at some time from the conception to the birth of the child.

b. The dispensation from the law requiring renewal of consent can be granted even without the knowledge of one or both of the parties. (Can. 1138 § 3.)

Sanations made without the knowledge of either of the parties are usually such as are granted *in globo,* v.g., sanations of marriages invalidly contracted due to lack of jurisdiction in the priest officiating (cf. sanations granted in this way by S.C.Sacr.,

21 July, 1919), or sanations of marriages previously invalidly sanated by bishops lacking the requisite faculties (cf. sanations made in this way by the S.O., 22 Dec., 1916). Also in cases where the invalidity of the marriage is the fault of an ecclesiastical personage; thus the Holy Office sanated a marriage contracted by an erroneous application of the Pauline privilege. (S.O., 19 June, 1947.)

2. *Conditions for Radical Sanation*

a. Any marriage entered into by parties with a mutual consent naturally sufficient but juridically inefficacious on account of a diriment impediment of ecclesiastical law or on account of the non-observance of the canonical form, can be radically sanated, provided the consent perseveres. (Can. 1139 § 1.)

Hence *the consent must be naturally valid*, i.e., not defective by reason of intentions contrary to the *bonum prolis, bonum sacramenti, bonum fidei*, nor by error of person, or by insanity, lack of knowledge of the purpose of the contract, etc. Note however, that the knowledge or belief that a marriage is null does not necessarily exclude a valid matrimonial consent, for, together with the knowledge or the opinion of nullity there can exist a will to enter marriage in so far as one can; true matrimonial consent can easily exist even though the marriage itself is known to be invalid by reason of some diriment impediment. (Cf. Can. 1085.)

Even though a marriage has been contracted invalidly because of an impediment, *the consent which has been given is presumed to persevere* until its revocation shall have been proved. (Can. 1093.) In a sanation, the consent must exist at the time the marriage is validated without a renewal of consent; however, if the consent was once given, it is presumed that it still exists unless one can prove that it was revoked.

b. But a marriage contracted with an impediment of the natural or divine law, even though the impediment has since ceased to exist, the Church does not radically sanate, not even from the moment of the cessation of the impediment. (Can. 1139 § 2.)

Although the Church does not sanate such marriages, nevertheless it has the power to do so once the impediment has ceased. (Sipos, § 142; Gasparri, II, nos. 1215-1219.) The rule of Canon 1139 § 2 is not adamant, since there are on record cases in which the Church has granted a sanation after the impediment had ceased. (Cf. Bouscaren-Ellis, p. 625.)

c. If the consent is wanting in both parties or in one party, the marriage cannot be radically sanated, whether the consent was lacking from the beginning or was originally given but later revoked. But if consent was lacking in the beginning but was later given, the sanation can be granted from the moment when the consent was given. (Can. 1140.)

d. A grave cause is necessary for the validity of a sanation granted by one inferior to the Holy See. (Cf. Can. 84 § 1.)

Such causes are: serious inconvenience involved in manifesting the invalidity of one's marriage to the other party; refusal of the non-Catholic party to renew consent; the fact that the nullity of the marriage arose from the ignorance or fault of an Ordinary, pastor or confessor.

3. Competent Authority for Radical Sanations

a. A radical sanation can be granted only by the Apostolic See. (Can. 1141.)

b. Local Ordinaries, in virtue of the quinquennial faculties, may also grant radical sanation in the following cases:

1) For marriages invalidly contracted because of some impediment of ecclesiastical law of major or minor degree, except the impediments resulting from the sacred order of the priesthood and from affinity in the direct line when the marriage has been consummated. (*Digest,* IV, p. 74.)

The sanation may be granted *if* there is a grave inconvenience in requiring a renewal of consent from the party who is ignorant of the invalidity of the marriage and *only provided* that the former consent continues to exist and that danger of divorce is absent. The Ordinary may use these faculties personally or through others specially deputed for the purpose; also in favor of his own subjects anywhere and of all other persons actually staying in his territory. (*Digest,* IV, p. 74.) This faculty does not extend to cases in which the marriage is invalid because of lack of canonical form or defective consent. (Cf. S.C. Sacr., reply, 10 March, 1937.)

2) For marriages attempted before a civil official or a non-Catholic minister where there was the impediment of mixed religion or disparity of cult, *provided that* matrimonial consent continues to exist in both parties and that the same cannot be legitimately renewed, either because the non-Catholic party cannot be informed of the invalidity of the marriage without danger of grave harm or inconvenience to the Catholic party, or because the non-Catholic party can in no wise be induced to renew consent before the Church or to give the guarantees as required by Canon 1061 § 2. (*Digest,* IV, p. 72.)

This sanation can be given *only if* it is morally certain that the non-Catholic party will not impede the baptism and Catholic education of all children who may be born, and *provided that* the Catholic party explicitly promise to provide, to the best of his ability, for the baptism and Catholic education of all children who may be born, and (if the case warrants it) for the conversion, baptism and Catholic education of children already born, that the parties did not, before the attempted marriage, bind themselves either privately or by public act to educate the children as non-Catholics, that neither party be actually insane, that at least the Catholic party know of the sanation and ask for it, and that there be no other canonical diriment impediment for which the Ordinary himself has not the faculty to dispense or to grant a sanation. This faculty may be used in favor of one's subject anywhere and in favor of all persons actually staying in the territory. However, it is the mind of the Holy Office that the Bishop exercise this faculty himself, that is, that he do not subdelegate it to anyone. (*Digest,* IV, pp. 72, 73.)

Note that local Ordinaries have faculties to sanate marriages invalid because of non-observance of the canonical form only in the case of mixed marriages or disparate cult marriages. The Apostolic Delegate has faculties to sanate the marriage of *two Catholics* invalid because of non-observance of the canonical form, if one of the parties refuses to renew consent according to the form prescribed by law or if grave harm or inconvenience accrue to one party if the other is required to renew consent in the prescribed form. (*Digest,* I, pp. 181-182.)

c. A Latin Ordinary may use his faculties in favor of

Orientals who are subject to his jurisdiction. (Cf. above, p. 220.)

4. *Oriental Law*

The same norms apply as regards radical sanation as in the Latin Code (Mp, Canons 127-130). A Patriarch, however, possesses faculties to grant a radical sanation if the obstacle to the validity of the marriage was the non-observance of the form, or an impediment from which the Patriarch can grant a dispensation. (Mp, Can. 130 § 2.)

III. COHABITATION AS BROTHER AND SISTER

The last refuge for those who are living in an invalid marriage is to obtain permission to live as brother and sister. That this permission may be given, four conditions must be verified:

1. *It is the only practical solution available.* This condition is verified when the couple can neither marry nor separate. They cannot marry because of some indispensable impediment, v.g., the bond of a previous valid marriage, impotence, etc. It is physically or morally impossible for them to separate, when: grave economic reasons will not allow it; or one of the parties is very sick; or children already born need the protection and care of the parents; or there is danger of scandal and infamy because others do not know of the invalidity of the marriage; or finally, cohabitation favors the conversion of one or both parties to the faith.

2. The second condition is that *no grave scandal will be occasioned by this cohabitation.* In these cases scandal can arise from a double source, namely, from an apparently sinful cohabitation, or from an apparent approbation of the Church if such persons are allowed to receive the sacraments.

a. Hence in cases *both materially and formally public* (both the fact of the invalidity of the marriage and the fact that the marriage cannot be convalidated are publicly known), the permission to live as brother and sister is not easily granted because scandal already exists. Nevertheless the parties may move to another local where the invalidity of the marriage is not known and the public case will then become occult. If this is not possible, scandal could still be avoided if the permission to cohabitate is kept secret. In this case the parties are allowed to receive the sacraments privately and secretly. In some cases scandal can be removed by discretely divulging the fact that the persons are living as brother and sister. This method of handling the case is permitted by the authors when the parties are of such age and virtue that the credulity of the faithful will not be overly taxed.

b. In cases *materially public but formally occult* (the invalidity of the marriage is well known, but it is not known that the marriage cannot be convalidated), scandal can usually be avoided by divulging the fact that their case has been happily "fixed up" by the pastor or the chancery. Indeed in some cases, the public reception of the sacraments will suffice to remove scandal because of the presumption on the part of the faithful that the marriage must have been convalidated.

c. In cases *altogether occult* (neither the fact of invalidity nor the reason of it are known), there is no question of scandal.

3. The third condition is *the absence of the proximate occasion of sin*. Objectively speaking, cohabitation is a proximate occasion of sin. In our case it is a necessary occasion (confer n. 1 above). If the occasion is voluntary, i.e., if the parties can separate, they must separate. If, however, the occasion is necessary, then the parties must use apt means to make the proximate occasion remote, because it can never be tolerated that one be allowed to remain in an occasion which places one in grave danger of eternal damnation.

The means to be used especially are: use of separate bedrooms, or if this is absolutely impossible, at least the use of separate beds; daily prayer; weekly reception of the sacraments; zeal in promoting works of charity; defense of the rights of the Church. Other reasons also may be at hand to render the occasion of sin remote, v.g., the age of the parties, the ill health of one of the parties, the presence of relatives in the home, etc.

4. The fourth condition is *the permission of the com-*

petent authority. The local Ordinary is the guardian of public morality, the judge of the reparation due for scandal and of the cessation of infamy, the protector of the reverence due to the sacraments, in his diocese. (Cf. Canons 335, 336, 343, 855, 893, 1130, 1131, 2295, etc.) Hence the Ordinary may, if he wish, reserve all "brother-sister" cases to his own judgment, without prejudice however to sacramental and professional secrecy, and without prejudice to the right of the parties to preserve their good name or to regain it. Since, however, the "permission" to live as brother and sister is not a dispensation or privilege, but rather a declaration that the law of God, all things considered, does not prohibit the cohabitation of this man and this woman, and therefore that they can be admitted to the sacraments, the decision on a particular case can be given *per se* also by the pastor or confessor.

In particular:

a. If the case is *both materially and formally public:* because of the reasons given above, the local Ordinary alone (or his delegate) is competent to give the permission to live as brother and sister.

b. If the case is *materially public but formally occult:* the pastor, as the guardian of public morality and the protector of reverence due to the sacraments in his parish, should be considered competent to give the permission, unless the Ordinary has expressly reserved these cases to his own judgment.

c. If the case is both *materially and formally occult:* the confessor is the competent authority, unless the Ordinary has expressly and lawfully placed some restrictions in these matters. If the Ordinary has placed restrictions on brother-sister arrangements in general, but has not specifically mentioned cases materially and formally occult, it seems to us that the confessor's powers in this matter are not restricted.

d. In altogether *extraordinary cases,* v.g., when there is question of a priest living in an invalid marriage, the case is to be referred to the Sacred Penitentiary.

Pastoral Note: The pastor and confessor may prudently hesitate to decide "brother-sister cases" without first referring the matter to the Chancery because of another problem involved. Most invalid marriages are invalid because of a previous bond.

Hence the legality of one's separation from a previous spouse is to be considered. Only adultery is sufficient reason for permanent separation. And even then the intervention of the Ordinary is sometimes required to make the separation altogether legal. Hence the pastor and confessor should first try to form a prudent judgment concerning the legality of the separation from a previous spouse, according to the rules given above under separation from bed and board. A further problem is presented by the legality of one's civil divorce from a former spouse. The Ordinary's permission is required for a divorce suit (cf. Balt. III, nos. 124, 126), and in some dioceses, those who have divorced without the Ordinary's permission, are debarred from the sacraments until they submit their case to the Ordinary. On the other hand, also keep in mind that moral theologians allow one to dissimulate on these problems if the circumstances warrant it (cf. rules on leaving a penitent in good faith). Also note that what some authors teach about the innocent spouse losing the right to maintain the separation if he also commits adultery after the separation is effected (when said separation was lawfully effected on his own authority) *is altogether uncertain.* It is solidly probable that once a perpetual separation is lawfully effected, subsequent adultery on the part of the innocent spouse in no wise affects the case. (Cf. Payen, II, n. 2476.) In a word: be slow to decide a case; be slow also in refusing to decide a case. There are many angles to consider.

APPENDIX

Second Marriages

1. Although chaste widowhood is more honorable, second and even further marriages are valid and lawful; however, it is not allowed to contract another marriage until the dissolution of the former shall have been established according to law and with certainty. (Canons 1142, 1069 § 2.)

Second marriages are permitted, in some circumstances recommended, but chaste widowhood is preferred, by the Apostle. (Cf. I Cor., 7, 40; I Tim., 5, 11 ss.)

2. A woman to whom the solemn nuptial blessing has once been given cannot receive it again in a subsequent marriage. (Can. 1143.)

If it is the second marriage for the man but the first for the woman, the blessing may be given again in places where it is customary to do so.

Whenever the nuptial blessing cannot be given, the substitute blessing contained in the ritual (*Appendix de matrimonio,* II) may be granted, but only in virtue of apostolic indult. The indult is contained in the Ordinaries' quinquennial faculties.

3. *Oriental law.* Second and further marriages are allowed just as in the Latin Church (Mp, Can. 131), but the solemn blessing at second and subsequent marriages is not forbidden.

4. *Civil Law.* In Puerto Rico, civil law forbids a woman to enter a second marriage until 301 days have elapsed since the dissolution of the former marriage, or until the birth of the child if she was pregnant before the death of her husband. In many States a restriction is made at the time a divorce is granted forbidding another marriage for a specified time. The restriction is generally not binding under pain of nullity, or if it is, it does not oblige outside of the State. (Alford, n. 455.)

PART IX

SACRED TIMES — PLACES — FURNISHINGS

CHAPTER I

Sacred Times

I. SUNDAYS AND HOLYDAYS

1. In the United States, besides Sundays, also the following feasts are celebrated as days of obligation: Christmas, Circumcision, Ascension, Assumption, All Saints, and Immaculate Conception.

2. On Sundays and Holy Days Mass must be heard; moreover, there is also an obligation to abstain from servile work, from judicial acts and, unless the contrary is permitted by lawful custom or particular indults, from public marketing, the holding of fairs, and any other kind of public commercial occupation involving buying and selling. (Can. 1248.)

a. One fulfills the *obligation of hearing Mass* by attending Mass celebrated in any Catholic rite, in the open air or in any church, public oratory, or semipublic oratory, and in the private cemetery chapels spoken of in Canon 1190; not however, in other private oratories unless this privilege has been granted by the Holy See. (Can. 1249.)

> If Mass is celebrated by a priest who has the personal privilege of a portable altar, those who attend the Mass by no means satisfy the obligation of hearing Mass on a day of precept, unless the indult granting the privilege of the portable altar expressly extends that favor to those attending the Mass.

If, however, the Mass is celebrated in the open (*sub dio*), the faithful who assist at it fulfill the obligation of hearing Mass as is expressly stated in Canon 1249. (S.C.Sacr., instr., 1 Oct., 1949 sub II, n. 8.)

If the Ordinary grants permission to say Mass outside a church or oratory, for a just and reasonable cause, in some extraordinary case, according to the norm of Canon 822 § 4, the law of hearing Mass is satisfied by one who assists at that Mass. (PCI, 26 March, 1952.) For example, a person taking care of a sick person could fulfill the obligation by hearing Mass in the private home of the sick if the Ordinary granted permission to have a Mass celebrated there.

b. In judging what type of work is *servile work,* the authors commonly look to the nature of the work, irrespective of whether a compensation is received or not. Accordingly, forbidden work is that which is performed more with the body than with the mind, v.g., plowing, harvesting, mining, masonry, and in general the work of factory employees.

Due to the recent development in the classification of forbidden work, it seems that some lighter manual work is at times permitted. Thus the tilling of a small garden by one whose occupation keeps him inside all week would be permitted. (Noldin, II, n. 267.) However, the custom of one's region must be considered and scandal must be avoided.

c. *Judicial acts* performed *cum strepitu iudiciali* whether the judicial process be civil or criminal, secular or ecclesiastical, are forbidden.

Hence, examining the witnesses, demanding the oath, passing a sentence and the like are forbidden. Acts which are performed *sine strepitu iudiciali* are not forbidden, v.g., consulting one's lawyer, preparing one's defense, etc.

d. Public marketing and *commercial occupation* as had in down-town and super-market shopping are forbidden on days of obligation.

In the United States custom permits the opening and operating of the corner grocery store for a few hours on Sunday morning.

II. FAST AND ABSTINENCE

A. *The Law of Fast and Abstinence*

1. *Abstinence.* The law of abstinence forbids the eating of flesh meat and broth made from meat, but not eggs, milk products, or seasoning, even though the latter be made from animal fat. (Can. 1250.)

> *Forbidden* are the fleshmeat of warm-blooded animals and all parts of such animals, v.g., blood, marrow, bones, brains, sweetbread, liver, kidneys, bouillon cubes, etc. Also forbidden are all liquid foods made from meat, v.g., chicken, mutton, beef broth; consomme or in general any kind of soup cooked or flavored with meat. Meat gravies or sauces are also forbidden.
>
> *Permitted* are fish and all cold-blooded animals, v.g., frogs and all shell-fish such as clams, turtles, oysters, crabs, lobsters, etc. Permitted also are eggs, milk and milk products such as butter and various kinds of cheese. Condiments even made from the *fat* of warm-blooded animals (not from the flesh meat of such animals or from their organic parts) are permitted. Thus oleomargarine, lard and like substances, provided no meat product enters into their composition, are permitted. Jello or gelatin even though made from meat are permitted by custom.

2. *Fast.* The law of fast prescribes that only one full meal a day be taken. It does not forbid the taking of some food in the morning and evening, but approved local usage must be observed in regard to the quantity and quality of the food. (Can. 1251 § 1.)

> The time of the full meal and the evening collation may be changed without any special reason. (Cf. Can. 1251 § 2.) An interchange between the evening collation and the breakfast snack, or between the breakfast snack and the main meal, etc., may be permitted for a reasonable cause, since the essence of the fast consists in this that only one full meal be taken in a day. The time of that full meal is not of the essence of the law.
>
> On a day of fast only, i.e., not also of abstinence, meat may be taken only *once.* (PCI, 29 Oct., 1919.) If a person is excused or exempted from the law of fasting, he may eat meat as often as he wishes on days of fast which are not also days of abstinence. (S.C.Conc., 17 Oct., 1923.) The same is to be said of those who are *dispensed* from the law of fast.

3. *Days of Fast and Abstinence.* According to the

common law (Canon 1252; S.C.Conc., 25 July, 1957):

a.   The law of abstinence alone must be observed on all Fridays;

b.   The law of both fast and abstinence must be observed on Ash Wednesday, the Fridays and Saturdays of lent, Ember Days, and the vigils of the feasts of Pentecost, Immaculate Conception, All Saints and Christmas;

c.   The law of fast alone must be observed on all the other days of lent;

d.   On Sundays and holydays of obligation, the law of abstinence, the law of fast, and the law of fast and abstinence together, are not binding, except on holydays during lent. The fast of a vigil is not anticipated; the lenten fast and abstinence now cease at midnight between Holy Saturday and Easter Sunday. (S.R.C., decr. 16 Nov., 1955.)

> In countries where not all the holydays of the universal Church are celebrated, the laws of fast and abstinence do not cease on the holydays not celebrated. (Cf. PCI, reply, 17 Feb., 1918.)

> The vigil of All Saints is still a day of fast and abstinence in the universal Church. (S.C.Conc., resp., 15 Feb., 1957.)

> Pope John XXIII granted to the faithful of the whole world the privilege of anticipating on December 23 the obligation of fast and abstinence proper to the vigil of Christmas. (S.C. Conc., 3 Dec., 1959.) Note that the faithful are given an option of observing the fast and abstinence either on December 23 or on December 24.

4.   *Those Bound to Fast and to Abstain*

a.   All those who are seven years old are bound to the law of abstinence. (Can. 1254 § 1.)

b.   The law of fast binds all who are twenty-one years old and not yet fifty-nine years old. (Can. 1254 § 2.)

> One is not bound to these laws on the very day of his seventh or twenty-first birthday respectively, but begins to abstain or fast on the next day. One is still bound to fast on the day of his fifty-ninth birthday; the obligation ceases at midnight be-

tween his birthday and the next day. (Cf. Canons 1254 and 34 § 3, 3°.)

B. *Manner of Fasting in the United States*

The following uniform norm for fast and abstinence in the United States is published by the Ordinaries in accordance with the provisions of Canon Law as modified through the use of special faculties granted by the Holy See (through the Sacred Congregation of Extraordinary Ecclesiastical Affairs on 19 December, 1941, and through the Sacred Congregation of the Council on 22 Jan., 1946, and 28 Jan., 1949). Note that each local Ordinary must approve this uniform norm for his own diocese. One must consult the norms given by the local Ordinary for his own diocese.

Uniform Norm of Fast and Abstinence
On Abstinence

1. Everyone seven years of age is bound to observe the law of abstinence.

2. *Complete* abstinence is to be observed on Fridays, Ash Wednesday and the vigils of the Immaculate Conception and Christmas. On days of complete abstinence meat and soup or gravy made from meat may not be used at all.

3. *Partial* abstinence is to be observed on Ember Wednesdays and Saturdays and on the vigil of Pentecost. On days of partial abstinence meat and soup or gravy made from meat may be taken only *once* a day, at the principal meal.

On Fast

1. Everyone twenty-one years of age and under fifty-nine years of age is also bound to observe the law of fast.

2. The days of fast are the weekdays of lent, including Holy Saturday, Ember Days, and the vigils of Pentecost, the Immaculate Conception, and Christmas.

3. On days of fast only one full meal is allowed. Two other *meatless* meals, sufficient to maintain strength, may be taken according to each one's needs; but together they should not equal another full meal.

Meat may be taken at the principal meal on a day of fast except on Fridays, Ash Wednesday, and the vigils of the Immaculate Conception and Christmas.

4. Eating between meals is not permitted, but liquids, including milk and fruit juices, are allowed.

When health or ability to work would be seriously affected, the law does not oblige. In doubt concerning fast or abstinence, a parish priest or confessor should be consulted.

Notes: a) Pope Pius XII, through the decree of the Sacred Congregation of the Council, 28 Jan., 1949, permitted that everywhere on the days of fast and abstinence eggs and milk products may be eaten in the morning and in the evening.

b) If on a day of *partial abstinence* meat is eaten outside the time of the principal meal, the law of abstinence is violated formally or materially, but one may still eat meat at the principal meal because the dispensation for the principal meal is not nullified by that fact. On a *day of fast only* if a person obliged to fast should inadvertently eat meat at one of his lesser meals, his doing so does not make that repast his principal meal, and if he has not yet taken his full meal, he may still do so and he may eat meat at that full meal.

c) Only ordinary or homogenized milk is allowed between meals. Such combinations as malted milk, milk shakes, and the like are not included in the term "milk." On the other hand, combinations based on skim milk and a coloring or special flavoring such as the so-called "chocolate milk" are considered a drink rather than a food and are allowed. (Report of Episcopal Committee, 14 Nov., 1951.)

C. *Fasts of Religious*

1. The canons of the Code effect no change in the constitutions and rules of religious institutes or of approved societies of men or women living in common but without vows. (Cf. Can. 1253.) The particular fasts or days of abstinence prescribed by the constitutions of a religious institute remain in force.

Asked whether the law of fast contained in the rule of the Friars Minor ceases on feast days of obligation outside of lent according to the norm of Canon 1252 § 4, the Sacred Congregation of Religious replied: "in the negative." (22 March, 1921.)

2. Concerning the quantity and quality of food allowed at the breakfast snack and the evening collation in fasts imposed by the constitution, unless a contrary usage prevails in the institute, the religious are to follow the ap-

proved usage of the place according to the norm of Canon 1251 § 1.

> Note that Pope Pius XII by the decree of 28 Jan., 1949 permitted that everywhere on days of fast and abstinence, eggs and milk products may be eaten in the morning and in the evening.

3. The faculties used by the local Ordinaries in the composition of the uniform norm for fast and abstinence apply to religious, even exempt. (Cf. *Digest,* III, p. 500.) Religious therefore may observe the fasts and days of abstinence prescribed by the Code in the same manner as the rest of the faithful in the diocese.

> The Holy Office declared that the lent before Easter as well as the other fasts and days of abstinence of the Church are to be observed according to the general laws of the Church or the particular indults granted for the countries in which the Friars Minor live. (S.O., decl., 20 Dec., 1870.)

> An indult lawfully granted by the local Ordinary relaxing an obligation of the common law is enjoyed also by all religious living in the diocese, without prejudice to their vows or to the particular obligations of their institute. (Can. 620.) Thus, if the local Ordinary grants a dispensation from fasting on St. Patrick's Day, religious living in the diocese are also dispensed, unless their constitutions impose a special obligation to fast at that time.

> The Friars Minor who, with the permission of their superiors and for a just cause, are outside the monastery on a day of fast imposed by the Rule, may, in the evening collation, accommodate themselves to the table of their host in regard to the quality of the food, observing, however, the limited quantity imposed by the fast. This privilege is usually renewed every five years, and was most recently renewed on 13 Feb., 1957. (*Acta Minorum,* LXXVI, p. 651.) It has been reported to the author that the late Valentine Schaaf, of revered memory, formerly Dean of the School of Canon Law at the Catholic University of America, and formerly Minister General of the Order of Friars Minor, taught that the above-mentioned privilege was granted by St. Francis in his rule when the saint says: "And according to the Holy Gospel, they may eat of all foods placed before them."

D. *Dispensations for the Military*

By indult, military chaplains and their subjects are dis-

pensed from the law of fast and abstinence on all days of
the year except the vigil of Christmas, Ash Wednesday,
and Good Friday. (Milit. Ord. U.S., Nov., 1957, n. 34.)
The subjects dispensed are, especially: all the faithful who
are actually enlisted in the armed forces of the Army,
Navy and Air Force together with their wives, children,
relatives and servants who habitually live with them; the
faithful who belong to the "Coast Guard," "National
Guard," "Air National Guard," or "Civil Air Patrol,"
provided they are living in common in the military fashion;
all the faithful staying within the limits of a military post
or in houses reserved for the armed forces; all the faithful
who are attached to military hospitals; all priests who are
subjects of the military vicar, by reason of service with the
armed forces; etc., etc. (S.C.Consist., 8 Sept., 1957; cf.
Digest, IV, p. 159 for more details.)

E. *Feasts and Fasts of Orientals in the United States*

All Orientals in the United States and Canada may observe *feasts* and *fasts* according to the prescriptions of the
Latin rite if the observance of the prescriptions of their
own rite causes them inconvenience. (Cf. S.C.E.O., reply,
19 Dec., 1928; decr., 1 March, 1929; decr., 24 May,
1930.)

> Latin rite pastors and Ordinaries may grant dispensations to
> individuals and families subject to them from Oriental rite reg-
> ulations concerning feasts and fasts. (Pospishil, p. 61.)

F. *Faculties to Dispense from Feasts and Fasts*

1. Because of a special large gathering of people or for
reasons of public health, Ordinaries may dispense an entire
diocese or place from the law of fast or of abstinence or
even from both together. (Can. 1245 § 2.)

> By special indult, Ordinaries in the United States may dis-
> pense their subjects from the laws of fast and abstinence on
> civil holidays whenever any of the civil holidays now observed
> occur on a day of fast and abstinence, or of abstinence alone.

(S.C.Conc., 15 Feb., 1957.) *Peregrini* may avail themselves of the dispensation granted for the place where they happen to be, even though the dispensation was not granted in their own diocese.

2. Not only local Ordinaries but also pastors, in single cases and for a just cause, can dispense individual persons and families subject to them, even outside their territory, and in their territory also *peregrini,* from the common law of the observance of feast days, and also of the observance of fast or of abstinence or of both. (Can. 1245 § 1.)

Hence, a general dispensation for the whole parish cannot be given by the pastor. He may, however, by one and the same act dispense several individuals or several families, v.g., a number of families taking part in a wedding celebration, and also the various individuals invited to the same celebration.

The faculty of the Ordinary and of the pastor to dispense from feasts and fasts is ordinary jurisdiction, and may be delegated to others, even habitually. Assistant pastors and confessors have no power to dispense from feasts and fasts except if it be delegated to them by others. The diocesan *pagella* will often grant such a faculty, at least for the sacramental forum.

3. In clerical exempt institutes, the superiors (even local) enjoy the same faculty to dispense as pastors. This faculty may be used in favor of their own subjects and also in favor of those who are not their subjects but who stay in the religious house day and night as servants, pupils, guests, or patients. (Cf. Canons 1245 § 3; 514 § 1.)

The faculty of religious superiors in clerical exempt institutes to dispense from feasts and fasts is ordinary power and may be delegated to others.

III. PASCHAL PRECEPT

1. Everyone of the faithful of both sexes, after he has reached the age of discretion, that is, has obtained the use of reason, is obliged to receive the sacrament of the Eucharist once a year, at least at Easter, unless perhaps upon the advice of his own priest, he is led to temporarily abstain from receiving because of some just cause. (Can. 859 § 1.)

Likewise, everyone of the faithful of both sexes, after he has reached the age of discretion, that is, has obtained the use of reason, is obliged to confess all his sins at least once a year. (Can. 906.) This precept obliges only those who have mortal sin on their conscience. In practice the faithful satisfy this obligation when they make their Easter Duty.

2. In the United States, by special concession of the Holy See, the time for fulfilling one's Easter duty extends from the first Sunday of lent till Trinity Sunday, unless the Ordinary restricts the time. (Cf. Balt. II, n. 257.)

The pastor or confessor may in individual cases, and for some reasonable cause extend the time for the reception of Easter Communion beyond the appointed time. (Cf. Can. 859 § 1.)

Easter Communion need not be received in one's own parish; however, the Code counsels that it be received there. (Cf. Can. 859 § 3.)

CHAPTER II

Sacred Places

I. CONSTITUTION

1. *Sacred places* are those which are destined for divine worship or for the burial of the faithful through the consecration or blessing prescribed for this purpose by the approved liturgical books.

2. The *consecration of a place* [church, bells, immovable altar], even though it belongs to regulars, is reserved to the Ordinary of the territory in which the place is located, provided that he possesses the episcopal character; not however to the Vicar General unless he has a special mandate. If the Ordinary of the territory lacks the episcopal character, he may grant any bishop of the same rite [as the place to be consecrated] permission to consecrate in his territory. (Can. 1155 §§ 1, 2.)

3. *The right to bless* a sacred place belongs to the Ordinary in whose territory the place is located, if the

place to be blessed belongs to the secular clergy, to a non-exempt clerical institute, or to a lay religious institute; if the place belongs to an exempt clerical institute, then the right pertains to the major superior. Both may delegate another priest for the blessing. (Can. 1156.) The same rules obtain when there is question of blessing and laying the cornerstone of a church. (Can. 1163.)

4. *Permission* to consecrate or bless a sacred place: notwithstanding any privilege, no one can consecrate or bless a sacred place without the consent of the Ordinary (Can. 1157), that is, the local Ordinary, or if the place belongs to an exempt institute, the religious Ordinary.

II. CHURCHES

1. *Definition*

By the name "church" is understood a sacred building dedicated to divine worship for this purpose especially, namely, that it can be used by all the faithful in the public exercise of divine worship. (Can. 1161.)

2. *Building of a Church*

a. No church may be built without the express written permission of the local Ordinary, and this cannot be given by the Vicar General without a special mandate. Even religious, although they have already been permitted by the local Ordinary to establish a new house in the diocese or city, are required to obtain the permission of the local Ordinary before they can build a church or a public oratory on a certain and determined location. (Can. 1162 §§ 1, 4.)

> The permission to establish a religious house carries with it, for clerical institutes, the right to have a *church* or *public oratory,* in connection with the house, as well as the faculty to carry out the sacred functions. (Can. 497 § 1.) The permission of the local Ordinary is required for the choice of the exact place in which this church or public oratory is to be built. (Can. 1162 § 4.) Nonclerical institutes need the permission of

the local Ordinary to open a church or oratory in connection with a religious house. (Cf. Canons 1162, 1191, 1192.)

b.   The right to bless and lay the cornerstone pertains to those mentioned in Canon 1156. (Can. 1163.)

c.   In a church no entrance or window shall be opened to [i.e., connect with] the houses of lay persons; if there are places underneath or above the church, these shall not be used for merely profane purposes. (Can. 1164 § 2.)

> *Merely profane:* dances, movies, plays, sleeping quarters, etc. Quite allowable would be, for instance, meetings of parish societies and sodalities, plays of a religious nature, catechetical instruction, parochial school classes, parish library, etc.

> The prescriptions of Canon 1164 § 2 pertain also to public oratories. (Can. 1191 § 1.) Ideally the same should be said of semipublic oratories; however legally, the attic and basement may be used for bedrooms, refectory and other profane uses. (Cf. Abbo-Hannan, II, n. 1192; V.C., II, n. 501; Coronata, II, n. 767; Beste, at Canon 1192 § 2.)

3.   *Consecration or Blessing*

Cathedral churches shall be dedicated by solemn consecration, and as far as possible, also collegiate, conventual, and parish churches. It is required that together with the church, the main altar (or if the main altar is already consecrated) one of the side altars be also consecrated. To be consecrated, the church must be constructed of stone, brick, or reinforced concrete; churches built of wood, iron or of some other metal may be blessed but not consecrated. (Can. 1165 §§ 3, 4, 5; S.R.C., 12 Nov., 1909.)

4.   *Name*

Every consecrated or blessed church must have its own title; after the dedication of the church this title cannot be changed. Churches cannot be dedicated to one who is only beatified [i.e., not yet canonized] without an apostolic indult. (Can. 1168 §§ 1, 3.)

5. *Bells*

It is appropriate that every church should have bells, which bells must also be either consecrated or blessed according to the rites prescribed in approved liturgical books. The use of the bells is subject exclusively to the ecclesiastical authority, and the bells are not to be used for merely profane uses except by reason of necessity, or by permission of the Ordinary or finally by reason of lawful custom. (Can. 1169 §§ 1, 2, 3, 4.)

> The right to consecrate or bless bells follows the rules of Canons 1155 and 1156. (Can. 1169 § 5.)

> It is left to the prudent judgment of the Ordinary to decide whether electrophonic bells may be used as a substitute for church bells of bronze. (S.R.C., 3 Feb., 1951.)

6. *Use of Churches*

a. Divine services may not be held in a new church before it has been dedicated to divine worship either through consecration or through blessing. (Can. 1165 § 1.)

> Authors commonly allow the Ordinary to permit divine services to be held in the church before its dedication, but only on a temporary basis, and to meet a real need of the faithful.

b. Once a sacred edifice is lawfully dedicated, all ecclesiastical rights may be formed, without prejudice, however, to parochial rights, to privileges and to lawful customs; the Ordinary, for a just cause, may establish limitations especially as to the hours for divine services, provided the church involved does not belong to an exempt religious institute, the prescription of Canon 609 § 3 remaining intact. (Can. 1171.)

> Concerning the right of the local Ordinary to establish limitations as to hours of divine services or to forbid certain services in churches or oratories of religious confer: Goyeneche in CRM, XXXIV (1955), pp. 357-364; Goyeneche, II, pp. 316ss, 327ss.

c. All those whose duty it is, shall see to it that churches are marked with that cleanliness which is becoming to the house of God; business transactions and public selling, even those conducted for pious purposes [bake sales, etc.] shall be kept out of them; and in general the same is required in regard to anything that is out of harmony with the holiness of the place. (Can. 1178.)

> Selling of religious articles and pamphlets in the church vestibule is permitted if it is done quietly.

> Banners and flags of societies not manifestly hostile to the faith and which carry no prohibited design may be admitted into the church. (S.R.C., instr., 26 March, 1924.)

> The use of the church may be allowed for meetings of Catholic societies, sacred concerts, distribution of parochial school diplomas. If possible, the Blessed Sacrament should be transferred to another repository. (Cf. V.C., II, n. 491; Abbo-Hannan, II, n. 1178.)

> Motion pictures and slides, even though of an edifying or religious character, may not be shown in a church. (S.C.Consist., 10 Dec., 1912.)

d. Admission to a church for divine services shall be entirely without charge, and every contrary custom is reprobated [i.e., rejected as unreasonable]. (Can. 1181.)

> Pew rent is not forbidden; however it is not to be taken up at the entrance of the church.

7. *Violation and Reconciliation*

a. A church is violated only by the following acts, and only provided that it is certain that they have occurred, that they are notorious, and that they have taken place in the church itself:

1) The crime of homicide.

2) The unjust and serious shedding of blood.

3) Impious and sordid uses to which the church has been subjected.

4) The burial of an infidel or of a person excommunicated by declaratory or condemnatory sentence. (Can. 1172.)

By violation the church does not lose its consecration; it remains a sacred place but is regarded as polluted and unfit for divine service until due expiation has been made by reconciliation.

The crime must take place in the church itself, therefore not in the attic, belfry, tower, sacristy, vestibule. Homicide includes suicide. If a person undergoes the mortal attack in church, the church is violated even though the assailant were outside and the victim died outside. Impious and sordid uses are, for instance, the stabling of animals, the holding of orgies, etc. An isolated impious or sordid act does not cause the church to be violated; repeated and protracted impious or sordid use is required.

b. Until the church is reconciled it is unlawful to conduct divine services, to administer the sacraments, or to bury the dead in a church that was violated. If the violation occur during divine services, the services are to be discontinued at once; if before the canon or after the communion of the Mass, the Mass is to be discontinued; otherwise the priest shall continue the Mass up to the communion. (Can. 1173.)

c. A church that was only blessed, when violated, can be reconciled by its rector or by any priest with at least the presumed consent of the rector. With regard to consecrated churches, the right of reconciliation belongs to the Ordinary in whose territory the place is located, if the place to be reconciled belongs to the secular clergy, to a non-exempt clerical institute or to a lay religious institute; if the place belongs to an exempt clerical institute, then the right of reconciliation pertains to the major superior. Both may delegate another priest for the reconciliation. Finally, in a case of grave and urgent need, if the Ordinary cannot be reached, the rector of a consecrated church is permitted to reconcile it, but he must then inform the Ordinary of his action. (Can. 1176 §§ 1-3.)

The reconciliation of a church that was only blessed can be effected with ordinary holy water; but the reconciliation of a consecrated church is to be effected with water especially blessed for this purpose according to the liturgical laws; however, not only bishops, but also priests who reconcile a church can bless this water. (Can. 1177.)

8. *Desecration*

A church does not lose its consecration or blessing except by total destruction, by the collapse of the greater part of its walls, or by its being turned over to profane (secular) uses by the local Ordinary according to the norm of Canon 1187. (Can. 1170.)

9. *Secularization*

If a church cannot in any way be used for divine worship and there is no possibility of repairing it, it can be turned over to secular, but not sordid, uses by the local Ordinary; and the local Ordinary shall transfer to another church its obligation and its income, as well as its title if it is a parish church.

A decree of the local Ordinary, without further ceremony, suffices to produce the effect here contemplated; thereafter the church is no longer a sacred place. (Cf. Can. 1170.)

III. ORATORIES

A. *General Concepts*

1. *An oratory* is a place destined for divine worship but *not* with the principal purpose that it serve the use of all the faithful in the public exercise of religion. (Can. 1188 § 1.)

2. *A public oratory* is one which is built principally for the convenience of a definite community or even of private individuals, but in such manner that all the faithful have the right, upheld in law, to enter it at least at the time of divine services. (Can. 1188 § 2, 1°.)

Doubts as to whether an oratory is public or not, may be solved by presumptions which show the probability that the oratory is a public one, v.g., the entrance faces a public street, the tower is equipped with bells, etc.

A permanent chapel aboard ship is considered a public oratory. (*Cod. Rubr.*, n. 279.)

3. *A semipublic oratory* is one which is erected for the convenience of some community or group of faithful, and the faithful at large have no right to enter it. (Can. 1188 § 2, 2°.)

Oratories in convents, retreat houses, seminaries, hospitals, military camps, prisons, are classified as semipublic. Some of these could be public, v.g., an oratory in a military camp, if the oratory is open to all the faithful at times of divine services.

4. *A private oratory* is one which is erected in private homes for the benefit of only one person or family and the members of their household. (Can. 1188 § 2, 3°.)

Permission for a private oratory where Mass may be celebrated must come from the Apostolic See. The entire discipline of requesting indults for private oratories is detailed in an instruction of the Sacred Congregation of the Sacraments, 1 October, 1949. (Cf. *Digest*, III, p. 318ss.)

B. *Erection, Blessing, Use*

1. *Public oratories* are governed by the same rules as are churches. Therefore, provided an oratory has been perpetually dedicated to the public worship of God through blessing or consecration, on the authority of the Ordinary, all sacred functions may be celebrated in it, with the exception of those that are forbidden by liturgical law. (Can. 1191 §§ 1, 2.)

The permission to establish a religious house carries with it, for clerical institutes, the right to have a *church* or *public oratory,* in connection with the house, as well as the faculty to carry out the sacred functions. (Can. 497 § 1.) The permission of the local Ordinary is required for the choice of the exact place in which this church or public oratory is to be built. (Can. 1162 § 4.) Nonclerical institutes need the permission of the local Ordinary to open a church or oratory in connection with a religious house. (Cf. Canons 1162, 1191, 1192.)

2. a. *Semipublic oratories* may be erected only with the permission of the Ordinary. Once the permission to establish the oratory has been granted, the oratory may not

be turned over to profane uses without the authorization of the same Ordinary. (Can. 1192 §§ 1, 3.)

> The major superior in a clerical exempt institute may, therefore, authorize the erection of semipublic oratories in houses of his institute.

In colleges or boarding schools, in high schools, barracks, forts, prisons, hospitals, etc., besides the principal oratory, no *secondary oratories* shall be erected unless some need or great advantage, in the judgment of the Ordinary, warrants it. (Can. 1192 § 4.) In case a secondary oratory is erected, the Blessed Sacrament may not be reserved there. (Can. 1267.)

> The Ordinary here includes also the major superior of a clerical exempt institute. (Can. 198.)

b.   All divine services and ecclesiastical functions may be celebrated in semipublic oratories lawfully erected, unless something to the contrary is demanded by the rubrics or by special limitations imposed by the Ordinary. (Can. 1193.)

c.   Semipublic oratories may be blessed or consecrated, or may be blessed with a simple blessing for a house; however no blessing is necessary. (Cf. Can. 1196 §§ 1, 2.) But even when the oratory is not blessed, it must be reserved exclusively for divine worship, and not devoted to any domestic use whatever. (Can. 1196 § 2.)

3.   a.   In *private oratories* erected in virtue of an apostolic indult, unless it is otherwise provided in the indult itself, there may be celebrated (after the oratory has been visited and approved by the Ordinary or his delegate) one low Mass daily, with the exception of more solemn feast days; but other ecclesiastical functions shall not be performed there. (Can. 1195 § 1.)

> The Ordinary may, but only in individual instances, permit the celebration of Mass even on more solemn feasts, for just and reasonable causes distinct from the causes for which the privilege of the oratory was granted. (Can. 1195 § 2.)

At the Mass celebrated in these private oratories, it is permitted to distribute Holy Communion unless the indult expressly provides otherwise. (S.C.Sacr., instr., 1 Oct., 1949, n. 11.)

The entire discipline on asking for the indult of a private oratory is regulated by an instruction of the Sacred Congregation of the Sacraments, 1 October, 1949, *Digest,* III, pp. 320-327.

b.   Private oratories may not be consecrated or blessed in the manner of churches. (Can. 1196 § 1.) There is no blessing prescribed for private oratories, however they may be blessed with an invocative blessing. (Formula for this blessing in *Rit. Rom.,* Appendix, Benedictiones Non Reservatae, n. 16.) Even though the private oratory has received no blessing, it must nevertheless be reserved exclusively for divine worship, and not devoted to any domestic use whatever. (Can. 1196 § 2.)

c.   The obligation of hearing Mass on Sundays and holydays can be fulfilled through attendance at Mass celebrated in a private oratory *only by the beneficiaries of the indult, i.e., those who are mentioned in the indult;* hence usually the petitioners, their children, close relatives by blood and marriage, servants, house guests, the celebrant and server of the Mass. (Cf. S.C.Sacr., instr., 1 Oct., 1949, n. 10.)

IV.   ALTARS

1.   *General Concept*

An altar is a sacred, i.e., consecrated table or stone on which Mass is celebrated. An immovable or fixed altar is a table placed on bases which, with the table, are consecrated as a single object; a movable or portable altar is a stone, generally small, which is alone consecrated, or even a stone placed on bases when the latter has not been consecrated along with it. (Can. 1197 § 1.)

In a consecrated church at least one altar, preferably the

high altar, must be immovable; in a church that is merely blessed, all the altars may be movable. (Can. 1197 § 2.)

The requisites for the construction of immovable and movable altars are given in Canon 1198. Commentary may be found in Abbo-Hannan, II, n. 1198.

2.   Consecration

In order that the Sacrifice of the Mass may be celebrated on it, the altar must be consecrated according to the liturgical laws, either the entire altar in case of an immovable one, or the altar stone if it is a movable altar. (Can. 1199 § 1.)

Without prejudice to particular privileges, all Bishops can consecrate movable altars; as to immovable altars, the requirements of Canon 1155 shall be observed. (Can. 1199 § 2.)

In virtue of the quinquennial faculties, local Ordinaries may depute priests to consecrate both immovable and movable altars. (*Digest,* IV, p. 77.)

3.   Desecration or Loss of Consecration

a.   An immovable altar loses its consecration by even a temporary separation of the table from its support; in which case, however, the Ordinary [local or religious] can grant permission to a priest to again consecrate the altar with the use of the shorter rite and formula. (Can. 1200 § 1.)

b.   Both an immovable and a portable altar lose their consecration:

1)   If they are badly broken, either by reason of the extent of the break or by the fact that anointed portions of the stone are affected. (Can. 1200 § 2, 1°.)

Examples: the altar table breaks into several pieces; an altar stone is broken in half; two or more anointed crosses are broken off, etc.

2)   If the relics are removed or if the lid of the sepulcher is broken or removed, except in the case in which the

bishop or his delegate removes the lid for the purpose of fastening it, repairing it, or replacing it, or for the purpose of inspecting the relics. (Can. 1200 § 2, 2°.)

> Consecration is not lost if the lid merely works loose, provided it is not removed; any priest may apply the cement needed to fasten it securely. (Abbo-Hannan, II, n. 1200.)

c. A slight break, i.e., a crack, in the lid of the sepulcher does not cause loss of consecration, and any priest may fill up the crack with cement. (Can. 1200 § 3.)

4. *Privilege of a Portable Altar*

The entire discipline on asking for the *privilege* of a portable altar is regulated by the instruction of the Sacred Congregation of the Sacraments, 1 October, 1949, *Digest,* III, pp. 328-334.

NOTE: Many liturgical details on altars may be found in *Matters Liturgical* (Wuest, Mullaney, Barry; Pustet Co., N.Y.; 1956), nos. 58-80.

CHAPTER III

Sacred Furnishings

I. CONCEPT

Sacred furnishings are all the things destined for use in the ceremonies associated with divine worship; in the strict sense, furnishings that have been consecrated or blessed with a constitutive blessing; in the broad sense all other movable property with which the house of God is furnished.

> Sacred furnishings include: *sacred vessels,* v.g., chalice, oil stocks; *coverings and ornaments* of vessels and altars, v.g., chalice veil, corporal, altar cloths; *priestly vestments,* v.g., stole, chasuble; *utensils* of the altar and church, v.g., crucifix, bells, missal, pews, etc.

II. MATERIAL — FORM — USE

1. Sacred furnishings, especially such as must be

blessed or consecrated according to the norm of liturgical law and which are used in public worship, shall be carefully kept in the sacristy of the church or in some other safe and reputable place, nor shall they be used for profane purposes. (Can. 1296 § 1.)

> The prohibition of using sacred furnishings for profane purposes refers primarily to the profane use of consecrated or blessed articles. To use a chair, carpet, etc. from the church would be easily excusable.

2. As to the material and form of sacred furnishings, the requirements and prescriptions of liturgical law, of ecclesiastical tradition and of sacred art are to be observed. (Can. 1296 § 3.)

> References to *Matters Liturgical* (ed. 1956) on the material and form of sacred furnishings:
>
> a. Vestments: Surplice (n. 131), amice (n. 120), alb (n. 121), cincture (n. 122), maniple, stole, dalmatic, chasuble, cope, humeral veil (nos. 123-125; 128-130), altar cloths (n. 135), corporal (n. 138), pall (n. 140), purificator (n. 141), tabernacle veil (n. 148).
>
> b. Chalice, paten, ciborium (nos. 94-101).
>
> c. Other vessels: Sick call pyx (n. 105), lunula (n. 108), monstrance (n. 108), tabernacle (n. 147), also altar crucifix (n. 152).

III. BLESSING AND CONSECRATION

1. The blessing of those sacred furnishings which, in accordance with liturgical laws, must be blessed before they can be put to their proper use, can be imparted by:

a. Cardinals, and all bishops;

b. Local Ordinaries who lack the episcopal character, for churches and oratories of their own territory;

c. The pastor for the churches and oratories located within the limits of his parish, and by rectors of churches for their own churches;

d. Priests delegated by the local Ordinary within the limits of the delegation and of the jurisdiction of the one delegating;

e.   Religious superiors and priests of their own institute delegated by them, for their own churches and oratories and for the churches of nuns subject to them. (Can.
1304.)

> A reserved blessing imparted by a priest who is not author-
> ized to bless, is unlawful, but valid. (Can. 1147 § 3.)

> The vestments and furnishings to be blessed are: the chas-
> uble, stole, maniple, alb, amice, and cincture; also the pall and
> the corporal, the altar cloths and the tabernacle.

> No blessing is prescribed for the chalice veil, the purificator,
> burse, surplice, cope, humeral veil, dalmatics, ciborium and
> lunula. However it is recommended that the ciborium and
> lunula be blessed. (Abbo-Hannan, II, n. 1304.)

> Note that all sacred furnishings either must or may be blessed
> except altar stones, chalices and patens, which must be conse-
> crated.

2.   Chalices and patens must be consecrated. This can
be done only by cardinals, bishops, and even though they
lack the episcopal character, Vicars Apostolic, Prefects
Apostolic, Abbots and Prelates *nullius*. Any one else
needs an apostolic indult to consecrate validly. (Cf. Can.
1147 § 1.)

IV.   LOSS OF BLESSING OR CONSECRATION

1.   Blessed or consecrated furnishings lose their blessing or consecration:

a.   If they are so damaged or altered that they lose their
original form and become unsuitable for their designated
use;

b.   If they have been put to unbecoming uses or exposed to public sale. (Can. 1305 § 1.)

> The common opinion holds that one or the other violation
> would not cause loss of sacred character, but that only habitual
> unbecoming use causes desecration.

> Private sale does not cause desecration.

2.   A chalice or paten does not lose its consecration
through the loss or renewal of the gold plating; but if it

wears off, there is a grave obligation to have the object replated. (Can. 1305 § 2.)

V. WASHING OF SACRED LINENS

1.   Care must be taken that the chalice and the paten, and, previous to washing, purificators, palls and corporals used in the Sacrifice of the Mass, shall not be touched except by clerics or by those entrusted with the custody of these furnishings. (Can. 1306 § 1.)

It is touching of these objects with the bare hand that is forbidden.

The custody of these objects may be entrusted even to a layman, for instance, a layman who serves the church as sacristan.

2.   Purificators, palls, and corporals used in the Sacrifice of the Mass shall not be given to lay persons, even religious, for washing, unless they have first been washed by a cleric in major orders; the water of the first washing is to be poured into the sacrarium, or if there is no sacrarium, into the fire. (Can. 1306 § 2.)

By papal privilege, lay brothers of the Order of Friars Minor, as long as they have charge of the sacristy, may handle the sacred vessels and also perform the first washing of the corporals and purificators if it seems expedient. (Cf. Capobianco, n. 353.) The Holy See usually grants the privilege of performing the first washing of purificators, palls and corporals to brothers and sisters of religious institutes following the Rule of the Third Order Regular of St. Francis, who serve as sacristans in their chapels. This privilege was renewed *ad quinquennium,* by the Sacred Congregation of Rites on 7 July, 1956. (*Acta Minorum,* LXXV, p. 189.)

PART X

INDULGENCES

CHAPTER I

Indulgences in General

I. NATURE OF INDULGENCES

1. Indulgences are a remission in the sight of God of temporal punishment due to sin, the guilt of which is already forgiven, granted from the treasury of the Church by ecclesiastical authority, to the living in the manner of absolution, to the faithful departed in the manner of suffrage. (Cf. Can. 911.)

2. An indulgence may be:

a. *Plenary* or *Partial.* A *plenary* indulgence is one which remits all the temporal punishment due to sins whose guilt is already forgiven; a *partial* indulgence is one which remits only a part of the punishment.

> To gain a plenary indulgence the person must be without even a venial sin, because the temporal punishment due that sin cannot be remitted until the sin is forgiven. (Genicot, II, n. 403.) A plenary indulgence, however, is understood to be so granted that if the person wishing to gain it cannot gain it in full, he can gain it partially in proportion to the dispositions of his soul. (Can. 926.) Partial indulgences are expressed in periods of time which designate the equivalent of the temporal punishment remitted in terms of the canonical penances formerly practiced in the Church. Since the severity of the old canonical penances varied in different places, the amount of the temporal punishment remitted is necessarily somewhat indefinite. (Bouscaren-Ellis, pp. 374-375.)

b. *Local, Personal* and *Real.* An indulgence is *local* if

330

directly attached to some place and a visit to such a church, oratory, shrine, etc., is one of the conditions for gaining the indulgence. It is *personal* if granted directly to a person or a determined class of persons (e.g., tertiaries, members of a pious union, etc.) independent of any particular place or thing. It is *real* if attached to some object or thing (e.g., rosaries, crucifixes, etc.).

c. Applicable to *oneself* or to the *deceased*. Indulgences can be applicable to oneself only, to the deceased only, or to either oneself or the deceased.

> No one gaining indulgences can apply them to other living persons; all indulgences granted by the Roman Pontiff are applicable to the souls in Purgatory unless the contrary is evident. (Can. 930.)

II. SUBJECTS CAPABLE OF GAINING INDULGENCES

In order to be *capable* of gaining indulgences for himself a person must be baptized, not excommunicated, in the state of grace (at least at the end of the prescribed works), and a subject of the one who grants the indulgence. (Can. 925 § 1.)

> It is sufficient if the last of the prescribed works be performed in the state of grace (S.P., 28 Feb., 1933), since at that moment the indulgence goes into effect. It is disputed whether the state of grace is required in gaining indulgences for the departed.

> Unless the contrary should appear from the terms of the grant, *peregrini, vagi,* and all who are exempt may gain indulgences granted by a bishop, provided they are within his diocese, and his subjects may gain them even when they are outside his diocese. (Can. 927.)

> Orientals can gain all indulgences granted by the Holy Father in a general decree. (S.P., 7 July, 1917; cf. S.P., 29 April, 1930; 31 Jan., 1931.)

III. CONDITIONS FOR GAINING INDULGENCES

A. *Conditions in General*

In order that a person actually gain indulgences he must have at least a general intention of gaining them and must perform the prescribed works at the appointed time and in the proper manner according to the terms of the grant. (Can. 925 § 2.)

1. *The intention.* At least a general intention to gain the indulgences is required.

> Once a person has made the habitual intention to gain all the indulgences connected with certain good works, he gains these indulgences as long as he has not retracted his intention, even though he does not think of the individual indulgences or is ignorant of them. Also a habitual intention of applying appropriate indulgences to the souls in Purgatory is sufficient. However, in practice, these intentions should be frequently renewed. (Cf. Genicot, II, n. 405.)

2. *The prescribed works*

a. A work which one is obliged to perform by law or precept under pain of sin cannot serve for the gaining of an indulgence, unless the grant expressly states that it can; but if a work is enjoined as a sacramental penance and happens also to be enriched with indulgences, a person can at the same time satisfy the penance and gain the indulgences. (Can. 932.)

> Community prayers of religious not prescribed under sin, are sufficient. (Beringer, I, n. 94.)

b. Several indulgences may be attached, on the basis of various titles, to one and the same place or thing; but by the performance of *one work* to which indulgences are attached on the basis of several titles, more than one indulgence cannot be gained, unless the act is confession or the reception of Holy Communion or unless the contrary has been expressly provided. (Can. 933.)

> Accordingly, one confession and one Communion may satisfy for gaining several indulgences. On the other hand, one visit to a church, v.g., on All Souls' Day, would not suffice for the gaining of several plenary indulgences even if the prescribed prayers are repeated. As has been expressly provided for, the apostolic indulgences can be gained simultaneously with the other indulgences attached to the same objects or works to which the apostolic indulgences are attached. (S.P., 14 June, 1922;

11 Mar., 1939; 22 Nov., 1958.) The Crosier and the Dominican indulgences can be gained by one recitation of the Rosary on beads enriched with both indulgences. (S.C.Indulg., 12 June, 1907.)

c. An indulgence is not gained if there is a *substantial* omission or change in the prescribed work or prayer. (Cf. Can. 934 § 2; S.P., 26 Nov., 1934.)

A slight omission (e.g., one or two Hail Marys of the Rosary) does not hinder the gaining of an indulgence. (Beringer, I, n. 92.)

Even one who through ignorance or impossibility omits to fulfill the prescribed conditions, does not gain the indulgence. (Noldin, III, n. 319.)

If various works are prescribed, one may generally perform them in any order one pleases. (Cf. S.C.Indulg., 19 May, 1759.)

d. If a particular prayer has been assigned, the indulgences can be gained by reciting that prayer in any language, provided the correctness of the translation be certain from a declaration of the Sacred Penitentiary or of one of the Ordinaries of places where the language in which the prayer is translated is commonly used; but the indulgences cease entirely by reason of any substantial addition, subtraction, or interpolation. (Can. 934 § 2; S.P., 26 Nov., 1934.)

It is only through a substantial change that the indulgences cease. (S.P., 26 Nov., 1934.) The custom of inserting the mystery of the Rosary in the Hail Mary is tolerated where the custom prevails.

The exactness of the translation suffices for the gaining of the indulgence without the authentic declaration of that exactness, at least in the case in which the translation has not been printed in any published work. (Abbo-Hannan, II, n. 934.)

For an authorized English translation of indulgenced prayers, consult: *The Raccolta or A Manual of Indulgences, Prayers and Devotions Enriched with Indulgences,* New York: Benziger Brothers, Inc., 1957.

e. When some particular vocal prayer is prescribed for the intention of the Supreme Pontiff it must be said *orally*. But to gain the indulgences it is sufficient to recite the prayer alternately with a companion, or to follow it mentally while it is recited by another person. (Can. 934 §§ 1, 3.)

Deaf-mutes can gain indulgences attached to public prayers, if together with the rest of the faithful who are praying in the same place, they raise their minds and pious affections toward God; in the case of private prayers it is sufficient that they recall them mentally, or say them in signs, or merely read them ocularly. (Can. 936.)

Indulgences attached to ejaculations can be gained by saying them mentally. (S.P., 7 Dec., 1933.)

f. Kneeling is necessary only in case it is expressly prescribed. (S.R.C., *Decr. Auth.,* n. 398.)

When the recital of prayers is enjoined with some bodily act which mutilated persons are unable to perform, they may gain the indulgences merely by the recital of the prayers. (S.P., 22 Oct., 1917.)

3. *The prescribed time*

a. A plenary indulgence, unless express provision to the contrary is made, can be gained only once a day, even though the prescribed work is performed several times. A partial indulgence, if there is no express provision to the contrary, can be gained several times a day upon repetition of the same work. (Can. 928 §§ 1-2.)

Several *different* plenary indulgences can be gained on the same day. Moreover, by express provision, some plenary indulgences (e.g., Portiuncula, All Souls, etc.) are *toties-quoties indulgences,* i.e., gained as often as the prescribed work is performed.

b. To gain an indulgence which is attached to a certain day, if a visit to a church or oratory is required, it may be made from noon of the preceding day to midnight which terminates the day named. (Can. 923.)

If no visit to a church is prescribed, the prayers may be said at any place, but during the natural day prescribed, from midnight to midnight.

c. A plenary indulgence granted for feasts of Our Lord Jesus Christ or for feasts of the Blessed Virgin Mary, is understood as granted only for feasts which are in the universal calendar. An indulgence, plenary or partial, granted for feasts of the Apostles, is understood as granted only for their natal feast. (Can. 921 §§ 1-2.)

The Code seems to extend the indulgence even to secondary feasts of our Lord and His Blessed Mother, but only if they are found in the universal calendar, not on the particular feasts of an order or diocese. (Abbo-Hannan, II, n. 921, note 41.) The natal feast of the Apostles is the day of their death or martyrdom. Hence, the feast of the Chair of St. Peter, the Conversion of St. Paul, etc. are not included.

d. A plenary indulgence granted as *quotidiana perpetua* or *ad tempus* to those who visit some church or public oratory is understood as to be gained by any of the faithful on any day of their choice, but only once in the year, unless the decree expressly provides otherwise. (Can. 921 § 3.)

e. Indulgences attached to feasts or to pious devotions or novenas, seven-day exercises and tridua which precede the feast or follow it, or to octaves, should be understood as *transferred* to the day to which the feast is lawfully transferred: 1) if the feast is transferred permanently, even if the feast as transferred, while possessing its proper office and Mass, does not enjoy the original solemnity and the external pomp; or 2) if the solemnity and the external pomp are transferred, whether the transfer is perpetual or temporary. (Can. 922.)

Hence, if the transfer is temporary, the indulgence remains attached to the original feast day, even if this should be Good Friday (S.P., 18 Feb., 1921), *unless* the external solemnity is also transferred. The external solemnity consists in some ecclesiastical ceremonies even non-liturgical ones; mere civil celebration is not sufficient (S.P., 14 Dec., 1937.) It suffices that the transfer affects only a single religious house; but in that case the indulgence is transferred only for the members of that house. (Abbo-Hannan, II, n. 922.)

When All Souls' Day is transferred to November 3, the indulgences are also transferred. (S.O., 13-14 Dec., 1916.)

B. *The Usual Conditions*

When the conditions for gaining an indulgence are expressed by the phrase "on the usual conditions" (*suetis conditionibus*), they are: confession, Communion, a visit to a church or public oratory, (or, in the case of those who may lawfully use it according to Canon 929, a semipublic oratory) and prayers for the intentions of the Supreme Pontiff. In cases, however, where all the aforesaid conditions are not required, those which are necessary are separately mentioned in the proper places. (*Raccolta,* p. IX.)

1. *Confession and Communion*

a. When confession and Communion are required for gaining indulgences, the confession can be made within eight days immediately preceding the day to which the indulgence is attached; Communion can be received on the day before the specified day; both confession and Communion may also be made on any of the seven days following the feast. (Can. 921 § 1.)

> Confession made on a Saturday is sufficient for the two following Sundays to which an indulgence is attached. The confession prescribed to gain an indulgence must be made even though there be no mortal sin to confess; absolution, in this case, is not necessary. (S.R.C., *Decr. Auth.,* nos. 214, 253, 359.)
>
> Holy Communion need not be received in the church in which the visit must be made. If Holy Communion is received in the church in which the visit must be made, no extra visit is prescribed as long as the prescribed prayers are recited. (Noldin, III, n. 322.)
>
> One confession and Communion will satisfy for several indulgences falling within the above stipulated time, provided the other prescribed conditions are fulfilled. (Cf. Can. 933.)

b. For indulgences attached to certain pious exercises of three or more days duration (triduums, retreats, missions, novenas), confession and Communion can be performed also on one of the seven days immediately following the conclusion of the exercises. (Can. 931 § 2.)

The visits to the church and the prescribed prayers may be performed during the exercises; but they are performed preferably on the day of the reception of the sacraments. (Beringer, I, n. 110.)

c. The faithful who are accustomed, unless lawfully impeded, to go to confession at least twice a month, *or* to receive Holy Communion daily in the state of grace and with a good intention though they may not receive once or twice a week, can, even without the actual confession, gain all the indulgences for which otherwise confession would be necessary, with the exception of ordinary and extraordinary jubilee indulgences or indulgences *ad instar iubilaei.* (Can. 931 § 3.)

Those who receive Communion daily, can gain all the indulgences without the obligation of going to confession, provided they perform the other prescribed works. Likewise those who habitually go to confession twice a month (it need not be at two week intervals) can gain all the indulgences even without receiving Communion, provided the other conditions are satisfied. Only the jubilee and *ad instar* jubilee indulgences are excepted; all other indulgences are included, even the Portiuncula indulgence. (Coronata, *De Sacr.,* I, 524.)

2. *Visit to a Church*

a. By a visit to a church or oratory is meant going to a church or oratory at least with some general or implicit intention of honoring God in Himself or in His saints, and saying some prayer, the one prescribed if any has been imposed by the one who granted the indulgence, otherwise, any prayer, oral or even mental, according to each one's piety and devotion. (S.P., 20 Sept., 1933.)

The visit to a church or public oratory in itself (i.e., independent of the other usual conditions: confession, Communion and prayer for the intentions of the Supreme Pontiff) must include its own prayer. Accordingly, besides the prayer according to the intention of the Supreme Pontiff, some other prayer must be said. This additional prayer for the visit is necessary to gain any indulgence requiring the ordinary conditions (S.P., 15 June, 1954), even when the prayer according to the intention of the Holy Father has been definitely determined, as for example, in the case of the Portiuncula indulgence. (Cf. *Acta Minorum*, LXXIII, pp. 212-213). This additional prayer for the visit may be a brief ejaculation. The following prayer of St. Francis is suggested: "We adore You, O most holy Lord Jesus Christ, here and in all the churches which are in the whole world, and we bless You, because by Your holy cross You have redeemed the world."

Visiting a church on Sundays in order to hear Mass may also serve as the prescribed visit to gain the indulgences, since only assistance at Mass, but not visiting a specified church, is obligatory on Sundays. (Gennari, *Questioni Teologico-Morali*, n. 613.) The visit prescribed for gaining the indulgences may also be made in connection with the reception of the sacraments.

If the *church is closed,* or if because of the throng it is impossible to enter the church, the prayers may also be said outside of the church. Also in the choir, or the sacristy, attached to the church by means of a door or window, the visit may be made to the church. (*Monit. Eccl.,* 1918, p. 129.)

b. If *no special church* is designated, the visit may be made to any church or public oratory.

c. The faithful of either sex who, for the pursuit of religious perfection, or for training, education, or for health's sake, live a common life in houses established with the consent of the Ordinaries, but which have no church or public chapel, and likewise all persons who live in the same place for the purpose of ministering to them, whenever a visit to any *unspecified* church or public oratory is prescribed for gaining indulgences, may make the visit in that chapel of their own house where they can legitimately satisfy the obligation of hearing Mass, and thus gain the indulgences, provided that they duly perform the other works prescribed. (Can. 929.)

d. If *a special church* is designated (e.g., parish church, church of certain religious or of a confraternity), the visit must be made to the church specified unless special privileges to the contrary be enjoyed, or unless a confessor has commuted this condition according to Canon 935.

By the *parish church* is meant one's own parish church, or

also the parish church of the place where one happens to be. (Bouscaren-Ellis, p. 387.)

By a *church of the regulars* is meant not only a church which is theirs by property right but also a church which, though it does not belong to them, has been assigned to them perpetually and legitimately for divine service and unrestricted use. Accordingly, if regulars reside at churches which are not their own, and in them carry on their ministry, provided that the churches are public and that the concession of the use of these churches is legitimate, stable and unrestricted, then the aforesaid churches enjoy the same privileges and indulgences which have been granted to the churches of the Order of the regulars. (Moccheggiani, pp. 428, 429.) However, those churches which have not been given over to them for their unrestricted use (mission churches, chapels of hospitals, etc.), even though they preach and administer the sacraments in them, cannot be considered churches of the order, and do not enjoy the privileges of the order. Churches, moreover, which at some previous point in history belonged to regulars, no longer enjoy the privileges of regulars, unless a special concession has been made to that effect. (Beringer, I, n. 177.)

3. *Prayers for the Intention of the Holy Father.* If it is prescribed that to gain an indulgence one must pray for the intentions of the Roman Pontiff, a merely mental prayer does not suffice; but, unless some special prayer is assigned, the oral prayer may be selected at the pleasure of the faithful. (Can. 934 § 1.)

To satisfy the condition "of praying according to the intention of the Supreme Pontiff," it suffices ordinarily to add to the other prescribed works the recitation of *one* Our Father, Hail Mary and Glory for the intentions of the Holy Father; and it rests with the individual, in accordance with Canon 934 § 1, to recite any other prayer that his esteem and attachment for the Holy Father may suggest. (S.P., 20 Sept., 1933.) The general intention to pray for the intention of the Holy Father, contained in the intention to gain the indulgence, is sufficient.

Particular prayers (six Our Fathers, Hail Marys and Glorys) for the intentions of the Holy Father are assigned for all *toties-quoties* plenary indulgences where a visit to church is prescribed, and no other prayer may be substituted. (S.P., 5 July, 1930; cf. S.P., 10 July, 1924; 13 Jan., 1930.)

C. *Power to Commute the Prescribed Works*

Confessors have the power to commute the pious works

which have been prescribed for gaining indulgences to other works, for persons who are unable to perform them because of some lawful impediment. (Can. 935.)

Confessor here means any priest who is approved for confessions and this power can be used even outside of confession but only in the internal forum. (Coronata, *De Sacr.*, I, n. 538.) The faculty to commute extends to all the good works prescribed, including the visit to the church even for the indulgences known as the *toties-quoties* and of the Portiuncula. (PCI, 19 Jan., 1940.) The visit to the church can be commuted if a church in the locality is to be visited, but not when the visit is prescribed to a church situated elsewhere. (Cf. S.C. Indulg., 18 Sept., 1862.)

CHAPTER II

Particular Indulgences

The *Enchiridion Indulgentiarum (Preces et Pia Opera)* is the authentic collection of prayers and devotions which have been indulgenced by the Sovereign Pontiffs. For the authorized English translation of the *Enchiridion Indulgentiarum* (Typis Polyglottis Vaticanis, 1950), one is referred to *The Raccolta or a Manual of Indulgences, Prayers and Devotions Enriched with Indulgences* (New York: Benziger Brothers, Inc., 1957).

I. THE PAPAL BLESSING

A. *The Papal Blessing for Feast Days*

1. Every bishop may, in his own diocese, impart the papal blessing with a plenary indulgence using the prescribed formula, and this three times a year, i.e., Easter and on two other solemn feasts designated by the bishop, even though he has merely assisted at the Solemn Mass; abbots and prelates *nullius,* Vicars Apostolic and Prefects Apostolic, even though they lack episcopal consecration, can do the same in their respective territories but on only two of the more solemn days of the year. (Cf. Can. 914 and S.P., 20 July, 1942.)

The bishops cannot delegate this faculty (S.P., 25 April, 1922); nor can they transfer the Easter blessing to another day. (PCI, 17 Feb., 1930.)

2. Regulars who have the privilege of imparting this papal blessing, not only are obliged to observe the prescribed formula but also cannot use this privilege except in their own churches and in churches of the nuns or tertiaries legitimately aggregated to their order; but not on the same day and in the same place where the bishop gives it. (Can. 915.)

The prescribed formula (*Rit. Rom.*, Tit. VIII, cap. 32) is required for the validity of the blessing. (S.C.Indulg., 22 March, 1879.) This formula must be used by all priests, secular as well as regular, who have a special indult from the Holy See for imparting this papal blessing. (S.R.C., 12 March, 1940.)

Those who are present when the papal blessing is given gain a plenary indulgence provided they receive the sacraments and pray for the intention of the Holy Father. On Easter, the Easter Communion is sufficient. (Coronata, *De Sacr.*, I, 485.) Those who cannot be present to receive the Papal Blessing given by the Supreme Pontiff to the City and to the World (*Urbi et Orbi*) on solemn occasions together with the plenary indulgence, can nevertheless gain the plenary indulgence if they receive the blessing with pious and devout minds by radio, on the usual conditions. (S.P., 15 June, 1939.)

B. *The Papal Blessing for Missions and Retreats*

1. Regulars (Benedictines, Dominicans, Franciscans, Capuchins, Conventuals, Jesuits, etc.), as well as Redemptorists and Passionists, have the faculty to impart the Papal Blessing with a plenary indulgence attached, at the end of missions and retreats. (Cf. Campelo, pp. 423-424.)

In addition to confession and Communion, the faithful must attend at least half of the sermons and instructions. This last condition is not required for the Papal Blessing at missions and retreats given by the Jesuits and Redemptorists.

The missionaries of regular orders and of congregations which communicate privileges with them, may delegate to another priest (regular and secular clergy of higher rank are to be preferred) the power of bestowing, in their stead, at the end of missions, the Papal Blessing. (Pius IX, 19 Jan., 1851; 4 May, 1851; Pius X, 11 March, 1908. Cf. Ubach, I, n. 464.)

2. The formula for this blessing is given in the *Roman*

Ritual, (Appendix, *Benedictiones Reservatae,* II, n. 4), and it consists in a single *sign of the cross* made over the people *with a crucifix* while saying: "Benedictio Dei omnipotentis, Patris, et Filii, † et Spiritus Sancti, descendat super vos, et maneat semper. (R.) Amen." (S.R.C., 11 May, 1911.)

> This blessing is not restricted by Canon 915 which does not apply to it. (Bouscaren-Ellis, p. 379.)

II. INDULGENCES FOR MISSIONS AND RETREATS

1. *Attending the Mission or Retreat.* The faithful who attend a mission or retreat can gain an indulgence of 7 years for each sermon and a plenary indulgence on the usual conditions if they devoutly assist, at least, at one third of the sermons in a spirit of devotion. (*Raccolta,* nos. 689, a; 692, c.)

2. *Renewing the Vows of Baptism.* The faithful who at the end of a mission or retreat or any other time of the year with the permission of the Ordinaries and according to the formulas prescribed by them, solemnly renew their baptismal vows, can gain a plenary indulgence, if in addition, they make their confession, receive Holy Communion, and pray for the intentions of the Holy Father. (*Raccolta,* n. 679.)

3. *The Papal Blessing.* Confer above, I, B.

4. *The Mission Cross*

a. *Erection and blessing:* The Holy Office, August 13, 1913, abrogated all former regulations for the erection of the mission crosses at the end of missions and laid down the following regulations: The mission cross must be made of solid material, must have a specified location with a solid base or be attached to a wall in some way, and must be blessed by a missionary who has preached the mission sermons. The consent of the bishop is required.

In case the mission cross becomes worn or is destroyed, it may, with the permission of the bishop, be replaced with another cross. The indulgences of the mission cross are of a local character.

No special formula for the blessing of the mission cross is prescribed. The formula mentioned in the Ritual for the blessing of crucifixes may be used.

b. *Indulgences*

1) The faithful who devoutly make a visit to a mission cross can gain a plenary indulgence under the usual conditions, on the day of the erection or blessing of the mission cross, on the anniversary of the same, on the feasts of the Finding (May 3) and of the Exaltation (September 14) of the Holy Cross, or on any of the seven days following any of the above. (*Raccolta,* n. 635.)

If the mission cross is in church, the visits to the church and to the cross may be combined.

2) A partial indulgence of five years can be gained by the faithful who by any outward sign of devotion salute the mission cross and say one Our Father, Hail Mary, and Glory, in memory of the sufferings of Our Lord. (*Raccolta,* n. 635.)

III. INDULGENCES FOR THE DYING

A plenary indulgence granted for the hour of death is gained at the moment the soul leaves the body. Even though there be several titles for gaining such an indulgence at the moment of death, it can by its very nature be gained only once. (Cf. S.C.Indulg., 23 Jan., 1901.)

A. *The Apostolic Blessing in the Hour of Death*

1. The pastor or any other priest who assists the sick has the faculty of imparting to them the apostolic blessing with a plenary indulgence at the hour of death, according to the form given in approved liturgical books; and he should not fail to do so. (Can. 468 § 2.)

2. The prescribed *formula* (*Rom. Rit.,* Tit. V, cap.

6) is required for validity. (S.C.Indulg., 5 Feb., 1841; 22 March, 1829.)

> In the case of necessity the short formula is sufficient: "Ego, facultate mihi ab Apostolica Sede tributa, indulgentiam plenariam et remissionem omnium peccatorum tibi concedo, et benedico te. In nomine Patris, et Filii, † et Spiritus Sancti. Amen."

3.   The apostolic blessing should be bestowed *upon all the faithful* in danger of death from any cause, also on those who are unconscious or in delirium, or who have lost their mind; only to those who are excommunicated and to those who die in manifest mortal sin, this great grace must be denied. (Cf. *Rom. Rit.,* Tit. V, cap 6; Iorio, III, n. 715.)

> This blessing can be given in every true danger of death even though death should not ensue immediately. The priest should not postpone this blessing till the last hour. It is customary to connect the apostolic blessing with the administration of the last sacraments. Since this indulgence can be gained only once, and that at the moment of death, the apostolic blessing can be given only once in the same infirmity, even though extreme unction may be repeated if there be a new danger of death. Only in case the patient entirely recovers from the sickness and then relapses again into a new danger of death from any cause, is the apostolic blessing to be repeated. (S.C.Indulg., 24 Sept., 1838.)

> The fact that a person can gain a plenary indulgence in the hour of death under some other title, is no hindrance to the imparting of the apostolic blessing by the priest. (Beringer, I, nos. 831, 1031.)

4.   To gain this indulgence *two conditions* are required: resignation to God's holy will, accepting death as a penalty for one's sins and the sufferings of death as coming from the hand of God; the invocation of the name of Jesus with the lips, or if this is impossible, at least in the heart. (S.C. Indulg., 23 Sept., 1775; 22 Sept., 1892.)

> Confession, Communion and extreme unction should precede the apostolic blessing, but they are not essential conditions for gaining the indulgence. One, however, must be in the state of grace. (Iorio, III, 716.)

If these conditions have not been fulfilled (for instance, on account of unconsciousness) when the apostolic blessing is imparted, the only thing necessary is to supply them later on, because the indulgence is gained at the moment of death.

The ejaculations, "My Jesus, mercy," or "My Jesus, for Thee I live, for Thee I die," contain these two essential conditions.

B. *Other Plenary Indulgences in the Hour of Death*

Even without the assistance of a priest, the faithful can gain a plenary indulgence in the hour of death from various other titles, namely:

1. With an object blessed with the apostolic indulgences.

2. With a crucifix blessed with the so-called *toties-quoties* indulgence for the dying.

3. With the recitation of various ejaculations and prayers (cf. e.g., *Raccolta,* nos. 4, 36, 113, 292, 332-334, 452, 638, 694). Of special note is the plenary indulgence granted originally by Pius X (9 March, 1904): The faithful who at any time in their lives, from a sincere spirit of love of God and with at least a contrite heart, express their intention of accepting calmly and gladly from the hand of God whatsoever manner of death it may please Him to send them, together with all its pains, anguish and suffering, may gain a plenary indulgence at the hour of death, if they have devoutly made such an act at least once in their lifetime, after having fulfilled the usual conditions. (*Raccolta,* n. 638.)

No prescribed formula is required and the act may be elicited anytime during one's life; the plenary indulgence is gained at the moment of death.

IV. TOTIES-QUOTIES INDULGENCES

A. *The Portiuncula Indulgence*

1. *Time.* The time within which the Portiuncula indulgences can be gained is from 12 o'clock noon of August 1 till midnight of August 2. (Cf. Can. 923.)

Local Ordinaries, pastors, and rectors of churches which have the privilege, can, if they judge it expedient, transfer the privilege of the Portiuncula indulgence to the following Sunday in case the second of August does not fall on a Sunday. (S.P., 10 July, 1924.) One and the same person can gain the Portiuncula indulgences on both days, on the feast in one privileged church where the indulgence is not transferred, and on the following Sunday in another where it is legitimately transferred. (S.P., 13 Jan., 1930.)

During the time appointed for gaining the Portiuncula indulgence, a relic or a picture or a statue of St. Francis or of the Queen of Angels should be exposed for public veneration. Furthermore, *public devotions* are to be held, including prayers for the intention of the Holy Father, invocation of the Blessed Virgin and St. Francis, the Litany of All Saints, and Benediction of the Blessed Sacrament. The pastor or the rector of the privileged church or oratory is obliged to carry out these provisions. But the omission of some or even all of these devotions would not invalidate the indulgence. (Schaaf, *Eccl. Rev.*, LXXXI, p. 18.)

2. *Conditions.* The works prescribed for the gaining of the indulgence are: confession and Communion, a visit to a church or chapel enriched with this privilege, six Our Fathers, Hail Marys and Glorys in each visit for the intention of the Holy Father.

a. *Confession and Communion.* Confession can be made within eight days immediately preceding the day to which the indulgence is attached; Communion can be received on the day before the specified day; both confession and Communion may also be made on one of the seven days following the feast. (Cf. Can. 931 § 1.)

b. *Visit to a church or chapel enriched with this privilege.* The visit to a church or chapel includes some prayer (e.g., even an ejaculation) *besides* the six Our Fathers, Hail Marys and Glorys for the intention of the Holy Father.

Originally granted to the Chapel of the Portiuncula at Assisi, the indulgence was later extended. Today this privilege *can be obtained* for all cathedral and parochial churches, and moreover for the churches and oratories for which, in the judgment of the local Ordinary, the convenience of the faithful seems to demand it. (S.P., 1 May, 1939.) Since the decree of July 10, 1924, of the Sacred Penitentiary, petitions for this privilege, which must be recommended by the local Ordinary, must be sent to the Sacred Penitentiary. This 1924 decree abrogated all privileges for the Portiuncula indulgence which had been previously granted for a time or at the Sacred Penitentiary's *beneplacitum*. Privileges, however, given perpetually were retained in force with the provision that the rules laid down in the decree for gaining the indulgence must be observed in using such privileges.

The perpetual privileges of the various branches of the Order of St. Francis are:

1) *All the faithful* can gain the Portiuncula indulgence in the churches and public chapels:

a) Of the Friars Minor, Conventuals, Capuchins and Tertiaries Regular (Campelo, n. 426);

b) Of the Poor Clares and of nuns of the Third Order having solemn vows (Campelo, nos. 427, 212);

c) Of Religious Tertiaries of St. Francis with simple vows (both men and women) who are legitimately aggregated to the First Order (Campelo, n. 427);

d) Of the secular Tertiaries of St. Francis if the church actually belongs to them; not therefore, if the Third Order is only canonically established there (Campelo, n. 427);

2) *Religious Tertiaries* of either sex who are legitimately aggregated to the First Order, and persons in their care or living under the same roof with them, can gain the Portiuncula indulgence also in their principal semipublic oratory provided there is no church or public oratory attached to their house. (Cf. Campelo, nos. 637, 638.)

3) *Secular Tertiaries* can gain the Portiuncula indulgence:

a) In the churches or public oratories in which the Third Order is canonically established (Campelo, n. 826);

b) In their parish church if where they live there is no

church or public oratory of the Third Order of St. Francis, nor any other church which enjoys the privilege of the Portiuncula indulgence or in which the Third Order is canonically established (Campelo, n. 806);

c) In the chapels (semipublic) of colleges, hospitals and similar institutions, if they live in these institutions, and are legitimately prevented from visiting a church of any of the three orders or their parish church. (Campelo, n. 808.)

c. *Prayers for the Intention of the Holy Father.* The six Our Fathers, Hail Marys and Glorys at each visit for the intention of the Holy Father are prescribed for gaining the Portiuncula indulgence, and no other prayer may be substituted. (S.P., 5 July, 1930; 10 July, 1924; 13 Jan., 1930.)

B. *The All Souls' Day Indulgence*

1. The faithful, as often as they visit a church or public oratory, (or even a semipublic oratory under the conditions specified in Canon 929) in order to pray for the dead on All Souls' Day may gain a plenary indulgence applicable only to the souls detained in purgatory. (S.O., 25 June, 1914; *Raccolta,* n. 590.)

> The prescribed *time* for gaining the indulgence is *either* November 2 (or the 3 if the office is transferred—S.O., 16 Dec., 1916) or for individuals who did not gain the indulgences on All Souls' Day, the following Sunday (S.P., 2 Jan., 1939.) The indulgence can be gained from 12 o'clock noon of the preceding day. (Cf. Can. 923.)
>
> The *conditions* are confession (which may be made from October 25 to November 9 inclusive; Communion (which may be received from November 1 to 9 inclusive); visit to a church which includes some prayer (e.g., even an ejaculation); six Our Fathers, Hail Marys, and Glorys at each visit for the intentions of the Sovereign Pontiff.

2. During the octave of All Souls' Day all the Masses said at any altar by any priest are privileged for the souls

to which they are applied. (*Raccolta,* n. 591.) The faithful who during the period of eight days from the commemoration of All Souls inclusive, visit a cemetery in a spirit of piety and devotion, and pray, even mentally, for the dead, may gain a plenary indulgence on the usual conditions, on each day of the octave, applicable only to the dead. (*Raccolta,* n. 592.) Those who make such a visit, and pray for the Holy Souls, on any day in the year, may gain an indulgence of 7 years, applicable only to the departed. (*Raccolta,* n. 592.)

C. *Other Toties-Quoties Indulgences*

There are many other such grants of *toties-quoties* plenary indulgences, for example, on the feast of the *Transitus* of St. Benedict the abbot (March 20) in all the churches of the Order of St. Benedict; on the feast of St. Ignatius (July 31) in the churches of the Jesuits; on the feast of St. Augustine (August 28) in the churches of the Order of St. Augustine, etc. In all these cases, the conditions are: confession, Communion, visits to the privileged church or public oratory, six Our Fathers, Hail Marys and Glorys at each visit for the intention of the Holy Father. (Cf. Regatillo-Zalba, III, n. 611; Cappello, *De Sacr.,* II, n. 689.)

V. GENERAL ABSOLUTION TO RELIGIOUS

1. General Absolution is a blessing of the Church to which a plenary indulgence is attached. Confession, Communion, and prayer for the intention of the Holy Father are required conditions. (Campelo, n. 375.) Contrary to the teaching of older authors, the Sacred Congregation of Indulgences (22 Aug., 1906) declared that this plenary indulgence can be gained not only for the suffering Souls, but also for the living, i.e., by the religious themselves.

2. For imparting General Absolution to regulars and nuns the formula *Ne reminiscaris* has been prescribed by Leo XIII, July 7, 1882. All other formulae have been abrogated. The formula *Ne reminiscaris* must also be used when General Absolution is imparted to religious of the Third Order legitimately aggregated to the First Order

(S.C.Indulg., 11 Nov., 1903) and to religious even though not members of the Third Order but who are aggregated to the First Order (S.R.C., 3 Aug., 1953.) The formula *Ne reminiscaris* must be used even on days when the religious receive it by virtue of communication of indulgences with the secular tertiaries. (S.R.C., 7 June, 1919.)

> Religious of the First and Second Order of St. Francis who are present in a church or oratory where the blessing is being given to tertiaries under the formula *Intret oratio,* can receive it, if on that day they are unable to do so under the formula *Ne reminiscaris.* (S.R.C., 7 June, 1919.) The condition that a religious can no longer that day conveniently receive the general absolution with the formula *Ne reminiscaris* certainly bears a liberal interpretation. (*Acta Minorum,* XLII, p. 24.)

3. When General Absolution is imparted privately (i.e., immediately after sacramental absolution), the confessor may use the short formula: "Auctoritate a Summis Pontificibus mihi concessa plenariam omnium peccatorum tuorum indulgentiam tibi impertior. In nomine Patris, et Filii, † et Spiritus Sancti. Amen." (S.R.C., 22 March, 1905.)

4. Various regulations and practices obtain in different orders for imparting General Absolution. For the Franciscan Family mark the following:

a. *Days.* For the days on which General Absolution may be given cf. p. 440. General Absolution can be imparted to the community as such publicly and also to individuals privately on the day itself as also on the entire day preceding. (S.C.Indulg., 26 Aug., 1895.)

> Those religious who are legitimately prevented from receiving General Absolution on the appointed days (the legitimately impeding cause must be recognized by the superior), can receive it on one of the seven days immediately following. (S.C. Indulg., 26 Aug., 1895.)

b. *Minister*

1) For *clerical religious* the office to impart General

Absolution to the community belongs to the superior. With his permission, also any other religious priest can impart it.

General permission is sufficient; for instance, where it is customary that in the absence of the superior the senior priest imparts it. For imparting General Absolution after confession no special permission is required.

The superior, or his delegate, who imparts General Absolution to his community himself receives General Absolution. (S.C.Indulg., 1 Feb., 1905.)

2) For *nuns,* the confessor, ex officio, and also any other priest appointed by the nuns' Ordinary (provincial or bishop) is the minister of General Absolution.

The sick nuns can receive General Absolution within the octave of the feast, on the day on which the confessor enters the enclosure to hear their confessions. (S.C.Indulg., 21 May, 1892.)

3) *Other religious* (brothers and sisters of the Third Order) receive General Absolution as a community *publicly* from their confessor (ordinary or extraordinary). Other priests, also priests of the First Order, need the faculty from the bishop to whom these religious are subject, not from the regular superior. For these religious, however, the indult of the Holy Office (15 Dec., 1910) also obtains, according to which in the absence of the authorized priest, any priest, whether secular or regular, having the faculties of the diocese, can also impart General Absolution to the community. Any confessor who lawfully hears the confessions of these religious can also impart General Absolution to them in confession.

APPENDIX

Special Privileges of the Franciscan Family

1. Pius X (Ap. Lett., 4 Oct., 1909) granted the three families of the First Order (Friars Minor, Conventuals, Capuchins) the mutual communication of all indulgences,

favors, and privileges, excluding the faculties for the Way of the Cross, Scapular of St. Joseph, Cord of St. Francis and pious associations and sodalities, which faculties were reserved to the proper Minister General. (Cf. *Acta Minorum*, XXIX, p. 104.)

> All indulgences, therefore, which were and will be granted to any one of the three families of the First Order are enjoyed by all. Indulgences granted to a particular church, province, or region are not communicable. Also excluded are indulgences granted to one of the families *ad tempus*. (Campelo, nos. 202-204.)

2.   Pius X (5 May, 1909 and 17 May, 1909) directly granted to all the children of St. Francis of the First, Second and Third Orders the communication of all indulgences. (*Acta Minorum*, XXVIII, pp. 174, 177.) In a response of June 9, 1919, the Sacred Congregation of Religious expressly declared this communication as still existing.

> Accordingly, members of Third Order Congregations which are aggregated to the First Order, enjoy all the indulgences granted to the First, Second, and Third Order Regular or Secular. (Cf. *Jus Seraphicum*, II, pp. 604-606.)

> A Religious Congregation which does not belong to the Third Order of St. Francis but which is aggregated to the First Order, enjoys all the indulgences and spiritual favors that are enjoyed by aggregated Congregations of the Third Order. (S.C.Rel., 17 Oct., 1957 — *Acta Minorum*, LXXVI, p. 349.)

3.   The Friars Minor who because of old age, infirmity, and senility dwell in infirmaries, can gain all the indulgences granted to Franciscan churches if they visit the chapel of the infirmary and fulfill the other prescribed conditions. (Campelo, n. 643.) The same privilege holds for those who have to stay with the sick. (*Summarium O.F.M.*, n. 54.) The sick, convalescent, and decrepit brethren who cannot well visit the church, can gain all the indulgences for which a visit to the church is required, in their cell or in the sick-room if they say five Our Fathers and five Hail

Marys in addition to the ordinary prayers for the intention of the Holy Father, and fulfill the other conditions prescribed for gaining the indulgences. (*Summarium O.F.M., n. 4.*)

CHAPTER III

Indulgenced Objects

Introduction: A simple blessing can be given to various things, even those which are incapable of receiving indulgences. Thus in the *Roman Ritual* are found various formulae for blessing water, homes, cars, fields, persons, etc. Some of the listed blessings are not reserved and these can be given by any ordained priest; others of these blessings are reserved. This chapter, however, deals only with those objects to which indulgences may be attached and the conditions necessary to attach these indulgences.

I. OBJECTS IN GENERAL

Holy Church permits indulgences to be attached to certain objects. Such objects are rosaries, crosses, crucifixes, medals, small statues, and scapulars. According to the practice of the Church various conditions are required before one of the above objects can be enriched with indulgences.

1. *Material and Form Prescribed*

a. For the validity of the blessing with indulgences, the object must be of *durable material,* hence not made of tin, lead, or glass which is inflated and hollow. (S.P., 11 March, 1939.) Any material that is easily broken, defaced, or destroyed, is not admissable: for instance, pictures printed or painted on paper or canvas; crosses, statues, medals made of zinc, lead, plaster. Pearl, mother-of-pearl, marble, iron, aluminum and other hard metals may be used; for the beads of rosaries, even hard glass or cord are permitted. (S.P., 21 Dec., 1925; 15 May, 1948.) Plastic also is considered durable material. (Cf. S.P., 6 May, 1959.)

On crucifixes the indulgences are attached to the corpus; on rosaries to the beads, and the above regulations refer only to these parts.

b. Medals and statues must represent canonized saints or at least those whose names are contained in approved martyrologies. Medals must bear the image of such saints at least on the one side, while on the other side may be represented the image of a beatified person, a church, or a celebrated personage, such as the Pope, etc. (Cf. S.P., 17 Feb., 1922.)

2. *The Faculty to Bless with Indulgences*

a. The faculty to attach indulgences to objects can be obtained directly from the Sacred Penitentiary, or through the bishop or one's major superior, or through membership in certain pious associations, etc.

b. In the grant of these faculties, the clause "with the consent of the local Ordinary" is sometimes added. The consent of the local Ordinary (in whose diocese such faculties are used) is necessary for *lawful,* not for the *valid* use of the faculties. Express consent is preferred, but tacit or implied, even presumed consent, is sufficient. (Cf. S.C. Indulg., 14 June, 1901.)

Religious may use such faculties within the monastery with the consent of their superiors.

Also other clauses which may have been added, must be observed. He who has permission to use certain faculties only *privately,* should not exercise them publicly in the presence of a congregation which presents the articles for blessing.

The customary clause "as long as the priest is approved for hearing confessions" designates any confessor approved for confessions of men and women or only children, and he can use his faculty to bless even outside the diocese in which he is a confessor. (Regatillo-Zalba, III, 616.)

c. A reserved blessing given by a priest without the necessary faculty is illicit but valid unless in the reservation the Holy See expressly states that it can be given validly only by those who have special faculties. (Can.

1147.) *For endowing objects with indulgences,* this regulation does not hold. In this latter case faculties are necessary for the validity of the act.

3. *The Rite of Blessing*

a. In the case of some objects a *special formula* must be used for the blessing, for instance, for the Dominican Rosary. If this formula is not used, at least essentially, the blessing is invalid. (Can. 1148.)

If no formula is prescribed, the blessing is made in the ordinary manner, that is, with one sign of the cross. No formula is required, no sprinkling with holy water.

When, however, these blessings are given *publicly,* the priest should adhere to the ceremonial customary for the administration of sacramentals: surplice and stole (at least for secular priests), holy water, and a general formula of the Ritual.

b. A priest who has faculties to bless with indulgences various objects for each of which the sign of the cross without a special formula is sufficient, can attach all these various blessings to the objects *with one sign of the cross.* (S.O., 18 May, 1914; cf. Regatillo-Zalba, III, n. 617, 2°.)

Hence, he need not repeat the sign of the cross for each blessing, even though the objects to be blessed are of a different nature. It is sufficient to make one sign of the cross over rosaries, crucifixes and statues for the purpose of attaching to rosaries the Crosier indulgence, to the crucifixes the indulgences of the Stations of the Cross, and to all these objects the Papal indulgences. An exception is made with regard to the *scapular medal* for which a distinct sign of the cross is required. (S.O., 4 June, 1913.) Moreover, the sign of the cross must be repeated for every scapular represented by the medal. (S.O., 16 Dec., 1910.)

c. To the *same object* various indulgences can be attached if only the object is adapted to them. Thus, for instance, to one and the same rosary of five decades, the Dominican, Crosier, and Papal indulgences can be attached, not, however, those of the seven decades of the Sorrowful Mother. Thus also the Papal indulgences, but not the Dominican indulgences, can be attached to the crown of the Seven Joys.

d. The priest need not see the objects which are to be blessed. These objects need be *only morally present,* for instance, in the same church in which the faithful are having their objects blessed, even though not exposed for blessing.

4. *The Use of Indulgenced Objects.* To gain the indulgences all the conditions in using the objects must be fulfilled, for instance, wearing the blessed object, prayer in presence of the object, and so on. And to gain indulgences of a different nature attached to the same object the specific conditions must be repeated. Cumulation of indulgences has been permitted only in special cases.

5. *Cessation of Indulgences.* Indulgences attached to rosaries or other objects cease only when the rosaries or other objects are entirely destroyed or sold. (Can. 924 § 2.)

> Blessed objects may now be loaned or given to another without loss of even the apostolic indulgences (cf. S.P., 18 Feb., 1921). Gradual substitution of beads does not impede the indulgences attached to a rosary. (Coronata, *De Sacr.,* I, n. 504.) With crucifixes, the indulgence is attached to the image, and accordingly the image may be transferred from one cross to another without loss of indulgence. (Cf. S.C.Indulg., 11 April, 1840.)

> These objects lose their indulgence even if the alms is only sufficient to defray their cost, but not if the buyer has become the owner before the indulgence is attached, even though he pays the price only after the attaching of the indulgence. (Abbo-Hannan, II, n. 924.)

II. OBJECTS IN PARTICULAR

A. *The Apostolic Indulgences*

1. Soon after his coronation the new Pope approves and promulgates the list of apostolic indulgences. Thus also John XXIII. (S.P., 22 Nov., 1958.) The Holy Father

attaches these indulgences to objects which he blesses at the time of his audiences, unless he expressly declares otherwise. (S.O., 12 June, 1913.) Other priests can obtain the faculties of attaching the apostolic indulgences from the Sacred Penitentiary. The blessing is given with one sign of the cross.

2. With regard to the material and form of objects to be blessed with the papal indulgences the same thing holds as for indulgenced objects in general. (S.O., 22 Nov., 1958.) To gain the papal indulgences, in addition to other ordinary conditions, it is required that one carry the indulgenced object on his person or becomingly keep it in his home. (S.P., 22 Nov., 1958.)

3. The entire list of apostolic indulgences can be found in the *AAS*, LI, pp. 48-50. Among the apostolic indulgences that can be attached to pious objects is the plenary indulgence in the hour of death which is gained on these conditions: that the person in the hour of death, after confession and Communion or at least an act of contrition, shall invoke the Name of Jesus, orally if possible, or at least in his heart, and accept death from the hand of the Lord with resignation as being the wages of sin.

It should be noted that these conditions are exactly the same as those for gaining a plenary indulgence in the moment of death with the *death crucifix* which has been blessed with the so-called *toties-quoties* indulgence, which is not gained as often as the person kisses the crucifix, but only once and that at the moment of death. (S.O., 10 June, 1914; S.P., 23 June, 1929; 22 Sept., 1942.) However, a small distinction is to be made: for gaining the indulgence of the dying by means of the objects to which the papal indulgences are attached, it is necessary that the sick person carry the object on his person or becomingly keep it in his home; whereas the condition for the gaining of the *toties-quoties* indulgence simply reads: "whoever kisses such a crucifix or touches it in any mannr." Hence, the last-mentioned crucifix need not remain with the dying person after he has kissed it. (Cf. S.P., 23 June, 1929; 22 Nov., 1958.)

Both the apostolic indulgence and the so-called *toties-quoties* indulgence can be attached to a crucifix with a single sign of the cross by a priest having both faculties.

4. Note that the apostolic indulgences are no longer personal, but *real,* so the objects to which they have been attached, may be given away, lent or bequeathed to others. (S.P., 18 Feb., 1921.)

5. The Papal indulgences can now also be gained together with other indulgences which may be attached to the same objects or the same good works. (S.P., 14 June, 1922.)

B. *Rosaries and Crowns*

Technically, Rosary (*Rosarium*) means the Dominican Rosary. Other so-called Rosaries are called crowns (*coronae*).

1. *The Dominican Rosary*

a. The Dominican Rosary is made up physically of five, ten or fifteen decades. Each decade consists of one Our Father and ten Hail Marys. The cross, etc., are not necessary. Meditation on the main mysteries of the life, suffering and glorification of Christ is prescribed during the recitation of the respective decades.

b. The *prayers of the Rosary* must be said on a blessed Rosary, held in the hand, in the customary way. In the common recitation of the Rosary, which may be done alternately, it is enough that one person (the leader) holds the blessed rosary in his hand. Those who participate in the common recitation of the Rosary, may also perform light hand work while saying the Rosary. The single decades may be separated; however, in order to gain the indulgences it is necessary that at least five decades be recited during one natural day. (S.O., 8 June, 1908.)

> The faithful can gain the indulgences attached to the Rosary if they recite it with a companion who is present only radiophonically. (S.P., 8 Oct., 1958.)

If on account of manual labor, or any other reasonable cause, the faithful cannot hold the rosary in their hand according to the prescribed form, they can gain the indulgences attached to it provided that while saying the prescribed prayers they carry the rosary in any manner on their person. (S.P., decr., 9 Nov., 1933.)

c. The superiors of the Dominican order have the faculty to bless this Rosary. Since April 1, 1933, the generals and provincials of the Dominican order can no longer delegate this faculty to priests outside of the order; but those priests who had received this delegation prior to April 2, 1933, can still make use of it. (S.P., decr., 20 March, 1933.) A special formula is required for the blessing.

d. *Indulgences.* For the indulgences attached to the Rosary cf. *Raccolta,* nos. 395-398. Note that one can gain a plenary indulgence, on condition of confession and Communion, as often as he recites five decades of the Rosary in the presence of the Blessed Sacrament, even reserved in the tabernacle. (Apost. Brief, 4 Sept., 1927.)

2. *The Crosier Rosary*

a. This Rosary has the same form as the Dominican Rosary. Meditation on the mysteries and uninterrupted recitation are not prescribed to gain the Crosier Rosary indulgence (five hundred days for every Our Father and Hail Mary, Leo X, 20 Aug., 1516). The indulgence is connected with every bead and is gained even if the entire Rosary is not said. (Campelo, n. 549.) The blessing is attached with one sign of the cross.

If a rosary has received the blessing for the Dominican Rosary indulgences as well as for the Crosier Rosary indulgence, the Crosier Rosary indulgence can be gained together with the indulgences of the Dominican Rosary. (Cf. S.P., 23 May, 1921; Campelo, n. 549.)

b. Since April 1, 1933, the general of the Crosier Fathers can no longer delegate the faculty to bless the Crosier Rosary to priests outside of the Order, but those priests who had received this delegation prior to April 2, 1933, can still make use of it. (S.P., decr., 20 March, 1933.)

3. *The Franciscan Crown of the Seven Joys*

a. This Crown consists of seven decades, each having one Our Father and ten Hail Marys; and in addition two Hail Marys (seventy-two years of Mary's life) together with one Our Father and Hail Mary and Glory for the intention of the Holy Father. Hence, the material Crown is composed of eight large and seventy-two small beads.

b. Meditation on the mysteries is not required. For the recitation of this Crown in common, the same concessions have been made as for the Dominican Rosary. The decades may also be said separately, provided they are said within one natural day.

c. Since April 1, 1933, the generals of the Orders of Friars Minor, Capuchins, Conventuals can delegate the faculty to bless the Franciscan Crown only to members of the Order; but priests outside of these Orders who had received this delegation prior to April 2, 1933, can still use it. (S.P., decr., 20 March, 1933.) The blessing of this Crown is attached with one sign of the cross.

d. The following are the indulgences attached to this Crown:

1) *A plenary indulgence* is granted to the members of the three orders of St. Francis, including the Third Order Secular, each time they recite the Franciscan Crown and add a Pater and Ave for the intention of the Holy Father. (Leo XIII, 7 Sept., 1901.)

No beads are required to gain this plenary indulgence. But all the faithful (also those belonging to one of the three orders of St. Francis) must have Crowns specially blessed for the purpose in order to gain the indulgences listed below, granted by Pius X, 15 Sept., 1905. In the *public recitation* of the Crown, however, in the churches of the three orders, all who join in the prayers gain the plenary indulgence whether they have blessed beads or not. Moreover, if two or more say this Crown in common (for instance, at family prayers), it suffices if the leader holds a blessed Crown in his hand. (S.C.Indulg., 12 Sept., 1906.)

2) *Other plenary indulgences* the faithful gain (Campelo, n. 538):

a) A plenary indulgence for taking part in the *public recitation* of the Crown in any church of the three orders of St. Francis.

b) A plenary indulgence, if, after confession and Communion (no other conditions), they recite the Franciscan Crown on the following days: Christmas (December 25), Epiphany (January 6), Sunday during the octave of Epiphany, Easter, Immaculate Conception (December 8), Annunciation (March 25), Purification (February 2), Visitation (July 2), Assumption (August 15), feast of the Seven Joys of the Blessed Virgin Mary (August 27), Nativity of the Blessed Virgin Mary (September 8).

c) A plenary indulgence once a month on any day after confession and Communion, if they say the Franciscan Crown every Saturday of the year.

d) A plenary indulgence in the hour of death on the usual conditions, if one has the Crown in his possession and has prayed it frequently.

3) *Partial indulgences* which the faithful can gain (Campelo, n. 538):

a) Seventy years and seventy quarantines every time they say the Franciscan Crown on any day of the week except Saturday.

b) One hundred years every time they say it on any Saturday of the year.

c) Two hundred years when they say it on the holy days of obligation.

d) Three hundred years when they say it on any feast of the Blessed Virgin not mentioned above for the plenary indulgences.

e) Ten years for every good work they perform for the honor of God or for the love of their neighbors, provided they carry the rosary about on their person and often recite it.

f) Ten years every time they say seven Hail Marys in honor of the Seven Joys, provided they carry the Crown about on their person and often recite it.

C. *Scapulars*

There are in all sixteen approved scapulars, the best

known are: the *white* (of the Most Holy Trinity—Trinitarian), the *red* (of the Passion—Vincentian), the *brown* (Mount Carmel—Carmelite), the *black* (of the Seven Dolors of Mary—Servite), the *blue* (of the Immaculate Conception of Mary—Theatine). These scapulars are ordinarily worn together as the four- or five-fold scapular.

1. *Material and Form.* The scapulars must be of woven wool material, having the respective color. (S.C.Indulg., 18 Aug., 1868.) The white scapular has in the middle a red-blue Cross of the Trinitarians; the black has on the one side the image of the Crucified and on the other the image of the two Sacred Hearts.

The form must be square. The connecting bands may be of any material, and color; only for the scapular of the Passion they must be red wool. If the scapular of the Passion is worn in connection with the others, the bands must be red wool.

> If several scapulars are worn together, the individual scapulars must be distinguishable; hence, they may not be sewed together on all sides. Only on one side may they be sewed together and sewed to the common connecting bands. To protect the scapulars from perspiration, they may be put in a cover.

2. *Manner of Wearing.* The scapular must worn like the habit of the order it represents, so that one part hangs down on the breast and the other down the back. (S.C. Indulg., 12 Feb., 1840.) It may be worn over or under the clothes. Except in case of special privilege it cannot be substituted in the case of religious by the habit they wear.

3. *Blessing and Imposition*

a. *For the rite of blessing,* a mere sign of the cross is *per se* not sufficient; the proper formula must be used. The *Roman Ritual* (Benedictiones Propriae, nos. 3, 6, 7, 8, 11-13) gives separate formulas for each of the five scapulars. That part of the formula which contains the blessing and the imposition (reception into the confraternity of the scapular) is essential. Also, holy water must be used in the rite. For the simultaneous blessing and imposition of the fivefold scapular, the *Roman Ritual* (Benedictiones Propriae, n. 14) contains a *collective formula,* which, however, can licitly be used only by those with a special faculty, validly by all who have the faculty of blessing and imposing the individual scapulars, since the collective formula contains the substance of the individual formulas.

b. *Manner of Imposition.* The scapulars must be blessed and imposed by the *same authorized priest*. The imposition of the scapular is effected by laying it around the neck or on one shoulder. The same blessed scapular may be used for imposition upon many persons successively.

> The formula for the enrollment as well as for the blessing may be used in the *plural* form if several persons are to be enrolled at the same time, and the actual enrollment may take place before or after the formula is pronounced. For the several-fold scapulars one enrollment is sufficient.

> The first scapular worn must be blessed, after which any new scapular worn by the person enrolled need not be blessed. (Bouscaren-Ellis, p. 394.)

> Also children who have not yet arrived at the years of discretion, can be enrolled in the scapular. The priest who has the faculties to enroll others, can also enroll himself. (Beringer, I, n. 931.)

4. *Enrollment.* The priest should keep a private register in which he records the names of those enrolled by him, and from time to time, perhaps once a year, send the names to the respective generals in Rome or to another place where there is a canonically established confraternity. The sending and recording of the names to a canonically erected confraternity of the respective scapular is required for validity in the case of the white, black, and brown scapulars (cf. Can. 649 § 2; Bouscaren-Ellis, p.

394), unless one has received special faculties of omitting the registration.

A validation of invalid enrollments in the scapular is granted every five or ten years.

5. *Special Faculties*

a. By enrollment in the Missionary Union of the Clergy every priest approved for confessions has the faculty to bless the five-fold scapular, using the one collective formula and without the obligation of making the enrollment in the register of the respective confraternity.

b. By the quinquennial faculties, local Ordinaries have the faculty to bless and impose the five scapulars with the one formula, with power to subdelegate; likewise the faculty to bless and impose the five scapulars with the one formula without the obligation of inscribing the names in cases of a great concourse of people during the time of retreats and missions, with the power to subdelegate. (*Digest,* IV, p. 77.)

c. Preachers of the Order of Friars Minor who have the faculty of blessing and imposing the five-fold scapular with the one collective formula when requested to do so, can use this formula in the plural, omit the imposition of the scapulars (which the faithful place upon themselves), and also omit the inscribing and sending of the names to the respective confraternities. (S.C. Indulg., 22 Aug., 1906; S.R.C., 23 May, 1917; Campelo, n. 683.)

In order that one rightly uses this indult, he must already possess both the faculty to bless the respective scapulars, and also the faculty to use the one collective formula.

D. *Scapular Medals*

Instead of the scapular (Third Order scapular excepted), the faithful may wear a medal and thereby gain all the indulgences and privileges attached to the wearing of the scapular. Faithful of the Oriental rites can also substitute the scapular medal for the scapular. (S.C.E.O., 25 March, 1935.)

For *soldiers* Pius X made the concession that they partake of all the indulgences and privileges of the respective scapulars all the world over if they wear a blessed scapular medal, even though they had not been enrolled in the scapular and their names had not been inscribed in the register of a canonically established confraternity. This also holds after their time of service is over. (Beringer, I, n. 939.)

1. *Material, Form, Use*

a.   Only such medals can be blessed as scapular medals as bear on the one side the image of the Sacred Heart (i.e., Our Lord showing his heart), and on the other the image of the Mother of God.

b.   The scapular medal must be made of a metallic substance. (S.O., 16 Dec., 1910; cf. also Beringer, I, n. 938; Danagher, *HPR,* LIV, p. 172.)

c.   These medals must be worn hung from a chain around the neck, or carried in a pocket, or sewed in one's clothing (in some way carried on one's person). It also seems necessary to have the scapular medal on one's person at night. (Beringer, I, n. 938.)

2. *The Blessing.* The medal can be blessed by any priest who has the faculty to bless the respective scapulars. A simple sign of the cross is sufficient for this blessing, which however, must both be distinct from the sign of the cross by which other indulgences are attached (S.O., 4 June, 1913), and repeated for every scapular represented by the medal. (S.O., 16 Dec., 1910.) He who has the faculties to bless the five-fold scapular with one formula must therefore make the sign of the cross five times over the medal. It is not required that one and the same priest bless both the scapulars and the medals.

The blessing of the scapular medals may also take place publicly in church; it is not, however, necessary that the medals be visible.

A large number of scapular medals may be blessed at once, to be distributed to various persons later on. It is not necessary that these medals be specified for determined persons, or that those for whom the medals are intended have already been enrolled in the scapular. A blessed scapular is, however, necessary for the enrollment.

A person who has been enrolled in a blessed scapular need not, when getting a new scapular, have the new scapular blessed; a new scapular medal, however, does not substitute for the old one unless it is also blessed. (S.O., 5 June, 1913; 10 May, 1916.)

E.   *The Medal of St. Benedict*

The model of St. Benedict bears on one side the image of St. Benedict with crucifix and rule book, on the other, a larger cross and inscription. For those who wear this medal, Holy Church implores a special protection against diabolic attacks.

The faculties to bless this medal are vested in every professed priest of the Benedictine order. Abbots who are at the head of the various congregations, can give this faculty to other priests whether secular or regular. (*Manual for Oblates of St. Benedict,* 1937, p. 273.)

CHAPTER IV

Stations of the Cross

I.   MATERIAL AND FORM

The stations of the way of the cross consist of fourteen *wooden* crosses, which must be fastened in place, with spaces between the several stations. These requisites are all *ad validitatem.* (S.C.Indulg., 23 Nov., 1879, 28 Aug., 1752.)

Iron crosses completely encasing and obscuring wooden crosses are not sufficient. (S.C.Indulg., 23 Nov., 1878.) The place between the stations must not be so scant that the entire way of the cross can be made with just a few steps. Pictures representing the sufferings of Christ are not essential. Customarily, no corpus is attached to the crosses. (Cf. Campelo, n. 708.)

II. ERECTION

1. *Faculties to erect.* The following can validly erect the stations of the cross:

a. Cardinals, with one sign of the cross, even in private oratories. (Can. 239 § 1,6°; Campelo, n. 692.)

b. Bishops, whether residential or titular, observing the prescribed rite. (Can. 349 § 1,1°.)

Vicars General do not possess the faculty. (S.P., 10 Nov., 1926.)

Bishops can delegate their faculty to others only if they themselves have obtained the faculty to delegate from the Sacred Penitentiary. (S.P., 18 July, 1919 and 10 Nov., 1926.)

c. The Minister General, Provincials, and local superiors (guardians and praesides) of the Order of Friars Minor in their respective territories. These may erect stations in churches, public places, semipublic oratories, private oratories in which Mass may be celebrated, and in other places which are not of an entirely private nature, such as cemeteries, mountainsides, hospitals, corridors of religious houses, etc. (Campelo, nos. 685, 704.)

1) The superiors of the Capuchins and of the Conventuals do not possess this faculty. The Provincials of the Capuchins can erect stations only in churches and oratories of their Order. They can also delegate local superiors to do the same. (Campelo, n. 696.)

2) The Minister General of the Order of Friars Minor can delegate all the priests of the Order, not, however, other priests. whether secular or regular. The Provincials and local superiors can delegate only *their own subjects* who have the faculties to preach and hear confessions. The Provincials and local superiors can exercise this power only in their respective territory. In the absence of the local superior, his legitimate representative has the same power. (Campelo, n. 685; *Const. Gen. O.F.M.,* ed. 1953, nos. 518 § 3, 526.) As their respective territory are to be considered places within the area to which they send their subjects to assist in the sacred ministry.

The above delegation need not be in writing for validity.

(S.P., 12 March, 1938.) The superiors can not only delegate in particular cases but also grant a general delegation for an indefinite number of cases. (Cf. *Acta Minorum,* anno 1940, p. 127.)

3) By special faculties granted by the Sacred Penitentiary, the superiors (even local) of the Order can delegate, in their respective territories, other priests of the Order, even those who are not their subjects, but provided they are members of the Order and are approved for confessions, to bless and erect the stations of the cross. It is not necessary that these priests be approved for hearing confessions in the place where the stations are to be erected. (S.P., 15 Dec., 1954.) This special faculty is given for seven years, and is usually renewed.

Note: the permission of the bishop is not required for valid erection of the stations. However, in keeping with ecclesiastical discipline, this permission should be obtained for places subject to his jurisdiction. If it is not convenient to procure the express permission, the presumed permission is sufficient. (S.P., 12 March, 1938.)

2. *Manner of erecting*

a. The blessing of the fourteen crosses is necessary for validity. The blessing of the crosses alone is essential. To go the way of the cross in connection with the erection, though prescribed by the *Roman Ritual,* is not essential. (Campelo, nos. 710-713.)

b. For validity, the priest who blesses the stations, must be morally present in the place where the stations are to be erected. He cannot, for instance, bless the stations in the parsonage, and then send them to the church where they are to be erected. In the houses of cloistered nuns it is sufficient to bless the crosses at the grate. (Campelo, n. 714.)

c. It is immaterial whether the blessing of the crosses takes place before or after they are fixed in their places, whether the crosses are fixed in place by the priest who blesses them or by others, at the same time or later. (Campelo, nos. 711, 715.)

d. Several stations of the cross can be erected at the same place, or in the same church. (Cf. Campelo, n. 706.)

N.B. Periodically, usually at five-year intervals, invalidly erected stations are validated by the Sacred Penitentiary. (Thus v.g., S.P., 13 Oct., 1956 — *Acta Minorum,* LXXV, p. 266.) The validation, however, has reference only to the blessing and the prescribed formalities. Other defects, such as the use of iron crosses, must be remedied by the substitution of wooden crosses, unless a special validation for such defects be also obtained from Rome. (*Acta Minorum,* LVII, p. 206.)

3. *Document of erection.* After the blessing and erection of the stations of the cross, the priest who performed the ceremony should sign a document attesting the canonical erection of the stations. (S.C.Indulg., 10 Feb., 1844.) This document is to be preserved in the archives or sacristy of the church.

4. *Removal and replacing of crosses.* If seven or more of the crosses are destroyed, lost, or permanently removed and replaced by others, either simultaneously or successively, the stations have been morally changed and a new blessing and erection is necessary. However one or the other cross can certainly be substituted without a new blessing. (S.C.Indulg., 20 Sept., 1839; Campelo, nos. 720, 726.)

5. *Transferal of stations*

a. A change in the order of crosses or a change of position in the same church or in the same place, is permissible. (S.C.Indulg., 20 Aug., 1844.)

b. If the stations are transferred to a morally different place, the same formalities are required as in the original erection. (S.C.Indulg., 30 Jan., 1839.)

If, however, a new church is built on almost the same spot and under the same title, the stations can without further ado be transferred from the old to the new church. (S.C.Indulg., 7 June, 1905.)

c. If a new way of the cross is erected in the *same*

place in which the stations have already been canonically erected, the only thing necessary is that a priest authorized by competent authority repeat that part of the rite which contains the blessing of the crosses.

> The privilege to have the stations of the cross in a private oratory is of a personal nature and hence ceases with the death of the one who had the privilege of the private oratory. Also, if the stations are to be transferred to another oratory a new canonical erection is necessary. (Cf. Campelo, nos. 728-729 for details.)

III. INDULGENCES OF THE STATIONS OF THE CROSS

1. *The indulgences gained*

a. All the faithful can gain *a plenary indulgence every time* they make the stations with a contrite heart.

b. If they receive Holy Communion on the same day, or make the stations ten times within a month and receive Holy Communion once, they can gain another plenary indulgence.

c. If, for a reasonable cause, they do not complete the exercise, they can gain a partial indulgence of ten years for every station they have made. (*Preces,* n. 194.)

All other indulgences heretofore attached to the stations of the cross are abrogated. (*Preces,* n. 194.)

2. *Conditions for gaining the indulgences*

a. *Meditation on the Passion* of Our Lord Jesus Christ, however brief and according to one's capacity, is required. Oral prayers, or meditation on specified phases of the sufferings of Christ, are not required. For the common people a pious remembrance and veneration of and affection for, our suffering Savior are sufficient. (Campelo, nos. 600-601.)

b. *Physical change of place* from one station to another.

1) When the stations are made *privately,* moving from station to station is always required. Contrary indults have

been abrogated. (Cf. S.O., 24 July, 1912 and S.P., 14 Dec., 1917; Campelo, n. 598.)

2) When the stations are made *publicly* in a church, and disturbance and disorder may easily be caused by moving about, it is sufficient if the priest accompanied by two clerics or servers goes from station to station, pausing at each station and saying the prayers while the congregation answer from their places. (S.C.Indulg., 6 Aug., 1757.) If the priest cannot be understood on account of the size of the church or other conditions, it is permissible that one priest recite the prayers from the pulpit or some other suitable place while another priest accompanied by two clerics or servers moves from station to station. (Campelo, n. 597.) The faithful usually rise and kneel for every station, or at least genuflect.

When the stations are thus made publicly, a religious who is not a priest may *not* take the place of a priest. (S.P., 18 June, 1954.)

3) When the stations are made in common by a religious community in its oratory or in a church which the community uses as an oratory, it is sufficient, where space is limited, that one religious (man or woman) move from station to station. (S.P., 20 March, 1946, 18 June, 1954.) Where, however, it can be conveniently done, all must move from station to station.

c. *Uninterrupted visiting* of the stations is required. Notable interruption breaks the moral unity of the devotion and one must begin the devotion anew. Short interruptions do no destroy the unity of the devotion. Interruptions made to assist at Mass, to listen to a sermon, to go to confession and Communion, are not considered notable. (S.C.Indulg., 17 Dec., 1760.)

Confession, Communion, and prayer for the Holy Father are not prescribed.

IV. THE STATION CRUCIFIX

All those who are legitimately hindered from making the stations of the cross, can gain the indulgences of the stations if they hold in their hand a crucifix blessed for that purpose and contritely and devoutly say twenty Our Fathers, Hail Marys and Glorys, namely one for each station, five in memory of the sacred wounds of Our Lord Jesus Christ, and one for the intentions of the Supreme Pontiff. (*Preces,* n. 194.)

1. *Material and form.* The figure of the crucified Savior must be attached to a cross or at least stand forth in relief. (S.C. Indulg., 24 May, 1883.) The *corpus* must be made of solid material (v.g., brass or solid wood); fragile materials are excluded. (S.C. Indulg., 16 Sept., 1859.) A plastic crucifix is acceptable. (S.P., 6 May, 1959.) The indulgences are not attached to the cross, but to the *corpus.* Hence the cross itself may be made of any kind of material, and may also be substituted without a new blessing. (Cf. Campelo, n. 543.)

2. *Faculty to bless*

a. By virtue of their office, the Minister General, all Provincials, and all local superiors (guardians and praesides) of the Order of Friars Minor and in their absence, their representatives as specified in the General Constitutions (custos, vicar, discreet), have the faculty to bless the station crucifix. (Campelo, nos. 730, 732.)

b. Only the Minister General of the Order of Friars Minor can delegate this faculty, and only to priests of the Order. (S.C. Indulg., 15 March, 1884; S.P., 20 March, 1933; Campelo, n. 733.) However, priests (whether secular or religious) who had obtained this delegation prior to April 2, 1933 can continue to use their faculty. (Cf. S.P., 20 March, 1933.) Likewise the faculty can be obtained by members of the Missionary Union of the Clergy, by application for the special faculties of the Union.

c. Concerning the faculty of cardinals and bishops, the same rules obtain as regulate their faculty to erect the stations of the cross. (Cf. Campelo, n. 734.)

3. *Formula of blessing*

Since no special formula is prescribed for the blessing of the station crucifix, it is sufficient to make one sign of the cross over the crucifix to be blessed. (S.C. Indulg., 10 April, 1840 and 7 Jan., 1843.) If several crucifixes are being blessed at the same time, they can all be blessed with one and the same sign of the cross. (S.C. Indulg., 12 March, 1855.) Finally, other indulgences can be applied to the crucifix (v.g., the apostolic indulgences, the plenary indulgence for the hour of death, etc.), together with the indulgences of the stations of the cross: in which case, also, if the priest has the faculty to attach all these indulgences, it is sufficient if he use one and the same sign of the cross for attaching all of them. (S.O., 18 May, 1914; S.C. Indulg., 29 Feb., 1820; Campelo, n. 737.)

4. *Conditions for gaining the indulgences*

a. The one using the station crucifix must, at the time, be legitimately prevented from making the way of the cross. It is required that one then recite twenty Our Fathers, Hail Marys, and Glorys without a notable interruption. While the person says the prescribed prayers, he must hold the crucifix in his hand. When several persons who are legitimately hindered from visiting the stations, say these prayers in common, it is sufficient if the leader holds the crucifix in his hand while the others pray along, or alternate, or follow mentally. (S.C. Indulg., 19 Jan., 1884, and 13 Nov., 1893.)

If on account of manual labor or any other reasonable cause the faithful cannot hold the station crucifix in their hand according to form, they can gain the indulgences attached to it if, when saying the prescribed prayers, they carry the station crucifix in any manner on their person. (S.P., 9 Nov., 1933.)

The latest decree on the use of the station crucifix no longer stresses the need of meditation on the Passion to gain the indulgences. To neglect this salutary practice, however, would be to defeat the purpose of the Stations. (S.P., decr., 25 March, 1931.)

Confession and Communion are not necessary conditions for the gaining of the indulgence.

If for a reasonable cause one does not complete the prescribed Our Fathers while using the station crucifix, one gains an indulgence of ten years for every Our Father said with its Hail Mary and Glory. (*Preces,* n. 194.)

b. The sick who cannot without grave inconvenience or difficulty make the stations either in the ordinary form or by reciting twenty Our Fathers, etc., can gain all indulgences of the stations of the cross by contritely kissing or looking at a crucifix blessed with the indulgences of the stations (which a priest or any other person may hold before them), and saying some short aspiration or prayer in memory of the passion and death of Christ. (*Preces,* n. 194.)

The sick who cannot without great inconvenience say the prescribed aspiration or prayer in memory of the passion and death of Christ, can gain the indulgences by contritely kissing or looking at a station crucifix. (*Preces,* n. 194.)

c. The indulgences of the station crucifix are no longer personal, but real. Hence these crucifixes may be loaned or given to others. (Cf. S.P., 18 Feb., 1921, in reference to objects endowed with the apostolic indulgence.)

CHAPTER V

Special Faculties of Priests Belonging to Certain Societies

I. MEMBERSHIP IN SOCIETIES

In order to become a member of *The Pontifical Society for the Propagation of the Faith* or of *The Missionary Union of the Clergy,* one must have himself enrolled. The secular clergy wishing to join one or both of these societies should make their petition through their chanceries or write directly to The Society for the Propagation of the Faith, National Office, 366 Fifth Avenue, New York 1, New York. The religious clergy are to make the petition through their major superiors.

II. DUTIES OF MEMBERS

1. The obligations of a member of *The Pontifical Society for the Propagation of the Faith* are as follows: a. to make an annual offering of at least one dollar; b. to recite daily one Our Father, Hail Mary and the invocation, "St. Francis Xavier, pray for us."

2. The obligation for a member of *The Missionary Union of the Clergy* are as follows: a. to pray, and to stimulate others to pray for the missions, and to remember them in the Holy Sacrifice of the Mass; b. to encourage vocations for the missions; c. to read books and reviews that treat of the missions and to aid in their distribution; d. to refer to the missions frequently in sermons, talks, catechism classes, etc.; e. to promote The Society for the Propagation of the Faith, The Work of St. Peter the Apostle for Native Clergy, The Association of the Holy Childhood, and other works that benefit the missions.

3. In order to enjoy the rights, privileges, indulgences, and other spiritual favors of an association, it is necessary and sufficient that one has been validly received into it according to the association's own statutes, and has not been lawfully expelled from it. (Can. 692.)

These rights, privileges, etc. are not lost by failure to observe the statutes of the association. Even the failure of a member to observe the statutes for a long period of time does not result in his expulsion. Moreover, the statutes of the association do not bind under pain of even venial sin. (Abbo-Hannan, I, n. 692.) However, to gain indulgences, the special works prescribed, if any, must be done. (Cf. Can. 925 § 2.) The same is true of the other rights, privileges, and spiritual favors of the association only if some special works are legitimately prescribed for enjoying them. (PCI, 4 Jan., 1946.)

III. FACULTIES OF MEMBERS

A. *The Pontifical Society for the Propagation of the Faith*

1. *All priest members* enjoy the following faculties:

a. The faculty of blessing with a single sign of the cross, crowns, rosaries, crosses, crucifixes, small religious statues and sacred medals, (without compensation of any kind, and with consent of the local Ordinary at least reasonably presumed) and of attaching to these same articles the apostolic indulgences. This faculty may be used outside of Rome only, privately at any time, but publicly only when preaching during Advent, Lent, Retreats and Missions.

b.   The faculty of blessing rosaries and attaching to them a partial indulgence of five hundred days, to be gained by the faithful, as often as they, while holding one of these coronae in the hand, shall devoutly recite the Lord's Prayer or the Hail Mary, provided, however, that the coronae thus to be blessed have been made according to the model of the coronae of the Most Holy Rosary of the Blessed Virgin Mary.

The members of those Religious Orders or Congregations, of both men and women, *who have some of their members engaged in mission work in pagan countries,* may enjoy all the favors, (indulgences, privileges, faculties) granted to those enrolled in The Pontifical Society for the Propagation of the Faith, provided they recite daily the prescribed prayers, that is, one Our Father, one Hail Mary, with the invocation: St. Francis Xavier, pray for us.

The members of such Orders or Congregations, *who have none of their members employed in the missions,* may gain the same spiritual favors (indulgences, privileges, faculties) by the recitation of this daily prayer, provided the religious house in which they live make an annual contribution to the Pontifical Society.

2.   Priests who enroll as *special* or *perpetual members* of the society and *Priest Zelators* (i.e., diocesan or parochial directors and those who collect for the society) enjoy, in addition to the favors mentioned in n. 1, the following faculties:

a.   The faculty of blessing everywhere the medal of the Immaculate Conception, proper to the Congregation of the Mission, and applying thereto the usual indulgences.

b.   The faculty of blessing with the annexed indulgences

the medal of St. Benedict in places where there are no monasteries or houses of said Saint enjoying these privileges.

c. The faculty of blessing and imposing even with a single formula, the scapular of the Holy Trinity, of Our Lady of Mount Carmel, of Our Lady of Dolors, and of enrolling the faithful in these Confraternities under the usual conditions; the scapular of the Passion of Our Lord, using the red color, which is proper to the Congregation of the Mission; that of the Immaculate Virgin, using the blue color proper to the Theatine Fathers, provided that in the place where this faculty is to be used there are no houses respectively of the Trinitarians, Carmelites, Servites or Theatines.

d. The faculty of enrolling the faithful in the Confraternity of Cordigers, and of blessing and imposing the Cord of St. Francis in places where there are no religious houses of the Conventual Fathers.

e. The faculty of enrolling the faithful in the Third Order Secular of St. Francis in places where there are no canonically erected houses of the said Order, and of blessing of the scapular and cincture.

f. The faculty of enrolling the faithful in the Confraternity of the Angelic Warfare (Militia Angelica) in places where there is no religious house of the Friars Preachers, and of blessing and imposing the cord and medal of St. Thomas Aquinas.

3. Special and perpetual members who enrolled *as priests prior to April* 1, 1933, enjoy the following faculties:

a. The favor of the privileged altar four times a week.

b. The faculty of giving to the faithful at the hour of death a plenary indulgence.

c. The faculty of applying by a single sign of the cross

the apostolic indulgences to beads, crosses, crucifixes, statues and medals, and the brigittine indulgences to rosaries.

d.   The faculty of attaching by a single sign of the cross the crosier and brigittine indulgences to rosaries.

e.   The faculty of attaching to crucifixes the indulgences of the way of the cross.

f.   The faculty of investing the faithful with the scapulars of the Most Holy Trinity, The Passion of Our Lord, the Seven Dolors, the Immaculate Conception, and Our Lady of Mount Carmel.

g.   The faculty of enrolling into the Third Order Secular of St. Francis of Assisi.

h.   The faculty of enrolling in the Archconfraternity of the Cord of St. Francis of Assisi.

i.   The faculty of enrolling in the Sodality of the Angelic Militia.

j.   The faculty of blessing the medal of the Immaculate Conception.

k.   The faculty of blessing the medal of St. Benedict.

1.   Lastly, to those Priests Zelators who, with the permission of their Ordinary, give a series of conferences or sermons in the form of spiritual exercises, the faculty of giving the apostolic blessings with plenary indulgences attached on the last day of the conferences to be gained by all who have been present at five at least of the exercises on condition of confession, Communion and prayers for intention of the Pope.

B.   *The Missionary Union of the Clergy*

1.   *All members* by enrollment in the Missionary Union of the Clergy enjoy the following faculties:

The faculty (provided one has been approved for the hearing of confessions),

1) to bless and to impose with the rites prescribed by the Church the scapulars of the Passion of Our Lord Jesus Christ, of the Immaculate Conception, of the Most Holy Trinity, of the Seven Dolors of Mary, and of Our Lady of Mount Carmel;

2) to bless and impose with one formula the scapulars, which as members of the Pious Union they have the faculty to impose;

3) to impose the above-mentioned scapulars without the obligation of enrollment in the register of the Confraternity.

All priests of the Order of Friars Minor and *all those who were theological students* in the Order before January 1, 1957, have been enrolled *in perpetuum* and enjoy, accordingly, the above privileges. Since January 1, 1957, the accustomed general enrollment in Rome of theological students of the said Order has been abrogated and each theological student must be enrolled individually with the National Director of the Missionary Union of the Clergy. (*Acta Minorum,* LXXV, p. 72.)

2. *Special faculties* (as listed below) may be obtained from the General Secretary of the Missions in Rome *by special petition* for each enrolled member individually.

The List of Special Faculties

a. The faculty (provided one has been approved for the hearing of confessions) *to bless with a single sign of the cross,* with at least the reasonably presumed consent of the local Ordinary in whose territory the power is to be exercised:

1) crowns, rosaries, crosses, crucifixes, small religious statues and sacred medals, outside of Rome, privately any time, publicly, however, only during the seasons of Advent and Lent, and on the occasion of spiritual exercises and missions, in which the priest shall deliver sermons; and of applying to these objects the *apostolic indulgences;* also of

attaching to rosaries the *brigittine indulgences.*

2) crucifixes of metal or other durable material and of applying to them a *plenary indulgence* to be gained by any of the faithful *in the hour of death,* even if the crucifix does not belong to the dying Catholic, provided that the dying person kisses or in some way touches the crucifix and provided that he has gone to confession and Communion or if this is impossible the dying person shall at least contritely invoke the name of Jesus with his lips, if he is able, but if not, shall devoutly invoke the name of Jesus in his heart and accept death patiently from the hand of the Lord as the wages of sin.

b. The faculty *to bless with a single sign of the cross,* with at least the reasonable presumed consent of the local Ordinary in whose territory the power is to be exercised:

1) crosses with a figure of metal, ivory, wood, or other durable material bearing the image of our Lord nailed to the cross, and of applying to them all the *indulgences of the stations of the cross* for the sick, for those making a journey by ship, for prisoners, and for all others legitimately hindered from making the stations of the cross, provided that those legitimately impeded, holding the blessed crucifix in their hand, recite, at least with a contrite heart and with pious recollection of the Passion of our Lord, twenty Our Fathers, Hail Marys, and Glorys, one that is, for each station, five in memory of the sacred wounds of our Lord, and one according to the intention of the Holy Father; or if there is question of the sick, who because of the nature or seriousness of their condition, are not able to recite these prayers without grave inconvenience, it suffices that with love and a contrite heart they kiss or even only look upon one of these blessed crucifixes, handed to them by a priest or another person, and recite, if they can, some prayer or

ejaculation in memory of the Passion of our Lord Jesus Christ.

2) crowns made according to the exemplar of the crowns of the Most Holy Rosary of the Blessed Virgin and of attaching to them an *indulgence of five hundred days* to be gained by the faithful as often as they devoutly recite the Our Father or the Hail Mary while holding one of these crowns in their hands.

c. The personal indult of a privileged altar four times a week, provided they have not received a similar indult for another day.

The secular clergy are to make the petition for these special faculties through their bishops; the religious clergy are to make the petition through their major superiors. However, all priests who were enrolled *as priests* prior to April 1, 1933, enjoy perpetually all these additional special faculties without any need to petition or to renew them. Likewise, in virtue of number thirteen of the revised statutes of the Missionary Union of the Clergy, all members (also those enrolled after April 1, 1933), who have entered the mission field among non-Catholics obtain all the faculties granted to the members and retain them for life, provided they do not give up mission work of their own accord. (S.C.P.F., 14 April, 1937.) Number thirteen refers not only to missions under the jurisdiction of the Sacred Congregation for the Propagation of the Faith, but to all missions among non-Catholics, whether these be non-Christians or dissident Christians. (S.C.P.F., 14 April, 1937.)

PART XI

THE PRE-CENSORSHIP AND PROHIBITION OF BOOKS

CHAPTER I

The Pre-Censorship of Books

The provisions of this section of Canon Law regarding books are to be applied also to daily publications, periodicals, and other published writings of whatever kind, unless the contrary is evident. (Can. 1384 § 2.)

I. THE REQUIRED NIHIL OBSTAT AND IMPRIMATUR

A. *Publications Needing Previous Censorship*

1. The following shall not be published, even by laymen, unless *ecclesiastical censorship* has taken place:

a. Books of the Sacred Scriptures or annotations and commentaries of the same;

b. Books which treat of Holy Scripture, sacred theology, church history, Canon Law, natural theology, ethics, or other such religious or moral branches; also books and booklets of prayers, devotions, or of instruction and training in religion, morals, asceticism, mysticism, and the like, even though they seem to favor piety; and in general all writings which contain anything of special importance to religion and good morals;

c. Sacred pictures, no matter by what process they are to be printed, whether to be published with prayers or

382

without them. (Can. 1385 § 1.)

> Slides and films are not included under the general law of the Church (Wiest, CUA, n. 329, p. 99); the accompanying printed texts, however, require censorship.

2. The *permission* to publish books and pictures mentioned in Canon 1385 § 1 can be given either by the proper local Ordinary of the author, or by the Ordinary of the place where the books or pictures are published, or by the Ordinary of the place where they are printed; but if one of these Ordinaries has refused the permission, the author may not ask it of any of the others without informing him that it has been so refused by the former. Moreover, religious must obtain in advance the permission of their major superior. (Can. 1385 §§ 2, 3.)

3. Some publications require a more special permission:

a. Translations of the Sacred Scriptures into the vernacular may not be printed unless they have been approved by the *Holy See,* or unless they are published under the *vigilance of the bishops and with annotations,* especially such as are taken from the Fathers of the Church and from learned Catholic writers. (Can. 1391.)

> Both the supervision of the bishops *and* the insertion of notes is required. (PCI, reply, 20 May, 1923.) There is question here of new translations into the vernacular. Ancient versions and a modern version which has already been approved require only the permission of one of the Ordinaries mentioned in Canon 1385 § 2.)

b. The expressed permission of the *Holy See* is required in order to publish in any language either an authentic collection of prayers and pious works to which the Holy See has attached indulgences; or the list of Apostolic indulgences; or a summary of indulgences, whether already arranged but never approved, or to be compiled anew from various sources. (Can. 1388 § 2.)

> A summary of indulgences is any list or group of indulgences.

Special permission of the Holy See is required only if the list has not already been approved. If, on the other hand, a list or collection of indulgences which has been approved by the Holy See, or one taken from an Apostolic brief or rescript, is to be printed, the Ordinary may give permission to do so. (Coronata, II, n. 956.) Accordingly, all books of indulgences, summaries, booklets, leaflets, etc., in which the grants of indulgences are contained need only the permission of the local Ordinary (Can. 1388 § 1), as long as the authenticity of the indulgence is evident from an Apostolic brief or rescript or from summaries approved by the Holy See. (Coronata, II, n. 956.) The local Ordinary may be any one of the three mentioned in Canon 1385 § 2. (Abbo-Hannan, II, n. 1388.)

c. In publishing liturgical books or parts thereof, as well as litanies approved by the Holy See, the agreement of the text with approved editions *must be proved by the attestation* of the Ordinary of the place in which they are published or in which they are printed (Can. 1390); moreover, any publisher whether pontifical or not, editing the Roman Breviary, Missal, Ritual, Pontifical, Martyrology, etc., *must obtain the special permission* of the Sacred Congregation of Rites as often as he desires to publish these books, and the local Ordinary shall attest that the intended edition conforms to the typical *Vatican* edition. (S.R.C., decr., 10 Aug., 1946.)

Although the canon speaks only of the Ordinaries of the place of publication and printing, there seems to be sufficient extrinsic authority for allowing the proper local Ordinary of the editor to make the required attestation. (Coronata, II, n. 956.)

B. *New Editions and Translations*

1. The approval of the original text of a work does not extend to translations of that work into another language nor to new editions of the work; consequently both translations and new editions of an approved work must be approved anew. (Can. 1392 § 1.)

Re-printing from the original plates or standing type does not require new approval. However, reprint editions from new type or by some other process more probably require new approval.

(Wiest, CUA, n. 329, pp. 130-131.)

2. Excerpts taken from periodicals as chapters [titles, etc.] and published separately are not considered new editions and hence do not need new approval. (Can. 1392 § 2.)

> If a work was published serially and the chapters are later assembled and published as a separate work, this is a new edition and needs new approval. (Bouscaren-Ellis, pp. 756-757.)

C. *Making the Imprimatur Public*

The permission by which the Ordinary allows the publication [i.e., the *imprimatur*] is to be given in writing, and must be printed at the beginning or end of the book, magazine, or picture, giving the name of the one granting the permission, and also the place and date of the grant. (Can. 1394 § 1.)

> This canon refers to the *imprimatur* required in A and B above, not to the permission required in n. II below. That permission need not be published.

> The formula "with ecclesiastical permission," though not in strict conformity with the text of the law, may be regarded as sufficient for books and booklets of minor importance, and for most reviews and magazines. (Cf. Bouscaren-Ellis, p. 759.)

> The Code does not demand that the *nihil obstat* of the ecclesiastical censors be printed in the book along with the *imprimatur* of the Ordinary.

II. PERMISSION TO WRITE

1. *Secular clerics* without the consent of their Ordinaries, and *religious* without the permission of their major superiors *and* of the local Ordinary, are forbidden even to publish books treating of profane subjects and to contribute to or edit papers, magazines, or reviews. (Can. 1386 § 1.)

> Secular clerics are obliged to seek permission from "their Ordinaries," i.e., the Ordinary of the place of their incardination, or of their residence if they have a domicile or quasi-domicile outside their diocese. For religious, once the permission of their major superiors is obtained, their local Ordinary includes not only the Ordinary of the author's residence, but

probably also the Ordinaries of place of publication and place of printing. (V.C., II, n. 728.)

To "contribute to" designates a habitual or notable contribution, not an occasional brief letter to the editor or a single article of lesser moment.

Writings which contain anything of special importance to religion and good morals require moreover previous censorship according to Canon 1385.

If a book or article requiring censorship is approved by one of the three Ordinaries mentioned in Canon 1385 § 2, it seems that a secular cleric needs no further permission unless his own proper Ordinary has determined otherwise. (Cf. *The Jurist*, XV, pp. 293-294.)

2. In newspapers, magazines, and reviews which habitually attack the Catholic religion or good morals, *even Catholic laymen* must write nothing whatever, unless there is a just and reasonable cause, approved by the local Ordinary, for doing so. (Can. 1386 § 2.)

Although the proper local Ordinary is the one most obviously intended, some authors permit the option of obtaining this permission from any of the three Ordinaries mentioned in Canon 1385 § 2. (Bouscaren-Ellis, p. 754.)

CHAPTER II

The Prohibition of Books

The provisions of this section of Canon Law regarding books are to be applied also to daily publications, periodicals, and other published writings of whatever kind, unless the contrary is evident. (Can. 1384 § 2.)

I. EFFECTS OF PROHIBITION

1. The prohibition of books has this effect that, unless due permission is obtained, the forbidden books may not be published, nor read, nor retained, nor sold, nor translated into another language, nor communicated in any way to other persons. (Can. 1398 § 1.)

To communicate includes the giving, lending, restoring and reading of the forbidden book to another, not however the dramatic representation of it on stage or screen.

A book which has been in any way forbidden may not again be published unless it has been corrected and permission has been given by the one who forbade the book or by his superior or successor. (Can. 1398 § 2.)

2. Booksellers shall not sell, lend, or keep books which treat professedly of obscene matters; as to other forbidden books, they must not have them for sale without having obtained due permission from the Holy See, nor sell them to anyone unless they can prudently judge that the buyer is asking for them lawfully. (Can. 1404.)

Permission of the Holy See is required for the public selling of forbidden books, i.e., publicly displaying, advertising, etc. It seems, however, that a bookseller does not need permission of the Holy See to privately retain and sell forbidden books to persons lawfully requesting them. Books dealing with obscenities are absolutely forbidden. (Coronata, II, n. 966; V.C., II, n. 732.)

II. FORBIDDEN BOOKS

A. *By Common Law*

The following twelve numbers of Canon 1399 enumerate the classes of books forbidden by the common law:

1. Editions of the original text and of ancient Catholic versions of Sacred Scripture, even of the Oriental Church, published by non-Catholics; also all translations of Sacred Scripture into any language, made or published by non-Catholics;

2. Books, no matter who the authors are, which propound heresy or schism, or which in any way attempt to subvert the very foundations of religion;

Books of heretics who wrote before the Reformation and whose errors are entirely obsolete may be read. Thus the collections of Labbe and Migne are not forbidden. (Bouscaren-Ellis, p. 767.)

3. Books which professedly and of set purpose attack religion or good morals;

4. Books by any non-Catholic which treat professedly

of religion, unless it is certain that they contain nothing against the Catholic Faith;

5. *If published without observing the requirements of the canons:*

a. Books of Sacred Scripture, or annotations and commentaries of the same, and translations of Sacred Scripture into the vernacular;

b. Also books and booklets which tell of new apparitions, revelations, visions, prophecies, miracles; or which introduce new devotions even on the plea that they are private;

> Other works lacking the required censorship are not by that fact forbidden. Since the Code mentions booklets in the second half of this number, periodicals and newspapers are not included in the prohibition since these latter are neither books nor booklets.

6. Books which attack or ridicule any of the Catholic dogmas, or defend errors proscribed by the Holy See, or disparage divine worship, or strive to overthrow ecclesiastical discipline, or of set purpose insult the ecclesiastical hierarchy or the clerical or religious state;

7. Books which teach or approve of any sort of superstition, fortune telling, divination, magic, spiritism, or other such practices;

8. Books which hold duelling, suicide, or divorce to be licit, or which, treating of Masonic sects and other societies, contend that they are useful and not harmful to the Church and civil society;

> The Holy Office declared that it is forbidden by Canon 1399 to publish, propagate, or read books, periodicals, daily papers, or leaflets which promote the doctrine or action of Communists, or to write in them. Persons who persist in doing so are to be denied the sacraments. (S.O., 1 July, 1949.)

9. Books which professedly treat of, narrate, or teach lascivious or obscene matter;

10. Editions of liturgical books approved by the Holy

See, in which anything has been changed so that they do not agree with the authentic editions approved by the Holy See;

11. Books containing indulgences which are apocryphal or which have been proscribed or revoked by the Holy See;

> *Raccoltas* which are out of date, though certainly unreliable for present use, are not forbidden. (Bouscaren-Ellis, p. 769.)

12. Pictures, no matter how printed, of our Lord Jesus Christ, the Blessed Virgin Mary, the Angels and Saints, or other Servants of God, which are foreign to the mind and decrees of the Church.

Note: Orientals are also bound by Canon 1399. (S.C. E.O., 20 Jan., 1944.)

B. *By the Index of Forbidden Books*

The Index is an alphabetical catalogue of those works which Rome has seen fit to proscribe by name. As a rule books explicitly contained in the Index are already by their very nature condemned by virtue of Canon 1399. Since it is impossible to list all books forbidden by Canon 1399, the Index is reserved for those works only which, due to circumstances, necessitate an explicit condemnation. Since 1897, the modern version of the Index has gone through a number of editions which in turn incorporate the more recent condemnations published in the *Acta Apostolicae Sedis*. Usually it is the Holy Office which now issues the condemnation. Books condemned by the Roman Pontiff himself are marked with the cross or dagger (†) which reminds one of the censure involved in reading such books. (Cf. Can. 2318.)

> Books condemned by the Holy See are to be considered as forbidden everywhere and into whatever language they may be translated. (Can. 1396.) Orientals are also bound by the decrees of the Holy Office prohibiting books. (S.C.E.O., 26 May, 1928.)

III. PERMISSION TO READ FORBIDDEN BOOKS

1. Cardinals of the Holy Roman Church, bishops, even titular ones, and other Ordinaries, using the necessary precautions, are not bound by the ecclesiastical prohibition of books. (Can. 1401.)

2. In regard to books forbidden by Canon 1399 or by decree of the Apostolic See, Ordinaries can grant to their own subjects permission only for particular books and only in urgent cases. (Can. 1402 § 1.)

> Ordinaries here include major superiors in clerical exempt religious institutes.
>
> Local Ordinaries, in virtue of the quinquennial faculties, can grant general permission, but for not more than three years, to their individual subjects, excepting for works which professedly advocate heresy or schism, or which attempt to undermine the very foundations of religion, or which are professedly obscene. This permission is to be granted only with discrimination and for a just and reasonable cause (cf. Can. 1402 § 2); that is, to such persons only as really need to read the said books and papers, either in order to refute them, or in the exercise of their own lawful functions, or in the pursuit of a lawful course of studies. (*Digest,* IV, pp. 69-70.) This faculty must be exercised by the bishop personally.

3. Those who have obtained Apostolic permission to read and keep forbidden books are not thereby permitted to read and keep any books forbidden by their Ordinaries, unless the Apostolic indult expressly gives them the faculty to read and keep books no matter by whom forbidden. (Can. 1403 § 1.)

4. The use of books mentioned in Canon 1399, 1° (namely, editions by non-Catholics of the original text or of ancient Catholic versions of Sacred Scripture, and all translations of Scripture by non-Catholics), and of books published contrary to the prescription of Canon 1391 (i.e., translations of Sacred Scripture into the vernacular published without the requisite permission), is permitted only to persons who are in any way engaged in theological or

scriptural study, provided the books are faithfully and
completely edited and that their introductions or annotations do not attack Catholic dogmas. (Can. 1400.)

> Those *in any way* engaged in theological or scriptural study
> include all seminary students of theology, all priests engaged
> in private study, and even lay persons who are studying these
> subjects.

Note: Permission, from whomsoever obtained, in no wise
exempts one from the precept of natural law forbidding
the reading of books which place one in proximate danger
of sin. (Can. 1405 § 1.)

PART XII

PASTORS

CHAPTER I

Some Rights and Duties of Pastors

The pastor obtains the care of souls from the moment of taking possession according to the norm of Canons 1443-1445; and before taking possession or in the very act thereof he shall make the profession of Faith mentioned in Canon 1406 § 1, 7°. (Can. 461.)

> Taking canonical possession [i.e., installation] is done in the manner prescribed by particular law or legal custom, unless the Ordinary dispenses from this manner expressly and in writing; in which case, the dispensation amounts to the taking of canonical possession. (Can. 1444 § 1.)

I. FUNCTIONS RESERVED TO THE PASTOR

Unless otherwise provided by law, the following functions are reserved to the pastor:

1. The solemn administration of baptism. (Can. 462, 1°.)

> No other priest or deacon may solemnly baptize without the permission of the pastor or local Ordinary; in case of necessity this permission may be presumed. (Canons 738, 741.)
>
> *Peregrini* are to be baptized by their own pastor and in their own parishes, if it can be done easily and without delay; otherwise a peregrine may be baptized by any pastor within the limits of his territory. (Can. 738.)
>
> In another territory no one may confer solemn baptism without the proper permission, not even to residents of his own territory. (Can. 739.)
>
> If baptism was conferred neither by the pastor nor in his

presence, the minister of the baptism shall as soon as possible notify the pastor of domicile of the fact of the administration of baptism. (Can. 778.)

2.   The *public* carrying of the Blessed Sacrament to the sick in his parish. (Can. 462, 2°.)

The right to carry the Blessed Sacrament publicly to the sick is proper to the pastor also in regard to those who do not belong to his parish but who are staying within its limits. (Can. 848 § 1.)

Other priests may carry the Blessed Sacrament to the sick *publicly* only in case of necessity or with at least the presumed permission of the pastor or the Ordinary (Can. 848 § 2), as for instance, in a hospital at an hour when the pastor is occupied elsewhere.

Any priest may carry Holy Communion to the sick *privately* with at least the presumed permission of the priest to whom the custody of the Blessed Sacrament has been entrusted. (Can. 849.) In our country Holy Communion is practically always carried privately to the sick, except in religious houses and hospitals, etc. Hence, any priest may carry out this function with the permission of the priest who has charge of the church from which he takes the Blessed Sacrament, not necessarily, therefore, of the pastor.

3.   The *public* or *private* carrying of the Blessed Sacrament as Holy Viaticum to the sick and the administration of extreme unction to those in danger of death. (Can. 462, 3°.)

Other priests are authorized to carry out these functions only in case of necessity or with the permission, at least presumed permission, of the pastor or local Ordinary. (Canons 848, 850, 938.)

Holy Communion as Viaticum refers to the Viaticum of precept, which one is obliged to receive in danger of death (cf. Can. 864 § 1), and it is only this Viaticum in the strict sense which is reserved to the pastor of the territory in which the sick person is staying. Hence, either before or after this Viaticum, any priest may bring Communion privately to the person in danger of death, with the permission, at least presumed, of the priest to whom the custody of the Blessed Sacrament has been entrusted. (Cf. V.C., II, n. 114.)

As to the proper minister of Holy Viaticum and extreme unction *in religious houses* confer our commentary above, in the chapter on extreme unction, p. 151.

4. The proclamation of forthcoming ordinations and marriages; the assistance at marriages; the imparting of the nuptial blessing. (Can. 462, 4°.)

The names of those to be promoted to the individual *sacred* orders, with the exception of religious in perpetual vows, whether solemn or simple, are to be publicly announced in the proper parish church of each candidate. (Can. 998.)

The solemn nuptial blessing may be imparted by the priest who licitly and validly assists at the marriage. (Can. 1101 § 2.) Hence, any priest legitimately delegated for the marriage by the pastor, can impart this blessing.

5. Funerals in accordance with Canon 1216. (Can. 462, 5°.)

Confer the chapter on Christian Burial for details.

6. The blessing of homes according to the rules of the liturgical books on Holy Saturday or on some other day according to the custom of the place. (Can. 462, 6°.)

It is only the special Easter blessing of homes or the blessing on some fixed day of the year that is reserved to the pastor. The ordinary blessing of a home may be imparted by any priest.

7. The blessing of the baptismal font on Holy Saturday, the leading of public processions outside the church, the imparting of blessings with pomp and solemnity outside the church, unless these functions are reserved to the chapter of a capitular church. (Can. 462, 7°.)

The blessings of the ashes, palms and candles are not reserved to the pastor. The rite of churching of women is not reserved.

II. STOLE FEES AND OFFERINGS

1. The pastor has a right to the fees which are allotted to him by legitimate custom or by the lawful schedule of taxes determined by a provincial council or by a meeting of the bishops of the province according to Canon 1507; and even if some duty or function of the pastor has been fulfilled by someone else the fees belong to the pastor, unless the contrary is evident from the will of the donor in

reference to the amount in excess of the tax or fee. (Can. 463 §§ 1, 3.)

Hence if a religious assisting the pastor on a feast day administers baptism, the stole fee goes to the pastor and not to the religious.

The contrary will of the donor in reference to the amount in excess of the fee may be expressed, or it may be implied in the circumstances, v.g., because of special friendship, consanguinity, gratitude to a priest who has done much for the donor, etc. Pastors should note that *the celebrant of the nuptial Mass has a right to the stipend for the Mass,* even though the pastor has the right to the stole fee for the wedding.

In the case of *obligatory* offerings, that is, of offerings *prescribed* by lawful custom or by the lawful schedule of taxes in the diocese or province, the pastor has a strict right to demand them, in such wise, however, that he may not refuse his services to persons who are not able to make offerings. (Can. 463.) Other offerings which are not prescribed by law or custom but which are nevertheless made by the faithful are called *voluntary* offerings. When these offerings are made on the occasion of a function which is reserved to the pastor, the latter has no right to demand them, but he has a right to them against others. Hence, if a reserved function is legitimately performed by some other priest and a purely voluntary offering is given, the offering goes to the pastor unless the will of the donors evidently demand that it go to the officiating priest. Hence, offerings made on the occasion of functions reserved to the pastor, if these offerings are purely voluntary and not prescribed by any law or custom, will presumably go to the pastor, unless the donors intend them as a gift to the officiating priest. (Bouscaren-Ellis, pp. 205-206.)

Custom or particular law may dispose of stole fees or part of them otherwise than by assigning them to the pastor. The right of assistant pastors to share in stole fees depends on custom, diocesan law, or on the will of the pastor. (Bouscaren-Ellis, p. 207.)

2. Gifts Made to Rectors of Churches:

a. Unless the contrary is proved, it is to be presumed that donations made to rectors of churches, even of churches of religious, are made to the church. (Can. 1536 § 1.)

The contrary may be proved either by the express will of the donor or by the circumstances of the donation. This canon does not affect the stole fees, which go to the pastor according to the norm of Canon 463, but treats rather of donations made outside the time of those parochial services for which a fee or offering is made to the pastor personally.

b. A donation made to a church may not be refused by the rector or superior without the permission of the Ordinary. (Can. 1536 § 2.)

> The Ordinary is the major superior in the case of exempt clerical religious; in all other cases, the local Ordinary. (Bouscaren-Ellis, p. 820.)

III. VACATIONS AND ABSENCES

1. The pastor is allowed to be away from his parish for, at most, two months within the year, either continuous or interrupted, unless a grave cause, in the judgment of the Ordinary, requires a longer absence or permits only a shorter one. The days spent in retreat are not computed in the days of absence. (Can. 465 §§ 2, 3.)

2. Whether the absence is to be continuous or interrupted, if it is to last for more than a week the pastor must have both a legitimate cause and the written permission of the Ordinary, and he must leave a vicar substitute in his place, which substitute is to be approved by the Ordinary; if the pastor is a religious, he needs, besides, the permission of his superior, and the substitute must be approved by both the Ordinary and the superior. (Can. 465 § 4.)

3. If for a grave and unforeseen cause the pastor must leave hurriedly and will be forced to be absent for more than a week, he shall as soon as possible inform the Ordinary by letter, indicating also the reason for departure and the identity of the supplying priest. (Can. 465 § 5.)

> In this case, the priest whom the pastor designated as his substitute has the parochial powers even before the approval of the Ordinary provided the Ordinary has been notified of his designation and has not provided otherwise. (Cf. PCI, reply, 14 July, 1922.)

4. If the pastor is to be absent for only a week or for

less than a week, he should see to it that the needs of the
faithful are taken care of in his absence. (Cf. Can. 465
§ 6.)

> For these short absences the Code does not demand the per-
> mission of the Ordinary. The priest who supplies for the pastor
> in these cases receives no special parochial jurisdiction from the
> Code. Whatever jurisdiction he needs must be delegated to him
> by the Ordinary or by the pastor according to the norms of law.

IV. MASS FOR THE PEOPLE

1. The pastor is bound to apply Holy Mass for the intentions of the people committed to his care on all Sundays and holydays, even suppressed holydays. (Canons
466 § 1, 339 § 1.) The list of these days can be found in
one's Directory or Ordo. If a pastor rules several parishes,
or besides his own parish, holds another or others as administrator, he must celebrate only one Mass on the prescribed days for all the people committed to his care.
(Can. 366 § 2.)

2. The pastor shall offer this Mass personally; if he is
impeded from doing so, he shall have it said by another
priest but on the prescribed day; and if even this is impossible, he shall say it on another day as soon as possible,
personally or through another. (Canons 466 § 1, 339 § 4.)

3. For a just cause the Ordinary may permit the pastor
to offer the Mass for the people on another day rather than
on the day prescribed by law. (Can. 466 § 3.)

4. The pastor is to offer the Mass in the parish church,
unless circumstances demand or suggest that it be offered
elsewhere. (Can. 466 § 4.)

5. A pastor who is lawfully absent may either apply
the Mass personally in the place where he is, or provide
that it be said at the parish by the priest who is taking his
place. (Can. 466 § 5.)

CHAPTER II

Pastor and the Administration of Church Property

Administrators of church property are obliged to fulfill their office with the care and diligence of a good *paterfamilias*. Hence they must observe the following:

1. Be vigilant that the church property entrusted to their care suffer no harm or perish in any way;

2. Observe the regulations of Canon and civil law, as well as regulations imposed by a founder or donor or by legitimate authority;

3. Collect the income and fruits accurately and in due time, keep them in a safe place, and use them according to the mind of the founder or according to established laws or norms;

4. With the permission of the Ordinary, to invest or use for the benefit of the church money which may be left over after all expenses are paid;

5. Keep well-ordered accounts of receipts and expenditures;

6. Keep in good order in the archives or in a convenient safe all documents and legal papers upon which the rights and property of the moral person depend. Authentic copies of all such papers should be deposited in the archives or safe of the curia. (Can. 1523, 1°-6°.)

I. ANNUAL ACCOUNT

Any custom to the contrary being reprobated, administrators, whether clerical or lay, of any church, even of a cathedral church, or of any pious place canonically erected, or of a confraternity, are obliged to give an account of their administration to the local Ordinary every year. (Can. 1525 § 1.)

This canon covers the property and funds also of a parish entrusted to regulars, not however of the parish church itself if the church is owned by regulars. (Cf. Can. 630 §§ 3, 4.)

This canon does not cover the property of a religious institute of pontifical right, nor does it refer to hospitals, orphanages, schools, etc. *owned* (not simply administered) by religious institutes of pontifical right. (Cf. Canons 1491, 1492.)

II. EXTRAORDINARY ADMINISTRATION - INVESTMENTS

Unless they obtain the previous permission of the local Ordinary, to be given in writing, administrators act invalidly when they place acts which exceed the limitations and manner of ordinary administration. (Can. 1527 § 1.)

Ordinary administration includes whatever is necessary for the upkeep of church property, v.g., paying bills, making necessary repairs, buying supplies etc.

Extraordinary administration covers acts which do not occur periodically or which are by their nature of greater importance, v.g., installing a new heating system, making investments, changing investments, and in general the actions listed under Canons 1529-1543.

In practice, diocesan regulations are to be consulted. An excellent article on the investment of church funds may be found in *The Jurist*, XI, pp. 3-27.

III. EXCHANGE OF STOCKS AND BONDS

The administrator of church property may exchange stocks and bonds for other stocks or bonds and probably also sell them for cash and purchase others, provided that even the appearance of speculation is excluded and that the permission of the Ordinary, of the diocesan council of administration and of the interested parties is obtained. (Cf. Can. 1539 § 2.)

These actions are not considered alienation but rather acts of administration; hence all the formalities demanded for alienation of church property need not be observed.

IV. ALIENATION AND DEBTS

1. For the alienation of precious objects or of other property the value of which exceeds 30,000 lire or francs,

and for debts or obligations contracted in excess of this sum, the permission of the Holy See must be previously obtained, otherwise the contract is void. (Canons 1532 § 1, 1533.)

> Precious objects are those which because of intrinsic worth (the material of which they are made) or because of historical or artistic appeal, are of notable value, i.e., about $335.
>
> 30,000 lire are equivalent to 6000 gold dollars or $10,000 in present devaluated money. For the time being the 30,000 lire or francs are reduced to 10,000 gold francs. This is a temporary expedient due to the fact that the changed value of money and the wavering of currency has occasioned in certain places special difficulties in applying the prescriptions of the Code of Canon Law. (S.C.Consist., 13 July, 1951.) The 10,000 gold francs of this decree are equivalent to $5,000 in American money. (S.C.Consist., 18 Oct., 1952.)

2. When the value of property to be alienated (or the debt to be contracted) does not exceed 1000 francs or lire, the local Ordinary may give the necessary permission after consulting the council of administration (unless the matter is of small importance) and after obtaining the consent of interested parties. (Can. 1532 § 2.)

> For the time being the sum of 1000 francs and lire is taken to be $167. (Cf. S.C. Consist., 18 Oct., 1952.)

3. When the value of property to be alienated (or the debt to be contracted) exceeds the sum of 1000 francs or lire but not of 30,000 francs or lire, the local Ordinary may grant the necessary permission after obtaining the consent of the diocesan consultors, the diocesan council of administration and the interested parties. (Can. 1532 § 3.)

4. When in one transaction there are alienated several pieces of church property belonging to the same moral person, if the value of the articles taken together is in excess of 30,000 lire, the permission of the Holy See is required. (PCI, 20 July, 1929.)

> Pieces of property are taken together, i.e., they coalesce for

the purpose of alienation either on account of the intention of the administrator or the short time between individual acts of alienation, or the purpose of the various alienations (Cf. Bouscaren-Ellis, pp. 817-818 for details.)

5. If the property to be alienated is divisible, one must mention all parts already alienated in the petition for permission or consent for further alienation, otherwise the permission is invalid. (Can. 1532 § 4.)

Note: By the quinquennial faculties, local Ordinaries may grant permission for alienation up to the sum of $10,000 in cases where there is an urgent necessity, evident utility, and danger in delay. (S.C.Consist., 27 April, 1953; *Digest,* IV, p. 73.) The Apostolic Delegate has the same faculty for alienation not exceeding $15,000. (*Digest,* IV, p. 393.)

V. Mortgage and Debts

When for good reasons church property is to be pledged or mortgaged, or when there is question of contracting a debt, the superior who is to give the permission as determined in Canon 1532 must first demand that all interested parties be consulted and must see to it that such debts are paid as soon as possible. For this reason the Ordinary is to determine the amount of money which is to be set aside annually for the payment of the debt. (Can. 1538 §§ 1, 2.)

The actions spoken of in this canon are all forms of alienation and hence the rules for alienation of church property must be observed. (Can. 1533.) Details may be found in Abbo-Hannan, II, n. 1538.

VI. Leasing Church Property

1. In the leasing of ecclesiastical real estate, the contract should determine the use the property may be put to, the nature of the care expected, the time and method of paying the rent, and the guaranties for the fulfillment of these conditions. (Cf. Can. 1541 § 1.)

2. In every lease of church property, the permission of the proper authority is to be obtained as follows:

a. If the value of the lease (i.e., the annual rental) exceeds 30,000 lire and the term of the lease runs beyond nine years, permission must be obtained from the Holy See; if the term of the lease does not run beyond nine years, from the local Ordinary with the consent of the diocesan consultors, the diocesan council of administration and of the parties interested.

b. If the value of the lease is between 1000 and 30,000 lire and the term of the lease runs beyond nine years, the permission must be obtained from the local Ordinary with the consent of the persons mentioned in a. above; if the term of the lease does not run beyond nine years, from the local Ordinary with the advice of the diocesan council of administration and with the consent of the interested parties.

c. If the value of the lease does not exceed 1000 lire and the term of the lease runs beyond nine years, from the local Ordinary with the advice of the diocesan council of administration and the consent of the interested parties; if the term of the lease does not run beyond nine years, the administrator of the property may grant the lease after he has informed the Ordinary. (Can. 1541 § 2.)

In all leases it is forbidden to anticipate the payment of rentals beyond six months without the special permission of the local Ordinary. (Cf. Canons 1479, 1541 § 2.)

VII. MONEY LOANS

To loan church funds to others is not an act of alienation, (provided the funds are at hand and do not represent invested capital) but is an act of administration of church property. If the loan is a large one, the act would be one of extraordinary administration and would therefore require the permission of the Ordinary. In making loans it is always allowable to make an agreement for the legal rate of interest provided such rate is not excessive. (Cf. Can. 1543.)

VIII. LOAN, SALE OR EXCHANGE OF SACRED THINGS

1. Sacred things, namely such as are destined for divine worship by consecration or blessing, are not to be lent for any use which is repugnant to their nature. (Cf. Can. 1537.)

> Hence it is not forbidden to lend sacred articles to another church for temporary use, v.g., on the occasion of a jubilee, first Mass etc.

2. In the sale or exchange of sacred things no account of the consecration or blessing is to be taken in determining the price. (Can. 1539 § 1.)

> Hence it is lawful to exchange or sell consecrated or blessed articles; these actions are however alienation and the permissions demanded by Canon 1532 must be obtained. Unless the articles are put up for public sale, the consecration or blessing is not lost. (Can. 1305 § 1, 2°.) However indulgences attached to sacred articles are usually lost by the sale of said articles. (Cf. Can. 924 § 2.)

IX. DONATIONS

The giving of alms is part of the ordinary administration of the goods of the church. Hence small and moderate donations sanctioned by local custom may be given by rectors of churches from the funds of their churches. Larger gifts may be made by reason of *remuneration,* v.g., in gratitude to benefactors, *piety,* v.g., out of a sense of duty to one's country or relatives, and *charity,* v.g., to the poor, the sick, orphans, etc. (Cf. Can. 1535.)

X. ADMINISTRATION OF PIOUS TRUSTS AND PIOUS FOUNDATIONS

a. A pious trust is property or money given for a charitable or religious purpose. A cleric or religious who has been entrusted by the donor, either during his lifetime or in a last will, with property to be devoted to pious causes, must inform the Ordinary of his trust and report to him all the items of movable or immovable property involved, together with the burdens imposed; the Ordinary must demand that the property be placed in a safe place, and if necessary, be safely invested, and he must see to it that the intentions of the donor are carried out. When pious trusts have been committed to a religious, if the property is given to a church of the place or diocese for the benefit of the people or of pious causes [v.g., for the benefit of a parochial school, an orphanage, hospital], it is the local Ordinary who must be informed and consulted; otherwise it is proper Ordinary of the religious. (Can. 1516.)

b. A *pious foundation* is property (money, stocks, land, etc.) given to a moral person (diocese, parish, college, etc.) in the Church with the obligation (either in perpetuum or for a long time) of investing the money and using the annual income either for the celebration of Masses or for carrying out certain specified works of religion, piety, or charity. A pious foundation cannot be accepted without the permission of the Ordinary; when accepted all monies which make up the endowment of the pious foundation are invested according to the prudent judgment of the Ordinary, and an annual account must be rendered to the Ordinary of the amount of income received from the endowment and of the fulfillment of the obligations imposed by the pious foundation. (Cf. Canons 1544-1549.)

> If the pious foundation is attached to a religious house, college, seminary, hospital, church, etc. belonging to exempt religious, the Ordinary spoken of in Canons 1544-1549 is the major superior; otherwise, it is the local Ordinary, even in cases where the foundation is attached to a parochial church committed to the care of exempt religious, but not owned by them. (Cf. Can. 1550.)

XI. Law Suits

Administrators are not to begin a law suit in the name of the church, or act as defendants in one, unless they first obtain the written permission of the local Ordinary or if the case is urgent, of the rural dean, whose duty it will be to immediately inform the Ordinary of the permission granted. (Can. 1526.)

CHAPTER III

Special Provisions for Religious Pastors

A religious may rule a parish as pastor or vicar. The religious is technically a pastor when the parish he rules has been entrusted to his religious community (house, province) but has not been united to it "pleno iure." When a parish has been united "pleno iure" to the religious community, the moral person (religious house or province) receives the title to the parish and is the habitual pastor, whose representative in the actual administration of the parish and the care of souls is technically called *a vicar*. The same rights and duties are enjoyed by the religious priest whether he rules a parish as pastor or as vicar.

In reference to parishes entrusted to a religious community or united "pleno iure" to a religious community, the religious superior, according to the constitutions, shall present a priest of his institute to the local Ordinary for the office of pastor or vicar, and the local Ordinary, if he is satisfied that the priest possesses the necessary qualifications, shall grant him canonical institution. (Canons 456, 471 §§ 1, 2.)

> The religious pastor obtains the care of souls from the moment of taking possession, i.e., from his installation as pastor according to the norm of Canons 1443-1445. (Can. 461.) However the religious vicar to whom is entrusted the actual care of a parish united "pleno iure" to the religious community, needs

only the authentic notification of appointment by the local Ordinary to enter into possession of his office, installation is not required; but the profession of Faith must be made. (Cf. Abbo-Hannan, I, p. 456, footnote 44.)

I. OBLIGATIONS OF THE RULE

1. The religious pastor remains bound to the observance of his vows and constitutions in so far as the observance is compatible with the duties of his office. In matters of religious discipline he is subject to his superior whose right it is, to the exclusion of the local Ordinary, to inquire into his conduct regarding religious observance, and if necessary to correct him. (Can. 630 §§ 1, 2.)

Details can be found in the constitutions of each religious institute. The religious pastor as well as the local superior should confer the constitutions of their institute for these details.

2. All things coming to him in the name of the parish he acquires for the parish; other things he acquires in the same manner as other religious. (Can. 630 § 3.)

II. SUBJECTION TO THE VIGILANCE AND VISITATION OF THE LOCAL ORDINARY

1. Even though the religious pastor exercise the sacred ministry in the house or place in which the major superiors of the institute have their habitual residence, he is nevertheless wholly subject to the jurisdiction, visitation, and correction of the local Ordinary just as are secular priests who are pastors, with the sole exception of the regular observance. (Can. 631 § 1.)

Hence, the local Ordinary exercises jurisdiction over the person of the religious pastor in those things which pertain to the care of souls.

2. The local Ordinary may issue opportune orders and inflict due penalties on the religious pastor if the latter is found negligent in his office. In this matter, however, the authority of the local Ordinary is not exclusive of, but is

cumulative with, that of the religious superior, in such wise, however, that if one thing is commanded by the superior and something else by the local Ordinary, the decree of the Ordinary must prevail. (Can. 631 § 2.)

Since religious are subject to the jurisdiction of the local Ordinary with regard to their parochial ministry, by virtue of Canon 619 they are subject to penalties which the local Ordinary may inflict for any delinquencies committed in parochial work, unless the religious are exempt by law or by privilege from the penalties imposed by the local Ordinary. For the special privileges of regulars and mendicants in this regard, confer below pp. 419-420.

III. ADMINISTRATION OF TEMPORALITIES

1. The vow of poverty notwithstanding, the religious who is pastor may receive, collect, administer and expend the alms offered *for the good of the parish,* i.e., for Catholic schools, pious places connected with the parish, the good of the parishioners, but under the vigilance of his superior. (Can. 630 § 4.)

A religious (or cleric) who has been entrusted by the donor, either during his lifetime or in a last will, with property to be devoted to pious causes, must inform the Ordinary of his trust and report to him all the items of movable or immovable property involved, together with the burdens imposed; the Ordinary must demand that the property be placed in a safe place, and if necessary, be safely invested, and he must see to it that the intentions of the donor are carried out. When pious trusts have been committed to a religious, if the property is given to a church of the place or diocese for the benefit of the people or of pious causes [v.g., for the benefit of a parochial school, an orphanage, hospital], it is the local Ordinary who must be informed and consulted; otherwise it is the proper Ordinary of the religious. (Can. 1516.)

2. If the *parish church* belongs to the religious community it pertains to the religious superior to accept, collect and administer funds for the building, maintenance, repair and ornamentation of the church; if the church does not belong to the religious community these things pertain to the local Ordinary. (Can. 630 § 4.) Both the superior

and the local Ordinary may delegate their right in these matters to the religious pastor, retaining the right of supervision. (V.C., I, n. 789.)

> The temporal care of the parish church itself pertains to the religious superior only if the church belongs to the community in such wise that the community can be called its proprietor; on the contrary, the care of the church pertains to the Ordinary if the church retains its own juridic personality, independent of the religious community, even though the care of souls there is entrusted perpetually to the religious. The mere fact of a complete union of the parish with a religious institute does not necessarily mean that the church belongs to the institute. Many churches in the United States retain their own separate juridic personality and are not owned by the religious even though the religious have been entrusted, perpetually, with the care of souls there. (Beste, p. 426.)

3. Any religious, even a regular, must obtain the permission of the local Ordinary for *the investment* of money given to a *parish* or *mission* or to the religious himself but for the benefit of the parish or mission. (Can. 533 § 1, 4°.) The local Ordinary also has the right to inquire into the administration of these moneys. (Can. 535 § 3, 2°.)

> When a fund or legacy is given to a religious parish *church,* if the church is the property of an *exempt institute,* or has been handed over to it for its permanent use, i.e., the institute has at least the "dominium utile et perpetuum," it is the religious superior and not the local Ordinary whose consent must be obtained for the investment of the fund and who has the right to inquire into its administration. In all other cases it is the local Ordinary who must be consulted concerning the investment of such funds, lands, etc. and who has the right to inquire into their administration. (Cf. Canons 630 § 4, 1550; PCI, reply, 25 July, 1926; Beste, p. 427.)

4. The superior of a house of a religious congregation must obtain the consent of the local Ordinary for the *investment* of funds which have been donated or bequeathed *to the house* for expenditure in behalf of divine worship or works of charity in the place in which the house is located. (Can. 533 § 1, 3°.) The local Ordinary has also the right to inquire into the administration of such

funds. (Can. 535 § 3, 2°.)

The consent of the local Ordinary is required only by non-exempt congregations, not by exempt clerical congregations or orders.

The consent of the local Ordinary is necessary only when the money is to be spent in the house or in the city, or diocese where the house is located. The local Ordinary's consent is not required if the funds may be spent in any place at the discretion of the religious superior, v.g., for the foreign or home missions of the institute.

APPENDIX

Choral Recitation of the Divine Office

Since in many religious institutes the religious pastor is obliged also to attend the choral recitation of the Divine Office, we include the canonical doctrine on this subject.

1. In institutes of men and women bound by the obligation of choir duty, the divine office must be recited daily in common, in accordance with the constitutions, in every house with at least four religious bound to choir service and not legitimately excused, or with even fewer religious bound to choir service if the constitutions so provide. (Can. 610 § 1.)

The obligation of choral recitation is a grave one, but it affects the community directly, the individual religious only indirectly. No religious in particular is under grave obligation to be present in choir unless his presence is necessary to make the choral recitation of office possible. (Schaefer, n. 1202; Coronata, I, n. 616.)

In houses which are not canonically considered religious houses, even though they belong to the religious, v.g., summer villas, there is no obligation of choir, even though four religious bound to choir service be in residence there. (Schaefer, n. 1201.)

2. Religious obliged to the choir service are all the professed, whether in temporary or perpetual vows, not, however, the novices.

The obligation of choir ceases whenever because of a legitimate cause the required number cannot be present even though they may actually be in the house. Legitimate causes impeding presence in choir are studies, sickness, works of the sacred ministry. Once the daily *horarium* is legitimately established, the superior is not bound to make frequent changes so that the religious may be present at the choral service. If the religious cannot be present at the time established, the obligation of choral recitation of the parts of the office recited at that time ceases for that day.

It is probable that the obligation of the choral service can be fulfilled if only two professed religious are present; probably also if
the office is recited by two novices. (Schaefer, n. 1201.) Of course,
there is no *obligation* to recite the office in common in cases in
which four professed members cannot be present, unless the constitutions of the institute provide otherwise. (Can. 610 § 1.)

If one of the four religious bound to choir is not attached to the
religious house, but is merely living there for a time by reason of
some ministry or by holy obedience, the choral obligation does not
urge, unless the constitutions provide otherwise, for the obligation
of choir arises only when four religious bound to choir are present
who are members of that community. (Schaefer, n. 1201.) This
principle would seem to hold also in institutes where the constitutions specify that visitors in houses of the institute are bound to
attend choir after spending a definite number of days in the house.

3. The recitation of the divine office must take place in the
choir of the church, not, however, in a private oratory of the religious house, unless such an oratory connects with the church
through an open wall or some other open approach. (S.R.C., 12
Dec., 1879.)

4. A religious who is away from the house to which he is attached, if he stays for a time at another house of his institute, is
obliged to follow the calendar of that house when he attends choir,
but in the private recitation of the office he follows the calendar of
his own house. (*Cod. Rubr.*, nos. 151-152.) If the religious is away
from his own monastery and is not staying in a house of his own
institute, he follows the calendar of his own religious province.
(Cf. S.R.C., 31 Aug., 1839; 27 June, 1896.)

PART XIII

CANONICAL STANDING OF RELIGIOUS IN REGARD TO THE SACRED MINISTRY

Religious superiors shall ensure that their subjects when designated by them willingly undertake, without prejudice to religious discipline, labors of the sacred ministry, especially in the diocese in which they reside, as often as their services are needed by local Ordinaries and pastors, even outside their own churches or oratories. (Can. 608 § 1.) In turn, local Ordinaries and pastors shall willingly call upon the services of religious, especially those residing in their diocese, for the work of the sacred ministry, especially the hearing of confessions. (Can. 608 § 2.)

In the exercise of the sacred ministry, religious, even regulars, are in many things subject to the jurisdiction of the local Ordinary and are bound to observe the regulations published by him. In this section are placed the more important canons of the Code defining the relationship between the local Ordinary and religious priests who carry on the sacred ministry in his diocese.

I. THE WORD OF GOD

A. *Preaching*

1. Local Ordinaries have the right to preach in any church in their territory, even an exempt one. (Can. 1343 § 1.)

Except in the case of large cities, a bishop is also authorized to forbid preaching to the people in other churches of the same place at the time when he himself is preaching or at which he has arranged that a sermon be delivered in his presence to a congregation of the faithful, for a public and extraordinary reason. (Can. 1343 § 2.)

2. For every sermon to be preached to the laity or to religious, even to nuns subject to regulars, the faculty to preach is given, even to exempt religious, by the Ordinary of the place in which the sermon will be delivered. (Canons 1337, 1338 § 2.)

If the sermon is to be delivered to exempt nuns, the preacher needs also the permission of the regular superior to whom the nuns are subject. If the sermon is delivered to the members of any other religious institute, the preacher needs also the consent of the religious superior of that institute. (Cf. Can. 1338 §§ 2, 3.)

3. If, however, the sermon is to be given only to *exempt men religious* or to those who live day and night in their houses as defined in Canon 514 § 1, the faculty to preach, *in a clerical institute,* is granted by the superior, as determined by the constitutions. The superior can grant this faculty also to those who belong to the secular clergy or to another institute, provided they have been judged qualified by their own Ordinary or superior. (Can. 1338 § 1.)

4. Priests of another diocese, whether secular or religious, shall not be invited to preach unless the permission of the Ordinary of the place in which the sermon is to be given has been previously obtained; the latter is not to grant permission unless he is either already certain of their qualifications, or has received from the preacher's own Ordinary testimonials asserting the preacher's learning, piety and integrity. (Can. 1341 § 1.)

5. Ordinaries shall see to it that at least once every ten years pastors provide a sacred mission, as it is called, for the flock entrusted to their care. The pastor, even a reli-

gious pastor, must abide by the regulations of the local Ordinary in providing these missions for the people. (Can. 1349.)

> The Ordinary is to see to it that the mission be held *at least* once every ten years; hence, he may command that they be held oftener. Since all must abide by his regulations in the conducting of the mission, pastors must observe whatever he has decreed in regard to the method, time, place and the personnel connected with the mission. (Cf. Abbo-Hannan, II, n. 1349.)

B. *Catechetical Instruction*

1. If in the judgment of the local Ordinary the aid of religious is needed for the catechetical instruction of the people, religious superiors, even exempt, when requested by the Ordinary, are bound either personally or through their religious subjects, without detriment, however, to religious discipline, to give this instruction to the people, especially in their own churches. (Can. 1334.)

2. It is the right of the local Ordinary to regulate in his diocese everything pertaining to the training of the people in Christian doctrine; and even exempt religious, in teaching non-exempt persons, are obliged to abide by his regulations. (Can. 1336.)

> It is desired that at the Masses which are celebrated in churches and public oratories on Sundays and holy days, a short explanation be given of the gospel or of some portion of Christian doctrine; and if the local Ordinary has commanded this to be done and has provided special instructions with regard to it, his law binds not only priests of the secular clergy, but also religious, even exempt, and even in their own churches. (Can. 1345.)

3. Local Ordinaries have the right and the duty to guard lest in any schools in their territories anything should be taught or should happen contrary to faith or good morals. They have the right to approve the instructors in religion and the textbooks of religion; and also in the interests of religion and morals, to demand that both instructors and textbooks be removed. (Can. 1381 §§ 2, 3.)

Local Ordinaries either in person or through delegates have the right to visit, in reference to whatever involves religious and moral training, all schools as well as all oratories, recreation centers, etc.; and from his visitation the schools of any religious whatsoever are not exempted, unless there be question of internal schools conducted for the professed members of an exempt institute. (Can. 1382.) As to schools conducted for non-professed persons, this canon does not expressly abrogate privileges that were granted prior to the Code and which therefore may still be in force. Thus schools and colleges in the care of *regulars* are exempted from the visitation of the local Ordinary, even though they are conducted not for the members of the institute but for seculars. (Bouscarn-Ellis, p. 748.)

C. *Writing*

1. Religious may not publish books on moral, religious, or theological topics, holy pictures, books or booklets of devotion, of prayers, etc., unless they first obtain the permission of their major superior and then also obtain the *nihil obstat* and the *imprimatur* of the local Ordinary. (Cf. Can. 1385 for details.)

The local Ordinary in question is either the local Ordinary of the author, or of the place in which the books, etc., are published, or of the place in which the books, etc., are printed. If one of these Ordinaries refuses his permission to publish, the author may not ask it of any of the others without informing him that it has been refused by the former. (Can. 1385 § 2.)

2. Secular clerics are forbidden without the consent of their Ordinaries, and religious without the permission of their major superior and of the local Ordinary, to publish books that deal with profane subjects, or to write for or edit papers, magazines or periodicals. (Can. 1386 § 1.)

This canon speaks of a simple permission or consent, *not* of a previous censorship of the book or article.

The permission to contribute to periodicals may be given habitually so that one need not apply for it as often as he may write an article. Likewise, it is probable that the permission required by this canon is not needed for a single article, but only in the case of a cleric or religious who is an habitual contributor. (Abbo-Hannan, II, n. 1386.)

3. The permission by which the Ordinary grants au-

thorization for publishing (the *imprimatur*) is to be given in writing and is to be printed at the beginning or at the end of the book, magazine, or sacred image, giving the name of the one granting the permission and also the place and date of the grant. (Can. 1394.)

> This canon refers to the *imprimatur* required in n. 1 above, not to the permission required in n. 2 above. That permission need not be published.

> The formula "with ecclesiastical permission," though not in strict conformity with the text of the law, may be regarded as sufficient for books and booklets of minor importance, and for most reviews and magazines. (Cf. Bouscaren-Ellis, p. 759.)

> The Code does not demand that the *nihil obstat* of the ecclesiastical censors be printed in the book along with the *imprimatur* of the Ordinary.

II. DIVINE WORSHIP

A. *Divine Services*

1. Religious superiors should see to it that the divine services in their churches do not prove detrimental to the catechetical instruction or to the explanation of the gospel given in the parochial church; the judgment as to whether the services are detrimental pertains to the local Ordinary. (Can. 609 § 3.)

> The local Ordinary cannot suspend or forbid the divine services in the churches of *regulars,* but in case of conflict must have recourse to the Holy See. (Cf. Coronata, I, n. 615.)

> Concerning limitations as to the hour of divine services, confer pp. 50-51.

2. Local Ordinaries must see to it that the prescriptions of the sacred canons concerning divine worship are accurately observed, and especially that superstitious practices are not introduced into public or private worship or into the daily lives of the faithful, and also that nothing be introduced which is foreign to the faith, in conflict with ecclesiastical tradition or which savors of sordid profiteering. If the local Ordinary enacts laws on these matters for

his territory, all religious, including the exempt, are obliged to observe them, and the Ordinary can visit their churches and public oratories to see to it that they are observed. (Can. 1261 §§ 1, 2.)

> This visitation of the Ordinary is not to be made as a matter of course with regard to the churches of *regulars*. Ordinarily he is to use his right of visitation only when he has positive information that the particular laws enacted by him are not being observed in the churches of regulars. (Cf. PCI, reply, 8 April, 1924.)

3. Prayers and exercises of devotion are not permitted in churches or oratories until the local Ordinary has approved of them. (Can. 1259 § 1.)

> This provision holds only for such prayers and devotions as have not yet been approved, not for such as are already in use and well known; it does not seem to refer to prayers and devotions held in semipublic oratories of regulars. (Bouscaren-Ellis, p. 689.)

B. *Blessings*

Confere above pp. 315 ff.

C. *Sacred Images*

No one may place or cause to be placed in churches, even exempt, or in other sacred places, any unusual image, unless it has been approved by the local Ordinary. (Can. 1279 § 1.)

> If images which are exposed for public veneration are to be solemnly blessed, the blessing is reserved to the Ordinary, who can, however, delegate any priest to impart it. If the place where the image is to be exposed belongs to clerical exempt religious, the major superior has this right. (Canons 1279 § 4, 1156.)

D. *Relics*

Only those relics can be publicly venerated in churches, even exempt churches, which are certified to be genuine through an authentic document issued by a cardinal, by a local Ordinary, or by some other ecclesiastical person to whom the faculty of authenticating relics has been granted by an apostolic indult. (Can. 1283 § 1.)

If the documents for certain relics have been lost, the relics are not to be exposed for public veneration until the local Ordinary decides to allow it. Ancient relics, for which no documents can be found, may be accorded the same veneration they have enjoyed in the past, unless in a particular case it is evident from incontestable proof that they are false or spurious. (Cf. Can. 1285.)

E. *Processions*

1. Unless there is an immemorial custom to the contrary, or unless in the prudent judgment of the bishop, local circumstances require something different, on the feast of Corpus Christi there shall take place in any given place only one solemn procession through the public streets, and that from the principal church; in it all the clergy must take part, as well as all religious communities of men even those enjoying exemption; only those regulars are excused from participation who live perpetually in the strict enclosure or who dwell more than three miles from the city. (Can. 1291 § 1.)

2. The other parishes and churches, including those belonging to regulars, can have their own processions outside the church during the octave; but where there are more churches than one, it pertains to the local Ordinary to specify the day, the hour and the route for each procession. (Can. 1291 § 2.)

3. Religious, even exempt, are not allowed to hold processions outside their churches or cloisters without the permission of the local Ordinary, except in the case mentioned in n. 2 above. (Cf. Can. 1293.)

4. Neither a pastor nor anyone else can introduce new processions or transfer or abolish customary ones without the permission of the local Ordinary. (Can. 1294 § 1.)

F. *Public Prayers*

If the local Ordinary orders the ringing of bells, the recitation of certain prayers, or the carrying out of certain sacred functions for a public purpose, all religious, even exempt, must obey, without prejudice, however, to the constitutions and privileges of each institute. (Can. 612.)

III. EXORCISM

No one may lawfully perform exorcisms over those who are obsessed unless he has obtained special and express permission from the Ordinary. (Can. 1151 § 1.) The major superior in a clerical exempt religion may grant this permission if the obsessed person is his subject.

> The ministers of the exorcisms which occur in baptism and in consecrations or blessings are those who are the lawful ministers of these sacred rites. (Can. 1153.)

IV. HOLY MASS

1. *The Imperata, etc.* Religious, even exempt, when they celebrate Mass must say the *oratio imperata* prescribed by the bishop of the diocese as well as the special oration to be said on the anniversary of the bishop's election and consecration; they must also include the bishop's name in the canon of the Mass, and in the *preces* of the divine office.

2. *The Celebret.* Special regulations made by the local Ordinary in the matter of admitting priests to the celebration of Mass in a church not their own, providing these regulations are not contrary to the Code of Canon Law, must be observed also by exempt religious except if there is question of admitting religious priests to celebrate in a church of their own institute. (Cf. Can. 804 § 3.)

3. *Stipends and Fees*

a. Religious, even exempt, must conform to the regulations of the local Ordinary or the custom of the diocese in the matter of manual Mass stipends. (Can. 831 § 3.)

b. The local Ordinary is to draw up a list of funeral fees and offerings for his territory (cf. Can. 1234), and the terms of this list are binding on even exempt religious. (PCI, 6 March, 1927.)

c. It pertains to a provincial council or a meeting of the bishops of the province to specify the stole fees which may be received upon the occasion of the administration of the sacraments or the sacramentals. Such a schedule of fees must be approved by the Holy See. (Can. 1507.)

V. THE SACRAMENT OF PENANCE

For the obtaining of jurisdiction in regard to the hearing of confessions confer above, pp. 80-81.

Note that a priest, even a secular, who is to give a retreat in a house of a clerical exempt institute, may obtain faculties to hear confessions and faculties to preach from the religious superior according to Canons 875 and 1338 § 1, and hence need not recur to the chancery of the diocese, providing that the retreat is given to the religious or to those who stay at the religious house day and night as servants, students, guests, or patients.

VI. SUBJECTION TO THE COERCIVE POWER OF THE LOCAL ORDINARY

1. In all matters in which religious are subject to the local Ordinary he may coerce them even with penalties. (Can. 619.)

Penalties, whether medicinal or vindicative, established by the local Ordinary do not affect *regulars* even in matters in which they are subject to him, unless they are specifically mentioned as liable to them. (Coronata, I, n. 626.) However, regulars *unlawfully* dwelling outside their houses, even under pretext of going to their superiors, do not enjoy the privilege of exemption (Can. 616 § 1), and hence are subject to the coercive power of the local Ordinary in all matters in which nonexempt religious are subject to him.

Mendicants, because of a special privilege, cannot be punished with *censures* by the local Ordinary except in three cases, namely:

a. If they presume to preach without the permission of the bishop in churches not their own or even in their own churches in cases where the bishop's permission is needed.

b. If they presume, without the approval of the Bishop, to hear confessions of seculars.

c. If they expose for public veneration images that are depicted in an unusual or scandalous manner. (Cappello, *De Cens.*, n. 21.)

2. Even though a regular may have been outside his house lawfully and even though he has already returned to it, he can be punished by the local Ordinary for a delict committed outside the religious house, if the superior, when notified of the crime, fails to punish him. (Can. 616 § 2.)

3. If abuses have crept into the houses or the churches of regulars, or of other exempt religious, of which the superior has been informed but which he has neglected to correct, the local Ordinary is obliged to refer the matter to the Holy See immediately. (Can. 617 § 1.)

Every nonformed house (*domus non formata*) remains under the special vigilance of the local Ordinary, and the latter may himself deal provisionally with abuses which may have arisen to the scandal of the faithful. (Can. 617 § 2.)

4. A local interdict must be observed by all in the interdicted place, even by strangers and exempt persons, unless one can prove that he possesses a special privilege exempting him from the observance of the interdict. (Cf. Can. 2269.)

VII. Participation in Favors Granted by the Local Ordinary

An indult lawfully granted by the local Ordinary relaxing an obligation of the common law is enjoyed also by religious living in the diocese, without prejudice, however, to the vows and constitutions of their own institute. (Can. 620.) Hence, a religious, even exempt, may use a dispensation granted to the diocese by the local Ordinary from the laws of fast and abstinence; however, in a case in which the religious is bound to fast or to abstain on a given day by an additional obligation imposed by his vows or by the rule or constitutions of his institute, the Ordinary's grant does not dispense him from the obligation of his vow, rule or constitutions.

Religious may avail themselves of the dispensations, favors, etc., which the local Ordinary grants also by *delegated* power, unless the one from whom he received the power has limited its use in regard to religious or to the exempt.

In the internal forum, religious, even exempt, may ordinarily request from the local Ordinary dispensations, absolutions, etc., from obligations imposed by common law, for instance, in regard to censures, irregularities, fast, abstinence.

Part XIV

SPECIAL PRIVILEGES OF REGULARS

Each religious institute enjoys only those privileges which are contained in the Code of Canon Law or which have been directly granted to it by the Apostolic See; every communication of privileges is excluded for the future. (Can. 613 § 1.) Privileges acquired through communication and peacefully enjoyed by religious institutes before the Code are not abrogated by this canon. (PCI, reply, 30 Dec., 1937.)

The privileges enjoyed by a regular order belong also to the nuns (*moniales*) of that order, in so far as they are capable of enjoying them. (Can. 613 § 2.)

> This ruling contains an exception to the norm of paragraph one of Canon 613 which excludes the communication of privileges. But, note that the concession of Canon 613 § 2 does not affect sisters of the Third Orders but only nuns; however, it affects the latter even if they are immediately subject to the local Ordinary and even if, through Apostolic indult, they take only simple vows, though their constitutions provide for the solemn profession of the institute's members. (Abbo-Hannan, I, n. 613; Schaefer, n. 1241.)

I. DIVINE OFFICE

1. *Dispensation.* By privileges granted by Clement VII, Paul IV, and St. Pius V, *regular* superiors may dispense their subjects who are occupied with preaching, hearing confessions, teaching or studying Sacred Theology or Canon Law, or who are sick or who are taking care of the sick, from the recitation *of the divine office*. The superior

must, however, impose instead the recitation of at least six or seven psalms, of seven Our Fathers and the Creed twice. (Schaefer, n. 1213; Coronata, I, n. 619 bis.)

The superior general and in particular cases, other superiors also, may, according to their prudent judgment, exempt professors and students from some community exercises, even from *choir service,* especially during the night, whenever this seems necessary for the pursuit of their studies. (Can. 589 § 2.) These exemptions may be granted also during vacation periods, if they serve the purpose of promoting effective study. (Pruemmer, q. 220; Abbo-Hannan, I, n. 589.) The superior general may grant a *general* dispensation from the obligation of choir; the other superiors may grant dispensations only in particular cases. For dispensations for others who are not students or professors see the constitutions of the individual institutes. The General Constitutions of the Order of Friars Minor grant to local superiors the power to dispense from choir service for a short time; if the dispensation is to be of long duration it must come from the provincial superior, who can grant it only for a grave cause. (Art. 149 § 4.)

2. *The Sick.* The Friars Minor and the Poor Clares, when they are sick, may say seven Hail Marys and one Our Father, or something else assigned them by their confessor, instead of the divine office; and if the illness be serious, in the judgment of the doctor, they are not even bound to this, but it suffices that they have the intention to recite the office. (Schaefer, n. 1214; Coronata, I, n. 619 bis.) This privilege is enjoyed also by other regulars. (Coronata, I, n. 617.)

3. *The Brothers' Office.* Innocent IV granted this privilege to the Poor Clares that for a reasonable cause they may recite the office of the lay sisters instead of the divine office. Hence, by virtue of the communication of privileges, the Friars Minor may for a reasonable cause recite the office of the lay brothers instead of the divine office. (Trienekens, n. 181.)

A reasonable cause is had if one is occupied with urgent business, is quite scupulous in reciting his office, is given to headaches, has difficulty in reading; also, if one is fatigued from the hearing of many confessions or the preaching of sermons.

The office of the lay brothers consists of twenty-four Our Fathers for Matins, for Lauds five, for Prime, Tierce, Sext and None, for each of these seven, for Vespers, however, twelve, for Compline seven; in all, seventy-six.

Lay brothers of the Order of Friars Minor fulfill their obligation of reciting the various canonical hours of the Office of the Our Fathers when they recite either in whole or in part the divine office according to the Roman Seraphic Breviary or any other breviary approved for the faithful by the Holy See. (S.C. Rel., 24 March, 1958.) The lay brothers may fulfill their obligation by reciting the Little Office of the Blessed Virgin; they may use a vernacular breviary; the breviary they use need not be approved by the Holy See itself but it suffices if it be approved by some other ecclesiastical authority; the privilege may be used also by nuns of the Second Order and by women religious of Congregations aggregated to the Order of Friars Minor or in any way affiliated with it. (S.C.Rel., 21 Aug., 1958 — Acta Minorum, LXXVII, p. 324.)

4. *Mental Recitation. Regulars,* by virtue of a privilege granted to the Friars Minor by Leo X, may recite the office mentally when reciting it *privately.* This privilege to recite the office mentally may be used for the recitation of the entire office, and not only for the recitation of such parts as are said secretly in the public recitation. (Schaefer, n. 1214; Trienekens, n. 181; Goyeneche, II, pp. 58-61.)

5. *Little Office of the Blessed Virgin.* By reason of privileges granted by Benedict XIV, Pius IV and Gregory XVI, the Friars Minor may recite the little office of the Blessed Virgin instead of the divine office, while they are conducting missions, retreats, triduums, and other continuous courses of sermons. (Capobianco, n. 157).

II. HOLY MASS

1. *All regulars* enjoy the privilege of beginning the celebration of Mass from two hours before dawn to two hours after midday, probably also three hours after midday. Regulars may use this privilege anywhere; other priests, even seculars, may enjoy this privilege when they

celebrate Mass in a church or oratory of regulars. (Capobianco, nos. 66-68; Lyszczarczyk, p. 174, n. 2; confer also Schaefer, n. 1220.)

> In *their own churches* regulars may, for a just cause, begin the celebration of Mass from two hours after midnight to three hours after midday. Secular priests celebrating Mass in the churches of regulars enjoy the same privilege. (*Caeremoniale O.F.M.*, n. 188; Lyszczarczyk, p. 174, n. 3.)

2. A cleric in minor orders or in tonsure may, for a reasonable cause, act as subdeacon in a solemn Mass providing he does not wear the maniple, pour water into the chalice at the offertory, touch the chalice during the canon, or cleanse the chalice after the communion. Non-clerics are not allowed to act as subdeacon at Mass and every contrary privilege and custom is hereby revoked and abrogated. (S.R.C., decr., 14 March, 1906.)

> It is probable that a cleric in a religious institute who is not yet tonsured may act as subdeacon in Mass, in case of necessity, provided he does not place the four acts mentioned above. The religious, by receiving the habit of religion, certainly partakes of the rights and privileges of clerics (Can. 614), and is in a certain sense taken into the ranks of the clergy. Hence, the religious is in no wise on the same level with the layman, and it is the layman whom the decree of the Congregation of Rites seems to exclude absolutely from the function of subdeacon in the solemn Mass. (Kurtscheid, *Provincial Chronicle* [of the St. John the Baptist Province O.F.M., Cincinnati], II [1930], pp. 104-105.

III. ORATORIES

1. Major superiors of *clerical exempt religions* may erect semipublic oratories, and besides the principal oratory they may erect also secondary oratories in the religious house or in an institution connected with the religious house (v.g., a college, hospital) if some need or great advantage demands it. (Cf. Can. 1192 §§ 1, 4.)

2. Gregory XIII granted to the Society of Jesus the privilege to erect semipublic oratories in villas and hos-

pices (small houses not canonically erected as religious houses). By communication, this privilege is enjoyed by other *regulars,* so that the major superiors may authorize the erection of semipublic oratories in these houses. (Schaefer, n. 1371; Coronata, II, n. 765; V.C., I, n. 785.)

> The oratories spoken of under numbers 1 and 2 are semi-public oratories (cf. Can. 1188 § 2, 2°), and hence the faithful may fulfill the precept of hearing Mass on days of obligation in these oratories. (Can. 1249.)

IV. THE SACRAMENT OF PENANCE

A. *Privilege to Confess to any Confessor*

Professed members of a religious Order, when legitimately staying outside of the monastery, or when on a journey, may confess to a priest of their own Order who is suited for the hearing of confessions, even though not approved by the superior. In defect of such a confessor, the regular may confess to any other priest, even though this priest does not have the faculties of the diocese, provided, however, that the priest is suited for confessions, that no priest of his Order suited for confessions is present, and that the constitutions of the Order do not expressly forbid such a choice. (Shuhler, CUA, n. 186, p. 66.)

> Any religious, even exempt, may for peace of conscience, go to confession to any priest who has the faculties of the diocese, and the confession made to this priest is valid and licit, in spite of any contrary privilege; and the confessor may absolve the religious even from sins and censures reserved in the institute. (Cf. Can. 519.)

B. *Privileges of Regular Confessors*

1. Regular confessors, approved for the hearing of confessions by the local Ordinary, can dispense the faithful from private *non-reserved* vows, provided that the dispensation does not infringe upon the vested rights of others; they may also dispense from all *oaths,* except in the case where the dispensation from an oath tends to the prejudice

of other persons who refuse to remit the obligation. (Schaefer, n. 1332.)

For the distinction between reserved and non-reserved vows, see p. 144.

The vow of perfect and perpetual chastity made by a married person after marriage, is not reserved (Coronata, II, n. 897), and hence the regular confessor may dispense from it. If both husband and wife make such a vow, many authors think it to be reserved. Though it may be such, it could be annulled and suspended by the parties themselves. Although there is not much reason to think that a husband can directly annul the vows of his wife, nevertheless, there is sufficient authority defending the opinion that he can do so, provided that the vows were made by the wife during marriage (Coronata, II, n. 895); hence, the husband can directly annul the vow of the wife and the wife can then suspend the vow of her husband and thus both can ask for and enjoy the conjugal debt. (Arregui, n. 213; Coronata, II, n. 897.)

2. Regular confessors, approved by the local Ordinary for the hearing of confessions, can dispense all the faithful from *irregularities* resulting from a secret crime (*ex delicto occulto*), except in cases of irregularities which result from voluntary homicide or effectively procured abortion, and cases which have been taken to court. The use of this faculty is restricted to the sacramental forum, but is not restricted to urgent cases. It may be used both to permit the penitent to receive Holy Orders as well as to allow him to exercise Orders already received. (Coronata, *De Sacr.,* II, n. 169.)

3. Regular confessors, approved by the local Ordinary for the hearing of confessions, can, in the sacramental forum only, absolve the faithful (laymen, religious, clerics), *from censures* reserved by the common law to the local Ordinary. (Schaefer, n. 1334.)

In the Code, censures are reserved, sometimes simply to the *Ordinary,* at other times to the *local Ordinary,* and again to one's *proper Ordinary.* The regular confessor can absolve from all these censures except in the case where the absolution is reserved to the *proper* Ordinary and that Ordinary happens to be a major superior in a clerical exempt religion. In such a case, the regular confessor does not possess the faculty to absolve.

This faculty may be used for both public and occult cases; however, it should not be used for public cases until the penitent repairs the scandal he has given or lets it be known that the scandal will be repaired shortly.

For instance, in case of a censure contracted because of an invalid marriage, the penitent is instructed to contact his pastor concerning the convalidation of the marriage; he may then be absolved by the regular confessor without any scandal being caused.

4. A regular confessor *who is on a journey,* provided that he possesses jurisdiction delegated by some local Ordinary (i.e., that he has jurisdiction for confessions in some diocese), *can probably hear the confessions of the faithful,* even though he does not have jurisdiction in the diocese in which the confessions are heard; but this is true only if in the case he cannot conveniently present himself for faculties to the Ordinary of the place through which he is traveling, and also, only provided that the pastor is not opposed to his act of hearing confessions. (Cf. McCartney, CUA, n. 280, pp. 70-79.)

PART XV

THIRD ORDERS — ESPECIALLY
THE THIRD ORDER OF ST. FRANCIS

Special References:

1. *Constitutiones Tertii Ordinis Saecularis Sancti Francisci Assisiensis.* These constitutions were approved by the Sacred Congregation of Religious on August 25, 1957. The authorized English translation was published in the year 1959, by the Franciscan Herald Press, 1434 West 51st Street, Chicago 9, Illinois. Hereafter the authorized translation will be referred to as *Constitutions of the Third Order of St. Francis.*

2. *Ritual for Public Functions of the Franciscan Third Order,* by Fr. Mark Hegener, Franciscan Herald Press, Chicago, Illinois, 1955. Hereafter referred to as *Ritual of Franciscan Third Order.*

I. NATURE

1. *A Third Order Secular* is an association of persons (tertiaries) who in the world strive after Christian perfection, under the guidance of and according to the spirit of some order, in a manner compatible with life in the world and according to rules approved by the Holy See. (Cf. Can. 702 § 1.)

> Third Orders Secular are called so to distinguish them from Regular Third Orders. These latter are true religious institutes with the three public vows and the obligation of living in community. Since tertiaries do not live in community, Third Orders Secular are also distinguished from those societies of men or women living in common without public vows. (Cf. Canons 673-681.) Moreover, Secular Institutes which neither admit the three public vows of religion, nor the obligation of living in community, must be distinguished from Third Orders Secular. Members of Secular Institutes besides having their own specific regulations must make a profession by a private vow, oath, or consecration of chastity, poverty, and obedience, binding in

conscience. Third Orders Secular do not have such vows. Finally, Third Orders Secular are distinct from those other associations of the faithful whose purpose consists in the exercise of some work of piety or religion (pious unions) or the furtherance of public worship (confraternities). (Cf. Can. 707.)

The purpose of a Third Order Secular is to make progress in Christian perfection according to the spirit of the Order (Franciscan, Dominican, etc.) to which it is affiliated. The Third Orders Secular are not as such to engage in questions of a social or political nature. Even charitable activities should not be considered the main object and purpose of a Third Order Secular. The individual members of a Third Order Secular, however, should take part in all good works of the social, economic and political order.

2.   If a Third Order Secular is divided into several societies, each legitimately established branch is called a *sodality or fraternity* of tertiaries. (Can. 702 § 2.)

A person may belong to a Third Order Secular without belonging to any of the smaller groups into which it may be divided. Ordinarily tertiaries of the same Third Order unite, where it is feasible, into a local association, i.e., a fraternity of tertiaries. The Third Order as a whole is not erected into a moral person, whereas the fraternities of tertiaries are erected. (Cf. Bouscaren-Ellis, p. 358.) Moreover, by its own particular law a Third Order Secular may be divided into regions, provinces, nations.

The Third Order Secular of St. Francis in North America: since the seventh centenary of the Third Order, in 1921, the various tertiary provinces of the country have federated into a Tertiary Organization known officially as The Third Order of St. Francis in North America. The office of the Tertiary Organization's Secretary, The Third Order of St. Francis in North America, Central Office of the Federated Provinces, 29 S. La Salle Street, Chicago 3, Illinois, Suite No. 1043, has been designed to serve as a clearing house for information regarding the Third Order in all its phases: literature; applications for faculties to receive and profess members of the Third Order; application for canonically establishing new fraternities; affiliation of fraternities with existing tertiary provinces, etc.

3.   *The Rules* of Third Orders Secular have been approved by the Holy See; hence, they are not subject to modification, corrections or changes by the local Ordinary. (Cf. Can. 689 § 2.)

According to the Constitutions of the Third Order of St. Francis, directors can dispense individual members, for a just cause, from any precept of the rule or constitutions. (Art. 112, 60.) The visitator, during the visitation, can likewise dispense from or commute regulations of the rule and of the constitutions, for a just cause. (Art. 117, 4°.) This power of dispensing does not affect those things which are prescribed under pain of nullity, for instance, the duration of the novitiate.

II. ESTABLISHMENT OF THIRD ORDER FRATERNITIES

By *apostolic privilege* the following religious Orders can have affiliated Third Order Seculars: the Franciscans (all branches), Dominicans, Praemonstratensians, Carmelites, Augustinians, Minims, Servites, Trinitarians, Mercedarians, Benedictines.

1. The right to erect a fraternity of tertiaries belongs to the religious superiors of the First Order according to their constitutions.

Several fraternities of a Third Order Secular can be canonically established in the same place, even in the same church. (S.C. Indulg., 21 Jan., 1893; 8 March, 1905). Fraternities which have been established by one family of the First Order, cannot without the consent and knowledge of those who established them, go over to the authority of another family. (S.C.Rel., 24 Nov., 1911.)

According to the Constitutions of the Third Order of St. Francis, the religious superiors (generals, provincials, local superiors) of the three Families of the First Order and of the Third Order Regular may, within the limits of their proper jurisdiction, establish fraternities either personally or through their delegates, even outside the churches of the order. (Cf. Arts. 97-99.)

2. For the valid erection of a fraternity of tertiaries, the religious superior needs the *written permission of the local Ordinary.* (Cf. Canons 703 § 2; 686 § 3.)

The written permission of the local Ordinary is required for the establishment of a Third Order fraternity even in the churches of religious. However, the consent given by the local Ordinary for the erection of a religious house is good also for the erection in the same house or in the church annexed to it, of an *inorganic* Third Order fraternity. (Cf. Can. 868 § 3; Coronata, I, nos. 671, 689.) A Third Order fraternity is classified as inorganic if it lacks a President and Assistants or Councilors as required by common law and particular statutes.

3. A *formal decree* of erection by the legitimate ecclesiastical superior is necessary for the establishment of a Third Order fraternity. (Cf. Can. 687.)

The formal decree of erection should be in writing; this is probably not a requisite to validity. (Bouscaren-Ellis, p. 347.) The decree of erection gives a fraternity the status of a legal person in the Church with the canonical right to its own officers, to possess temporal property and to transact legal acts (elections, etc.). (Cf. Can. 687.)

Since a fraternity is erected as a moral person, this erection becomes an act of public authority, *and it is therefore necessary that public proof be available.* (Can. 99; Chelodi, *Jus de Personis,* n. 98.) This proof of the existence of a fraternity can be secured through the decree of erection, the method advised by Benedict XIII (Benedict XIII, *Paterna Sedis,* 10 Dec., 1725); or through an enactment of the one who has erected the fraternity, with the officials of the fraternity as witnesses, the method given in the *Rituale Romano-Seraphicum Ordinis Fratrum Minorum,* 3rd. ed., 1955, pp. 487-488.

4. The *rite* of erecting a fraternity of the Third Order of St. Francis is given in the Ritual of Franciscan Third Order, pp. 68-73. There is nothing mentioned, however, concerning the necessity of this form for a valid or licit erection; therefore, any act of competent authority with the intention of erecting a fraternity would suffice for validity. (Gennari, *Quaestioni Theologico-Morali,* n. 336.)

5. The Constitutions of the Third Order of St. Francis (Art. 93) enumerate the following as necessary requirements for establishing a fraternity as an organic body:

a. At least three professed members (Can. 100 § 2);

b. The consent of the local Ordinary, given in writing (Canons 703 § 2, 686 § 3);

c. The document of establishment signed by the competent superior of the Family on which the fraternity depends (Can. 687; cf. Can. 100 § 1);

d. A register for the names of the tertiaries (cf. Can. 694 § 2);

e. A church, oratory, or an altar, where the fraternity carries out its religious functions;

f. The appointment of the director and of the prefect together with the council, as enjoined by common law and by these constitutions.

Validation of invalidly established fraternities, as well as of invalid receptions and professions in the Third Order of St. Francis is granted severally to the four jurisdictions of the Franciscan First and Third Orders Regular, usually at five year intervals.

III. GOVERNMENT OF THIRD ORDERS

1. *The Religious Superior.* The religious superiors of the First Order have the right (which may be delegated wholly or in part) as regards their respective Third Orders:

a. To establish fraternities within the limits of their jurisdiction but only with the previous consent of the local Ordinary (Cf. Can. 703 § 2);

b. To visit and regulate what concerns internal discipline and spiritual direction (cf. Can. 690 § 2);

c. To dismiss tertiaries (cf. Can. 696 § 3), and for a grave cause to suppress fraternities. (Bouscaren-Ellis, p. 354.)

> Concerning the Third Order of St. Francis, the superiors of the four Franciscan families govern the Third Order normally through provincial commissaries and local directors. The *provincial commissary* is appointed by the minister provincial on the advice of his definitory. Some of the principal duties of the provincial commissary are to make a visitation of all the fraternities personally or through a delegate yearly or at least every three years; to preside at the election of the council in the triennial visitation, unless for a just cause the election takes place at another time; to send an annual report to the minister provincial, to the general commissary, and also to the national commissary. The *local director* of a fraternity is appointed by the bishop or provincial according to the rules given below. It should be noted that it is permissible to unite the appointment to a certain office, for instance, to that of the pastor of a certain parish, making the pastor and his lawful successors the directors of the Third Order.

2. *The Local Ordinary.* The local Ordinary, to whom all tertiaries owe obedience and reverence, has, according to common law, the right:

a. To grant permission for the establishment of a fraternity of tertiaries in his diocese (cf. Canons 703 § 2, 686 § 3);

b.   To make a visitation of the churches or oratories or of the altars that are the property of the Third Order; to examine the books of administration, and to ask for an account of the temporal goods and Mass obligations of the fraternity itself (cf. Canons 690 and 691 § 1);

It is not permitted, however, that local Ordinaries visit with respect to internal discipline or spiritual direction, i.e., the observance of the rules or the statutes, dispensation from the latter, admission to the novitiate and profession. (Cf. Can. 690 § 2.) Moreover, local Ordinaries are lacking in authorization to visit an oratory or chapel that belongs to and is maintained by the exempt religious. (Abbo-Hannan, I, n. 690.)

c.   To grant permission to wear the habit during public sacred functions (cf. Can. 703 § 3);

d.   To dismiss tertiaries (cf. Can. 696 § 3), and for a grave cause to suppress fraternities (cf. Can. 699 § 1.)

3.   *Third Order Directors*

a.   The *appointment* of the director and chaplain of the Third Order pertains to the local Ordinary; however, in fraternities erected in churches of the First Order, the appointment pertains to the religious superior, who must have the consent of the local Ordinary if a secular priest is to be chosen. (Cf. Can. 698 § 1.)

In the Third Order of St. Francis, according to a long-standing custom, the religious superior appoints the director for fraternities established even outside of Franciscan churches. Secular priests, however, or those of another religious institute may not be appointed directors unless the local Ordinary (cf. Can. 698 § 1) or the respective religious superior is consulted.

b.   The director and chaplain can, during their term of office, bless the habit, insignia, scapulars, etc., of the fraternity and impose them upon the persons to be enrolled. (Can. 698 § 2.)

Article 113 of the Constitutions of the Third Order of St. Francis outlines the director's chief duties as follows:

1) To admit postulants to the habit and novices to profession, on the advice of his council;

2) To receive the above-mentioned both to the habit and profession, in accordance with the ceremonial;

3) To preside at the monthly meetings of the fraternity and at the sessions of the council;

4) To see to it that the councilors and the officers fulfill their duties diligently;

5) To impart the papal blessing and the indulgenced blessing on the appointed days;

6) To dispense individual members, for a just cause, from any precept of the rule or of these constitutions;

7) To examine the registers of the fraternity and the books concerned with administration, to see also that obligations are fulfilled — without however, involving himself in financial matters except to the extent enjoined by articles 131 and 144;

8) To preside at the election of the council if this takes place outside the time of visitation.

4. *Officers.* Third Order fraternities which are legitimately erected have the right, according to their statutes and the sacred canons, to elect administrators of property, officials and helpers. In matters concerning the convocation to the meeting and elections, the common law as stated in Canons 161-182 and the statutes not in conflict with the common law are to be observed. (Cf. Can. 697 §§ 1-2.)

The internal government of a fraternity in the Third Order of St. Francis belongs to the *council* which consists of the prefect and of at least four councilors. According to the Constitutions of the Third Order of St. Francis (Art. 122), at the establishment of a new fraternity, the council is appointed by the one who establishes the fraternity, after consultation with the director already appointed; in other cases the council shall be elected at a general meeting by the professed tertiaries, who have not been deprived of the right to vote. For details concerning the election of officers, confer *Constitutions of the Third Order of St. Francis,* Articles 125-129. Elections may not be held in the absence of the visitator or of the director.

At least once a month, the council shall hold a session, presided over by the director or, in his absence, by the prefect or the vice-prefect or the councilor who is senior by reason of profession. All the councilors who have not a legitimate reason for being absent are bound to attend; and a session may not be held unless the majority of the council, not counting the director, is present. If the director was not present at the session of the council, its decisions require his approval. (Arts. 130-131.) It is the duty of the council:

1) To promote the gospel perfection of the members, and to put forward every means suitable for achieving this end;

2) To strengthen the bonds of fraternal love among the members and among the fraternities, and to carry on works of charity and of the apostolate, so that all the tertiaries may show themselves, both in the Church and in civil society, to be true heralds of the charity of our Lord Jesus Christ and of our holy Father Francis;

3) To admit, after discussion, postulants to the habit and novices to profession;

4) To carry out the wishes of the superiors;

5) To administer the goods of the fraternity and to distribute the alms;

6) To admit into the fraternity isolated tertiaries or those coming from another fraternity;

7) To propose to the director the dismissal of those who remain incorrigible despite three admonitions, and also of delinquent members;

8) To confer offices on the councilors or on other tertiaries;

9) To examine and approve the books of the fraternity;

10) To see to it that the officers fulfill their duties well;

11) To prepare the annual report for submission to the superiors. (Art. 133.)

IV. MEMBERSHIP IN THIRD ORDERS

1. *Requirements for Membership.* According to common law, the following are *invalidly* admitted to a Third Order:

a. One who has taken vows, either perpetual or temporary, in a religious institute; if he is released from his vows and returns to the world, his former membership in a Third Order revives (Can. 704 §§ 1-2);

b. Those enrolled and remaining in another Third Order, if they have not obtained an apostolic indult to belong to both; however, individual tertiaries may for a just cause transfer either from one Third Order to another or from one fraternity to another fraternity of the same Third Order (cf. Can. 705);

c. Non-Catholics and members of condemned societies or persons notoriously under censure, and in general public sinners (Can. 693 § 1);

d. Those refusing to join or not knowing what is being done, e.g., infants (cf. Can. 693 § 3.)

According to the Constitutions of the Third Order of St. Francis, those are invalidly admitted to the novitiate who have not yet completed their fourteenth year. (Art. 13.) The following are, moreover, illicitly admitted: married women without the husband's knowledge or contrary to his will, unless their spiritual director or the director of the fraternity judges otherwise; those who through their own fault are burdened with debts which they cannot pay; those who are not of a kindly and peaceful disposition, but are prone to bickering, gossip, detraction, and calumny, or to unusual forms of devotion. (Art. 14.)

2. *Reception and Enrollment*

a. The reception of members must be done according to law and the statutes of each Third Order. In order that the reception may be proved, the names must by all means be inscribed in the register; this enrollment is necessary for valid membership in a particular fraternity. (Cf. Can. 694 §§ 1-2.)

The Constitutions of the Third Order of St. Francis make the following stipulations:

1) *Novitiate.* Postulants are received into the novitiate by means of the clothing in the habit, which consists in receiving a blessed scapular and cord. (Art. 16.) The rite for the reception is contained in the Ritual of Franciscan Third Order, pp. 23-32. Essential is the blessing of the scapular and the cord. The scapular of woven wool may be brown, black or gray in color. The connecting bands may be of any material and color. The cord may be made of wool or hemp or linen. The formula by which the scapular and cord are handed over is also essential. The reception by the use of the formula in the plural is permissible.

At the time of clothing each tertiary shall be given a certificate of membership with the appropriate information, signed by the one who officiated at the ceremony. (Art. 18.) The novitiate shall last one complete year. (Art. 19.) If a novice through his own negligence has not attended the majority of the instructions, or if it remains doubtful that he is worthy and suitable, the novitiate shall be prolonged, but not beyond six months. If, however, when the year of novitiate is completed, a novice through his own negligence fails to make profession within two years, the novitiate must be repeated if he wishes to be admitted to the order. (Art. 23.) For the reception into a particular fraternity the advice of the fraternity council is required. (Art. 133, 3°.)

2) *Profession.* For the profession to be valid it is required that those who are about to make it:

a)   Be fifteen years old;

b)   Have duly completed the novitiate;

c)   Do so freely and expressly in the presence of the lawful superior or another who has the proper faculties. (Art. 25.)

The year of probation begins with the day of reception. The profession cannot take place validly till a day later in the following year. (Cf. Can. 34.) As such, the profession to keep the rule does not bind under sin. For the profession into a particular fraternity, the advice of the fraternity council is required. (Art. 133, 3°.) The rite of profession is contained in the *Ritual of Franciscan Third Order,* pp. 33-43.

b.   The religious superiors (even local superiors of non-formed houses) of the First Orders can receive individual persons into their respective Third Order. (Cf. Can. 703 § 2.) This power is ordinary and can be delegated. The reception of a member, however, into a *fraternity* of tertiaries pertains to the director according to the statutes. (Cf. Canons 694 § 1, 698 § 2.)

3.   *Dismissal.* No one who has lawfully become a member is to be dismissed except for a just cause as specified by the statutes. Anyone who has become an apostate, heretic or schismatic, or who has joined a society condemned by the Holy See, or who has notoriously incurred a censure, or who is living as a public sinner, after previous warning shall be dismissed according to the statutes and

with right of recourse to the Ordinary. Even though there is no express provision in the statutes, the local Ordinary as well as the religious superior have the right to dismiss members from the Third Order. (Cf. Can. 696 §§ 1-3.)

According to the Constitutions of the Third Order of St. Francis, erring members, if after the third warning they do not amend, shall be dismissed *from the fraternity* by the director with the consent of the council. The names of the dismissed tertiaries shall be forwarded to the provincial or regional commissary. (Art. 148.) The imposition of dismissal must always be communicated in writing, and must be noted in the register of the fraternity and in the minutes of the council. (Art. 151.) Dismissal *from the Third Order itself* pertains to the provincial and the general commissaries (Art. 150), or the local Ordinary (Can. 696 § 3).

V. Indulgences and Spiritual Favors

1. In order to enjoy the rights, privileges, indulgences, and other spiritual favors of a Third Order, it is sufficient that one has been validly received into it and has not been lawfully expelled from it. (Cf. Can. 692.)

Admission into a Third Order is effected by *means of the investment or reception*. Reception is valid even though a person does not affiliate with any particular fraternity (S.C.Indulg., 14 July, 1891). Indulgences can be gained from the day of reception, even before the name has been recorded. (Cf. Bouscaren-Ellis, pp. 351-352.)

To gain the indulgences, the special works prescribed, if any, must be performed (cf. Can. 925 § 2). The same is true of the other rights, privileges, and spiritual favors only if some special works are prescribed for acquiring them. (PCI, 4 Jan., 1946.) In general the good works prescribed by the rules or statutes are not enjoined as necessary conditions for gaining the spiritual favors or indulgences. The wearing of the Third Order habit, however, is a condition for gaining the indulgences. Moreover, the scapular of the Third Order cannot be substituted by a medal except by apostolic indult. (S.C.Rel., 25 March, 1922.)

According to the Constitutions of the Third Order of St. Francis (Arts. 159 and 17), in order to gain the indulgences granted to the Order, tertiaries must wear the scapular and cord habitually, but for a reasonable cause, they may lay aside the cord and scapular for a short time. In individual cases and for a just cause, the director may dispense from wearing them, or he may allow to be used in their stead a metal medal bearing the image of our Lord Jesus Christ or of the Blessed Virgin Mary or of our holy Father Francis. In the case of individual fraternities the major superiors of the Franciscan Order have the same faculty, provided that the reasons, submitted in writing by the director and council of the fraternity, are really sufficient.

2. As such the Third Orders do not enjoy the communication of indulgences with their respective First Orders; they can gain only those indulgences which have been directly granted to them. (Cf. S.C.Indulg., 31 Jan., 1893; 18 July, 1902.)

To the Third Order Secular of St. Francis, however, Pius X, May 5, 1909, granted perpetually the communication of indulgences and spiritual fruits with the First and Second Orders of St. Francis.

3. The Ursulines enjoy all the privileges and indulgences of the Third Order of St. Francis. (S.C.Rel., 19 May, 1917.)

VI. INDULGENCES AND SPIRITUAL FAVORS OF FRANCISCAN TERTIARIES

A. *The General Absolution or Indulgenced Blessing*

1. *General Rules.* General absolution is a blessing of the Church to which a plenary indulgence is attached under the ordinary conditions (confession, Communion, and prayer for the intention of the Holy Father). This indulgence is applicable to the Souls in Purgatory.

The days on which general absolution may be given to Franciscan tertiaries are:

January 1, Octave of Christmas	August 27, Seven Joys of B.V.M.
	September 8, Nativity of B.V.M.
January 6, Epiphany	September 17, Stigmata of St. Francis
February 2, Purification	
First Friday in March, Feast of the Stations of the Cross	October 4, St. Francis
	November 1, All Saints
March 19, St. Joseph	November 19, St. Elizabeth
March 25, Annunciation	November 21, Presentation of B.V.M.
All the days of Holy Week	

Easter Sunday
Ascension Thursday
Pentecost
Holy Trinity
Corpus Christi
Sacred Heart
June 29, Sts. Peter and Paul
July 2, Visitation
August 12, St. Clare
August 15, Assumption
August 25, St. Louis

November 25, St. Catherine
December 8, Immaculate
Conception
December 25, Christmas
Once every year at the end of canonical visitation
Four times a year on any convenient day
On the day canonical visitation is held in the cloister attached to the church where the fraternity meets.

General absolution can be given to all the tertiaries publicly or privately not only on the day assigned, but also on any day of the week (within the octave) following the day on which general absolution is permitted. (Benedict XV, Brief *Quae Omnia,* 14 April, 1917.) Furthermore it can be imparted *privately* already on the preceding day. (S.C. Indulg., 21 July, 1888.)

Imparting the general absolution is considered *public* if it is given to a number of tertiaries together outside of the confessional. It is not necessary that these tertiaries represent a canonically established fraternity. The tertiaries can also receive general absolution in a fraternity not their own, even if it belongs to a different branch of the order. The giving of general absolution is *private* if done in the confessional. Sacramental confession is not prescribed for the private reception of general absolution. (Coronata, I, n. 691.)

2. *Minister of General Absolution*

a. The Franciscan superiors can *publicly* impart general absolution as well as the papal blessing to the tertiaries of their territory; the director to the tertiaries of his fraternity.

Moreover, Franciscan superiors can delegate to priests of their Order even though the latter are not approved for hearing confessions, the faculty to impart in their own churches the general absolution and the papal blessing to tertiaries. (S.O., 27-28 May, 1914; cf. Campelo, n. 811.)

b. In the absence of a delegated priest, any approved confessor can impart *publicly* to a gathering of tertiaries general absolution as well as the papal blessing. (S.O., 15 Dec., 1910.)

> The tertiary priest who lawfully imparts general absolution or the papal blessing publicly, receives it himself also. (S.C. Indulg., 18 June, 1876; 1 Feb., 1905.)

c. *Privately* (in the confessional or in the sacrament of penance) every approved confessor can give the general absolution.

3. *Rite of General Absolution*

a. In *privately* imparting the general absolution the short formula is sufficient: "Auctoritate a Summis Pontificibus mihi concessa plenariam omnium peccatorum tuorum indulgentiam tibi impertior. In nomine Patris † et Filii et Spiritus Sancti. Amen."

b. In imparting the general absolution to secular tertiaries *publicly,* the priest uses the violet stole, and the formula *Intret oratio.* The first prayers are said kneeling at the foot of the altar; the *Misereatur,* etc., standing on the Gospel side of the altar.

> Religious who are present in a church or oratory where the blessing is being given to tertiaries under the formula *Intret oratio,* can receive it, if on that day they are unable to do so under the formula *Ne reminiscaris,* and *vice versa.* (S.R.C., 7 June, 1919.)

> The Minorite provinces, custodes and commissariats in the United States and Canada have the indult to impart publicly the general absolution to tertiaries of the Third Order Secular of St. Francis under the short formula: "Auctoritate a Summis Pontificibus mihi concessa, etc." (S.R.C., 2 March, 1959.)

B. *The Papal Blessing*

1. The papal blessing (not to be confused with the general absolution) has a plenary indulgence attached to it for the faithful who are present when it is imparted, provided they have received the sacraments and pray for the intention of the Holy Father. By grant of Leo XIII (Const., *Misericors,* 30 May, 1883) the papal blessing can be given publicly to tertiaries twice a year. It cannot be given in the

same city on a day when the bishop confers it. (Cf. Can. 915.)

The papal blessing can be given *only publicly,* i.e., if a number of tertiaries are gathered together; not, however, privately to the individual tertiaries. Those tertiaries who live in places where no fraternity of the Third Order has been established can receive the general absolution in place of the papal blessing twice a year. (S.C.Indulg., 31 May, 1893.)

2. Every priest who is authorized to impart publicly the general absolution, can also give the papal blessing. (Cf. above VI, A, 2, a and b.)

3. The papal blessing must be imparted according to the formula of the Roman Ritual, Tit. VIII, chap. 32. (S.R.C., 12 March, 1940.) This formula is also found in the *Ritual of Franciscan Third Order,* pp. 49-50.

The prescribed formula is required for the validity of the blessing. (S.C.Indulg., 22 March, 1879.)

C. *Special Indults for Franciscan Tertiaries*

1. *For tertiary priests*

a. Tertiary priests enjoy the indult of a privileged altar three times a week unless they have a similar indult from another source. (Leo XIII, Const., *Misericors,* 30 May, 1883.) All the Masses which are said for deceased tertiaries are privileged.

b. Those tertiary priests who are not bound to choral office enjoy the privilege of using the breviary of the Franciscan Family to which they are attached. (S.R.C., 2 May, 1880; 15 April, 1904.) When they celebrate Mass in a private oratory they may use the Missal of that Franciscan Family. (S.R.C., 15 April, 1904.) They are always allowed to add the name of our holy Father Francis in the *Confiteor.*

If they use the Seraphic calendar in reciting the breviary they may say the votive Mass of the Immaculate Conception on Saturdays, provided they celebrate Mass in a private oratory and observe the liturgical rules. (S.R.C., 9 Dec., 1903; 22 March, 1905.) Priest-tertiaries who use the Roman Missal and breviary may follow the Roman-Seraphic Missal and breviary on the principal Franciscan feastdays.

The privilege enjoyed by the First Order whereby the divine office may be recited mentally in private recitation, is not enjoyed by secular priests who are members of the Third Order. (*Clergy Review,* XLII, pp. 369-371.) Likewise, secular priests belonging to the Third Order do not enjoy the privilege of substituting the Brothers' Office for the divine office.

2.   *For directors.* Directors of the Third Order who cannot join it because they have taken vows in some religious institute or are members of another Third Order, can, during their term of office, share in all the indulgences and other favors enjoyed by the fraternity which they direct. (S.P., 13 Dec., 1928; 26 Feb., 1954.)

3.   *For all Franciscan tertiaries*

a.   Members who are ill or convalescing and who cannot easily leave the house, can gain all the indulgences attached to Franciscan or Third Order churches by reciting five Our Fathers and Hail Marys and adding at least one Our Father, Hail Mary and Glory be to the Father, for the intention of the Sovereign Pontiff. (Leo XIII, Brief, 7 Sept., 1901.) Such tertiaries, too, can receive the general absolution and can also gain every plenary indulgence granted for stated days, on any day within the octave of the feast to which the general absolution or plenary indulgence is attached, provided they fulfill all the other conditions. (S.C.Indulg., 13 Aug., 1901.)

b.   In places where there is no Franciscan church or public oratory and no fraternity of the Third Order has been established, tertiaries can gain all the indulgences of the order in the parish church or its dependent church. (S.R.C., 31 Jan., 1893; cf. also *Ius Seraphicum,* II, p. 365.)

c.   Tertiaries who live in seminaries, colleges, hospitals, hospices, etc., and who cannot easily visit a parochial or a Franciscan church, can gain the indulgences of the order in the oratory of the house, even when this is a semipublic oratory only. (S.C.Indulg., 18 July, 1902; 22 March, 1905; 8 Aug., 1906.)

ABBREVIATIONS

Series I

AP. CONST.—Apostolic constitution.

AP. LETT.—Apostolic letter.

CAN.—Canon.

COD. RUBR.—*Novus Rubricanum Codex—Rubricae Breviarii et Missalis Romani,* 1960.

MP—The *motu proprio, Crebrae allatae.* Codification of the marriage legislation for the Oriental Church.

PCI—Pontifical Commission for the Authentic Interpretation of the Canons of the Code.

PC OR—Pontifical Commission for the Redaction of the Code of Oriental Canon Law.

S.C. CONC.—Sacred Congregation of the Council.

S.C. CONSIST.—Sacred Consistorial Congregation.

S.C.E.O.—Sacred Congregation of the Oriental Church.

S.C. INDULG.—Sacred Congregation of Indulgences.

S.C.P.F.—Sacred Congregation for the Propagation of the Faith.

S.C. REL.—Sacred Congregation for Religious.

S.C. SACR.—Sacred Congregation of the Sacraments.

S.O.—Sacred Congregation of the Holy Office.

S.P.—The Sacred Penitentiary.

S.R.C.—Sacred Congregation of Rites.

S.R.R.—The Sacred Roman Rota.

Series II

Abbreviation   *Work and Author*

ABBO-HANNAN—Abbo, J.—Hannan, J., *The Sacred Canons,* 2 vols., St. Louis: B. Herder Book Co., 1952.

ACTA MINORUM—*Acta Ordinis Fratrum Minorum,* Ad Claras Aquas, Florentiae.

ALFORD—Alford, Culver, *Ius Matrimoniale Comparatum,* Rome, Italy: Anonima Libraria Cattolica Italiana, 1938.

Abbreviation   *Work and Author*

ANGLIN, CUA—Anglin, T., *The Eucharistic Fast,* The Catholic University of America Canon Law Studies, n. 124, Washington, D.C.: The Catholic University of America Press, 1941.

ANLER—Anler, Ludwig, *Comes Pastoralis,* 10. ed., Fulda: Verlag Parzeller & Co., 1947.

ARREGUI—Arregui, Antonio, *Summarium Theologiae Moralis,* 13. ed., Westminster, Maryland: The Newman Bookshop, 1944.

AYRINHAC—Avrinhac, H.-Lydon, P., *Matrimonial Legislation in the New Code of Canon Law,* revised ed., New York: Benziger Bros., 1932.

BALT. II—*Concilii Plenarii Baltimorensis II, Acta et Decreta,* Baltimore: John Murphy, 1868.

BALT. III—*Acta et Decreta Concilii Plenarii Baltimorensis Tertii,* Baltimore: John Murphy and Associates, 1886.

BARRETT, CUA—Barrett, John, *A Comparative Study of the Third Plenary Council of Baltimore and the Code,* The Catholic University of America Canon Law Studies, n. 83, Washington, D.C.: The Catholic University of America Press, 1932.

BERINGER—Beringer, Franz, *Die Ablaesse ihr Wesen und Gebrauch,* 1. ed., 2 vols., Paderborn: Verlag Ferdinand Schoeningh, 1922.

BESTE—Beste, Udalricus, *Introductio in Codicem,* 2. ed., Collegeville, Minn.: St. John's Abbey Press, 1944.

BOUSCAREN-ELLIS — Bouscaren, T.-Ellis, A., *Canon Law, a Text and Commentary,* 3. ed., Milwaukee: Bruce Publishing Co., 1957.

BRYS—Brys, J., *Juris Canonici Compendium,* 10. ed., 2 vols., olim ab Exc.mo De Brabandere et R.dis Adm. Van Coillie et DeMeester editum, Brugis: Desclée, 1947-1949.

CAEREMONIALE O.F.M.—*Caeremoniale Romano-Seraphicum Ordinis Fratrum Minorum,* 2. ed., Ad Claras Aquas: Ex Typographia Collegii S. Bonaventurae, 1927.

CAMPELO—Campelo, Joseph, *De Indulgentiis Seraphici Ordinis,* 2. ed., Compostellae: Typis "El Eco Franciscano," 1943.

CAPOBIANCO—Capobianco, Pacificus, *Privilegia et Facultates Ordinis Fratrum Minorum,* 3. ed., Romae: Pontificium Athenaeum Antonianum, 1956.

Abbreviation   *Work and Author*

CAPPELLO—Cappello, Felix, *Summa Iuris Canonici,* 3 vols.,
Romae: apud Aedes Universitatis Gregorianae, 1940-1945.
Vols. I and II, 4. ed., 1945; Vol. III, 2. ed., 1940.

CAPPELLO, DE CENS.—Cappello, Felix, *Tractatus Canonico-
Moralis de Censuris,* 4. ed., Romae: Marietti, 1950.

CAPPELLO, DE SACR.—Cappello, Felix, *Tractatus Canonico-
Moralis de Sacramentis,* 5 vols., Romae: Marietti, 1949-1953.
Vol. I, 6. ed., 1953; Vol. II, 6. ed., 1953; Vol. III, 3. ed., 1949;
Vol. IV, 3. ed., 1951; Vol. V, 6. ed., 1950.

CHELODI—Chelodi, Joannes, *Ius Canonicum de Personis,* 3. ed.,
Vicenza: Societá Anonima Tipographica, 1942.

CLERGY REVIEW—*The Clergy Review,* London: 1931—.

CLORAN—Cloran, Owen, *Previews and Practical Cases,* Milwaukee: The Bruce Publishing Company, 1951.

COUSSA I—Coussa, A., *Epitome Praelectionum de jure Eccle-
siastico Orientali, Vol. I,* Pontificium Institutum Utriusque
Iuris: Typis Monasterii Exarchici Cryptoferratensis, 1948.

COUSSA III—Coussa, A., *Epitome Praelectionum de Iure Eccle-
siastico Orientali, Vol. III De Matrimonio,* Romae: apud Cus-
todiam Librariam Pontificii Instituti Utriusque Iuris, 1950.

CORONATA—Coronata, Matthaeus Conte a, *Institutiones Iuris
Canonici ad Usum Utriusque Cleri et Scholarum,* 2. ed., 5
vols., Romae: Marietti, 1939-1947.

CORANATA, DE SACR.—Coronata, M., *Institutiones Iuris Canonici ad Usum Utriusque Cleri et Scholarum, De Sacramentis,
Tractatus Canonicus,* 3 vols., 2. ed., Romae: Marietti, 1948-
1951.

CREUSEN—Creusen, J.-Garesche, E. F.-Ellis, A. C., *Religious
Men and Women in the Code,* 4. ed., Milwaukee: Bruce, 1940.

CRM—*Commentarium pro Religiosis et Missionariis,* Romae:
1920—.

DECR. AUTH.—*Decreta Authentica Sacrae Congregationis Indulgentiis Sacrisque Reliquiis* etc., Ratisbonae: Tipographica Frid-
erici Pustet, 1883.

DE SMET—De Smet, A., *Tractatus Theologico-Canonicus de
Sponsalibus et Matrimonio,* 4. ed., Bruges: Car. Beyaert, 1927.

Abbreviation   *Work and Author*

DIEDERICHS, CUA—Diederichs, M., *The Jurisdiction of the Latin Rite Ordinaries over their Oriental Subjects,* The Catholic University of America Canon Law Studies, n. 229, Washington, D.C.: The Catholic University of America Press, 1946.

DIGEST—Bouscaren, T., *The Canon Law Digest,* 4 vols., Milwaukee: Bruce, 1934, 1943, 1954, 1958.

ECCL. REV.—*American Ecclesiastical Review,* Washington, D.C.: 1889—.

GASPARRI—Gasparri, P., *Tractatus Canonicus de Matrimonio,* ed. post Codicem, 2 vols., Rome: Vatican Press, 1932.

GENICOT—Genicot, E.-Salsman, J.-Gortebecke, A., *Institutiones Theologiae Moralis,* 17. ed., 2 vols., Bruxellis, 1951.

GENNARI—Gennari, Casimiro, *Questioni Teologico-Morali,* 2. ed., Romae: Tipographia Pietro Veratti, 1907.

GOYENECHE—Goyeneche, S., *Quaestiones Canonicae de Iure Religiosorum,* 2 vols., Neapoli: M. D'Auria, 1954-1955.

HPR—*Homiletic and Pastoral Review,* New York: 1900—.

IORIO—Iorio, T., *Theologia Moralis,* 4. ed., 3 vols., Neapoli: M. D'Auria, 1953-1954.

JURIST—*The Jurist,* Washington, D.C.: 1941—.

JUS SERAPHICUM—*Jus Seraphicum,* Romae: 1955—.

LYSZCZARCZYK—Lyszczarczyk, V., *Compendium Privilegiorum Regularium,* Leopoli: Ex Typ. Catholica Josephi Checinski, 1906.

MATTERS LITURGICAL—Wuest, J.-Mullahey, T.-Barry, W., *Matters Liturgical,* 9. ed., New York: Frederick Pustet Company, 1956.

MOCCHEGGIANI—Moccheggiani, Petro, *Collectio Indulgentiarium Theologice, Canonice ac Historice Digesta,* apud Florentiam: Ex Typographia Collegi S. Bonaventurae, 1897.

MORIARITY, CUA—Moriarity, F., *The Extraordinary Absolution from Censures,* The Catholic University of America Canon Law Studies, n. 113, Washington, D.C.: The Catholic University of America Press, 1938.

Abbreviation   *Work and Author*

McCARTNEY, CUA—McCartney, M., *Faculties of Regular Confessors,* The Catholic University of America Canon Law Studies, n. 280, Washington, D.C.: The Catholic University of America Press, 1949.

NOLDIN—Noldin, H.-Schmitt, A.-Heinzel, G., *Summa Theologiae Moralis,* 3 vols., Oeniponte: Typis et Sumptibus Feliciani Rauch, 1953-1954. Vol. II, 30. ed., 1954; Vol. III, 30. ed., 1954; Vol. I, 31. ed., 1953.

PAYEN—Payen, G., *De Matrimonio,* 2. ed., 3 vols., Zikawei: Typographia Tou-se-we, 1935-1936.

PERIODICA—*Periodica pro Religiosis et Missionariis,* Bruges, 1905-1919; *Periodica de Re Canonica et Morali utilia praesertim Religiosis et Missionariis,* Bruges, 1920-1927; *Periodica de Re Morali, Canonica, Liturgica,* Bruges, 1927 and Rome, 1937—.

POSPISHIL—Pospishil, Victor, *Interritual Canon Law Problems in the United States and Canada,* Chesapeake City, Maryland: St. Basil's, 1955.

PRECES—*Enchiridion Indulgentiarum (Preces et Pia Opera),* Romae: Typis Polyglottis Vaticanis, 1950.

PRUMMER—Pruemmer, D.-Muenich, M., *Manuale Theologiae Moralis,* 11. ed., 3 vols., Friburg: Herder, 1953.

QUIGLEY—Quigley, J., *Matrimonial Impediments and Dispensations,* 2. ed., Philadelphia: Dolphin Press, 1945.

RACCOLTA—*The Raccolta,* New York: Benziger Brothers Inc., 1957.

REGATILLO-ZALBA—Regatillo, E.-Zalba, M., *Theologiae Moralis Summa,* 3 vols., Batriti: Biblioteca De Autores Cristianos, 1952-1954.

RV. REL.—*Review for Religious,* St. Marys, Kansas: 1942—.

RIT. ROM.—*Rituale Romanum Pauli V Pontificis Maximi Iussu Editum Aliorumque Pontificum Cura Recognitum Atque Auctoritate Pii Papae XI Ad Norman Codicis Iuris Canonici Accommodatum,* 2. ed., amplificata 1., New York: Benziger Brothers, 1945.

SARTORI—Sartori, Cosmos, *Enchiridion Canonicum,* 7. ed., Romae: Ex Typographia Augustiniana, 1944.

Abbreviation *Work and Author*

SCHAEFER—Schaefer, Timotheus, *De Religiosis,* 4. ed., Romae: Editrice Apostolato Cattolico, 1947.

SHUHLER, CUA—Shuhler, Vincent, *Privileges of Regulars to Absolve and Dispense,* The Catholic University of America Canon Law Studies, n. 186, Washington, D.C.: The Catholic University of America Press, 1943.

SIPOS—Sipos, S.-Galos, L., *Enchiridion Iuris Canonici,* 6. ed., Romae: Herder, 1954.

SLATER-MARTIN—Slater, T.-Martin, M., *A Manual of Moral Theology,* 2 vols., New York: Benziger Brothers, 1908.

SUMMARIUM O.F.M. — *Summarium Indulgentiarum Quibus Gaudet Ordo Seraphicus etc.,* 1841.

THEOLOGICAL STUDIES—*Theological Studies,* Woodstock, Md.: 1940—.

TIMLIN, CUA—Timlin, B., *Conditional Matrimonial Consent,* The Catholic University of America Canon Law Studies, n. 89, Washington, D.C.: The Catholic University of America Press, 1934.

TRIENEKENS—Trienekens, I., *Expositio Canonico-Moralis Regulae Fratrum Minorum seu ejusdem vota et Praecepta,* 3. ed., Werlensis Guestfalorum: Typis Officinae Typographicae S. Francisci, 1931.

UBACH—Ubach, Joseph, *Compendium Theologiae Moralis,* 2 vols., Friburg: Herder and Co., 1926.

V.C.—Vermeersch, A.-Creusen, J., *Epitome Iuris Canonici,* 3 vols., Mechliniae et Romae: H. Dessain. Vol. I, 7. ed., 1949; Vol. II, 7. ed., 1954; Vol. III, 6. ed., 1946.

VLAMING—Vlaming, T.-Bender, L., *Praelectiones Iuris Matrimonii,* 4. ed., Bussum: Paul Brand, 1950.

WALSH, CUA—Walsh, J., *The Jurisdiction of the Interritual Confessor in the United States and Canada,* The Catholic University of America Canon Law Studies, n. 320, Washington, D.C.: The Catholic University of America Press, 1950.

WELSH, CUA—Welsh, Thomas, *The Use of the Portable Altar,* The Catholic University of America Canon Law Studies, n. 305, Washington, D.C.: The Catholic University of America Press, 1950.

Abbreviation   *Work and Author*

WIEST, CUA—Wiest, D., *The Precensorship of Books,* The Catholic University of America Canon Law Studies, n. 329, Washington, D.C.: The Catholic University of America Press, 1953.

WOEBER, CUA—Woeber, E., *The Interpellations,* The Catholic
University of America Canon Law Studies, n. 172, Washington, D.C.: The Catholic University of America Press, 1942.

WOJNAR—Wojnar, M., *The Code of Oriental Law De Ritibus
Orientalibus and De Personis,* reprint from *The Jurist,* Washington, D.C.: The Catholic University of America, 1959.

WOYWOOD—Woywood, S.-Smith, C., *A Practical Commentary
on the Code of Canon Law,* 1 vol. ed., New York: Joseph
Wagner, Inc., 1952.

ALPHABETICAL INDEX

for the sick, 72-73, 393
time of, 69-70

COMMUNIST:
penalties, 112, 119
prohibition of writings, 388
marriage of, 192

COMMUTATION:
of conditions for indulgences,
337, 339-340
of oath, 148
of vow, 147
Computation of time, 17-18
Conditional consent, 240-243

CONFESSION: see penance
as condition for indulgences,
336-337

CONFESSOR:
absolution from censures, 98-
101
absolution of men religious,
426
absolution from reserved sins,
24, 91-92
and cohabitation, 303-304
commutation of good works,
339-340
convalidation of marriage,
392
dispensation from feasts and
fasts, 313-314
dispensation from irregularities, 142
dispensation from matri-
monial impediments, 223-
225, 227-229
dispensation from vindicative
penalties, 140
and dying non-Catholics, 156-
157
extraordinary, 85
and extreme unction, 151
faculties in danger of death,
82-83
faculty to impart general
absolution to religious, 350-
351
faculty to impart general
absolution to tertiaries, 442
faculties at sea, 83-84

ignorance of censures, 97
obtaining jurisdiction, 80-82
occasional, 86-87
ordinary, 85
Oriental, 24
privileges of regulars: see
regulars
regular: see regulars
and separation cases, 287, 291
supplementary, 86
supplied jurisdiction, 5-7
of women religious, 85-88

CONFIRMATION:
age, 40
faculty of pastors, 7, 41-44
record of, 41, 43
rubrics for, 43
sponsor for, 40-41
subject of, 40

CONSANGUINITY:
civil law impediment, 209
computation of, 207-209
dispensation from, 209-211
matrimonial impediment,
207-211
multiple, 208
in Oriental law, 211

CONSECRATION:
of altar, 315, 325
of bells, 315, 318
of chalice, 328
of church, 315, 317
illicit, of bishops, 105

CONSENT:
matrimonial: see marriage
renewal of, 293-296
Conspiring against ecclesiastical
authority, 115
Convalidation: see marriage

CONVERTS:
baptism of, 35-38
from Oriental dissident
churches, 37-38
reception of, 36-37
Cooperators in crime, 93-94
Corpus Christi, procession, 417
Council, appeal to, 115
Cremation, 159-160

of emigrants, 246
and engagement contract, 171
of extreme unction, 151
faculties:
  for apostolic blessing, 343
  assistance at marriage, 247-248, 253-255
  assistance at marriage of Orientals, 248-250, 254-255
  assistance at marriages of *vagi,* 253
  for blessing sacred utensils and vestments, 328
  for confessions, 79
  to confirm, 41-44
  to delegate to assist at marriage: see above
  to dispense: see above
  to reconcile violated church, 320
  over reserved sins, 90-92
functions reserved to, 392-394
instruction, premarital, 180-181
investigation, premarital, 173-175
matrimonial dispensations, 219, 223-225, 227-229
pious trusts, 403-404
proper, 16
religious: see religious
sick communion, 393
stole fees, 394-396
and Third Order Fraternity, 434
transfer of Portiuncula Indulgence, 346
vacations, 396
Viaticum, 393

PAULINE PRIVILEGE:
  extension of, 282-285
  interpellations, 277-280
  nature of, 275-277
Penalties: see censures, vindicative penalties

PENANCE, SACRAMENT OF:
  absolution from censures, 98-101
  absolution in danger of death, 82-83
  absolution of dying non-Catholic, 156-157
  absolution from reserved sin, 90-92, 137
  jurisdiction:
    aboard plane, 83-85
    aboard ship, 83-85
    delegated, 80-83
    hearing confessions without, 137
    for men religious, 80-81, 426
    ordinary, 79-80
    for Orientals, 81, 92
    supplied, 5-6
    for women religious, 85-88
  in papal enclosure, 88, 120-121
  place of, 86-88, 148-149
  violation of seal, 105-106
Peregrini, as subjects of law, 14-15, 314
Petition for dispensation, 219

PHYSICAL PRESENCE:
  for marriage, 238
  of witnesses at marriage, 246-247
Pious Union of the Clergy, 378-381

PLACE:
  for All Souls' Day indulgence, 348
  for baptism, 34, 392-393
  for Communion, 70-71
  for confession, 81, 86-88, 148-149
  for indulgence, 337-339
  of marriage, 266-267
  for Mass, 53
  for Portiuncula Indulgence, 346-348
  for reservation of Blessed Sacrament, 73-74
Plenary: see indulgences
Populis, papal constitution, 284-285
Portiuncula: see indulgences

PRAYERS:
  as condition for indulgences, 333-334